The Craft of Prolog

Logic Programming
Ehud Shapiro, Editor

Koichi Furukawa, Jean-Louis Lassez, Fernando Pereira,
and David H.D. Warren, associate editors

The Art of Prolog: Advanced Programming Techniques
Leon Sterling and Ehud Shapiro, 1986

Logic Programming: Proceedings of the Fourth International Conference
edited by Jean-Louis Lassez, 1987 (Volumes 1 and 2)

Concurrent Prolog: Collected Papers
edited by Ehud Shapiro, 1987 (Volumes 1 and 2)

*Logic Programming: Proceedings of the Fifth International Conference
and Symposium*
edited by Robert A. Kowalski and Kenneth A. Bowen, 1988 (Volumes 1 and 2)

Constraint Satisfaction in Logic Programming
Pascal Van Hentenryck, 1989

Logic-Based Knowledge Representation
edited by Peter Jackson, Han Reichgelt, and Frank van Harmelen, 1989

Logic Programming: Proceedings of the Sixth International Conference
edited by Giorgio Levi and Maurizio Martelli, 1989

Meta-Programming in Logic Programming
edited by Harvey Abramson and M. H. Rogers, 1989

Logic Programming: Proceedings of the North American Conference 1989
edited by Ewing L. Lusk and Ross A. Overbeek, 1989 (Volumes 1 and 2)

Concurrent Constraint Programming
Vijay A. Saraswat, 1990

Logic Programming: Proceedings of the North American Conference 1990
edited by Saumya Debray and Manuel Hermenegildo, 1990

Prolog and Its Applications
edited by Alan Bond and Basuki Soetarman, 1990

Logic Programming: Proceedings of the Seventh International Conference
edited by David H. D. Warren and Peter Szeredi, 1990

Prolog VLSI Implementations
Pierluigi Civera, Gianluca Piccinini, and Maurizio Zamboni, 1990

The Craft of Prolog
Richard A. O'Keefe, 1990

The Craft of Prolog

Richard A. O'Keefe

The MIT Press
Cambridge, Massachusetts
London, England

Library of Congress Cataloging-in-Publication Data

O'Keefe, Richard A.
    The craft of Prolog / Richard A. O'Keefe.

        p.   cm. —- (Logic programming)
    Includes bibliographical references.
    ISBN-13 978-0-262-15039-2 (hc.: alk.paper) — 978-0-262-51227-5 (pb.: alk.paper)
    1. Prolog (Computer program language) I. Title. II. Series.
QA76.73.P76038 1990
005.13'3—dc20   90-32345
                                               CIP

to my parents

Contents

Series Foreword

The logic programming approach to computing investigates the use of logic as a programming language and explores computational models based on controlled deduction.

The field of logic programming has seen a tremendous growth in the last several years, both in depth and in scope. This growth is reflected in the number of articles, journals, theses, books, workshops, and conferences devoted to the subject. The MIT Press Series in Logic Programming was created to accomodate this development and to nurture it. It is dedicated to the publication of high-quality textbooks, monographs, collections, and proceedings in logic programming.

Ehud Shapiro
The Weizmann Institute of Science
Rehovot, Israel

Preface

There are a lot of introductory Prolog books around. This is not one of them. Think of it as "second steps in Prolog". If you have already read one of the introductory books, if you have taken an introductory course on Prolog, if you have written one or two Prolog programs, and if you are wondering why it is still hard to write good Prolog programs, this book is meant to help you. The purpose of the book is to show you how you can write Prolog programs that work, that don't take an unreasonable amount of time, and that are clean enough to show to your friends.

Some of the material in this book was written when I was a student at the University of Edinburgh. The chapter on tokenising still shows traces of this. The chapter on search has changed beyond recognition, but that's where it started. I thought of my notes as supplements to Clocksin & Mellish [7].

Some of the material was written for Quintus Computer Systems Ltd, in order to clarify things for Quintus customers. The chapter on memory management and cuts, the chapter on all solutions predicates, and part of the chapter on sequences had this origin. Quintus remains my ideal of a company to work for as the AI department at Edinburgh remains my ideal of a place to do research.

Further material was written for a tutorial that I gave at the Fourth IEEE Symposium on Logic Programming in 1987 at San Francisco. By then the material had begun to take its present shape.

The notes have been used several times in "Advanced Prolog" courses given at Quintus, and once at AI Ltd in Watford, England. Additional material is presented at these courses which has not found its way into this book, such as how to use the Quintus Prolog module system, elements of relational data-base design, how to debug Prolog programs, and how to use various add-ons, though I don't teach the add-ons part. There is a lot to be said about debugging techniques; the cleaner you keep your code the easier it is to debug both by hand and with the aid of meta-programs. There is also a lot to be said about data-base design. If this book does well, I might try another.

Some of the notes were adapted for a short Prolog course given to second-year Computer Science students at the University of Auckland. That didn't work very well. I warned you that this is not an introductory Prolog book. I recommend "Programming in Prolog" [7] and "The Art of Prolog" [9].

The basic structure of the book is a loose collection of Prolog programming topics. The chapter on "Basics" was written to provide the background you'll need to understand the other chapters, but the other chapters can be read in any order.

Vocabulary issues

I have made an attempt to purge the words "optimise" and "bug" from this book. I have permitted "optimise" to remain in the phrase "tail recursion optimisation", because that is the commonly understood term for turning procedure calls into jumps. Instead of saying "optimise" I have tried to say "improve": it is more honest, better understood by outsiders, and easier to say and type. It is *important* that we should not mislead ourselves into believing that we have made our code as good as possible (which is what "optimise" means) when we have only made it a little less bad. Similarly, instead of of saying "bug" I have tried to say "mistake": it is more honest, and it is not jargon. It is important to understand that "bugs" are not things that happen to our programs without our cooperation, "mistakes" are things *we* put into our programs. Our response to mistakes should be to look for ways that we can learn to avoid making them, not to blame the nature of things.

What is the name of this book?

When I was asked to do the tutorial, the title offered to me was "Prolog for Hackers", which I rejected in favour of "Practical Prolog". Leon Sterling suggested "A Discipline of Prolog", and some day I would like to write a book which could live up to that title. I stuck with "Practical Prolog" until the day I was about to send the LaTeX sources to MIT Press, when I discovered that there was a new book out with that title. (I haven't read that book; my only comment is that it describes MProlog.) Then I had to think again, and think fast. "The Practice of Prolog" is catchy, and goes well with "The Art of Prolog". But that sounds like an authoritative textbook. I finally settled on "The Craft of Prolog". I wonder what the book will be called by the time you read it.

Acknowledgments

I would like to thank

- The Department of Artificial Intelligence at the University of Edinburgh, particularly my supervisor Alan Bundy, and the Prolog team who were there: David H. D. Warren, Fernando Pereira, Lawrence Byrd, Dave Bowen, and of course Chris Mellish and Bill Clocksin. I learned Prolog there from the people who made Edinburgh Prolog happen, so I've always found it simple.

- Quintus Computer Systems Inc, including Fernando Pereira, Lawrence Byrd, Dave Bowen, and Bob Keller, for letting me spend so much time on this. I am particularly grateful to Lawrence Byrd from whose sections of the Advanced Prolog course at Quintus I continued to learn.

- The University of Auckland: the Physics Department for lending me a copy of TEX which ran on a PC, the Computer Centre for lending me a PC to run TEX on, and the Computer Science Department for giving me an account so that I could still receive E-mail.

- The University of Melbourne, for letting me visit, try out my material one more time on some of their students, for lending me an office and a Sun to finish the book, and for letting me print hundreds of pages of drafts.

- The men and women who have attended courses based on this material.

- My father, who proofread a draft even though Prolog is as deep a mystery to him as the Law is to me.

- Mats Carlsson and Jeff Shultz who noticed mistakes in the text and told me about them. So did some other people, but with shifting from country to country a couple of times I'm afraid I've lost your names. Thank you anyway.

The Craft of Prolog

Introduction

This is not an introductory Prolog textbook. For introductions to Prolog and logic programming, you want to read

- "Logic for Problem Solving" [6]

- "Programming in Prolog" [7], or

- "Prolog: a Relational Language and its Applications" [8].

It isn't even a second Prolog textbook. There are two books which stand head and shoulders above a crowd of others:

- "The art of Prolog" [9]

- "Advanced Prolog, techniques and examples" [10]

No, this isn't a textbook at all. It's a book about *using* Prolog effectively for people who have already learned the basics of the language and are wondering whether Prolog programs have to run slowly.

I don't describe Prolog's syntax or built-in predicates. Your first and second Prolog books should have told you what you needed to know about them. If you need more detail, the Prolog system you are using has a manual. Some of the manuals I had available while writing this book are

- the Quintus Prolog manual [16]

- the SICStus Prolog manual [17]

- the NU Prolog manual [18]

I also had access to and used C Prolog, Stony Brook Prolog, ALS Prolog, LPA Prolog Professional, LPA Mac Prolog, and NIP (now confusingly renamed to "Edinburgh Prolog"). Much of this book should apply to those Prologs, except that the notation for character literals differs. At one time or another I had access to manuals for BIM_Prolog, IF/Prolog, MProlog, AAIS Prolog and ZYX Prolog. This book was *not* written with those Prologs in mind, which is not to say that there is anything wrong with them.

There are three main themes:

- hacking your program is no substitute for understanding your *problem*.

- Prolog is different, but it's not *that* different.

- Elegance is not optional.

Understanding, not hacking

You can speed a program up by attending to the fine details. This book has many examples of that. But the really big savings come from choosing inherently efficient algorithms, and exploiting the properties of your problem. To do that, you need a clear understanding of what you want to do, and this will show up in your program.

If you don't like mathematics, I have bad news for you: the most effective *kind* of understanding for this purpose is mathematical.

If I may intrude a personal element here, one of the things which distinguishes imperative programming in C, Pascal, Fortran or whatever from declarative programming in Prolog, Scheme, ML or whatever for me is a big difference in feeling. When I code in C, I feel that I'm on a knife-edge of "state"—I focus on statements and what they *do*. I'm worried about the behaviour of a machine. But when I'm writing Prolog, the predicates *feel* like geometric objects and the data flow between goals *feels* like lines of tension holding the goals together into an integrated whole, as if the program fragment I was working were a large Rubik's cube that I could handle and move from one configuration to another without destroying it. When I fix mistakes in a Prolog program, I look for flaws in the static "spatial" configuration of the program; a mistake feels like a snapped thread in a cobweb, and I feel regret for wounding the form. When I'm coding C, I worry about 'register' declarations and pointer arithmetic. When I'm coding Prolog, I worry about getting the interface of each predicate just right so that it *means* something and has the visible perfection of a new leaf.

This kind of mathematical feeling for programming really pays off in practice. Programs with lots of implicit connections in them (such as the assignment statement tends to introduce) tend to be hard to restructure. The more declarative a Prolog program is, the easier it is to manipulate "algebraically" and obtain large performance improvements.

As an example of the kind of thinking required, there are two rules for making a calculation cheap:

- Don't do it. Find a way of making do without. For example, if you want to find out whether $\sqrt{X} > Y$, the fastest method is not to tweak your square root calculation but to test for $X > Y^2$ instead.

- Don't do it again. If a result has been computed and is going to be needed again soon, hang onto it instead of recalculating it.

But in order to apply these rules, you need to understand when a computation can be replaced by a logically equivalent one, and when two computations are equivalent. Those aren't questions about your programming language, they are questions about your problem.

Prolog is not that different

At first sight, Prolog is very different from the programming languages you are used to. The thing most programmers appear to miss is the assignment command. There really is no direct equivalent of assignment in Prolog (no, you should *not* use the dynamic data base for this purpose) and for 99% of your Prolog programming you have no *use* for an assignment command. The fact that type declarations are not required is another source of confusion to some. (There is no shortage of type systems available for Prolog. Nu Prolog [18] comes with three of them!) There are no nested blocks. There aren't a lot of keywords with special syntax, only a small number of punctuation marks.

It is true that Prolog is different from other languages at the *coding* level. If you are a typical Pascal or C programmer (as judged by the code which gets published in books, public domain discs, and Usenet) you are going to have serious trouble with Prolog.

However, the "discipline of programming" method of *design* carries over directly to Prolog. Two books which every programmer should have read, whatever language s/he uses, and better programmers will own copies of and re-read, are

- "A Discipline of Programming" [1]

- "The Science of Programming" [2]

When should you have an 'if' (a case analysis) in your program? When should you have a loop (a recursive predicate) in your program? What should the loop invariant (the meaning of the predicate) be? What controls the loop (what is the recursion based on)? These are the kinds of question which this method tackles, and has answers (well, heuristics) for. I strongly recommend both of these books; if you master this approach you will be a much more effective programmer, and the techniques *do* apply to Prolog because for the most part they are concerned with logical formulas.

For many tasks there are algorithms in the standard literature which can be readily adapted to Prolog. This book uses Warshall's algorithm and Rem's algorithm, the semi-naïve method from the data base literature, a data structure for queues from the functional programming community, and others. There are some really beautiful algorithms and data structures, such as an implementation of random-access stacks where pushes and pops take constant time and random accesses take logarithmetic time, which I reluctantly left out. You don't have to invent everything yourself. One tip: look for algorithms which are efficient under the "pointer machine" model rather than ones which are only efficient under the "random access machine" model. Another tip: *never* use "quick"sort, plain old merge sort is quite a bit faster.

We have a lot to learn from the relational data base people. There are two books I am particularly attached to:

- "Principles of Database and Knowledge-Base Systems" [5]. This is a "must buy".

- "The Theory of Relational Databases" [4].

Finally, "Software Engineering" is not the same thing as programming. Software engineering is about making software products that work, on time, at a reasonable cost in development effort and future maintenance. Most of us have a *lot* to learn about that; I know I have. Many of the skills that set a software engineer apart from mere programmers have little or nothing to do with details of this programming language or that. As an elementary beginning, I would recommend

- "Professional Software" [3]

Such simple things as setting up consistent well-designed naming conventions have been ignored by standards committees, let alone programmers. I continue to try to improve my practice in this respect, and I believe that my programs are much easier to read now than they used to be, despite the authors of the books I learned from never having heard of Prolog. There is still more to software engineering than this, such as Quality Assurance, but I shall say no more, as the point is that most of the advice the better books offer applies quite directly to Prolog.

Elegance is not optional (1)

What do I mean by that? I mean that in Prolog, as in most halfway decent programming languages, there is no tension between writing a beautiful program and writing an efficient program. If your Prolog code is ugly, the chances are that you either don't understand your problem or you don't understand your programming language, and in neither case does your code stand much chance of being efficient. In order to ensure that your program is efficient, you need to know what it is doing, and if your code is ugly, you will find it hard to analyse.

Elegance is not optional (2)

What do I mean by that? I mean that there is no program so trivial that it will not one day need maintaining. A clear straightforward program is going to be easier to maintain than an ugly one. A good Prolog program will have surprising uses.

I don't care how long you have been writing Prolog, if you think you know how to write efficient code, you are probably wrong. I have seen programs written by people who are famous in the logic-programming community, people who have an excellent understanding of what logic programming is all about, and some of these programs were *shocking*. What makes me different? Nothing! I have often had the humiliating experience of writing a nice clean program and then "optimising" it, only to find that the "optimised" version ran slower. For this tutorial, I have checked each example to make sure that versions I claim to be faster really are faster.

Structure of the book

Since I assume you already know Prolog, most of the chapters stand on their own. You should read the first chapter first, as that establishes terminology that is used elsewhere. After that, dip in where you like; I hope the index and table of contents will help you find your way around, and if not, I've repeated myself a lot.

If I have done well, it is no more than the subject deserves. If I have done poorly, it is what I was capable of.

1 Basic Topics in Prolog

1.1   Introduction

In this chapter we're going to look at some of the things you need to know when writing Prolog code. In particular, there are several things you are used to in conventional languages like Pascal and Lisp which Prolog doesn't do in exactly the same way, but can do with procedure calls and argument passing, and there are some things which Prolog can do easily that Pascal can't.

Pascal feature	Lisp feature	Prolog feature
non-local variables	as Pascal	context arguments
assignment statements	as Pascal	accumulator passing
while statements	(do ...)	last call optimisation
for statements	(do ...)	counter arguments
arrays	as Pascal	trees
function arguments	as Pascal	call/N
var arguments	(values ...)	unification
-none-	-none-	partial data structures
-none-	-none-	difference lists

It is easier to think of something if you have a name for it. The point of this chapter is to give you names for some common ways that the arguments of predicates are used in Prolog, so that you can work out more easily what is going on in someone else's code, and so that you can more easily think of things to try in your own code.

1.2   Cases and Structural Induction

The most basic use of arguments is to discriminate between several cases. For example, suppose we have a data type "direction", with cases north, south, east, and west, and want to determine the appropriate Latinised adjective for each direction. We would write

```
%   direction_adjective(Direction, Adjective)
%   is true when Adjective is the Latinised adjective meaning
%   ''pertaining to Direction''.

direction_adjective(north, boreal).
direction_adjective(south, austral).
direction_adjective(east,  oriental).
direction_adjective(west,  occidental).
```

Here the first argument is being used to determine which case we have. The corresponding Pascal version would be

```
type
    Direction    = (north, south, east, west);
    String10     = packed array [1..10] of char;

function direction_adjective(d: Direction): String10;
    begin
        case d of begin
            north: direction_adjective := 'boreal    ';
            south: direction_adjective := 'austral   ';
            east:  direction_adjective := 'oriental  ';
            west:  direction_adjective := 'occidental';
        end {case};
    end {direction_adjective};
```

A particularly common case of this involves comparing two terms. The built-in predicate compare(R,X,Y) unifies R with '<', '=', or '>' when X precedes, is identical to, or follows Y in the standard order on terms. Suppose we wanted to compute the absolute value of the difference between two integers X and Y. We could do it thus:

```
abs_diff(X, Y, Diff) :-
        compare(R, X, Y),
        abs_diff(R, X, Y, Diff).
abs_diff(<, X, Y, Diff) :- Diff is Y-X.
abs_diff(>, X, Y, Diff) :- Diff is X-Y.
abs_diff(=, _, _, 0).
```

Things get more interesting when a recursively defined data type is involved. A list of Xs is either the empty list [] or a pair $[H|T]$ where H is an X and T is a list of Xs. The DEC-10 Prolog type checker uses the declaration

```
:- type list(T) ⟶ [] | [T|list(T)].
```

to express this.

A predicate defined on lists will often have two cases: one for the empty list [] and one for a pair $[H|T]$. The simplest predicate is one that recognises a list:

```
is_list([]).  % base case
is_list([_|Tail]) :- % step case
        is_list(Tail).
```

We say that a predicate like this is defined by *structural induction*: *induction* because it is defined recursively, *structural* because it is controlled by the *structure* of its argument rather than by numeric values or other means. The first clause of is_list/1 is called a *base case* or *non-recursive* case, and the second clause is called a *step case*, *recursive* case, or *inductive* case.

Consider arithmetic expressions defined like this:

```
:-    type expression  ⟶
            c(number)                          % a constant
      |     expression + expression            % addition
      |     - expression                       % negation
      |     expression - expression            % subtraction
      |     expression * expression            % multiplication
      |     expression / expression.           % (floating-point) division
%     arithmetic_value(Expr, Value)
%     is true when Expr represents an arithmetic expression and
%     Value is its numeric value.


arithmetic_value(c(N), N). % base case
arithmetic_value(E+F, Value) :- % step case
        arithmetic_value(E, Eval),
        arithmetic_value(F, Fval),
        Value is Eval + Fval.
arithmetic_value(-F, Value) :- % step case
        arithmetic_value(F, Fval),
        Value is -Fval.
arithmetic_value(E-F, Value) :- % step case
        arithmetic_value(E, Eval),
        arithmetic_value(F, Fval),
        Value is Eval - Fval.
arithmetic_value(E*F, Value) :- % step case
        arithmetic_value(E, Eval),
        arithmetic_value(F, Fval),
        Value is Eval * Fval.
arithmetic_value(E/F, Value) :- % step case
        arithmetic_value(E, Eval),
        arithmetic_value(F, Fval),
        Value is Eval / Fval.
```

In that example, the first clause is a base case, and the remaining clauses are all step cases. Note how the predicate and the type definition have much the same shape, and there is a clause for each of the cases.

Two things to watch out for are

- missing cases

- "duplicate" cases

For example, suppose we defined a formula to be "additive" if it didn't contain
any multiplications or divisions:

```
additive(c(_)).
additive(E+F) :-
        additive(E),
        additive(F).
additive(-F) :-
        additive(F).
additive(E-F) :-
        additive(E),
        additive(F).
```

There are no clauses here for the $E * F$ or E/F cases, and that is quite deliberate.
It's something worth noticing.

Of course, if you don't know what the possibilities are for the data structure, it
is hard to tell when a predicate has no clauses for some of those possibilities. That
is one reason why it is important to describe your data structures in comments in
your programs.

For an example of duplicate cases, consider member/2:

```
member(X, [X|_]).
member(X, [_|L]) :-
        member(X, L).
```

At first sight, it looks as though anything that matches the first clause head will also
match the second clause head. In fact it will, and even when Prolog has returned
from the first clause, it leaves a record behind (a so-called "choice point") so that
it can go back and try the second clause. The fact that both clauses match the
same case of the data structure is quite deliberate in this predicate. It is always
significant when two clauses can match the same case, either it is a mistake that
needs to be corrected, or it is an important fact about the predicate which you need
to understand.

1.3   Inputs and Outputs

There is nothing in the syntax of Prolog to indicate which arguments are inputs to a predicate and which arguments are outputs. That is not because Prolog's designers were sloppy, but because argument passing in Prolog uses **two**-way matching: one and the same rule may sometimes be given information in a particular argument, or return information through it.

Here is a table of the names of some people and their birthdays, expressed as date(Month,DayNumber) pairs:

```
birthday(byron,     date(feb, 4)).
birthday(noelene,   date(dec,25)).
birthday(richard,   date(oct,11)).
birthday(clare,     date(sep,15)).
```

If we put the question

?- birthday(byron, Date).

to Prolog, birthday/2 is then being called with its first argument known (bound, instantiated) and its second argument unknown (unbound, uninstantiated). In that case, the first argument is acting as an input, and the second argument is acting as an output. But if we put the question

?- birthday(Person, date(feb,4)).

to Prolog, birthday/2 is then being called with its first argument unknown (unbound, uninstantiated) and its second argument known (bound, instantiated). In that case, the first argument is acting as an *output*, and the second argument is acting as an *input*. Yet it is exactly the same fact which supplies the answer in both cases. Finally, if we put the question

?- birthday(Person, date(feb,Day)).

to Prolog, asking "who has a birthday in February, and on what day?" the second argument is partially filled in, but it isn't completely ground (there is still a variable in it). So that argument is partly an input, and partly an output. And it is still the same fact which supplies the answers.

It is quite common to have tables of facts like this in a Prolog program, and such tables can easily be used any way around. It is usual, however, for there to be one argument which uniquely determines the others. Here, for example, a birthday may be shared by several people, but a person has only one birthday. The convention is that you put that argument first.

In pure logic, there is no notion of input or output arguments at all. We just have variables which are constrained in various ways. But in Prolog, there are operations which cannot solve for variables in some of their arguments. A common example of that is the built-in predicate for evaluating arithmetic expressions:

Answer is Expression

That predicate is used to solve for Answer, and cannot solve for the Expression, because an Expression has only one value, but there are infinitely many expressions having the same Value. For example, if you want to compute factorials[1], you might write

```
factorial(0, 1).
factorial(N, N_Factorial) :-
        N > 0,
        M is N-1,
        factorial(M, M_Factorial),
        N_Factorial is M_Factorial*N.
```

The built-in predicate $E_1 > E_2$ is like is/2: it cannot solve for its arguments, but they must already be ground by the time it is called. So factorial/2 will not work unless its first argument is already instantiated to a number when it is called. This predicate, then, has got a definite input: its first argument must be given and cannot be solved for.

This example has two arguments. How do we tell which way around to put them?

The rule is

- **inputs** come first, then

- **outputs** come last.

If a predicate can solve for several of its arguments, but some of its arguments uniquely determine others, the ones which uniquely determine the others are reckoned as inputs, and the others are reckoned as outputs.

Arguments which are used to select a clause definitely count as inputs. If a predicate is doing a case analysis on one, two, or more of its arguments, those arguments do count as inputs, and should generally precede any other input arguments.

There is no reason why a Prolog predicate should have only one output. In Pascal, a computation which returns a single number can be written as a function, but a computation which returns two numbers has to be written as a procedure with two **var** arguments. For example:

---

[1] You probably don't. What one really uses in practice is the logarithm of the Γ function.

```
function min(x, y: integer): integer;
    begin
        if x < y then begin
            min := x;
        end else begin
            min := y;
        end;
    end {min};
```

```
(* BUT *)
procedure minAndMax(x, y: integer;
                    var min, max: integer);
    begin
        if x < y then begin
            min := x; max := y;
        end else begin
            min := y; max := x;
        end;
    end {minAndMax};
```

Common Lisp does not have this restriction. We can write

```
(defun our-min (X Y)
    (if (< X Y) X Y))
```

```
(defun our-min-and-max (X Y)
    (if (< X Y) (values X Y) (values Y X)))
```

However, *using* multiple results in Common Lisp is different from using single results:

```
(print (our-min 2 3))
```

doesn't need any explicit variables, but

```
(multiple-value-bind ((Min Max) (our-min-and-max 2 3))
    (print Min) (print Max))
```

In contrast, Prolog makes no distinction between operations with no results, operations with one result, and operations with more than one result: *all* results are just arguments that come last:

min(X, Y, X) :- X < Y.
min(X, Y, Y) :- X ≥ Y.

min_and_max(X, Y, X, Y) :- X < Y.
min_and_max(X, Y, Y, X) :- X ≥ Y.

If you just remember the rule **inputs before outputs** you won't go too far
wrong.

I have found it helpful to expand this basic rule into a more detailed argument
order convention. Just as legal theorists see what judges decide and then make up
legal principles to explain it, I made up my argument order convention to explain
the DEC-10 Prolog built-in predicates. When I write a predicate which is to be used
in other files or by other people, I try to stick to this convention. The expanded
convention is

- strict inputs come first. These are the things which the predicate cannot solve
  for but must be given. There are several kinds of strict inputs.

  1. Templates come first. A template is a term which is going to be used as
     a pattern for making or selecting things, so is likely to contain variables,
     but which will not be instantiated by the predicate. For example, the
     first argument of findall/3 and the first argument of retractall/1.

  2. Meta-arguments come next. A meta-argument is a term which stands
     for a goal, perhaps with some of its trailing arguments omitted. The
     first argument of the call/N family and the maplist/N family and the
     second argument of findall/3 are of this sort.

  3. Streams are terms which stand for open files. In systems which are
     compatible with DEC-10 Prolog they are atoms which have the form
     of file names (in DEC-10 Prolog you can have only one stream per file
     name), in more modern systems they may also be some other kind of
     term, typically returned by a command called open/3.

  4. Selectors or Indices come next. The first argument of arg/3 is a selector.
     These are arguments which are like an array subscript.

     With Selectors I group "induction arguments", the arguments which
     control the shape of a recursion. These are the arguments which would
     be loop control variables in Pascal or Lisp.

  5. Collections come next. These are arguments which are like an array or
     other kind of collection. Of course, almost any non-trivial data structure
     can be seen as a collection of some sort, the question is whether *this*
     predicate is using it that way.

With Collections I group "context arguments", the arguments which pass around data that a loop uses but does not change. See the next section.

6. Other strict inputs come last.

- Arguments which a predicate can either accept or solve for come after the strict inputs and before the strict outputs.

- Outputs come last.

There are some other guidelines:

sequence order Within each group, if you have several arguments which are positions in an abstract sequence (accumulator pairs, difference pairs, and so on—see later in this chapter), put those arguments side by side so that the first argument in the group represents the first position in the sequence and the last argument in the group represents the last position in the sequence.

code/data consistency Suppose you have a data structure with some attributes X, Y, Z which always appear in that order. That is, for each constructor function of that type, if it has an X and a Y argument, the X precedes the Y, and so on. Then when you pass these attributes to a predicate, they should appear in that order. For example, non-empty lists [Head|Tail] have the head before the tail, so when we pass the head H and the tail T of some list to a predicate we should usually put H before T. Similarly, functors are represented by Name/Arity pairs, so if we pass a name and arity separately to a predicate, the name (atom) argument should precede the arity (integer) argument.

function direction There are many predicates which are multidirectional, so that it is hard to say which arguments are inputs and which arguments are outputs. For example,

```
functor(Term, Symbol, Arity)
Term =.. List
atom_chars(Atom, Chars)
succ(NonNegativeInt, PositiveInt)
```

and so on. That is, they can solve for either argument given the other.

Typically, though, one of the directions is stronger than the other. Suppose we have a relation p(X, Y) for which for all non-variable X, there is at least one suitable Y but there is at least one non-variable Y having no suitable X. Then the argument order is X before Y.

Every non-variable Term has a principal Functor Symbol/Arity, but not every
constant/integer pair is the principal functor of a term (consider 2/1 or fred/(-
1)). So it has to be Term before Functor, and when we unpack the functor,
functor/3 has to be Term before function Symbol before Arity.

The Term argument has to precede the List argument of '=..'/2 for the same
reason: to each non-variable Term $f(X_1, \ldots, X_n)$ there corresponds a unique
List $[f, X_1, \ldots, X_n]$ but there are Lists such as [1,a] or [a+b,c] which do not
correspond to any Term.

name(Constant, Chars) is a function from Constant to Chars, but not conversely. E.g., name(0,"0") and name('0',"0") both succeed. The newer predicates atom_chars/2 and number_chars/2 are consistent with name/2, but note
that number_chars/2 follows this rule too: for any number there is a character
list, but not all character lists represent numbers.

Alas, the built-in predicates is/2 and compare/3 ignore this convention by putting
their output argument first, but they are the only "standard" predicates that put
an output first.

If you don't like my argument order convention, that's fine. Prolog doesn't care.
It's *my* convention, not Prolog's. The important thing is to *have* a convention and
to stick with it, because there are no syntactic labels to say which argument of a
predicate does what. With a convention like this, you spend less time designing
a predicate's interface and haven't as much to remember. For example, suppose
there were a predicate which was like findall/3 except that it returned a difference
pair. Following my convention, it would *have* to be

findall(Template, Goal, List0, List)

1.4   Context Arguments

Pascal has non-local variables: the body of a procedure or function can refer to
variables declared outside that procedure or function. The rule is that if a procedure
P is declared inside a procedure Q, then P has access to its own variables and to
all the variables that Q has access to.

Most functional languages are the same: Common Lisp, ML, and others are
lexically scoped just like Pascal.

There is no way that a Prolog predicate can be declared "inside" another Prolog
predicate. There is no reason in principle why a language based on logic couldn't
have some sort of nested variable scopes; after all the quantifiers $\forall X$ and $\exists X$
provide just such nested declarations in first-order logic. Prolog, however, is based
on a "flat" form of logic called Horn clauses. So what do you do instead?

This is a particularly pressing problem because something which would be a loop in Pascal is expressed as a recursive predicate in Prolog, so that the variables needed in the body of a loop are not local to that predicate.

Here is an example. Suppose we want to write a function which will take a list Xs and a scale factor Multiplier and return a new list whose elements are the elements of Xs multiplied by Multiplier. In Common Lisp we might write

```
(defun scale (Xs Multiplier)
    (map #'(lambda (X) (* X Multiplier)) List))
```

Here the lambda-function refers to 'Multiplier', which is an argument of the function 'scale'.

The scope of a variable name in a Prolog program is a single rule. We would have to code this example in Prolog as

```
scale([], _, []).
scale([X|Xs], Multiplier, [Y|Ys]) :-
        Y is X*Multiplier,
        scale(Xs, Multiplier, Ys).
```

where we keep passing Multiplier around as an argument. This is less convenient than Lisp's non-local variables, but it doesn't limit the computational power of the language. It would be quite possible to write a pre-processor which took

```
scale(List, Multiplier, Scaled) :-
        scale_1(List, Scaled)
where    {    scale_1([], [])
         ;    scale_1([X|Xs], [Y|Ys]) :-
              Y is X*Multiplier,
              scale_1(Xs, Ys)
         }.
```

and turned this into ordinary Prolog, and indeed this has been done. The point here is that

> A conventional procedure or function which refers to N distinct non-local variables can be transliterated to a Prolog predicate with N extra arguments.

This will help you to understand some Prolog code. If you see a variable being passed around unchanged, the chances are that you should think of it as a non-local variable. We call arguments used this way *context arguments*.

Here is another example. The task is to take a list of numbers and select the numbers which are greater than or equal to 10.

big_elements(Input, Output) :-
        big_elements(Input, 10, Output).

big_elements([], _, []).
big_elements([Nbr|Nbrs], Bound, Bigs) :-
        Nbr < Bound,
        big_elements(Nbrs, Bound, Bigs).
big_elements([Nbr|Nbrs], Bound, [Nbr|Bigs]) :-
        Nbr ≥ Bound,
        big_elements(Nbrs, Bound, Bigs).

In big_elements/3, the argument Bound is being passed around unchanged. In Lisp or Pascal, it would have been a non-local variable.

Quintus Prolog lets a predicate have 255 arguments. LPA Mac Prolog limits you to 31. Another Prolog for the Macintosh limits you to 14. The practical limit is the number of arguments you can keep straight in your head, which is likely to be smaller than that. If you find that a predicate (other than a table of facts) has more than 10 arguments, it's time to rethink your design.

If you have a lot of things that are being passed around as context arguments, it may be useful to package them up as a record, and pass that around, accessing fields of the record only when you need them.

For example, suppose that we have four context arguments which are being passed around:

c(...) :-
        init(..., A, B, C, D, ...),
        p(..., A, B, C, D, ...),
        ⋮

p(..., A, B, C, D, ...) :-
        ⋮
        use A,
        ⋮
        p(..., A, B, C, D, ...).
p(..., A, B, C, D, ...) :-
        ⋮
        use B,
        ⋮
        p(..., A, B, C, D, ...).

What we might do instead is to introduce some auxiliary predicates and do this:

context(context(A,B,C,D), A, B, C, D).

context_a(context(A,_,_,_), A).

context_b(context(_,B,_,_), B).

context_c(context(_,_,C,_), C).

context_d(context(_,_,_,D), D).

c(...) :-
        init(..., A, B, C, D, ...),
        context(Context, A, B, C, D),
        p(..., Context, ...),
        ⋮

p(..., Context, ...) :-
        ⋮
        context_a(Context, A),
        use A,
        ⋮
        p(..., Context, ...).
p(..., Context, ...) :-
        ⋮
        context_b(Context, B),
        use B,
        ⋮
        p(..., Context, ...).

We shall see later how the overhead of this procedure call to access parts of a context can be avoided, but even with a procedure call the clarity which can be obtained by this device is often well worth while. It is seldom worth bothering to package up two context arguments like this, but when you are using more than two context arguments it can make your code much easier to maintain.

Some programming languages have keyword arguments. For example, an Ada subroutine for drawing scatter plots might have an interface like

procedure ScatterPlot(
    Xs: **in** vector;
    Ys: **in** vector;
    X_Scale: **in** float := 1.0;
    Y_Scale: **in** float := 1.0;
    Label: **in** string := " ");

A clean way to hack something like this in Prolog is to pass a list of options, and have the interface predicate construct a suitable context argument. For example,

scatter_defaults(scop(1.0,1.0,"")).

scatter_option(x_scale, scop(X,_,_), X).
scatter_option(y_scale, scop(_,Y,_), Y).
scatter_option(label, scop(_,_,L), L).

set_scatter_option(x_scale(X), scop(_,Y,L), scop(X,Y,L)).
set_scatter_option(y_scale(Y), scop(X,_,L), scop(X,Y,L)).
set_scatter_option(label(L), scop(X,Y,_), scop(X,Y,L)).

set_scatter_options([], Scop, Scop).
set_scatter_options([Option|Options], Scop0, Scop) :-
        set_scatter_option(Option, Scop0, Scop1),
        set_scatter_options(Options, Scop1, Scop).

scatter_plot(Xs, Ys) :-
        scatter_plot(Xs, Ys, []).

scatter_plot(Xs, Ys, Options) :-
        scatter_defaults(Defaults),
        set_scatter_options(Options, Defaults, Scop),
        do_scatter_plot(Xs, Ys, Scop).

Comparable calls in Ada and Prolog would be

-- Ada
ScatterPlot(Xs, Ys);
ScatterPlot(Xs, Ys, 10.0, 5.0);
ScatterPlot(Xs, Ys, X_Scale ⇒ 10.0, Y_Scale ⇒ 5.0);
ScatterPlot(Xs, Ys, Label ⇒ "Income -vs- Year");

```
%% Prolog
scatter_plot(Xs, Ys, []),
scatter_plot(Xs, Ys, [x_scale(10.0), y_scale(5.0)]),
scatter_plot(Xs, Ys, [x_scale(10.0), y_scale(5.0)]),
scatter_plot(Xs, Ys, [label("Income -vs- Year")]),
```

The Ada approach is more conventional. The Prolog approach, though, is more "object-oriented"[2], and makes it straightforward to compute entire option clusters and pass them around. The Prolog approach shown here can be type-checked by the DEC-10 Prolog type checker. Another approach sometimes used would look like

```
scatter_plot(Xs, Ys, [x_scale=10.0, y_scale=5.0])
```

but that style costs more space and cannot be type-checked by the DEC-10 Prolog type checker.

1.4.1   Accumulator Passing

Imperative languages like C and Pascal have variables that can be changed. Neither pure functional languages nor Prolog have such variables. Instead, they use a technique called *accumulator passing* where the function or predicate receives as arguments the current values of the variables, and returns, amongst other things, the new values of the variables. Here is an example.

```
function len(x: list): integer;
    var n: integer;
    begin
        n := 0;
        while x <> mkNil do begin
            n := n+1;
            x := x^.tail;
        end {while};
        len := n;
    end {len};
```

In the imperative language Lisp, we would code it the same way:

```
(defun len (X)
    (let ((N 0))
        (while (consp X)
            (setq N (1+ N))
            (setq X (cdr X)))
        N))
```

---

[2] *Not* object oriented, just *more* object oriented.

But in a functional language, we would have to write

len(L) = len(L, 0).

len([], N) = N.
len([H|T], N) = len(T, N+1).

Here the local mutable variable N has turned into *two* things: an argument N which contains the current value, and a function result.

In Prolog, results are arguments just like inputs, and we would code the example as

len(L, N) :-
        len(L, 0, N).

len([], N, N).
len([H|T], N0, N) :-
        N1 is N0+1,
        len(T, N1, N).

The input argument corresponding to the initial state of a conventional variable (here the second argument of len/3) is called an *accumulator*. The output argument corresponding to the final state of a conventional variable (here the third argument of len/3) is called a *result*. Note that *one* conventional variable has turned into *two* Prolog arguments representing *two* states of the conventional variable. The two arguments together are called an *accumulator pair*.

Accumulator passing is a very common technique. For example, the usual definition of list reversal is

rev(List, Reverse) :-
        rev(List, [], Reverse). /* 1 */

rev([], Reverse, Reverse). /* 2 */
rev([Head|Tail], Reverse0, Reverse) :- /* 3 */
        rev(Tail, [Head|Reverse0], Reverse). /* 4 */

It should be clear by now that this is the equivalent of the Pascal

```
function rev(L: list): list;
    var Reverse: list;
    begin
        Reverse := mkNil;                      /* 1 */
        while L <> mkNil do begin              /* 3 */
```

```
        Reverse := mkCons(              /* 4 */
            L^.head, Reverse);
        L := L^.tail;                   /* 3 */
    end {while};
    rev := Reverse;                     /* 2 */
end {rev};
```

Suppose that for some reason we wanted to sum the positive and the negative elements of a list separately.

In Pascal we might write

```
procedure sumPosAndNeg(L: list;
                        var Pos, Neg: integer);
    begin
        Pos := 0;
        Neg := 0;
        while L <> mkNil do begin
            if L^.head >= 0 then begin
                Pos := Pos + L^.head;
            end else begin
                Neg := Neg + L^.head;
            end;
            L := L^.tail;
        end;
    end {sumPosAndNeg};
```

In Prolog, we implement the variables Pos and Neg as accumulator pairs:

sum_pos_neg(List, Pos, Neg) :-
        sum_pos_,neg(List, 0, Pos, 0, Neg).

sum_pos_neg([], Pos, Pos, Neg, Neg).
sum_pos_neg([X|Xs], Pos0, Pos, Neg0, Neg) :-
        $X \geq 0$,
        Pos1 is Pos0+X,
        sum_pos_neg(Xs, Pos1, Pos, Neg0, Neg).
sum_pos_neg([X|Xs], Pos0, Pos, Neg0, Neg) :-
        $X < 0$,
        Neg1 is Neg0+X,
        sum_pos_neg(Xs, Pos0, Pos, Neg1, Neg).

Note that the Pascal loop updates only one of Pos, Neg on each iteration, but the Prolog predicate has to specify the next values of all the variables.

Another example would be finding the sum of the elements of a list and the sum of their squares:

```
sum_and_ssq(List, Sum, SSQ) :-
        sum_and_ssq(List, 0, Sum, 0, SSQ).

sum_and_ssq([], Sum, Sum, SSQ, SSQ).
sum_and_ssq([X|Xs], Sum0, Sum, SSQ0, SSQ) :-
        Sum1 is Sum0 + X,
        SSQ1 is SSQ0 + X*X,
        sum_and_ssq(Xs, Sum1, Sum, SSQ1, SSQ).
```

If you have several accumulator pairs in a predicate, each recursive rule has to 'update' all of them. The recursive rules are like the body of the loop, and the outer predicate that calls the inner one is like the statements that initialise the loop variables.

Typically, an accumulator pair shows up as

```
p(..., Foo0, Foo, ...) :-
        ⋮
        q(..., Foo0, Foo1, ...),
        ⋮
        r(..., Foo1, Foo, ...),
        ⋮
```

where each of the "Foo*" variables appears twice in an execution path. Note the naming convention: the Prolog variables which correspond to successive "states" of a conventional variable "Foo" are given names beginning with "Foo". The initial state is given the name "Foo0", the next state after that "Foo1", and so on, the final state being given the name "Foo".

When you see

```
waterfall(Term0, Term) :-
        rewrite(Term0, Term1),
        !,
        waterfall(Term1, Term).
waterfall(Term, Term).
```

you can see at once that the two arguments of waterfall/2 form an accumulator pair, and that this is like the Lisp function

```
(defun waterfall (term)
    (while (rewritable term)
        (setq term (rewrite term)))
            term)
```

To summarise:

> variables which would be updated in a loop in an imperative lan-
> guage appear in Prolog as accumulator arguments of a recursive
> predicate.

1.4.2 Last Call Optimisation

Last call optimisation is an implementation technique which turns the last form in
a procedure body into a jump rather than a procedure call, if it would otherwise
have been a procedure call. It is not something that you have to do. It is not
something that you have to ask for specially in your source code. It is just an
efficient implementation technique which applies to every rule in your program.

Suppose we define len/2 thus:

```
len([], 0).
len([_|Tail], N) :-
        len(Tail, M),
        N is M+1.
```

How does the query len([a,b,c], X) work?

1 (Prolog tries to match it against len([], 0), which fails.
   Prolog tries to match it against len($[\_|Tail_1], N_1$), which succeeds, binding
   $Tail_1 = [b, c]$, $N_1 = X$.

   A stack frame is created, holding N_1 and M_1.

   Prolog now has the goal "len($[b, c], M_1$)".

2 (Prolog tries to match it against len([], 0), which fails.
   Prolog tries to match it against len($[\_|Tail_2], N_2$), which succeeds, binding
   $Tail_2 = [c]$, $N_2 = M_1$.

   A stack frame is created, holding N_2 and M_2.

   Prolog now has the goal "len($[c], M_2$)".

3 (Prolog tries to match it against len($[]$, 0), which fails.

Prolog tries to match it against len($[\_|Tail_3]$, N_3), which succeeds, binding $Tail_3 = []$, $N_3 = M_2$.

A stack frame is created, holding N_3 and M_3.

Prolog now has the goal "len($[]$, M_3)".

4. Prolog tries to match it against len($[]$, 0), which succeeds, binding $M_3 = 0$.

3) Prolog returns to the third frame, and executes the goal "N_3 is M_3+1", which succeeds, binding $N_3 = 1$.

The third stack frame is now released.

2) Prolog returns to the second frame, and executes the goal "N_2 is $M_2 + 1$", which succeeds, binding $N_2 = 2$.

The second stack frame is now released.

1) Prolog returns to the first frame, and executes the goal "N_1 is M_1+1", which succeeds, binding $N_1 = 3$, which binds $X = 3$.

The first stack frame is now released.

Note that this built a tower of stack frames, one for each element of the list. There is nothing incorrect about this, but it does tie up a lot of space. (At an absolute minimum, 4 cells per list element.)

If we code len/2 instead as

```
len(List, Length) :-
        len(List, 0, Length).
```

```
len([], N, N).
len([_|L], N0, N) :-
        N1 is N0+1,
        len(L, N1, N).
```

the query len([a,b,c], X) is now executed thus:

0 Prolog tries to match it against len(List, Length), which succeeds, binding List = [a,b,c], Length = X.

Prolog now **jumps** with the goal len([a,b,c], 0, X).

1a The clause len([_|L], N0, N) is selected, which binds L = [a,b,c], N0 = 0, N = X.

1b The goal N1 is N0+1 is executed, which binds N1 = 1.

Prolog now **jumps** with the goal len([b,c], 1, X). {if any stack frame was built, it is discarded now.}

2a The clause len([_|L], N0, N) is selected, which binds L = [b,c], N0 = 1, N = X.

2b The goal N1 is N0+1 is executed, which binds N1 = 2.

Prolog now **jumps** with the goal len([c], 2, X). {if any stack frame was built, it is discarded now.}

3a The clause len([_|L], N0, N) is selected, which binds L = [c], N0 = 2, N = X.

3b The goal N1 is N0+1 is executed, which binds N1 = 3.

Prolog now **jumps** with the goal len([b,c], 3, X). {if any stack frame was built, it is discarded now.}

4 The clause len([], N, N) is selected, which binds X = 3.

The difference is that this version took a constant amount of stack space, and can calculate the length of an arbitrarily long list. In Quintus Prolog, the tail-recursive version of len/3 is about twice as fast as the non-tail-recursive version of len/2. Since LPA Mac Prolog does last call optimisation, you might find a similar improvement.

Exercise. *Code both versions of len/2 and measure them.*

Note that the space and time savings of last call optimisation are obtained only when the predicate in question is determinate up to that point. If it is not, the stack frame must still be retained for the benefit of backtracking. (This is one of the things which makes Prolog optimising compilers interesting: live-dead analysis is *not* as trivial as it looks!)

As a matter of fact, it is not completely unfair to compare Prolog (or a pure functional language) to COBOL: both tend to have a lot of small named entities (predicates in Prolog, paragraphs in COBOL) which branch to one another. I think it was Landin who first pointed out that labels can be thought of as functions (J-functions).

1.4.3 Partial Data Structures

An extremely important feature of Prolog is the logical variable. It is of the utmost practical importance that a logical variable can occur anywhere in a data structure.

The following terminology I believe to be due to Leon Sterling. Suppose we have a recursively defined data type *Thing*. That is, a *Thing* is one of several kinds of terms, some of which have *Thing*s as arguments. Here are some examples:

- A list of Xs is either the empty list [] or a pair $[H|T]$ where H is an X and T is a list of Xs.

- A dictionary mapping Ks to Vs might be either an empty tree 'empty' or a quadruple 'node(Key,Val,Left,Right)' where Key is a K, Val is a V, and Left and Right are both trees mapping Ks to Vs.

- A $1 + 4$-tree of Xs (the 1 is the number of data items in a node, and the 4 is the number of subtrees) is either an empty tree 'el_4' or a quintuple 'nl_4(D,T1,T2,T3,T4)', where D is an X and T1, T2, T3, T4 are $1 + 4$-trees of Xs

A "proper" $Thing$ is a non-variable $Thing$ each of whose $Thing$ arguments is a proper $Thing$.

Thus a proper list is either [] or $[H|T]$ where H is any term and T is a proper list. [a,b,c] is a proper list, and so is [_,_], but [a|_] is not a proper list because it ends with a variable.

A proper dictionary is either empty or node(Key,Val,Left,Right) for any terms Key and Val, where Left and Right must be proper trees.

    node(1,2,empty,empty)

and

    node(3,_,node(4,_,empty,empty),empty)

are proper trees, but

    node(1,2,empty,_)

is not a proper tree because its Right son is a variable.

A proper $1 + 4$-tree is either 'el_4' or 'nl_4(D,T1,T2,T3,T4)' where T1, T2, T3, T4 are proper $1 + 4$-trees. D might be anything, including a variable.

A "partial" $Thing$ is either a variable or a $Thing$ at least one of whose $Thing$ arguments is a partial thing.

Thus a partial list is either a variable or $[H|T]$ where H is any term and T is a partial list. $[a, b, c]$ and [_, _] are not partial lists, but $[a, b, c|_]$ and _ are, because they do end with variables.

node(1,2,_,_) is a partial dictionary, but so is node(3,4,empty,_). Only one of the tree arguments of a node needs to be a partial tree to make the whole node a partial tree.

A $Thing$ is either a a proper $Thing$ or a partial $Thing$.

We could define

is_proper_list(Term) :-
        classify_list(Term, proper, proper).

is_partial_list(Term) :-
        classify_list(Term, proper, partial).

is_list(Term) :-
        classify_list(Term, partial, partial).

classify_list(V, _, X) :- var(V), !, X = partial.
classify_list([], X, X).
classify_list([_|T], X0, X) :-
        classify_list(T, X0, X).

is_proper_dictionary(Term) :-
        classify_dictionary(Term, proper, proper).

is_partial_dictionary(Term) :-
        classify_dictionary(Term, proper, partial).

is_dictionary(Term) :-
        classify_dictionary(Term, partial, partial).

classify_dictionary(V, _, X) :- var(V), !, X = partial.
classify_dictionary(empty, X, X).
classify_dictionary(node(_,_,Lson,Rson), X0, X) :-
        classify_dictionary(Lson, X0, X1),
        classify_dictionary(Rson, X1, X).

You will have recognised the last two arguments of the "classify" predicates as an accumulator pair. The accumulator is initialised to 'proper' and is set to 'partial' as soon as a variable is found.

Partial *Things* are sometimes called "incomplete" *Things*.

Why are partial data structures so useful? The answer is that they give us the freedom to build results from the top down, rather than from the bottom up.

Here is a very simple example.

append([], L, L).
append([H|T], L, [H|R]) :-
        append(T, L, R).

Here is a trace of the goal append([1,2], [3,4], X).

```
    (2) 0 Call: append([1,2],[3,4],_941) ?
    (3) 1 Call: append([2],[3,4],_1098) ?
    (4) 2 Call: append([],[3,4],_1131) ? g

[Ancestors:]
    (2) 0 : append([1,2],[3,4],[1,2|_1131]) <- partial last arg
    (3) 1 : append([2],[3,4],[2|_1131])     <- partial last arg

    (4) 2 Call: append([],[3,4],_1131) ?
    (4) 2 Exit: append([],[3,4],[3,4]) ? g

[Ancestors:]
    (2) 0 : append([1,2],[3,4],[1,2,3,4])
    (3) 1 : append([2],[3,4],[2,3,4])

    (4) 2 Exit: append([],[3,4],[3,4]) ?
    (3) 1 Exit: append([2],[3,4],[2,3,4]) ?
    (2) 0 Exit: append([1,2],[3,4],[1,2,3,4]) ?
```

That is, first X was bound to [1|_1098], and then the variable _1098 was bound to [2|_1131], and finally _1131 was bound to [3,4], which gave X the final value [1,2,3,4].

Suppose unification were unable to construct a compound term until all its arguments had been constructed, so that a term could be a variable or a ground term. Then we'd have to code append/3 thus:

```
append([], L, L).
append([H|T], L, X) :-
        append(T, L, R),
        X = [H|R].
```

which can append its first argument to its second, but cannot decompose its third argument, or as

```
append(X, L, R) :-
        L = R,
        X = [].
append(X, L, [H|R]) :-
        append(T, L, R),
        X = [H|T].
```

which can decompose its third argument, but isn't much use for appending two lists. Or we could rely on a smart compiler turning the original definition into whichever of these one-way variants were needed. However, *real Prolog does not have this restriction.*

It is both natural and efficient to use partial structures in Prolog programs. For example, suppose we want to apply a predicate p/2 to each element of a list and construct a list of the results. The obvious way to do it in Prolog is

```
map_p([], []).
map_p([X|Xs], [Y|Ys]) :-
        p(X, Y),
        map_p(Xs, Ys).
```

and this one predicate can construct either argument given the other, without the necessity of producing multiple copies of the code, whether manually or automatically.

Suppose we have a binary tree, with nodes b(Lson,Rson,Datum), and that we are given a list of 1s and 2s which specify a path from the root of the tree to some datum. There are at least two ways we could do this:

```
path_data([], Tree, Datum) :-
        b(d, Tree, Datum).
path_data([Arc|Arcs], Tree, Datum) :-
        b(Arc, Tree, Son),
        path_data(Arcs, Son, Datum).

b(1, b(Lson,_,_), Lson).
b(2, b(_,Rson,_), Rson).
b(d, b(_,_,Datum),Datum).
```

This is the obvious way. But another approach is to construct the entire path as a term, and then match it against the tree.

```
dynamic_pattern(Path, Tree, Datum) :-
        path_data(Path, Pattern, Datum),
        Tree = Pattern.
```

Note how this works: path_data/3 is called to produce a skeletal tree (only the nodes actually on the path to the datum are instantiated) and then that skeleton is matched against the whole tree.

Sometimes one approach is better, sometimes the other. Remember that you have the choice.

The great utility of partial data structures lies in the fact that you can construct a structure in any mix of top-down and bottom-up that is convenient, and you often don't need to care which.

1.5   Difference Lists

A common thing to do in Prolog is to carry around a partial data structure and
some of the holes in it. To extend the data structure, you fill in a hole with a new
term which has some holes of its own. (Of course, you have to remember where
the holes are!) For example, I once wrote an arithmetic expression simplifier which
worked with a sum as a tree with a hole at the end:

```
simplify_sum(Sum, Simplified) :-
        simplify_sum(Sum, TopOfTree, HoleAtBottom, 0, N),
        (    N =\= 0 →
             HoleAtBottom = N,
             Simplified = TopOfTree
        ;    var(TopOfTree) →
             Simplified = 0
        ;    TopOfTree = Simplified+HoleAtBottom
        ).

simplify_sum(A+B, Hole0, Hole, N0, N) :- !,
        simplify_sum(B, Hole0, Hole1, N0, N1),
        simplify_sum(A, Hole1, Hole, N1, N).
simplify_sum(C, Hole, Hole, N0, N) :- number(C), !,
        N is N0+C.
simplify_sum(X, Hole+X, Hole, N, N).
```

Difference lists are a special case of this technique, where the two arguments we
are passing around are positions in a list.

David Gries' superb book on programming [2] uses a pictorial notation for rea-
soning about arrays. I call this notation "Reynolds diagrams" after J. C. Reynolds,
who invented it. It is useful to draw Reynolds diagrams when working with lists.
For example, suppose we are writing a simple compiler, and want to translate

> **while** Expr **do** Stmt

to

```
        goto L2
label L1
        stmt
label L2
        expr
        goiftrue L1
```

It is useful to draw a Reynolds diagram:

```
[Code0                    |Code1 |Code2      |Code3 |Code4        |Code]
------------------------------------------------------------------
[goto(L2),label(L1),<stmt>,label(L2),<expr>,goiftrue(L1)]
```

from which it is relatively easy to derive

compile_stmt(while(Expr,Stmt), Code0, Code) :-
       Code0 = [goto(L2),label(L1)|Code1],
       compile_stmt(Stmt, Code1, Code2),
       Code2 = [label(L2)|Code3],
       compile_expr(Expr, Code3, Code4),
       Code4 = [goiftrue(L1)|Code].

Here we see the practical importance of incomplete structures: there is nothing to stop us processing the components of the while() in a more natural order:

compile_stmt(while(Expr,Stmt),
       [goto(L2),label(L1)|Code1],
       Code) :-
       compile_expr(Expr, Code3, [goiftrue(L1)|Code]),
       compile_stmt(Stmt, Code1, [label(L2)|Code3]).

The example is implicitly about the list segments Code0\Code1, Code1\Code2, Code2\Code3, Code3\Code4, and Code4\Code. This naming convention is not arbitrary. The idea is that

- successive positions in a list are called X_0, X_1, ..., X_n, and the far end of the list is called X.

- successive members of a logical sequence (such as states of a notional variable) are called X_0, X_1, ..., X_n, and the final state is called X.

This naming convention is, I believe, due to Fernando Pereira.

1.6 Counters

Suppose you want to process the set of integers 1–N. An example of this would be examining all the arguments of a term. There are three common ways of doing this in Prolog (which is not to say that there are no others). I shall illustrate this by showing how the test ground(Term) may be implemented.

```
count_down(0, ...args ... ) :- !,
        /* no more elements to process */.
count_down(N, ...args ... ) :-
        process(N, ...args ... ),
        M is N - 1,
        count_down(M, ...args ... ).
```

If non-negative integers were represented in unary form, that is as

- zero, representing 0, or

- succ(N), representing N+1

the natural way of defining recursive predicates over them would be to write

```
p(zero, ...) :- ...
p(succ(M), ...) :-
        ...,
        p(M, ...).
```

But Prolog *doesn't* represent non-negative integers that way. The counting-down
scheme shown above is as close as we can get.

Applied to the ground test, we obtain

```
%   ground(Term)
%   is true when Term contains no variables.

ground(Term) :-
        nonvar(Term),
        functor(Term, _, Arity),
        ground(Arity, Term).

%   ground(N, Term)
%   is true when Term (known to be a non-variable) has no
%   variables in its first N arguments.

ground(0, _) :- !. % no more elements to process
ground(N, Term) :-
        arg(N, Term, Arg), % process N
        ground(Arg),
        M is N-1,
        ground(M, Term).
```

Note that in this style, the argument N *means* "the number of unprocessed elements".

The second method counts up rather than down.

count_up(N, ... args ...) :-
   count_up(0, N, ... args ...).
count_up(N, N, ... args ...) :- !,
   /* no more elements to process */.
count_up(I, N, ... args ...) :-
  J is $I + 1$,
  process(J, ... args ...),
  count_up(J, N, ... args ...).

Applied to the ground test, we obtain

```
%    ground(Term)
%    is true when Term contains no variables

ground(Term) :-
        nonvar(Term),
        functor(Term, _, Arity),
        ground(0, Arity, Term).
```

```
%    ground(I, N, Term)
%    is true when Term (known to be a nonvariable term of arity N)
%    contains no variables in its arguments I+1...N

ground(N, N, _) :- !. % no more elements to process
ground(I, N, Term) :-
        J is I+1,
        arg(J, Term, Arg),
        ground(Arg), % process element J
        ground(J, N, Term).
```

Note that in this style, the argument I *means* "the number of elements which have been processed" and N *means* "the total number of elements".

The third method uses bisection.

bisection(N, ... args ...) :-
   bisection(1, N, ... args ...).

```
bisection(L, U, ... args ... ) :-
        L < U,
        !,
        M is (L + U)//2,
        N is M + 1,
        bisection(L, M, ... args ... ),
        bisection(N, U, ... args ... ).
bisection(N, N, ... args ... ) :- !,
        process(N, ... args ... ).
bisection(_, _, ... args ... ) :-
        /* no elements to process */.
```

Applied to the ground test, we obtain

```
ground(Term) :-
        nonvar(Term),
        functor(Term, _, Arity),
        ground(1, Arity, Term).
```

```
% ground(L, U, Term)
% is true when arguments L..U of Term are all ground.
```

```
ground(L, U, Term) :-
        (    L < U →
             M is (L+U) // 2,
             N is M+1,
             ground(L, M, Term),
             ground(N, U, Term)
        ;    L > U →
             true
        ; /*L = U */
             arg(L, Term, Arg),
             ground(Arg)
        ).
```

Just for variety, I have coded this to point out that you can use $if \rightarrow then; else$ in any of these methods.

In Prolog systems which support last call optimisation, counting down and counting up are superior to bisection. Bisection was often used in DEC-10 Prolog until David H.D. Warren implemented last call optimisation, because the other methods would build a tower of N local-stack frames, whereas the tower built by bisection is only $O(\log N)$ deep.

By actual measurement, the if-then-else version of counting down is the fastest way of coding ground/1 in Quintus Prolog. One uses this approach as a matter of course whenever it is appropriate.

Unfortunately, counting down traverses a term from right to left, while counting up and bisection traverse it from left to right. The standard predicate numbervars/3 is defined to number variables from left to right, so we have to code it thus:

```
numbervars('$VAR'(N0), N0, N) :- !,
        N is N0+1.
numbervars(Term, N0, N) :-
        /* nonvar(Term), otherwise clause 1 would have caught */
        functor(Term, _, Arity),
        numbervars(0, Arity, Term, N0, N).

numbervars(I, Arity, Term, N0, N) :-
    (   I =:= Arity → N = N0
    ;   J is I+1,
        arg(J, Term, Arg),
        numbervars(Arg, N0, N1),
        numbervars(J, Arity, Term, N1, N)
    ).
```

We see in this that (I,Arity) form a counting-up pair, and (N0,N) are an accumulator pair.

Something to bear in mind is that you can count with things other than numbers. For example, suppose you are given a list L1 and want to make a list L2 twice as long as L1. You could do

```
twice_as_long(L1, L2) :-
        length(L1, N1),
        N2 is N1*2,
        length(L2, N2).
```

When length/2 is given a length and asked to make a list, it probably uses a counting-down loop. In some Prologs, length/2 won't work that way at all. But we don't really need N1 or N2: L1 is a perfectly good representation of its own length as it stands. So we can write

```
twice_as_long([], []).
twice_as_long([_|L1], [_,_|L2]) :-
        twice_as_long(L1, L2).
```

A particularly important use of this is when we want to ensure that two lists are the same length. Consider the classical definition of permutation:

```
perm([], []).
perm([X|Xs], Ys1) :-
        perm(Xs, Ys),
        insert(Ys, X, Ys1).
```

```
insert(L, X, [X|L]).
insert([H|T], X, [H|L]) :-
        insert(T, X, L).
```

If the first argument of perm/2 is a proper list, it works well. But if you switch the arguments of perm/2, it misbehaves. The problem is that there is an infinite branch in the search tree where it keeps making wilder and wilder guesses for Xs. The cure is to constrain Xs and Ys to be the same length. But we don't need to compute the length explicitly: Ys itself will serve as an indication of its length. We obtain

```
permutation(Xs, Ys) :-
        permutation(Xs, Ys, Ys).
```

```
permutation([], [], []).
permutation([X|Xs], Ys1, [_|Bound]) :-
        permutation(Xs, Ys, Bound),
        insert(Ys, X, Ys1).
```

If Xs is proper, the third argument of permutation/3 doesn't do anything for us. But if Ys is proper, the third argument of permutation/3 is a list being used as a counter, counted down, and ensures that permutation/3 will terminate.

1.7 Backwards Correctness

When you are writing Prolog code it is important to realise that any predicate you write may be backtracked into. It is not sufficient to ensure that your predicate will compute the right answer when it is called: it must also behave sensibly if its caller fails.

You will recall that the counting methods I showed you earlier had cuts or if→ then;elses in them. Why is that?

Suppose we want a predicate to count the number of arguments of a term which are atoms. When I was starting to learn Prolog, I was tempted to write code like this:

```
count_atom_arguments(Term, Count) :-
        nonvar(Term),
        functor(Term, _, Arity),
        count_atom_arguments(Arity, Term, 0, Count).

count_atom_arguments(0, _, Count, Count).
count_atom_arguments(N, Term, Count0, Count) :-
        arg(N, Term, Arg),
        atom(Arg),
        Count1 is Count0+1,
        M is N-1,
        count_atom_arguments(M, Term, Count1, Count).
count_atom_arguments(N, Term, Count0, Count) :-
        M is N-1,
        count_atom_arguments(M, Term, Count0, Count).
```

If we call this, we shall see that it computes the correct answer.

```
?- count_atom_arguments(p(a,b,1,2,3,c,d,4,5,6,e,7,8,f), X).
X = 6
```

What's wrong with this? The answer is that if this solution is rejected, it will go away and never come back. The trouble is that nothing will ever stop the third clause.

There is of course a logical error in the third clause. It should only apply when there is an Nth argument, and it is not an atom. We might write the loop predicate as

```
count_atom_arguments(0, _, Count, Count).
count_atom_arguments(N, Term, Count0, Count) :-
        arg(N, Term, Arg),
        (       atom(Arg) → Increment = 1
        ; /*non atom*/ Increment = 0
        ),
        Count1 is Count0+Increment,
        M is N-1,
        count_atom_arguments(M, Term, Count1, Count).
```

Now this is safe because you can't get through the second clause unless Term has an Nth argument.

An important guide for Prolog programming is that you should look at each clause as you write it and say to yourself "when does it make sense to try this

clause? Have I ensured that Prolog knows when it doesn't make sense?" In this
example, you would have looked at the third clause. It makes sense only when
$N > 1$. But there is nothing there to tell Prolog that! You do not have to think
about *how* Prolog will execute the predicate, just *whether* it will try to execute the
clause, and if there is nothing to stop it, some day it *will* try it.

This example has the built-in protection of arg/3. But many similar loops lack
that protection. For example,

factorial(N, F) :-
       factorial(N, 1, F).

factorial(0, F, F).
factorial(N0, F0, F) :-
       F1 is F0*N0,
       N1 is N0-1,
       factorial(N1, F1, F).

We have to make this logically correct by inserting the condition that the second
clause is only to be applied when N0 > 0.

count_atom_arguments/4 is logically determinate because arg(N,Term,Arg) cannot succeed when $N = 0$, and it would be pleasant if Prolog compilers were smart
enough to realise this. Most aren't. In present systems, the first clause will leave a
choice point behind because it cannot tell that the second clause won't be useful.
The rule for efficiency is never to let a choice point live unless it will be useful, so
we have to add a cut to the first clause, or use an if→ then;else. We thus obtain

count_atom_arguments(N, Term, Count0, Count) :-
    (N =:= 0 →
       Count is Count0
    ;   arg(N, Term, Arg),
       (atom(Arg) → Increment = 1
       ; /*non atom*/ Increment = 0
       ),
       Count1 is Count0+Increment,
       M is N-1,
       count_atom_arguments(M, Term, Count1, Count)
).

The backwards correctness problem shows up elsewhere. You will recall the usual
definition of append/3:

```
append([], L, L).
append([H|T], L, [H|R]) :-
        append(T, L, R).
```

If the first argument of append/3 is a proper list we are safe. This will terminate no matter what we do. Similarly, if the third argument is a proper list, append/3 will terminate. But if we call

```
?- append(X, [], X).
X = [] ;
X = [_144] ;
X = [_144,_146] ;
X = [_144,_146,_148] ;
X = [_144,_146,_148,_150] ;
X = [_144,_146,_148,_150,_152] ;
    ⋮
```

There is very little we can do about this, because that it what it is *supposed* to do: it is enumerating all the solutions of that goal, and there are infinitely many. Coroutining systems like NU Prolog do a better job of coping with such queries, but what they do is to put them to one side and hope. The problem is that some queries genuinely have far too many solutions to be feasible. The answer is that you should make it clear in the comments of your predicates which ways around they are supposed to work.

> What will your predicate do if it is backtracked into?

2 Searching

2.1 Introduction

Suppose we have a graph defined by two predicates:

start(StartingPlace) this predicate identifies a starting point in the graph. Usually it will identify a unique node in the graph, one which has no predecessors, but that isn't strictly necessary.

child(ParentPlace, ChildPlace) this predicate is true whenever ParentPlace and ChildPlace are nodes of the graph and there is an arc leading directly from ParentPlace to ChildPlace.

and that we want to locates nodes which can be reached from a starting place by following "child" arcs and which satisfy a third given predicate:

solution(InterestingPlace) which is true of those nodes in the graph which we are interested in finding.

2.2 Simple Depth-First Search

The obvious way to code this in Prolog is as a transitive closure. Transitive closures are described further in section 5.4. Logically we want

answer(Y) $\Leftrightarrow$ start(X) & X child$^*Y$ & solution(Y)

which can be expressed directly in Prolog as

```
answer(Y) :-
        start(X),
        child_star(X, Y),
        solution(Y).

child_star(X, X).
child_star(X, Z) :-
        child(X, Y),
        child_star(Y, Z).
```

It is important to bear in mind the two readings of this piece of code: under the *declarative* reading it is a clear and concise description of exactly what we mean by Y being an answer, but under the *procedural* reading it is a program which can be executed to find answers. The text we have here doesn't say how it is to be executed: we bring to the reading our knowledge of how the Prolog system executes such specifications.

Considered as a *Prolog program*, this is a depth-first search which starts from the starting place and explores blindly, exploring each node's children before it explores its brothers. Considered as a *logical specification*, it is no such thing. An interpreter which started by enumerating the solutions and then searching up the graph to see which of them could be reached would be entirely consistent with the logic.

Before going any further, let's have an example of a graph. To keep things simple, I'll make it a tree. That is, there will be a unique starting place, and each node in the graph will be the child of at most one other node. Lines running down the page are to be read as saying that the lower node is a child of the upper node.

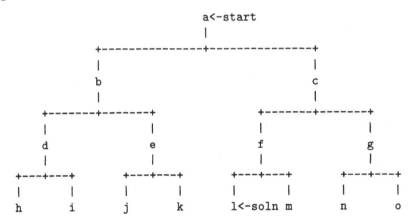

I have chosen to make node l the solution.

The program we have above will check the nodes in the order

a, b, d, h, i, e, j, k, c, f, l, m, g, n, o

That is what is meant by a depth-first search.

Depth-first search has many virtues. That is what makes Prolog so efficient as a programming language. But it is not always the best way of searching a graph. Sometimes other search orders are better.

Many people have stopped at this point, and said "This program did not specify a searching method. The searching method was inherited from Prolog. Prolog has depth first search and nothing else. Therefore this program has depth first search and nothing else. Therefore you cannot program other searches in Prolog." You may be surprised to see such bad logic from people who profess to be able to judge a logic programming language, but it is so: just such claims have appeared in print.

The difficulty lies in the fact that *this* program does not specify a search order in its logic, so *this* program defaults to using Prolog's depth first strategy. The solution lies in realising that we *can* specify the search order in the *logic* of a program instead of leaving it implicit in the interpreter, and that if we do so, we can obtain any search order we want.

2.3   Depth-First Search with explicit Open set

Let's start by making the depth-first program more explicit. Following standard terminology, we shall call the collection of nodes which have not been explored yet "Open". It turns out to be more convenient to pick up all the children of a node at once. You may be able to provide this operation directly. If that would not be easy, we can code it in Prolog:

```
children(ParentNode, ChildrenNodes) :-
        findall(ChildNode, child(ParentNode, ChildNode), ChildrenNodes).
```

The new program is

```
depth_first(Answer) :-
        start(Start),
        depth_star(/*Open*/ [Start], Answer),
        solution(Answer).
```

```
depth_star([X|_], X).
depth_star([X|Open1], Y) :-
        children(X, Children),
        append(Children, Open1, Open2),
        depth_star(Open2, Y).
```

Now the collection of unexplored nodes is visible as an explicit list, rather than being implicit in the stack frames of the child_star/2 predicate. We can see that depth_first/2 is popping nodes off the front of the list, and pushing the children back onto the front, so the Open set is being maintained as a stack.

2.4   Breadth-First Search

We begin to see how we could program other searching methods. We can choose other data structures to represent the Open set, use some other way of selecting a candidate from it, and insert the children into it some other way.

A particularly simple change is to add the children at the other end of the Open list. With this change we maintain the Open collection as a queue rather than a stack, and it is well known that this gives us breadth-first search.

breadth_first_1(Answer) :-
        start(Start),
        breadth_star_1(/*Open*/ [Start], Answer),
        solution(Answer).

breadth_star_1([X|_], X).
breadth_star_1([X|Open1], Y) :-
        children(X, Children),
        append(Open1, Children, Open2),
        breadth_star_1(Open2, Y).

If you run this program with the example graph shown above, and check the arguments given to solution/1, you will see that it explores the graph in the order

    a, b, c, d, e, f, g, h, i, j, k, l, m, n, o

This is what we mean by breadth-first search: all the nodes which are N steps away from the starting point will be explored before any of the nodes which are $N + 1$ steps away from the starting point. In this particular case, depth-first search checked fewer nodes than breadth-first search, but if 'b' had had more descendants the reverse would have been true.

This is a large difference in behaviour from a very small change in the code: we just swapped the first two arguments to append/3.

2.5   A Digression on Queues

The breadth-first search code written above is inefficient because it keeps copying the entire Open set. It is better to use a different data structure which makes queue operations more efficient.

A queue is a sequence just like a list. It is easy to add elements at one end of a list, and easy to remove them from the same end. Lists are a good way of implementing stacks. But with a queue we want to add elements at one end and remove them from the other.

A basic set of operations is

empty_queue(Queue) true when Queue represents an empty queue.

queue_head(Head, Queue1, Queue0) true when Queue1 and Queue0 represent queues having the same elements, except that Queue0 has an extra element at the left, namely Head.

queue_last(Last, Queue1, Queue0) true when Queue1 and Queue0 represent queues having the same elements, except that Queue0 has an extra element at the right, namely Head.

A very simple approach would be to use lists. We would then have the following definitions:

empty_queue_1([]).

queue_head_1(Head, Queue1, [Head|Queue1]).

queue_last_1(Last, Queue1, Queue0) :-
        append(Queue1, [Last], Queue0).

Making an empty queue costs unit time, as does adding or removing an element at the left of a queue. But adding or removing an element at the right of a queue having N elements costs $O(N)$ time and space. So if we add N elements at the right of a queue and then remove them from the left it will cost $O(N^2)$ time and space.

Something you should always look out for is an opportunity to *batch* updates. Suppose you have a list of M items to be added to a queue, or removed from it. We might do

queue_head_list_1(Heads, Queue1, Queue0) :-
        append(Heads, Queue1, Queue0).

queue_last_list_1(Lasts, Queue1, Queue0) :-
        append(Queue1, Lasts, Queue0).

Adding M elements at the right of a queue having N elements with these definitions costs $O(N)$ time, rather than the $O(MN)$ time that adding the elements one at a time would cost.

There is a technique well-known in functional programming circles. What you do is keep a back-to-back pair of lists L+R, where the sequence represented by the pair is the sequence represented by the list append(L,reverse(R)). With this representation, we have

empty_queue_2([]+[]).
queue_head_2(Head, L+R, [Head|L]+R).
queue_head_2(Head, L+[], []+R) :-
        reverse(R, [Head|L]).

queue_last_2(Last, L+R, L+[Last|R]).
queue_last_2(Last, []+R, L+[]) :-
        reverse(L, [Last|R]).

In order to make this faster, we might rewrite it as

empty_queue_2([]+[]).

queue_head_2(Head, L1+R1, L2+R2) :-
        queue_head_2(L2, R2, L1, R1, Head).
queue_head_2([], R, L, [], Head) :-
        reverse(R, [Head|L]).
queue_head_2([Head|L], R, L, R, Head).

queue_last_2(Last, L1+R1, L2+R2+) :-
        queue_head_2(R2, L2, R1, L1, Last).

Here is a trace:

```
?-    empty_queue_2(Q0) ,        % Q0 = []+[]
      queue_last_2(a, Q0, Q1),   % Q1 = []+[a]
      queue_last_2(b, Q1, Q2),   % Q2 = []+[b,a]
      queue_last_2(c, Q2, Q3),   % Q3 = []+[c,b,a]
      queue_head_2(U, Q4, Q3),   % Q4 = [b,c]+[]; [c,b,a] was reversed!
      queue_head_2(V, Q5, Q4),   % Q5 = [c]+[]
      queue_head_2(W, Q6, Q5).   % Q6 = []+[]
```

The cost of any individual operation can be $O(N)$ where N is the number of elements in the queue, but (as long as we don't backtrack), the *average* cost of an addition or deletion is $O(1)$.

This would be an ideal solution, but in Prolog it is possible for the reversal to be done many times. Consider

```
?-    ...
      many_solutions(X),
      queue_head_2(Element, Q1, Q),
      p(Element, X),
      ...
```

The queue_head_2/3 call can be repeated as many times as many_solutions/1 has solutions, so the $O(N)$ worst case cost of queue_head_2/3 can be repeated that many times.

Another approach would be to use difference lists. We might represent a queue by a pair Front-Back, where Back is a tail of Front.[1] The code we obtain is

---

[1] This is in general a bad idea; difference lists should almost always be represented by a pair of arguments, not by a data structure.

empty_queue_3(Queue-Queue).

queue_head_3(Head, Front-Back, [Head|Front]-Back).

queue_last_3(Last, Front-[Last|Back], Front-Back).

Here is a trace:

```
?-  empty_queue_3(Q0),          % Q0 = X1-X1
    queue_last_3(a, Q0, Q1),    % Q1 = X1-X2, X1 = [a|X2]
    queue_last_3(b, Q1, Q2),    % Q2 = X1-X3, X2 = [b|X3]
    queue_last_3(c, Q2, Q3),    % Q3 = X1-X4, X3 = [c|X4]
/* at this point, Q0 = [a,b,c|X4]-[a,b,c|X4] */
    queue_head_3(U, Q4, Q3),    % Q4 = [b,c|X4]-X4
    queue_head_3(V, Q5, Q4),    % Q5 = [c|X4]-X4
    queue_head_3(W, Q6, Q5).    % Q6 = X4-X4
```

This has some disadvantages, such as the fact that it is possible to remove more elements from such a queue than were inserted into it. I call this *hallucinating*; logical variables let you refer to terms that are not fully known yet, but when you take more things off a queue than are ever entered you are dealing with things which will never exist. For example:

```
?-  empty_queue_3(Q0),          % Q0 = X1-X1
    queue_head_3(X, Q1, Q0).    % Q1 = X2-[X|X2], Q0 = [X|X2]-[X|X2].
```

For several years, this was the representation of queues that I used, despite the disadvantages. Then Fernando Pereira showed me a technique that he attributes to Mark Johnson [20], who invented it while at Stanford. Johnson was contrasting two alternative analyses for a feature of Swiss German known as the "Double Infinitive Construction", and realised that he had to simulate queues in his (unification-based) grammar in order to generate this construction. The idea is that we use a difference list to hold the elements of a queue, but augment it with the current length of the queue, represented in unary notation. That is, a queue representation looks like

$$q(\underset{n}{s(\ldots \underset{1}{s(0)} \ldots)}, [\underset{1}{X1},\ldots,\underset{n}{Xn,Y1,\ldots}], [Y1,\ldots])$$

where the term 0 represents the integer 0, and $s(X)$ represents the integer after the integer X represents. So there are as many 's' constructors wrapped around the 0 in the first argument are there are elements in the queue.

Here is the queue package that I used to test the searching predicates described in this chapter.

```
%    queue(Queue)
%    is true when Queue is a queue with no elements.

queue(q(0,B,B)).

%    queue(X, Queue)
%    is true when Queue is a queue with one element.

queue(X, q(s(0),[X|B],B)).

%    queue_head(X, Queue1, Queue0)
%    is true when Queue0 and Queue1 have the same elements except
%    that Queue0 has in addition X at the front.
%    Use it for enqueuing and dequeuing both.

queue_head(X, q(N,F,B), q(s(N),[X|F],B)).

%    queue_head_list(List, Queue1, Queue0)
%    is true when append(List, Queue1, Queue0) would be true
%    if only Queue1 and Queue0 were lists instead of queues.

queue_head_list([], Queue, Queue).
queue_head_list([X|Xs], Queue, Queue0) :-
        queue_head(X, Queue1, Queue0),
        queue_head_list(Xs, Queue, Queue1).

%    queue_last(X, Queue1, Queue0)
%    is true when Queue0 and Queue1 have the same elements except
%    that Queue0 has in addition X at the end.

queue_last(X, q(N,F,[X|B]), q(s(N),F,B)).

%    queue_last_list(List, Queue1, Queue0)
%    is true when append(Queue1, List, Queue0) would be true
%    if only Queue1 and Queue0 were lists instead of queues.

queue_last_list([], Queue, Queue).
queue_last_list([X|Xs], Queue1, Queue) :-
        queue_last(X, Queue1, Queue2),
        queue_last_list(Xs, Queue2, Queue).
```

```
%    list_queue(List, Queue)
%    is true when List is a list and Queue is a queue and they
%    represent the same sequence.

list_queue(List, q(Count,Front,Back)) :-
        list_queue(List, Count, Front, Back).

list_queue([], 0, B, B).
list_queue([X|Xs], s(N), [X|F], B) :-
        list_queue(Xs, N, F, B).

%    queue_length(Queue, Length)
%    is true when Length is (a binary integer representing) the number
%    of elements in (the queue represented by) Queue. This version cannot
%    be used to generate a Queue, only to determine the Length.

queue_length(q(Count,Front,Back), Length) :-
        queue_length(Count, Front, Back, 0, Length).

queue_length(0, Back, Back, Length, Length).
queue_length(s(N), [_|Front], Back, L0, Length) :-
        L1 is L0+1,
        queue_length(N, Front, Back, L1, Length).
```

2.6 Back to Breadth-First Search

With the aid of the queue package described above, we can code breadth-first search
more efficiently.

```
breadth_first(Answer) :-
        start(Start),
        queue(Start, Open),
        breadth_star(Open, Answer),
        solution(Answer).
```

```
breadth_star(Open, Y) :-
        queue_head(X, Open1, Open),
        (    Y = X
        ;    children(X, Children),
             queue_last_list(Children, Open1, Open2),
             breadth_star(Open2, Y)
        ).
```

In fact, if we are sure that there is at least one solution in the tree, and if we only want one solution, we can use the difference list version. This amounts to replacing the call to append/3 in the first version of breadth_star/1 by a difference list.

```
breadth_first_2(Answer) :-
        start(Start),
        breadth_star_2([Start|Rest], Rest, Y),
        solution(Y),
        !,
        Answer = Y.
breadth_star_2([X|Open], Rest, Y) :-
        (    Y = X
        ;    children(X, Children),
             append(Children, Rest1, Rest),
             breadth_star_2(Open, Rest1, Y)
        ).
```

This is measurably faster than the version using queues, but there is a snag. One way of thinking about it is that there is a race between the producer of nodes (children/2 and append/3) and the consumer of nodes (breadth_star_2/3). As long as there is at least one node in the instantiated portion of the Open set which has any children, the producer will stay ahead, but eventually the nodes with children will run out and the producer will stop putting new nodes at the end. But nothing ever puts a nil ([]) there. So when the nodes have run out, breadth_star_2/3 will keep on going, hallucinating new nodes. Provided there is at least one solution, breadth_first_2/1 will find it, and the cut will then ensure that it doesn't go on forever, hallucinating. The version using queues does not have this problem, because at every step the queue of nodes is properly terminated.

2.7   Digression: Unpacking the 'queue' records

The version of breadth-first search which uses 'queue' triples works, but we would like it to go as fast as possible. A common method of speeding up a Prolog procedure is to note that one of its arguments is always a compound term of a certain form, and to pass the arguments separately instead. This I call "unpacking". The first argument of breadth_star/2, for example, is always a queue(N,F,B) triple, so we might investigate passing N, F, and B as separate arguments.

If we do this, and unfold the calls to queue/2 and queue_head/3, we get

```
breadth_first(Answer) :-
        start(Start),
        breadth_star(s(0), [Start|B0], B0, Answer),
        solution(Answer).

breadth_star(s(N1), [Node|F1], B1, Answer) :-
        (    Answer = Node
        ;    children(Node, Children),
             queue_last_list(Children, N1, F1, B1, N2, F2, B2),
             breadth_star(N2, F2, B2, Answer)
        ).

queue_last_list([], N, F, B, N, F, B).
queue_last_list([X|Xs], N0, F1, [X|B1], N, F, B) :-
        queue_last_list(Xs, s(N0), F1, B1, N, F, B).
```

A predicate with seven arguments is a bit unwieldy, so we restructure the program, defining

```
breadth_one(N, F, B, A) :-
        breadth_star(N, F, B, A),
        solution(A).

breadth_two(Xs, N0, F0, B0, A) :-
        queue_last_list(Xs, N0, F0, B0, N1, F1, B1),
        breadth_one(N1, F1, B1, A).
```

That's what the new predicates are to *mean*, here's how it all *works*:

```
breadth_first(Answer) :-
        start(Start),
        breadth_one(s(0), [Start|B], B, Answer).
```

```
breadth_one(s(N1), [Node|F1], B1, Answer) :-
        (    solution(Node),
             Answer = Node
        ;    children(Node, Children),
             breadth_two(Children, N1, F1, B1, Answer)
        ).

breadth_two([], N, F, B, Answer) :-
        breadth_one(N, F, B, Answer).
breadth_two([X|Xs], N, F, [X|B], Answer) :-
        breadth_two(Xs, s(N), F, B, Answer).
```

We can simplify this still further, by unfolding the call to breadth_one/4 in the first clause of breadth_two/5. Then we might as well call breadth_two/5 breadth_star/5 again.

```
breadth_first(Answer) :-
        start(Start),
        breadth_star([], s(0), [Start|B], B, Answer).

breadth_star([], s(N), [Node|F], B, Answer) :-
        (    solution(Node),
             Answer = Node
        ;    children(Node, Children),
             breadth_star(Children, N, F, B, Answer)
        ).
breadth_star([X|Xs], N, F, [X|B], Answer) :-
        breadth_star(Xs, s(N), F, B, Answer).
```

The original code constructed a new queue element every time a child was added to the queue (at a cost of 2 words for s(N), 2 words for [X|B], and 4 words for queue(_,_,_)) and every time a node was removed from the queue (at a cost of 4 words for queue(_,_,_)). This was a cost of 10 words per item ever in the queue. The new code costs 4 words per item. Where the nodes themselves are small, this may be a substantial saving. Where the nodes are large and costly to build, it may be negligible. This improvement speeded up the 8-puzzle by 8%.

If you want to code a breadth-first search in Prolog, this is the approach to use.

2.8 Keeping Track of Visited Nodes

Now we have breadth first and depth first search coded efficiently in Prolog. Efficiently, that is, for trees. When we have a graph, we may explore the same subgraph many times. Worse: if the graph contains a cycle, a depth-first search may never terminate. There is a standard solution for that. In addition to the collection of Open nodes which have yet to be explored, we carry around a collection of Closed nodes which are not to be generated again. The presence of a node in the Closed set does not mean that it has been explored entirely, or even at all. It only means that the node is never to be included in the Open set again.

How shall we represent the Closed set? The basic thing we want to do is to add a node to it and determine whether it was previously present. The Quintus library contains a predicate ord_union/4 which comes close: see section 5.2.

ord_union(+OldSet, +NewSet, ?Union, ?ReallyNew) given an OldSet and a NewSet, this returns their Union, and the ReallyNew elements, namely the elements of NewSet which were not already in OldSet.

This takes time proportional to the size of the input sets. We would really prefer something which took time proportional to the size of the New set. But this will do to be going on with.

We thus arrive at two new versions of depth first and breadth first search.

```
depth_first(Answer) :-
        start(Start),
        depth_star(/*Open*/ [Start], /*Closed*/ [Start], Answer),
        solution(Answer).
```

```
depth_star([X|_], _, X).
depth_star([X|Open1], Closed, Y) :-
        children(X, Children),
        ord_union(Closed, Children, Closed1, Children1),
        append(Children1, Open1, Open2),
        depth_star(Open2, Closed1, Y).
```

```
children(ParentNode, ChildrenSet) :-
        findall(ChildNode,
                child(ParentNode, ChildNode),
                ChildrenNodes),
        sort(ChildrenNodes, ChildrenSet).
```

```
breadth_first(Answer) :-
        start(Start),
        queue(Start, Open),
        breadth_star(Open, /*Closed*/ [Start], Answer),
        solution(Answer).
```

breadth_star(Open, Closed, Y) :-
      queue_head(X, Open1, Open),
      (Y = X
      ;   children(X, Children),
           ord_union(Closed, Children, Closed1, Children1),
           queue_last_list(Children1, Open1, Open2),
           breadth_star(Open2, Closed1, Y)
).

2.9   Local Heuristic Ordering

We have a degree of freedom in these two predicates. We can search the children
of a node in any order we please. So far we have considered searching them in the
order they happened to be generated, and searching them in an order determined
by their names. But if we can estimate how close a node is to a solution, we can
order the children of a node so they are searched in order of plausibility. If you
know the distance to a solution exactly, you don't need to do any searching because
you can just pick the closest node at each step. When the estimate is not know to
be exact, it is called a *heuristic* function. The heuristic is a new given (functional)
predicate:

estimated_distance_to_goal(+Node, -Estimate) given a node, this returns an
    estimate of how far it is from this node to a solution. Only the relative order
    (big is bad) matters.

We obtain two new searching methods:

h_depth_first(Answer) :-
      start(Start),
      h_depth_star(/*Open*/ [Start], /*Closed*/ [Start], Answer),
      solution(Answer).

h_depth_star([X|_], _, X).
h_depth_star([X|Open1], Closed, Y) :-
      children(X, Closed, Closed1, Children1),
      append(Children1, Open1, Open2),
      h_depth_star(Open2, Closed1, Y).

children(ParentNode, Closed, Closed1, RankedChildren) :-
      ordered_children(ParentNode, Closed, Closed1, OrdPairs),
      strip_ranks(OrdPairs, RankedChildren).

```
ordered_children(ParentNode, Closed, Closed1, OrdPairs) :-
        children(ParentNode, ChildrenSet),
        ord_union(Closed, ChildrenSet, Closed1, NewChildren),
        compute_ranks(NewChildren, RawPairs),
        keysort(RawPairs, OrdPairs).

compute_ranks([], []).
compute_ranks([Child|Children], [Estimate-Child|Pairs]) :-
        estimated_distance_to_goal(Child, Estimate),
        compute_ranks(Children, Pairs).

strip_ranks([], []).
strip_ranks([_-Child|Pairs], [Child|Children]) :-
        strip_ranks(Pairs, Children).

h_breadth_first(Answer) :-
        start(Start),
        queue(Start, Open),
        h_breadth_star(Open, /*Closed*/ [Start], Answer),
        solution(Answer).

h_breadth_star(Open, Closed, Y) :-
        queue_head(X, Open1, Open),
        (   Y = X
        ;   children(X, Closed, Closed1, Children1),
            queue_last_list(Children1, Open1, Open2),
            h_breadth_star(Open2, Y)
        ).
```

2.10 Global Heuristic Ordering

Why should we stop at ordering the children of a node by their distance estimates? Why not keep the whole Open set in such an order?

What we want is a data structure which represents a collection of nodes and cost estimates from which we can cheaply select the node with lowest associated cost estimate. The operations we want are

empty_heap(-Heap) make an empty heap.

add_to_heap(+Heap0, +Cost, +Node, -Heap) add a Node and its associated cost to a given Heap0, yielding a new Heap containing that Node and the contents of the old Heap0.

get_from_heap(+Heap0, -Cost, -Node, -Heap) remove from a given Heap0 the Node with the lowest associated Cost, and return the updated Heap.

A data structure providing such operations is called a *priority queue*, and the Quintus Prolog library contains an implementation using heaps. I shall not describe the implementation here, but shall simply take heaps as given; they are standard data structures described in all good data structure textbooks.

The code we obtain has the form

```
best_first(Answer) :-
        start(Start),
        initial_heap(Start, Heap),
        best_star(/*Open*/ Heap, /*Closed*/ [Start], Answer),
        solution(Answer).

initial_heap(Start, Heap) :-
        estimated_distance_to_goal(Start, Estimate),
        empty_heap(Empty),
        add_to_heap(Empty, Estimate, Start, Heap).

best_star(Heap, Closed, Answer) :-
        get_from_heap(Heap, _, Node, Heap1),
        (    Answer = Node
        ;    children_4(Node, Closed, Closed1, Heap1, Heap2),
             best_star(Heap2, Closed1, Answer)
        ).

children_4(ParentNode, Closed, Closed1, Heap, Heap1) :-
        ordered_children(ParentNode, Closed, Closed1, OrdPairs),
        add_children(OrdPairs, Heap, Heap1).

add_children([], Heap, Heap).
add_children([Estimate-Child|Children], Heap0, Heap) :-
        add_to_heap(Heap0, Estimate, Child, Heap1),
        add_children(Children, Heap1, Heap).
```

2.11 An Example

In this section, these searching methods are applied to a real problem. Or at any rate a real toy problem. A commonly used example is the "8-puzzle". We are given a little tray capable of holding 9 square tiles. There are 8 tiles, numbered 1 to 8, and there is a hole. There are thus $9! = 362,880$ different states. It turns out that they fall into two groups, such that any state in either group can be reached from any other state in the same group but from no state in the other group. Each group contains 181,440 states. Here is a picture of the starting state:

1	2	3
7	8	4
6	5	

Any of the tiles can slide horizontally or vertically, provided that it is moving into the hole. There is one solution:

1	2	3
8		4
7	6	5

Note that if you can get from a position P to a position C in this problem, you can get back from C to P by sliding the tile you just moved back the other way. So plain depth-first search is likely to get trapped in a loop. We'll try five methods on this puzzle:

- plain breadth-first search

- depth-first search with a Closed set

- breadth-first search with a Closed set

- depth-first search with a Closed set and ordered children

- breadth-first search with a Closed set and ordered children

The times reported here are for Quintus Prolog release 2.0 running on a Sun 3/50
under SunOS 3.2. They really don't mean a whole lot, because this is just one
rather small problem. I leave it as an exercise for the reader to work out how to
represent the board.

Time	#Nodes	Time/Node	Method
1.7s	64	27 ms	plain breadth first
1.1s	31	36 ms	breadth first with closed set
0.8s	22	36 ms	breadth first with distance estimate
0.4s	11	36 ms	depth first with distance estimate
0.2s	6	33 ms	best first

There is no point in trying simple depth-first search on this problem because the
state graph is full of cycles (if you move the tile, you can always move it straight
back). Depth-first search would usually fail to terminate on problems like this.

Since there are only four possible moves in any state, it is easy to calculate the
set of children directly rather than using findall/3. The results using this approach
were

Time	#Nodes	Time/Node	Method
0.27s	137	2 ms	bounded depth first (depth bound = 8)
0.20s	98	2 ms	depth first with iterative deepening
0.37s	64	6 ms	plain breadth first using difference list
0.44s	64	7 ms	plain breadth first using queue
0.28s	60	5 ms	iterative deepening + local ordering
0.25s	31	8 ms	breadth first with closed set
0.32s	22	14 ms	breadth first with distance estimate
0.15s	11	14 ms	depth first with distance estimate
0.09s	6	15 ms	best first

Although the different search methods seem to range from very simple to quite
complicated (if you don't regard the priority queue package as "given" you will

find the best-first search to be very complicated), we see that all of them spend about the same amount of time per node investigated. The only really important difference is how many nodes are investigated.

In order to work out which searching method to use in any particular case, we see that you don't need to understand the details of the Prolog code. What you need to understand is which method is likely to explore fewest nodes. The most important thing to understand is the space your program is searching.

2.12   Iterative Deepening

Depth-first search is attractive because it maps so directly to Prolog. The big problem with it is that it is prepared to explore infinite paths in the search space. Can we tame depth-first search?

It turns out that we can tame depth-first search very simply, obtaining a method which is as safe as breadth-first search, yet which can be used directly in Prolog.

The first step is to put a *depth bound* on depth-first search. Here is the code:

```
bounded_depth_first(Bound, Answer) :-
        Bound ≥ 0,
        start(Start),
        bounded_depth_star(Bound, Start, Answer),
        solution(Answer).

bounded_depth_star(Bound, Node, Answer) :-
        (     Answer = Node
        ;     Bound1 is Bound-1,
              Bound1 ≥ 0,
              child(Node, Child),
              bounded_depth_star(Bound1, Child, Answer)
        ).
```

This is a plain depth first search, except that as soon as the Bound is exhausted it abandons that path. The Bound being finite, if each Node has finitely many children, bounded depth-first search must terminate.

Following DEC-10 Prolog, the Quintus Prolog interpreter has a depth bound like this which you can set with maxdepth/1. That bound only applies to interpreted code, though. We'll see shortly how you can add a depth bound to compiled code.

Bounded depth-first search is fine, provided you can guess a suitable bound. If your guess is too large, it may waste a lot of time. If your guess is too small, it may fail to find a solution. We saw in the table above that bounded depth-first search with a depth bound of 8 explored 137 nodes, even though another variant of depth-first search was able to find a solution after exploring only 11 nodes. Most of that work was wasted. (Even so, it managed to be faster than most versions of breadth-first search.) If we had used a depth bound of 1, no solution would have been found.

The answer to the problem of guessing the bound is to try a succession of bounds. We thus obtain a method called *iterative deepening* (also called *consecutively bounded* depth-first search). We start off with a small bound, and keep on increasing it. Here is the code:

```
iterative_depth_first(Answer) :-
        iterative_depth_first(0, Answer).
iterative_depth_first(Bound, Answer) :-
        bounded_depth_first(Bound, Answer).
iterative_depth_first(Bound, Answer) :-
        Bound1 is Bound+1,
        iterative_depth_first(Bound1, Answer).
```

The initial depth Bound need not be 0. It could be bigger. We need not increment the bound by 1. We could increment it by 2 or more.

There are two problems with this version of iterative deepening. It does a lot of repeated work, and may report the same answer more than once. For example, if a solution is found with depth bound 3, it will also be found with all depth bounds greater than 3. It turns out that if the average number of children per node is B (this is known as the *branching factor* of the search space) it does about $\frac{B}{(B-1)}$ times as many operations as breadth-first search.

We can add the local ordering heuristic to bounded depth-first search (and thus to iterative deepening). This cut the number of nodes explored in the example above from 98 with plain iterative deepening to 60 with local ordering.

The exciting thing about iterative deepening is that it is easy to apply to Horn clause programs. Suppose we have a Horn clause program something like this, where *args*, and (–) are irrelevant details:

$p_1(args)$:- $b_{111}(-), \ldots, b_{11k}(\ )$.
$\vdots$
$p_1(args)$:- $b_{1n1}(-), \ldots, b_{1nk}(-)$.
$\vdots$
$p_m(args)$:- $b_{m11}(-), \ldots, b_{m1k}(-)$.
$\vdots$
$p_m(args)$:- $b_{mn1}(-), \ldots, b_{mnk}(-)$.

We can run this with a depth bound by adding two new arguments B0,B to every predicate, adding a check to every clause, and linking the body goals together thus:

$p_1(args,$B0,B) :-
       B0 > 0, B1 is B0-1, $b_{111}(-,$B1,B2), ..., $b_{11k}(-,$Bk,B).

$\vdots$

$p_1(args,$B0,B) :-
       B0 > 0, B1 is B0-1, $b_{1n1}(-,$B1,B2), ..., $b_{1nk}(-,$Bk,B).

$\vdots$

$p_m(args,$B0,B) :-
       B0 > 0, B1 is B0-1, $b_{m11}(-,$B1,B2), ..., $b_{m1k}(-,$Bk,B).

$\vdots$

$p_m(args,$B0,B) :-
       B0 > 0, B1 is B0-1, $b_{mn1}(-,$B1,B2), ..., $b_{mnk}(-,$Bk,B).

A well-known example of a simple Prolog program which can run into trouble is trying to find a path through a graph which has a loop in it. Here's a very simple version.

```
arc(/* from */ a, /* to */ b).
arc(/* from */ b, /* to */ c).
arc(/* from */ c, /* to */ b).
arc(/* from */ c, /* to */ d).

path(Node, Node).
path(From, To) :-
        arc(From, Next),
        path(Next, To).

?-    path(a, d).
```

This query leads to path/2 chasing around the b→ c→ b loop forever. But if we apply the depth-bound transformation to the program, we get

```
arc(/* from */ a, /* to */ b, B0, B) :- B0 > 0, B is B0-1.
arc(/* from */ b, /* to */ c, B0, B) :- B0 > 0, B is B0-1.
arc(/* from */ c, /* to */ b, B0, B) :- B0 > 0, B is B0-1.
arc(/* from */ c, /* to */ d, B0, B) :- B0 > 0, B is B0-1.

path(Node, Node, B0, B) :- B0 > 0, B is B0-1.
```

```
path(From, To, B0, B) :-
        B0 > 0, B1 is B0-1,
        arc(From, Next, B1, B2),
        path(Next, To, B2, B).
```

```
?-   path(a, d, 8, _), !.
```

The bound here is on the number of resolutions to be done. It is, in general, hard to predict this, so we should use iterative deepening.

```
id_call(Goal) :-
        id_call(Goal, 1).
```

```
id_call(Goal, Bound) :-
        call(Goal, Bound, _). % from library(call)
id_call(Goal, Bound) :-
        Bound1 is Bound+1,
        id_call(Goal, Bound1).
```

We can pervert the Definite Clause Grammar (DCG) notation to make it easy to write code in this style. We just add a predicate

```
tally(B0, B) :-
        B0 > 0,
        B is B0-1.
```

and then we can write

```
arc(/* from */ a, /* to */ b) ⟶ tally.
arc(/* from */ b, /* to */ c) ⟶ tally.
arc(/* from */ c, /* to */ b) ⟶ tally.
arc(/* from */ c, /* to */ d) ⟶ tally.
```

```
path(Node, Node) ⟶ tally.
path(From, To) ⟶ tally,
        arc(From, Next),
        path(Next, To).
```

```
?-   id_call(path(a,d)), !.
```

Note that abusing DCG notation this way gives us a way of calling built-in predicates, such as {X > Y}. A better approach would be to write a translator for such predicates similar to the DCG rule translator and plug it into term_expansion/2.

So if you have a logic program which you cannot run in plain Prolog because depth first search goes into a loop, you can use this approach to tame it.

2.12.1 Avoiding duplicate solutions

One snag with iterative deepening is that if we find a solution when the depth bound is B, we shall find and report it again when the depth bound is $B+1$, when it is $B+2$, and so on forever. We can't avoid *finding* such repeated solutions, but we *can* avoid *reporting* them.

A simple technique is to look at the final value of B: if it is less than the increment the solution cannot have been reported on any previous iteration. We don't need to change the translation of clauses, just id_call/2.

id_call(Goal) :-
        id_call(Goal, 1, 1).

id_call(Goal, Bound, Increment) :-
        call(Goal, Bound, Remaining),
        Remaining < Increment.
id_call(Goal, Bound, Increment) :-
        Bound1 is Bound+Increment,
        id_call(Goal, Bound1, Increment).

2.12.2 Pruning Earlier

A clause whose body contains N goals is going to require at least one resolution step for each of them, and it is going to require one resolution step for the head. This means that there is no hope of the clause succeeding unless $B > N$ when it starts. So instead of translating a clause as

$p(args,B_0,B)$:-
        $B_0 > 0$, % enough for head
        $B1$ is $B_0 - 1$,
        $b_1(-,B_1,B_2), \ldots, b_N(-,B_N,B)$.

we can translate it as

$p(args,B_0,B)$:-
        $B_0 > N$, % minimum needed for head and body
        $B1$ is $B_0 - 1$, % decrement by 1, not N
        $b_1(-,B_1,B_2), \ldots, b_N(-,B_N,B)$.

This can save some wasted work in any form of depth-bounded search. What we need here is a lower bound on the number of steps needed for each goal in the body; the better we can make those bounds the sooner we can cut off a search which is fated to exceed the depth limit.

2.12.3 Stopping

The big problem with the iterative deepening method is that it never gives up. Suppose the search space is of depth D, that is, there is at least one node at depth D and no nodes at greater depth. Once iterative deepening has increased the depth bound B to D or more, there is no point in continuing. As coded above, however, it will keep trying ever greater bounds, in vain.

We want iterative deepening to continue searching as long as at least one node was cut off because it exceeded the depth bound. This appears to be a case for side effects, as the backtracking search destroys any information we held as variable bindings.

The Quintus Prolog library contains a package called library(ctr), the interface of which was adapted from Arity/Prolog. It provides a small global array of integers. The operations we need are

ctr_set(+Counter, +Value) where Counter is an integer between 0 and 31, and Value is any integer. Like a[i]:=v.

ctr_is(+Counter, ?Value) where Counter is an integer between 0 and 31. Like v:=a[i] if Value is a variable or v=a[i] if Value is an integer.

Exercise. *Implement these two predicates using assert/1 and retractall/1.*

We're going to use counter 13 (why 13? why not?) to hold a flag. This flag is going to be 0 if no depth cutoff has occurred yet, or N if the depth bound needs to be increased by at least N.

We change the translation of a clause. Now, if the depth bound is too small, a clause will not simply fail, but will first update counter 13.

$p(args, B_0, B)$:-
        tally(N, B_0, B_1),
        $b_1(-, B_1, B_2)$, ..., $b_N(-, B_N, B)$.

where the predicate tally/1 is

tally(N, B_0, B_1) :-
    ($B_0 > N \rightarrow B_1$ is $B_0 - 1$
    ; D is $N - B_0 + 1$,
        ctr_is$(13, C)$,
        ($C = 0$; $C > D$),
        ctr_set$(13, D)$,
        fail
).

Now we modify id_call/1 to maintain and test this flag. The flag must be cleared each time we start a search. It tells us by how much we need to increase the depth bound, so we check it before increasing the bound.

```
id_call(Goal) :-
        id_call(Goal, 1).

id_call(Goal, Bound) :-
        ctr_set(13, 0),
        call(Goal, Bound, _).
id_call(Goal, Bound) :-
        ctr_is(13, Increment),
        Increment > 0,
        Bound1 is Bound+Increment,
        id_call(Goal, Bound1).
```

2.13 Returning the Path to a Solution

In the preceding material, we have just been looking for a solution. But sometimes we want to know how that solution was obtained. Let's assume that one of two operations is provided:

labelled_child(Parent, Label, Child) is true when Child is a child of Parent, and Label distinguishes it from the other children of Parent. (It is usual to think of Label as the name of an operation which converts the Parent "state" into the Child "state".)

labelled_children(Parent, LabelledChildren) where LabelledChildren is a list of Label-Child pairs, is true when LabelledChildren is a collection of all the children of Parent with their distinguishing labels, in no particular order.

If we are given labelled_child/3, we can find labelled_children/2 using findall/3, and we can find labelled_child/3 using member/2 if given labelled_children/2.
Simple depth-first search is easily augmented:

```
depth_first_search(Start, Path, Answer) :-
        start(Start),
        depth_star(Start, Path, Answer),
        solution(Answer).

depth_star(Answer, [], Answer).
```

```
depth_star(Parent, [Label|Path], Answer) :-
        labelled_child(Parent, Label, Child),
        depth_star(Child, Path, Answer).
```

Depth-first search with local ordering and iterative deepening are just as easy to augment, but the other searching methods require that we keep the paths as well as the nodes in the Open set. For example, we might code breadth first search using queues thus:

```
breadth_first_search(Start, Path, Answer) :-
        start(Start),
        queue(Start/[], Open),
        breadth_star(Open, RevPath, Answer),
        solution(Answer),
        reverse(Path, RevPath).
```

```
breadth_star(Open, RevPath, Answer) :-
        queue_head(Node/NodePath, Open1, Open),
        (     Answer = Node, RevPath = NodePath
        ;     labelled_children(Node, LabelledChildren),
              queue_last_labelled(LabelledChildren, NodePath, Open1, Open2),
              breadth_star(Open2, RevPath, Answer)
        ).
```

```
queue_last_labelled([], _, Queue, Queue).
queue_last_labelled([Label-Child|Children], Path, Queue0, Queue) :-
        queue_last(Child/[Label|Path], Queue1, Queue0),
        queue_last_labelled(Children, Path, Queue1, Queue).
```

Here I have chosen to make the Open set a queue of Node/ReversedPath pairs.

Exercise. *Why are these paths reversed? Why are they lists rather than queues?*

2.14   Explain the Method in your Comments

If you look back at the different searching methods we've explored above, you'll notice that they all look pretty much the same. They all look something like this:

```
search(Answer) :-
        start(Start),
        compute_initial_open_set(Start, Open),
        compute_initial_closed_set(Start, Closed),
        search_star(Open, Closed, Answer),
        solution(Answer).
```

```
search_star(Open0, Closed0, Answer) :-
        remove_candidate(Open0, Candidate, Open1),
        (     Answer = Candidate
        ;     generate_children(Candidate, Children),
              update_open_and_closed_sets(Children, Open1, Closed0,
                  Open2, Closed1),
              search_star(Open2, Closed1, Answer)
        ).
```

This has an important practical consequence: it may be obvious from your code that some sort of search is being done, but it will *not* be obvious *which* sort. Since the code doesn't make it obvious, the comments must. Never mind if you are the only person who will ever see the code, you'll have forgotten in a couple of months.

A comment should look something like this:

```
%   foo_generator explores a design tree using breadth first search
%   with local heuristic ordering and a Closed set.
```

No matter what sort of program you are writing or what programming notation you are using, the most important information to put in your comments is the information which is not in the program proper, and the second most important information is that which is there but hard to figure out.

2.15   The Algebra of Binary Relations

We can think of a binary relation r(X,Y) as a predicate, and with that mindset we would combine binary relations using logical symbols. But we can also think of a binary relation as a boolean matrix, and that would suggest using matrix algebra. The following definitions are quite common:

$$
\begin{aligned}
\mathbf{0} &= \emptyset \\
I &= \{(X,Y) \mid X = Y\} \\
r' &= \{(Y,X) \mid r(X,Y)\} \\
r+s &= \{(X,Y) \mid r(X,Y) \lor s(X,Y)\} \\
r\&s &= \{(X,Y) \mid r(X,Y) \land s(X,Y)\} \\
r.s &= \{(X,Y) \mid \exists Z\, r(X,Z) \land s(Z,Y)\} \\
r^0 &= I \\
r^{n+1} &= r.r^n
\end{aligned}
$$

$$r^* = \bigcup_{n=0}^{\infty} r^n$$
$$= I + r.r^*$$
$$r^+ = \bigcup_{n=1}^{\infty} r^n$$
$$= r.r^*$$

Suppose we have a binary relation parent(P,C) meaning "P is a parent of C", and a binary relation diff(X,Y) meaning "X and Y are not the same". Then we can write such definitions as

$$
\begin{aligned}
\text{childof} &= \text{parent}' \\
\text{sibling} &= (\text{childof.parent})\&\text{diff} \\
\text{cousin} &= \text{childof.sibling.parent} \\
\text{ancestor} &= \text{parent}^+ \\
\text{related} &= (\text{parent} + \text{childof})^*
\end{aligned}
$$

This is rather pretty. But it should also be familiar. The idea of suppressing the last two arguments is just what we know in Definite Clause Grammar rules. (This suggests that allowing the 'transpose' operator $'$ in grammar rules might be useful. Hmm.) More to the point, except for $r\&s$ and r', expressions in the algebra of binary relations are exactly the same as *regular expressions*, where binary predicates which are otherwise defined play the role of constants. There should be nothing surprising about using regular expressions (that describe sequences of constants) to describe paths in graph (sequences of edges) except that an edge corresponds to a transition from one state to another rather than to a state.

What use is that? The main use is that this algebra is well understood. There are algebraic laws that binary relations satisfy. For example, $(X')^* = (X^*)'$. Considering the application of such laws to a problem can lead to insight, such as realising that this means that instead of searching forwards from ancestor to descendant we can search backwards from descendant to ancestor. Thinking about manipulating expressions can suggest other ways of re-organising a program. I shall mention just one. For any fixed n and binary relation r,

$$r^* = I + r^1 + \cdots + r^{n-1} + (r^n)^+$$

What does that tell us? It tells us that we may recast any search as

1. compute $(I + r^1 + \cdots + r^{n-1})(\text{start})$, the set of nodes which can be reached from the start in fewer than n steps.

2. compute the relation r^n, which represents taking n steps at a time.

3. search the graph whose initial nodes were found in step 1, and whose edges result from applying the relation found in step 2.

Why is that useful? Because the number of states you can reach by taking two steps is often less than the square of the number of states you can reach by taking one step. This can greatly reduce the branching factor of the state space. The technique doesn't always pay off. The point is that if you think of graph search in terms of regular expressions you don't have to be a genius to think of such improvements.

3 Where Does The Space Go?

A good predictor of Prolog performance on a new machine is the memory bandwidth of that machine. Prolog performance, that is to say, is dominated by memory references. If you reduce the number of memory references made by a Prolog program, you are likely to increase its speed. If you want to make your Prolog programs efficient, don't waste time trying to simulate Pascal, put the effort into trying to make your data structures small and the decisions obvious.

As well as the amount of memory turned over, an important factor is the amount of space held at any one time. The trouble is that virtual memory is not the same thing as free memory. If the set of pages you are using actively is small enough to fit into your computer's physical memory, all will be well, but if not, you will get very poor performance. So if your problem is likely to process large amounts of data, it is important to represent those data compactly.

Where then does the space go?

There are two principal varieties of Prolog system:

- systems like DEC-10 Prolog and C Prolog structure-sharing

- systems like Quintus Prolog and LPA Prolog structure-copying

Both varieties have six major memory areas:

the run-time support area. This depends on the implementation, and there is nothing a Prolog programmer can do about it. If a foreign language interface is offered, conventional methods for writing efficient procedures in that language should be used. Remember to close files as soon as you have finished with them and to release dynamically allocated storage as soon as you have finished with it.

the clause store. Things like the atom symbol table, the procedure symbol table, dynamic clauses, index blocks, and compiled code go in here. Prolog systems tend not to reclaim space in the symbol tables. Still, even a PC implementation should cope with a thousand predicates and several thousand atoms. A structure-sharing system puts "skeletons" here.

the environment stack. This maps "local" variables to their bindings. It is just like the stack used in a C or Pascal implementation. In a structure-copying system, all source variables are local. Space in this stack is reclaimed on failure, on determinate exit, or on determinate last call if the compiler supports tail recursion optimisation (TRO).

the choice point stack. When Prolog cannot decide which of several alternatives to choose, it picks the first and pushes a record on the choice point stack so that it can go back and try the others. Space in this stack is reclaimed on failure, and by cuts.

the trail. This records which bound variables need to be reset on backtracking. Space in this stack is reclaimed on failure, on garbage collection, and in some systems, by cuts.

the global stack or copy stack. In a structure-sharing system, the sixth area is the global stack, which holds the bindings of "global" variables. In a structure-copying system, the sixth area is the copy stack, which holds compound terms that have been constructed at run-time. Mentioning an atom or a number does *not* result in space being allocated in this area, although calculating a *new* large number may. Space in this area is reclaimed on failure or garbage collection.

A good description of Prolog memory management can be found in "Computing with Logic" [12].

In order to reduce memory use, we need to reduce the amount of space *created* in these areas and the amount of space *retained* in these areas.

3.1   The Clause Store

Space in the symbol tables is created whenever a new entity is mentioned. Reading a new atom or asserting a clause for a new predicate does that. The space required to store an atom should be a little bit more than the space required to hold the name of the atom: this overhead can be 4 bytes on a 16-bit machine like a PC or 8 bytes on a 32-bit machine like a VAX. The space required to hold information about a predicate varies from system to system, but it should be comparable to the space for a smallish clause. You shouldn't have to worry.

The amount of space required for a clause varies enormously from Prolog system to Prolog system. In fact, you may have several choices within a particular system. Native code for Prolog tends to be bulky, so if your Prolog system offers a choice of code representations (as DEC-10 Prolog did, with its :-fastcode and :-compactcode directives) you are better off choosing threaded code for almost all of your program.

Some Prolog systems do not reclaim compiled code. (Access to compiled code is lost when you abolish/2 the predicate or load a new definition.) DEC-10 Prolog did not do this. Quintus Prolog does. Prolog systems such as Prolog-X and ALS Prolog which attempt to minimise the differences between compiled and interpreted code are likely to be good here.

Space is obviously allocated when a clause is created by assert/1. But when is the space for a clause released?

A structure-sharing system represents terms by so-called *molecules*. A molecule is like a little closure, saying how a skeleton is fleshed out by variable bindings. Clearly, a structure-sharing system cannot reclaim the storage of a clause until it is sure that there are no live molecules which reference any of the skeletons in that clause. clause/2 and retract/1 involve creating a term which unifies with the clause, so they intrinsically nail down the storage. A paradox: retract/1 says that you want a clause to go away, but it *can't* until you have no further use for the copy of the clause which retract/1 gives you.

The rule in DEC-10 Prolog and C Prolog, then, is that in order to reclaim the space of a clause, you have to backtrack over all the goals which are using (a copy of any part of) it. Unfortunately, this means that if you call

    retract(H)

it not only fails to reclaim the space for the matching clause, it nails it down so that the space *cannot* be reclaimed until the call to retract/1 is backtracked over. Many Prologs have a predicate

    retractall(H)

which retracts every clause whose head would have unified with H. This command is determinate, and if you know that there is a single clause whose head would match H, or if you would like to get rid of all such clauses, you should use retractall/1 rather than retract/1. If you are using a Prolog system which does not provide retractall/1, put the definition

```
retractall(Head) :-
        retract((Head :- Body)),
        fail
    ;    true.
```

in your library. If this use of retract/1 fails to remove unit clauses which would unify with Head, you have a seriously broken implementation of retract/1 and should demand that your Prolog vendor fix it.

C Prolog has a further rule: it will not reclaim the space for a clause as long as there is a data-base reference pointing to it.

Structure-copying systems have an easier time. A copy of a clause is independent of the original, and the space can be reclaimed almost at once. Why "almost"? Because the predicate being affected might be running, and a running predicate isn't supposed to notice a change to its own clauses, so the clause must be retained until no stack frame might backtrack into it.

As a rule of thumb, failure and return to top level will reclaim anything.

3.2   Variables

In a structure-sharing system, we distinguish between

global variables, which occur inside a compound term. DEC-10 Prolog discounted
   one level of structure in a mode "+" argument, and arithmetic expressions
   don't count.

local variables, which do not occur inside compound terms, but must survive a
   call.

temporary variables, which do not have to survive a call.

For example, in

```
:- mode
        conc(+, +, -).

conc([H|T], L, [H|R]) :-
        conc(T, L, R).
```

H and R occur inside a compound term, so must be global. T occurs inside a
compound term, but that is a mode "+" argument, so one layer of structure is
discounted. T and L do not have to survive a call, but are handed straight on. So
each time this clause is run, it will use 2 cells in the global stack, and no cells in
the local stack.

```
p(Context, X0, X) :-
        q(Context, X0, X1),
        r(Context, X1, X).
```

Here the variables Context and X must survive the call to q/3. So must X1. But
X0 is temporary. While q/3 is running, therefore, this clause will use 3 cells in the
local stack, plus whatever book-keeping overhead there is.
   In a structure-copying system, we distinguish between

permanent variables, which must survive a call

temporary variables, which do not have to survive a call

Of course, what counts as a call depends on what operations the compiler expands
into in-line code. Typically, type tests and arithmetic operations don't count. So
in

```
p(I, N, Term) :-
        J is I+1,
        arg(J, Term, Arg),
        q(Arg),
        p(J, N, Term).
```

"I" would be a temporary variable, and the other variables would be permanent.

Instead of global variables taking up space on the global stack, in a structure-copying system, copies of terms take up space on the copy stack. So in

```
conc([H|T], L, [H|R]) :-
        conc(T, L, R).
```

all the variables are temporary, but the construction of [H|R] on the copy stack will take up 2 or 3 cells. Prolog systems based on David H.D. Warren's "New Engine" (commonly called the WAM) will tend to charge

- 2 cells for a cons cell (.)/2

- $N + 1$ cells for any other compound term with N arguments.

Temporary variables take up no space that you need to worry about. Permanent ("local") variables take up space on the local stack, but that is reclaimed on failure, determinate exit, or determinate last call. Global variables or copies of terms take up space on the other stack, and this space is only reclaimed by failure or garbage collection.

I have seen programs whose programmers didn't really believe that Prolog could count. Instead of writing terms like

        node(NodeName, PreConds, Effects, Support)

these programmers would write

        node(name(X), precons(P), effect(E), support(S))

This style may have its merits, but space saving is not one of them. The first version will take 5 cells per node, but the second will take 13. In a structure copying system, there will be no difference in space cost, but it will still take longer to get to the arguments than it would without those wrappers.

Only use wrappers when several different wrappers could appear in a particular argument position, or when the wrapper adds information.

3.3   Box Diagrams

Here are some pictures to show you what terms look like in a structure copying
systems such as Quintus Prolog. These pictures do *not* apply to all Prolog systems,
in particular they do not apply to Poplog which uses rather bigger representations
so that Prolog and the host language (Pop-11) can use the same data structures,
nor to Prologs embedded in Common Lisp. Neither do they apply to all Prolog
systems based on David Warren's "New Engine". The details are not exactly what
Quintus Prolog does now, nor what it will do in the future. Despite these caveats,
the pictures are close enough to be a useful guide.

Each Prolog term is represented by a one-word cell which contains a tag and
either an immediate value or a pointer. Tags include

- Unbound variable

- Bound variable

- Integer

- Float

- Atom

- List

- Struct (= compound term other than list)

The representations might look like

```
+---+----------------+<--\
| U | pointer *------|---/  [cell points to itself
+---+----------------+


+---+----------------+        +---+----------------+
| B | pointer *------|----->|representation of value
+---+----------------+        +---+----------------+


+---+----------------+
| I | integer value  |
+---+----------------+


+---+----------------+
| F | float value    |
+---+----------------+
```

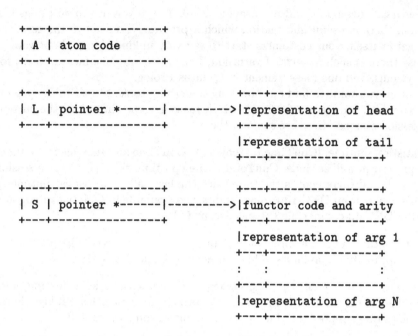

```
+---+---------------+
| A | atom code     |
+---+---------------+


+---+---------------+              +---+---------------+
| L | pointer *------|---------->|representation of head
+---+---------------+              +---+---------------+
                                   |representation of tail
                                   +---+---------------+


+---+---------------+              +---+---------------+
| S | pointer *------|---------->|functor code and arity
+---+---------------+              +---+---------------+
                                   |representation of arg 1
                                   +---+---------------+
                                   :   :              :
                                   +---+---------------+
                                   |representation of arg N
                                   +---+---------------+
```

You don't need to know any of this to use Prolog, and a Prolog program cannot get at any of this. The storage layout is not even visible to C code. If you want to learn more about how a Prolog system manages memory, read the Warren & Maier book [12]

3.4 Measuring Space Used

In some Prolog systems, your program can ask how much space it is using in each region. DEC-10 Prolog provided a command and a state function for this purpose:

statistics/0 writes a summary of the programs' time and space usage to the standard output stream.

statistics/2 takes a "measurement name" as first argument and returns a list of values.

Unfortunately, this is one of the less standardised areas of Prolog. C Prolog, for example, provided statistics/0, but instead of providing statistics/2, provided

T is cputime, % in seconds as a float
M is heapused % in bytes as an integer

The other measurements it did not provide at all. I urge you not to do things like that: when there is useful information which a program can send to the terminal but not get at itself, your customers start to say very unkind things about you.

Because there is such a range of variation, I shall describe one measurement for several systems, and one measurement in Quintus Prolog.

Quite often you want to find out how long something took. Most Prolog systems provide you with some sort of "clock" which measures the time since the current Prolog session started. Here are some of them:

- statistics(runtime, [CpuTime,Increment]). CpuTime and Increment are times expressed in milliseconds, CpuTotal is the cpu time since this Prolog session started, and Increment is the time since the last call to statistics(runtime,_). This comes from DEC-10 Prolog, and is also available in Quintus Prolog and other DEC-10-compatible Prologs except C Prolog.

- system_state(cpu_time, CpuTime). CpuTime is the time in milliseconds since startup, modulo two hours. This comes from Logicware's MProlog.

- CpuTime is cputime. CpuTime is expressed in seconds as a floating-point number. It comes from C Prolog, and is present in some other Prologs. Some Prologs don't report the time in seconds but in some other unit.

- time(CpuTime). This comes from LPA Prolog Professional. The time units are PC-specific and are approximately 18.2 seconds. Be careful not to call this predicate with CpuTime bound, it does something different then.

- ticks(CpuTime). This comes from LPA Mac Prolog. The time units are 60ths of a second. Be careful not to call this predicate with CpuTime bound, it does something different then.

The DEC-10 interface creates a list that we have no real use for. The C Prolog interface is inelegant: in Prolog, arithmetic expressions are supposed to be absolutely pure. Having random number generators or clocks in Prolog expressions is rather disgusting. If it weren't for the fact that they do something strange when given an instantiated argument, the LPA interfaces would be just about right.

Since these methods of getting at the time are not very portable, you might like to use the following three predicates when you want to write portable code. For some Prologs you may have to finish them yourself, alas.

- cpu_time(T) unifies T with the cpu time since the current Prolog session began. The time is expressed in seconds as a floating-point number. If the system distinguishes between 'user' time and 'system' time (as UNIX does) it is 'user' time and doesn't include time spent in child processes.

On PCs and Macintoshes, the usual measurement is clock time of some sort, including system and child time. Beware of this when comparing benchmarks on different systems. You should explain carefully in your own local porting guide what the measurement really means.

- cpu_time(Goal, T) unifies T with the cpu time taken to call Goal once until it either succeeds or fails. Any variables in Goal should be (or be thought of as) existentially quantified, as alternative solutions will pruned away, and cpu_time/2 will succeed even when Goal fails. cpu_time/2 should only be used when Goal takes a long time.

- cpu_time(N, Goal, T) unifies T with the cpu time taken to (call Goal until it either succeeds or fails) N times. Any variables in Goal should be (or be thought of as) existentially quantified, as there is a failure driven loop inside cpu_time/3 and variables in Goal will not be left bound. If Goal takes a short time, you should use cpu_time/3 with a large value of N to time it.

```
%    For ALS Prolog or C Prolog.

cpu_time(Time) :-
        Time is cputime.

cpu_time(Goal, Duration) :-
        Start is cputime, % in seconds as a float
        ( call(Goal) → true ; true ),
        Duration is cputime-Start.
cpu_time(N, Goal, Duration) :-
        T0 is cputime, % in seconds as a float
        ( call(( repeat(N), (Goal → fail) )) ; true ),
        T1 is cputime, % in seconds as a float
        ( call(( repeat(N), (true → fail) )) ; true ),
        T2 is cputime, % in seconds as a float
        Duration is (T1-T0) - (T2-T1).


%    For Logicware's MProlog Prolog.

cpu_time(Time) :-
        system_state(cpu_time, T),
        Time is T*0.001. % too bad about the modulus
```

```
/* I assume here that no Goal takes 2 hours or more */
/* but that the clock can wrap around on any occasion */

cpu_time(Goal, Duration) :-
        system_state(cpu_time, T0),
        ( call(Goal) → true ; true ),
        system_state(cpu_time, T1),
        (    T0 > T1 → % Oops, wrapped!
            Duration is ((7200000-T0)+T1)*0.001.

cpu_time(N, Goal, Duration) :-
        cpu_time((repeat(N), (Goal→ fail) ; true), D1),
        cpu_time((repeat(N), (true→ fail) ; true), D2),
        Duration is D1-D2.



%    For LPA Mac Prolog 2.5.

cpu_time(Time) :- !,
        ticks(T), % in (1/60) second units
        Time is T/60.0.

cpu_time(Goal, Duration) :- !,
        ticks(T1), % in (1/60) second units
        ( call(Goal) → true ; true ),
        ticks(T2), % in (1/60) second units
        Duration is (T2-T1)/60.0.

cpu_time(N, Goal, Duration) :- !,
        cpu_time((repeat(N), (Goal→ fail) ; true), D1),
        cpu_time((repeat(N), (true→ fail) ; true), D2),
        Duration is D1-D2.



%    For LPA Prolog Professional 2.5

cpu_time(Time) :- !,
        ticks(T), % in (1/18.2) second units
        Time is T/18.2.
```

```
cpu_time(Goal, Duration) :- !,
        time(T1), % in (1/18.2) second units
        ( call(Goal) → true ; true ),
        time(T2), % in (1/18.2) second units
        Duration is (T2-T1)/18.2.

cpu_time(N, Goal, Duration) :- !,
        cpu_time((repeat(N), (Goal→ fail) ; true), D1),
        cpu_time((repeat(N), (true→ fail) ; true), D2),
        Duration is D1-D2.


%    For Quintus Prolog (any release)

cpu_time(Time) :-
        statistics(runtime, [T|_]),
        Time is T*0.001.

cpu_time(Goal, Duration) :-
        statistics(runtime, [Start|_]),
        ( call(Goal) → true ; true ),
        statistics(runtime, [Finish|_]),
        Duration is (Finish-Start)*0.001.

cpu_time(N, Goal, Duration) :-
        statistics(runtime, [T0|_]),
        ( call(( repeat(N), (Goal → fail) )) ; true ),
        statistics(runtime, [T1|_]),
        ( call(( repeat(N), (true → fail) )) ; true ),
        statistics(runtime, [T2|_]),
        Duration is ((T1-T0) - (T2-T1))*0.001.
```

The implementation of cpu_time/3 depends on repeat/1. This is one of the very few known defensible uses of repeat/1.

```
%    For Prologs with last call optimisation.

repeat(N) :-
        integer(N), N > 0,
        repeat_1(N).

repeat_1(1) :- !.
```

repeat_1(_).
repeat_1(N) :- M is N-1, repeat_1(M).

%   For old Prologs without last call optimisation.

repeat(N) :-
          integer(N), N > 0,
          repeat_2(1, N).

repeat_2(I, I) :- !.
repeat_2(L, U) :- M is $(L + U) \gg 1$, repeat_2(L, M).
repeat_2(L, U) :- M is $(L + U) \gg 1 + 1$, repeat_2(M, U).

The Quintus-specific measurement I promised is the amount of space currently
used in the local stack. The query

        statistics(local_stack, [InUse,Free])

returns two numbers: the amount of memory in use by the local stack and the
amount of memory allocated for the local stack but not currently in use. Since
Quintus Prolog allocates more memory for the stack as needed, the Free measurement is not very interesting, but it is kept for compatibility with DEC-10 Prolog
and DEC-10 compatible Prologs. Both measurements are in bytes. In Quintus
Prolog, the local stack includes both the environment stack and the choice point
stack. The reason that this is useful is that a query leaves the InUse measurement
unchanged if and only if Prolog has detected that it is determinate. So we can
define

should_be_determinate(Goal) :-
          statistics(local_stack, [Before|_]),
          call(Goal),
          statistics(local_stack, [After|_]),
          Delta is After-Before,
          (Delta = 0 → true
          ;   write([Goal,left,Delta,bytes]), nl,
               ! % *make* it determinate
).

This can be quite useful for locating parts of your program that are leaving choice
points behind when they shouldn't.

3.5   A Hack

Many Prolog systems on the market do not have a garbage collector. You have to
read the fine print carefully; I have seen Prolog systems whose advertising glossies
said that they had a garbage collector, but where this turned out to mean that they
would eventually reclaim the storage of retracted clauses. The thing to ask is "does
it garbage collect the *stacks*?" This is especially important on small computers.

The following two hacks were developed for use in systems which do not have
a garbage collector. Often you have a computation which creates a great deal of
working storage which would eventually be garbage collected. You would like to
get the results and throw the working storage away at once.

```
%    gc_call(Goal)
%    acts like call(Goal), but discards all working storage.

gc_call(Goal) :-
        findall(Goal, Goal, GoalInstances),
        member(Goal, GoalInstances).

%    gc_once(Goal)
%    finds the first solution of Goal and discards working storage.

gc_once(Goal) :-
        findall(Goal, (Goal, !), [Goal]).
```

Using these operations is rather less nauseating than building calls to assert and
retract into your program, and will be less vulnerable to interrupts. When you move
up to a system with a garbage collector, you can just redefine these commands.

3.6   The Trail

You can ignore this. Each variable can appear in the trail at most once, and a good
system running a program with a lot of determinacy will keep the trail a good deal
smaller than that. Any measures you take to reduce the space in the other stacks,
especially increasing determinacy, will reduce space in this stack.

3.7   Choice Points and the Cut

To understand this topic, you need to have some idea of how a Prolog interpreter
works. This sketch is rather over-simplified, but you'll get the idea.

```
execute(Query) :-
        callable(Query),
        the_current_choice_point_stack_top_is(Mark),
        execute(Query, Mark).

execute(true, _) :- !.
execute(fail, _) :- !,
        fail.
execute(!, Mark) :- !,
        prune_the_choice_point_stack_back_to(Mark).
execute((A,B), Mark) :- !,
        execute(A, Mark),
        execute(B, Mark).
execute(((Test→ Then);Else), Mark) :- !,
        if_then_else(Test, Then, Else, Mark).
execute((A;B), Mark) :-
        execute(A, Mark).
execute((A;B), Mark) :- !,
        execute(B, Mark).
execute(¬(A), Mark) :- !,
        if_then_else(A, fail, true, Mark).
   ⋮
/* and so on */
execute(Goal, Mark) :-
        the_relevant_clauses_are(Goal, Clauses),
        execute_clauses(Clauses, Goal, Mark).

if_then_else(Test, Then, Else, Mark) :-
        execute(Test, Mark),
        !,
        execute(Then, Mark).
if_then_else(Test, Then, Else, Mark) :-
        execute(Else, Mark).

execute_clauses([Clause], Goal, Mark) :- !,
        execute_clause(Clause, Mark, Goal).
```

```
execute_clauses([Clause1,Clause2|Clauses], Goal, Mark),
        push_a_new_choice_point,
        (     execute_clause(Clause1, Mark, Goal)
        ;     rest_clauses(Clauses, Clause2, Mark, Goal)
        ).

execute_clause((Head:-Body), Mark, Head) :-
        execute(Body, Mark).

rest_clauses([], Clause, Mark, Goal) :-
        pop_the_current_choice_point,
        execute_clause(Clause, Mark, Goal).
rest_clauses([Clause2|Clauses], Clause1, Mark, Goal) :-
        modify_the_top_choice_point,
        (     execute_clause(Clause1, Mark, Goal)
        ;     rest_clauses(Clauses, Clause2, Mark, Goal)
        ).
```

You are to understand everything in this code as determinate except for the explicit disjunctions in the last clauses of execute_clauses/3 and rest_clauses/4.

The point is that the Prolog system is exploring a proof tree, and that a choice point is created when the system *thinks* that the current node of the proof tree *might* have more than one branch.

I repeat that Prolog is an efficient programming language because it is a very stupid theorem prover. Prolog systems differ in how good they are at noticing that the current node of the proof tree has only one branch. 'the_relevant_clauses_are' has in effect to execute *part* of each clause to determine whether it is relevant or not, and to filter out all the clauses which are bound to fail.

Prolog debuggers, by design, do not filter any clauses out. Some of them even let you see unsuccessful head unifications.

There has been a great deal of confusion about how :-dynamic code is to be handled. A lot of Prolog implementors have never had any clear idea about what should happen when a predicate which is running is changed. The definition used in DEC-10 Prolog, C Prolog (in some modes), and early versions of Quintus Prolog, was the "immediate update" view. This meant that as soon as a clause was asserted in or retracted from a predicate, each running copy of that predicate was supposed to notice the change. The trouble with that is that the Prolog system can *never* tell that it has come to the last branch of a node in the proof tree: while it is working on that branch, another clause might be added! The result is that

```
p :-
        clause(p, Body, Ref),
        assert((p :- Body)),
        erase(Ref),
        write(*),
        fail.
```

will run forever, once called. With this definition of the effect of assert/1 and
retract/1 on running code, there isn't any point in the system trying to be clever
about choice points.

I have been advocating the "logical view" since 1984. Tim Lindholm has implemented it in Quintus Prolog: we had a paper about it in the Melbourne conference
in 1987 [22]. The idea here is that the set of clauses relevant to a running goal is
the set of clauses which were there when it started. The interpreter sketched above
assumes (and implements) this view. According to this definition, every time 'p' is
called it prints a single * and fails.

This was an extremely important change, because it means that Quintus Prolog
now creates exactly the same set of choice points for static and :-dynamic predicates,
so that you need exactly the same cuts in your code whichever condition it was
running under. SICStus Prolog works like this too.

3.8   Uses of the cut

What a cut *does* is very simple operationally: it prunes the stack of choice points
back to where it was when the predicate which lexically contains the cut was called.
Another way of saying this is that *the cut succeeds and commits Prolog to all the
choices made since the parent goal was called.*

It is more difficult to understand cuts in terms of the proof tree. What they do is
prune away untried branches up to the parent node. Suppose for example we have
the clauses

```
p :- q, !.
p :- r.

q :- s.
q :- t.

s.
```

When the cut is executed, the OR tree looks like

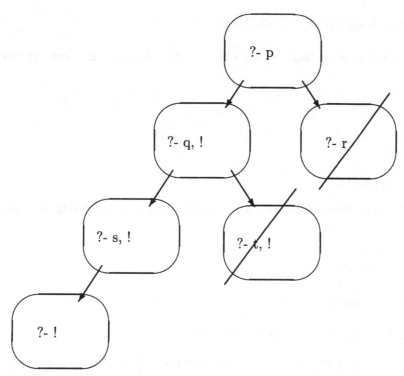

The labels on the nodes are conjunctions. The cut will prune away the branches whose nodes have slashes through them.

You may find it useful to think of the cut as doing two things:

commit: telling Prolog not to consider any more (later) clauses for this goal (here the second clause of p is to be ignored).

prune: throwing away all the alternative solutions for the goals to its left in its clause (here Prolog is not to look for another way of satisfying the goal 's').

You will often find yourself using a cut for one of these purposes but not the other.

You and I, as programmers, are interested in the *solutions* of queries, and Prolog reports solutions to top-level queries. But Prolog is really looking for *proofs*.

There are two kinds of cuts:

red cuts prune away solutions as well as proofs.

grue cuts prune away proofs but not solutions.

3.9   Cutting away Clauses

A cut that serves to select (commit to) a clause tends to appear in a context like this:

Head :-

    Test 1,

    ...

    Test n,

    !,

    Rest of clause.

where the Tests are determinate tests that will either fail, or succeed with only one solution. A common example is

p(X, *args*) :- var(X), !,

    /* X is unbound */.

p(X, *args*) :- number(X), !,

    /* X is a number */.

p(X, *args*) :-

    /* X is an atom or compound term */.

Cuts used to prune away alternative clauses are pretty harmless, but see below.

3.10   Pruning Alternative Solutions

A cut that serves to prune away alternative solutions to a particular goal tends to look like

Head :-

    Goal,

    !,

    Rest of clause.

where the *Goal* is typically a user-defined predicate or a conjunction of them.

If you use a cut in this way, you have to be very careful not to inadvertently commit to a particular clause. If you really have to do it, you may be better advised to use the 'once' control structure:

Head :-

    once(*Goal*),

    Rest of clause.

In some Prolog systems, this is given the pretentious name of "snips" and a special syntactic form. In others, you may have to use an if→ then form:

Head :-
      (*Goal* → true),
      Rest of clause.

But it is bad style to do any of these: if a predicate should be determinate, make *it* determinate, and don't pass the buck on to the caller.

Here is a fragment of Prolog code.

```
p(...) :-
        ⋮
        setof([Model,Count], to_be_processed(Model,Count), Pairs),
        make_model_menu(Pairs, Menu),
        !,
        ⋮
```

```
make_model_menu([], []).
make_model_menu([[_,0]|Pairs], Menu) :-
        make_model_menu(Pairs, Menu).
make_model_menu([[Model,_]|Pairs], [Item|Menu]) :-
        make_model_menu_item(Model, Item),
        make_model_menu(Pairs, Menu).
```

This is adapted from code which actually appeared in a real program. I have even seen very similar code exhibited by an instructor in a Prolog course. So the problem is real.

What is the matter with this fragment? After all, it works, and programs are works of engineering rather than art.

The symptom of the trouble is that the cut is not just in the wrong *place*, it's in entirely the wrong *predicate*. The intent of the cut is to ensure that we get only one solution from the predicate make_model_menu/2. But that should be part of the specification of make_model_menu/2, something which the caller can rely on without having to enforce it. Because of the way this fragment has been written, *we cannot understand* make_model_menu/2 *without examining all its callers.*

The rule of thumb you should follow is this:

> make cuts as local in their effect as possible.

If you want only one solution from a predicate, put the cuts in the predicate, not the calls to it. Put a cut in a clause *only* when it is there to make its parent predicate determinate, not to make subgoals determinate.

Let's see how this would affect the fragment in question.


```
p(...) :-
        ⋮
        setof([Model,Count], to_be_processed(Model,Count), Pairs),
        make_model_menu(Pairs, Menu),
        ⋮


%   make_model_menu(Model_Count_List, Menu)
%   takes a list of [Model,Count] pairs and returns a list of menu
%   items made from the Models with non-zero Count.

make_model_menu([], []).
make_model_menu([[_Model,0]|Pairs], Menu) :- !,
            %   The Count of this _Model is 0, so ignore it.
            make_model_menu(Pairs, Menu).
make_model_menu([[Model,_Count]|Pairs], [Item|Menu]) :-
            %   The _Count of this Model is not 0
            make_model_menu_item(Model, Item),
            make_model_menu(Pairs, Menu).
```


From this change we obtain two benefits. The first is that we can understand make_model_menu/2 on its own. It is good programming style to provide "header" comments for predicates like the one I have shown. Take a look at the Quintus Prolog library for more examples of this. If you have difficulty coming up with a short clear truthful description, this is generally a pretty good indication that there is something wrong with your design. Second, the clearer program is more efficient.

Here is another rule of thumb: if you have more than one cut in a clause, you are doing something *very* strange, and should try hard to eliminate some of them. One reason why you might have more than one cut in a clause is that it has more than one call to an "unfinished" predicate like the original version of make_model_menu/2. The program from which I drew this example actually read

```
q(...) :-
     ⋮
     setof([Model,Count], to_be_processed(Model,Count), Pairs1),
     make_model_menu(Pairs1, Menu1),
     !,
     setof([Model,Count], already_processed(Model,Count), Pairs2),
     make_model_menu(Pairs2, Menu2),
     !,
     append(Menu1, Menu2, Menu),
     !,
     ⋮
```

The first thing to note is that a cut is superfluous if the code is already determinate. If efficiency and determinacy are so important to you that you are prepared to put cuts all over the place, you should keep in mind which built in (and library) predicates are determinate, and when they are determinate, and you should provide comments for your own code to remind you of when your own code is determinate. append/3 is a library predicate (in library(basics)). When its first argument is a proper list, it is determinate. Since Menu1 is a proper list, the goal append(Menu1, Menu2, Menu) is determinate. In the pattern

     !, determinate_goal, ..., determinate_goal, !, ...

the second cut is always superfluous. So we don't need the cut after the append/3 goal. But there are still two cuts in this clause. However, we saw above that that was because they were in the wrong predicate, and should have been in make_model_menu/2 itself. We arrive at

```
q(...) :-
     ⋮
     setof([Model,Count], to_be_processed(Model,Count), Pairs1),
     make_model_menu(Pairs1, Menu1),
     setof([Model,Count], already_processed(Model,Count), Pairs2),
     make_model_menu(Pairs2, Menu2),
     append(Menu1, Menu2, Menu),
     ⋮
```

which is much easier to read.

The "p" fragment could be further improved in two ways. First, you should use lists sparingly. See, for example, my SIGPLAN Notices article "Prolog Compared

With Lisp?" [19]. A list cell costs 2 words in Quintus Prolog, so a list like [X,Y]
costs 4 words. A compound term with N arguments costs N+1 words, so a term
like X-Y (or X=Y or X/Y or foo(X,Y)) costs 3 words. Further, if you read David
Warren's SRI paper [14] describing the abstract Prolog instruction set which has
come to be known as "the WAM", you will find that unifying against [X,Y] costs 5
instructions:

```
get_list          arg
unify_variable    X
unify_list
unify_variable    Y
unify_constant    []
```

whereas unifying against X-Y costs 3 instructions:

```
get_structure     arg, '-'/2
unify_variable    X
unify_variable    Y
```

More generally, if you want to represent a record with N fields, using a list will cost
you $2N$ words and $2N + 1$ WAM instructions per match, while using a compound
term will cost you N+b1 words and $N + 1$ WAM instructions per match. The cost
ratio can approach 2 to 1!

Of course, the important thing is to write correct programs. We can worry about
the space and time costs later. If it were the case that using lists all over the place
made it easier to write correct programs, then it would be very wrong of me to use
space and time costs to dissuade you from using lists. But it is not the case!

> Using compound terms with well-chosen "record names" can make it
> much easier to write correct programs.

How so? First, if you accidentally swap two arguments of a predicate, or if you
pass an argument to the wrong chance, there is a fair chance that different "conceptual types" are involved. If you only use lists, they'll still match. If you use
compound terms with well chosen functors, you will be using different functors for
different conceptual types, and your program will promptly fail, indeed of succeeding with nonsensical answers. Second, it will be much easier for someone reading
your code (and this means you!) to see what is going on. Third, when you are
stepping through the program with the debugger, you will find it much easier to
read the arguments of goals, because they will "wear their names on their faces" as
it were. You can even customise the print/1 command by adding your own clauses
for portray/1.

A good functor to use for constructing pairs is (-)/2. It is good for two reasons: it is easy to type, and it is the functor which keysort/2 uses. But if you aren't planning to sort the result, it is an even better idea to use a different functor for each sort of pair.

Finally, note that make_model_menu/2 is rejecting Models with a zero Count, and makes no other use of Count. Why not move this test into the setof/3 goal, so that there never are such Models in the first place? Then we arrive at

```
p(...) :-
        ⋮
        setof(Model, to_be_processed(Model), Models),
        make_model_menu(Models, Menu),
        ⋮


to_be_processed(Model) :-
        to_be_processed(Model, Count),
        Count > 0.


make_model_menu([], []).
make_model_menu([Model|Models], [Item|Items]) :-
        make_model_menu_item(Model, Item),
        make_model_menu(Models, Items).
```

3.11 RED Cuts

Recall that red cuts prune away logical solutions. A clause with a red cut in it hasn't got a logical reading.

Red cuts are used for two principal purposes: to obtain the *first* solutions to a query, and to obtain an if→ then;else effect.

```
once(Goal) :-
        call(Goal),
        !.
```

When red cuts are used for the purpose of committing to the first solution found, you should have a comment explaining why this is ok.

One of the first "cut" examples new Prolog programmers are often shown is the max/3 predicate which finds the greater of two numbers. The pure version is

$\max(X, Y, X) :- X \geq Y.$
$\max(X, Y, Y) :- X < Y.$

We observe that if the first test succeeds the second can't (this is because $X \geq Y$ and $X < Y$ can't both be true), so that we can add a blue cut to the first clause:

$\max(X, Y, X) :- X \geq Y, !.$
$\max(X, Y, Y) :- X < Y.$

At this point, it is tempting to say that if the $X \geq Y$ test fails without reporting any error, we know that $X < Y$ must be true, so there is no point in testing it all over again. So we turn the blue cut (that is, a cut which is only useful with a dumb compiler) into a red one (that is, a cut *changes* the meaning of the code) by dropping the second test:

$\max(X, Y, X) :- X \geq Y, !.$
$\max(X, Y, Y).$

When red cuts are used to obtain an if$\rightarrow$then;else effect like this, it is a good idea to leave the negated goal there as a comment, so we should write the second clause of max/3 as

$\max(X, Y, Y)$ /* $X < Y$ */.

Unfortunately, it is possible to persuade this version of max/3 to give wrong answers. Consider the query

?- max(10, 0, 0).

The greater of 10 and 0 is 10, not 0, but that query will succeed. The reason for this is that we were relying on the $X \geq Y$, cut combination in the first clause to transfer the information that $X < Y$ to the second clause, but because the query max(10,0,0) doesn't match the *head* of the first clause, we never got as far as that test. We arrive in the second clause if *either* $X < Y$ or the query doesn't match $\max(X, Y, X)$.

We want our predicates to be "constant, firm, unwavering" about giving the right answers; we call the property of refusing to give wrong answers even when the query has an unexpected form (typically, as here, supplying values for what we normally think of as inputs) *steadfastness* and say that a good predicate is *steadfast*.

When a predicate is not steadfast, it is usually because you have not followed the rule for placing cuts correctly. Remember that the rule is

Place a cut precisely as soon as you know that this is the right clause to use, not later, and not sooner.

In this case, we know which clause to use as soon as we have examined the first two arguments; we're going to use a cut, we have no business looking at the third argument until we have done the cut. So a steadfast improved version of max/3 might look like

$$max(X, Y, Z) :\text{-} X \geq Y, !, Z = X.$$
$$max(X, Y, Y).$$

A rule of thumb which will help you get this right is

> Postpone output unifications until after the cut.

This problem only arises when your clauses are not self-contained but rely on (red) cuts earlier in the predicate. Postponing the output unifications is one way of fixing the problem. Leaving apparently redundant tests in place is a clearer way. Let's consider the problem of flattening a list (not something I've ever had a use for, but it's one of the standard examples).

```
flatten(Tree, List) :-
        flatten(Tree, List, []).
```

```
flatten([], List, List) :- !.
flatten([Head|Tail], List0, List) :- !,
        flatten(Head, List0, List1),
        flatten(Tail, List1, List).
flatten(Other, [Other|List], List).
```

The (red) cuts appear in the first two clauses, but they *really* convey meaning to the last clause. This would more properly be written as

```
flatten([], List, List).
flatten([Head|Tail], List0, List) :-
        flatten(Head, List0, List1),
        flatten(Tail, List1, List).
flatten(Other, [Other|List], List) :-
        Other ~= [],
        Other ~= [_|_].
```

When red cuts are used for this purpose, you should put a comment where the negated code should have appeared.

The 'plain' version of flatten/3 is not steadfast; it has just the kind of interaction between head unification and cuts that we have to watch out for. Here are two queries:

?- flatten([], X).
X = [] ;
no more answers

?- X = [_], flatten([], X).
X = [[]] ;
no more answers

What went wrong? The answer is that the *timing* of cuts matters: a cut should be executed as soon as it has been determined that the current path in the proof tree is correct, and not later. The code should have been written as

```
flatten([], List0, List) :- !,
        List0 = List. % MUST BE EXECUTED AFTER THE CUT
flatten([Head|Tail], List0, List) :- !,
        flatten(Head, List0, List1),
        flatten(Tail, List1, List).
flatten(Other, [Other|List], List).
%    Other ~= [], Other ~= [_|_].
```

There is a rather revolting hack which is worth noting. A lot of (meta-) predicates have the form

```
p(Var, args) :-
        var(Var),
        !,
        fail.
p(..., ...) :- ...
```

Avoid this if you possibly can. If you are processing arbitrary terms entered by the end-user, you may have no choice, but you should convert this to a pretty style as soon as you can. If, however, you do find yourself needing to do something like this, it is faster on some systems (such as Quintus Prolog) to do

```
p('*', args) :- !,
        fail.
p(..., ...) :- ...
```

where '*', is a constant chosen to be unacceptable to the remaining clauses. For example,

```
is_proper_list(0) :- !, fail. % catch variables
is_proper_list([]).
is_proper_list([_|L]) :-
        is_proper_list(L).
```

If you use this hack, be sure to include a comment which says what you're up to.

This hack does not work very well in coroutining Prologs like NU Prolog. The reason is that after the variable is bound to an "unacceptable" value but before the cut,fail is done, goals which were suspended while they waited for that variable to become bound may be woken. In such systems you should be using 'when' or 'wait' declarations anyway.

3.12 GRUE cuts

Grue cuts are ones which have no effect on the logic of a program, but improve its efficiency. We may divide grue cuts into two further classes:

Blue cuts are there to alert the Prolog system to a determinacy it *should* have noticed but wouldn't. Blue cuts do not change the visible behaviour of the program: all they do is make it feasible.

Green cuts are there to prune away attempted proofs that would succeed or be irrelevant, or would be bound to fail, but you would not expect the Prolog system to be able to tell that.

The trouble is that Prolog systems differ in the number of blue cuts they need. Suppose, for example, we have a table

```
capital(britain,      london)     :- !.
capital(australia,    canberra)   :- !.
capital(new_zealand, wellington) :- !.
```

where we expect queries capital(Country,Capital) with Country instantiated or Capital instantiated, so the calls are always determinate. These cuts are blue: we would definitely expect the Prolog system to manage without them.

In C Prolog, the cuts are necessary for efficiency.

In DEC-10 Prolog and Quintus Prolog, the cuts are necessary when the first argument is uninstantiated, but not when the first argument is instantiated.

In NU Prolog, we can dispense with the cuts by providing a 'when' declaration:

?- capital(Country, Capital) when nonvar(Country) or nonvar(Capital).

which causes a call to capital/2 to be delayed until at least one of the arguments is instantiated.

In order to know whether a blue cut is needed or not, you need to know how much indexing your Prolog system does. Most Prolog systems index on the principal functor (which includes the arity) of the first argument. Some will let you specify an indexing pattern.

When you have a fixed table like this, it is sometimes worth putting a protective envelope around it so that you get the requisite determinacy without compromising the logical purity of the table, e.g.,

```
capital(Country, Capital) :-
    (    nonvar(Country) →
         cap(Country, Capital),
         !
    ;    nonvar(Capital) →
         cap(Country, Capital),
         !
    ;    cap(Country, Capital)
    ).

cap(britain,      london).
cap(australia,    canberra).
cap(new_zealand, wellington).
```

If you often need this sort of thing, tell your Prolog vendor that more flexible indexing is important to you.

The most important rules about cuts are

> A cut should be placed at the exact point that it is known that this is the correct branch of the proof tree.
> Be very careful not to move calculations back over a cut, as they may fail and cause the cut to be missed.

If it's of interest, that's why grammar rule translation uses the 'C'/3 predicate.

3.13   How far do cuts reach?

A cut removes all the choice points introduced since the call to its "parent goal" was started. In the simplest case, the parent goal is just the head of the clause in which the cut is written. But when a cut occurs inside call/1 or setof/3 or some other control structures, its effect is local to that structure. For example, in

```
p(L) :-
        ( a, ! /* 1 */
        ; c, (d, ! /* 2 */, e), f
        ),
        call(( g, ! /* 3 */)),
        ¬ (h, ! /* 4 */, i),
        findall(X, (j(X), ! /* 5 */), L).
```

the cuts numbered 1, 2, and 4 can "see" the head of the clause p(L) as their parent goal, while the cuts number 3 and 5 are local to call/1 and findall/3 respectively.

How can you tell which cuts have which scope? The metaphor I use is that a cut reaches out as far as it can "see" and that some control structures are "transparent" and some are not. By a lucky accident, there is a simple rule for telling which which control structures are transparent to cut and which are opaque: cuts can't "see" through letters. Thus (A,B), (A;B), (A→B;C), ¬(A) are all "transparent" to cuts (that is, a cut inside one of these control structures will cut through it out to the head or the nearest opaque control structure), while call(A), (if A then B else C), not(A), findall(A,B,C), setof(A,B,C), bagof(A,B,C), once(A), forall(A,B)—such of these as your Prolog system provides—are all opaque.

Some Prolog systems (including Quintus Prolog) won't let you write a cut in the "A" position of ¬(A) or (A→B;C), but if they *did* allow it, such a cut would see through the control structure all the way out to the head.

3.14 Disjunction and If-Then-Else

3.14.1 Introduction

The if→ then;else control structure provides an alternative to the use of cuts. This section examines some of the control structures.

If you look in Chapter 5 of the Quintus Prolog Reference Manual you will find that it describes several "control structures":

- conjunction, "P, Q". Pronounce the comma as "and then".

- disjunction, "P ; Q". Pronounce the semicolon as "or else".

- cut, "!". Pronounce the exclamation mark as "cut".

- indirect (meta-) call, "call(X)".

- negation-as-failure, The form is actually written as "\ + P", which is as close as ASCII can get to "⊬ P". In this book I write it as "¬ P". Pronounce "¬" as "it is not provable that", or pronounce "¬ P" as "P has no provable instance". Do not confuse this with logical negation! See Chapter 5 of the Quintus Prolog Library Manual.

- if-then-else, "(P → Q ; R)". Pronounce the initial left parenthesis as "if", the right-pointing arrow as "then", and the semicolon as "else".

- if-then, "(P → Q)". If P fails, the whole form fails.

- true, otherwise, fail, false.

- indefinite repetition, "repeat".

However, chapter 5 only tells you what these operations are, and doesn't tell you how or when to use them. That's the purpose of this section.

3.14.2 Disjunction

The disjunction of several goals G_1, G_2, ..., G_n is indicated by writing

$$G_1 \; ; \; G_2 \; ; \; ...; \; G_n$$

You can also use the vertical bar "|", writing

$$G_1 \mid G_2 \mid ... \mid G_n$$

or any mixture of the two. In either case, this is read as the term

$$;(G_1, \; ;(G_2, \; ..., \; ;(G_m, G_n) \; ...))$$

which is, of course, another way you could write the goal.

Aside from questions of operator precedence, you can put a disjunction *anywhere* that a simple goal would have been allowed. ';' has wider scope than ",", so if you write

$$G_1,$$
$$G_2 \; ; \; G_3,$$
$$G_4$$

this will be read as

$$(G_1, \; G_2) \; ; \; (G_3, \; G_4)$$

To avoid confusion, you should *always* put parentheses around a disjunction, and *never* put parentheses around the individual disjuncts. (That is, write "(a,b ; c,d)", not "(a,b) ; (c,d)". The layout I recommend is

ⅼⅼⅼⅼⅼⅼⅼⅼ$(ⅼⅼⅼG_1$
ⅼⅼⅼⅼⅼⅼⅼⅼ$;ⅼⅼⅼG_2$
ⅼⅼⅼⅼⅼⅼⅼⅼ$;ⅼⅼⅼG_n$
ⅼⅼⅼⅼⅼⅼⅼⅼ$)$

This way you can tell as soon as you see the beginning of a line exactly what it is doing. Readers familiar with Ada will recognise the indentation style. Recalling that the disjuncts (the G_i) can be conjunctions, we see that the general pattern is

␣␣␣␣␣␣␣␣(␣␣␣$G_{1,1}$,
␣␣␣␣␣␣␣␣␣␣␣␣$G_{1,2}$,
␣␣␣␣␣␣␣␣␣␣␣␣$G_{1,p}$
␣␣␣␣␣␣␣␣;␣␣␣$G_{2,1}$,
␣␣␣␣␣␣␣␣␣␣␣␣$G_{2,q}$
␣␣␣␣␣␣␣␣;␣␣␣$G_{n,1}$,
␣␣␣␣␣␣␣␣␣␣␣␣$G_{n,r}$
␣␣␣␣␣␣␣␣)

Assuming that a disjunction like this doesn't contain any cuts, we can explain what it does by saying that it acts *as if* the disjunction were split out as a separate predicate

g(*shared variables*)

where

g(*shared variables*) :-
    $G_{1,1}$,
    $G_{1,2}$,
    $G_{1,p}$.
g(*shared variables*) :-
    $G_{2,1}$,
    $G_{2,q}$.
g(*shared variables*) :-
    $G_{n,1}$,
    $G_{n,r}$.

For example, suppose we want to test whether a variable P is one of {a,e,i,o,u}. We could write

```
(   P = a
;   P = e
;   P = i
;   P = o
;   P = u
)
```

or we could write vowel(P), where

```
vowel(a).
vowel(e).
vowel(i).
vowel(o).
vowel(u).
```

Which should we do?

In this case, there is no doubt that the better version is the one with the vowel/1 predicate. But how do I know that?

There are two grounds that we could base our choice on: *style* and *speed*. The *style* argument is that it is almost always cleaner to call a predicate than to have an internal if-then-else. This is especially true when we can arrange the code so that the new auxiliary predicate is likely to be useful elsewhere in our program. However, it is rather a pity to clutter up a program with lots of little auxiliary predicates that have no independent meaning. So the *style* argument leaves us saying "well, use an auxiliary predicate unless it would be much clearer as a disjunction", which leaves "much clearer" as a matter of taste.

If you examine the Quintus Prolog Library, you will discover that it uses disjunctions in the following ways:

- disguised if-then-elses. You can recognise these because they have a cut in all branches except possibly the last. There are two reasons why this pattern shows up. Many of them are old DEC-10 Prolog code, and the DEC-10 Prolog compiler could handle disjunctions with cuts, but couldn't handle if-then-else. The other reason for this pattern is that the then-part would have had a cut in it anyway, and "P→!,Q" has been "simplified" to "P,!,Q".

- "garbage collection failure". The pattern here is

```
p(args) :-
    (   do something hairy,
        fail
    ;   true
    ).
```

You can tell this from a failure-driven loop only by knowing that the "do something hairy" bit is determinate. The idea is that all the data structures built and bindings made in the "hairy" bit will be undone.

- failure-driven loops. An example can be found in library(files).

```
close_all_streams :-
    (   current_stream(_, _, Stream),
        close(Stream),
        fail
    ;   true
    ).
```

The difference between this and "garbage collection failure" is that the "hairy" part is not determinate.

- Deliberately pushing a choice point.

- Member/Union.

The last two uses of disjunction are genuine uses, where you can take the disjunction at face value, rather than as some sort of loop.

3.14.3 Pushing a choice point

This pattern crops up when you are making a non-determinate predicate out of determinate pieces. A good example is between/3, in library(between).

```
between(Lower, Upper, Index) :-
        (    var(Index), integer(Lower), integer(Upper) →
             Lower ≤ Upper,
             between1(Lower, Upper, Index)
        ;    integer(Index), integer(Lower), integer(Upper) →
             Lower ≤ Index,
             Index ≤ Upper
        ; /* the arguments are strange */
             Goal = between(Lower,Upper,Index),
             must_be(integer, Lower, 1, Goal),
             must_be(integer, Upper, 2, Goal),
             must_be(integer, Index, 3, Goal)
        ).
```

```
between1(Lower, Upper, Index) :-
        (    Lower =:= Upper → Index = Lower
        ;    Index = Lower
        ;    Next is Lower+1, % Lower < Upper
             between1(Next, Upper, Index)
        ).
```

3.14.4 Member/Union

A moderately common case is where you want to check whether a variable belongs to a set, which set can easily be expressed as the union of a smallish number of tests, but which would be excessively tedious to list with one clause per element. As an example, suppose we are using the ASCII character set, and want to express the idea "X is a letter". We could write a predicate with 52 clauses, one for each lower case and one for each upper case letter, but that would be tedious. Or we could write

```
(    between(0'a, 0'z, X)
;    between(0'A, 0'Z, X)
)
```

It is important to note that this is not an if→ then;else. If X is a variable, this disjunction is capable of enumerating all the solutions for X. Another way of thinking about this construct is described in the chapter on Sequences: it can be seen as concatenating the two sequences of solutions.

3.15   'repeat' loops

A "repeat" loop should in general have the form

```
p(args) :-
        initialise,
        repeat,
                obtain next datum(Datum),
                do something with the datum(Datum),
                fail unless this is the last datum(Datum),
        !,
        shut down.
```

For example, to read and print every term in a file, you might do

```
read_and_print(File) :-
        seeing(OldInput), % initialise
        see(File), % initialise
        repeat,
                read(Term), % obtain next datum
                expand_term(Term, Clause), % obtain next datum
                portray_clause(Clause), % do something
                Term == end_of_file, % fail unless last
        !,
        seen, % shut down
        see(OldInput). % shut down
```

Any "repeat" loop which isn't terminated by a cut almost certainly has something wrong with it. You should always bear in mind that the code that *follows* a call to your predicate might fail and backtrack into your code.

I have seen code written by people who thought they were competent Prolog programmers where there was a predicate containing a repeat loop, and every *call* to that predicate was followed by a cut. That is, they wrote something like

```
                /* DO NOT IMITATE THIS EXAMPLE */
p(args) :-
        initialise,
        repeat,
            obtain next datum(D),
            do something with(D),
            fail if not last(D).


                /* DO NOT IMITATE THIS EXAMPLE */
q(stuff) :-
            :
        p(args),
        !,
            :
```

That is not where the cut belongs. The cut belongs in the same clause as the repeat. This kind of code is very confusing for the reader, because the predicate with the repeat loop is incomplete. It is just like writing a predicate which opens a file and does something with it, but doesn't close it, so that every call has to close the file. You should be able to understand every predicate without understanding all its callers.

There is another way of using 'repeat', where you are turning a determinate generator into a backtrackable predicate. The shape of this is

```
p(args, Datum) :-
        initialise,
        repeat,
            obtain next datum(Datum),
            (   this is the last datum(Datum),
                !,
                shut down
                fail
            ;   true % yield Datum to caller
            ).
```

I'm not going to explain how this works, because you shouldn't do it. This is not just because the code is rather disgusting. The reason is that it is vulnerable in a special way: the caller might cut after finding an answer it likes, and that cut will prune away the choice point left behind by 'repeat' as well. So we run the risk of *never* getting to the *shut down* code.

This is also the reason why we do not include a "backtrackable assignment to global variables" operation in the Quintus Prolog Library: it can't be done in ordinary Prolog. (Some Prologs have additional impure hooks which do let you do it, but there is as yet no portable method.)

3.16   If-Then-Else

An if→ then;else has the form

```
(    Test₁ →
     WhenTrue₁
;    ...
;    Testₙ →
     WhenTrueₙ
; /* otherwise */
     WhenAllElseFails
)
```

This is exactly the same kind of thing as the if-then-else constructs of Fortran, Lisp, and Ada. Indeed, the syntax is identical to Lisp M-expr form, except for the use of () rather than [].

The tests can be any Prolog goals at all. You can even have an if→ then;else like

```
(    nl, tab(9), write(*), nl → true
;    abort /* cannot happen */
)
```

although that would be rather silly.

Read an if→ then;else as "if $Test_1$ has any solutions, commit to the first solution found, and then attempt $WhenTrue_1$, otherwise ...otherwise if $Test_N$ has any solutions, commit to the first solution found, and then attempt $WhenTrue_N$, otherwise attempt $WhenAllElseFails$." If $WhenAllElseFails$ is omitted, it is taken to be 'fail'. In general, you should use the if→ then;else form only when the tests are logically determinate.

In Quintus Prolog, a test which is a conjunction of type tests (such as var/1 and arithmetic tests (such as '>'/2 is especially efficient. For example, to add up the positive and negative elements of a list separately, write:

```
pos_and_neg_sums(Nums, Pos, Neg) :-
        pos_and_neg_sums(Nums, 0, Pos, 0, Neg).

pos_and_neg_sums([], Pos, Pos, Neg, Neg).
pos_and_neg_sums([Num|Nums], Pos0, Pos, Neg0, Neg) :-
    (    Num ≥ 0 →
         Pos1 is Pos0+Num,
         pos_and_neg_sums(Nums, Pos1, Pos, Neg0, Neg)
    ; /*Num < 0 */
         Neg1 is Neg0-Num,
         pos_and_neg_sums(Nums, Pos0, Pos, Neg1, Neg)
    ).
```

In particular, if you want to test whether a variable known to be bound to an integer has one of a small set of values, use '=:='/2, in your if→then;else, not '='/2.

3.17 Tips

The vertical bar "|" is accepted by the parser as a synonym for disjunction ';'. The original reason for this was that it makes Definite Clause Grammar rules look pretty. It will help you to make fewer mistakes if you use the vertical bar in list patterns only, and stick to ';' for disjunction.

Never put a disjunction sign at the end of a line. When the disjunction operator (whichever of the two you use) is being *used*, you should put it at the beginning of the line. Why? Because it is very hard to tell the difference between

```
        p,
        q
```

and

```
        p;
        q
```

when you are looking at one line out of thousands. Write the latter as

```
        p
    ;   q
```

and you'll have no trouble telling the two apart. When the disjunction operator is
being *mentioned* (that is, when it is part of a pattern to be matched) you should
put a space on either side of it and ensure that it is not the last token on a line.
You will never put spaces around the vertical bar when it is being used as part of a
cons cell, so that will make it easy for you to tell the difference between these two
clauses:

p([X|Y]) :- ...

p((X | Y)) :- ...

You are advised not to use 'false', because it is not available in most other Prologs.
Stick to 'fail'. About the only use you'll ever have for the operation is immediately
after printing an error message (or immediately after where you *should* have printed
an error message) , so you *mean* 'fail' rather than 'false' most of the time anyway.

You are advised not to use 'otherwise'. There are two reasons. One is that most
other Prolog's haven't got it. The other is that in several Prolog-like languages
which have it, it means something else. It is very tempting to think that 'otherwise'
in Prolog is like 'default' in C. For example, you would expect

```
switch (i) {
     default: return 1;
     case 1:  return 0;
     case 2:  return -1;
}
```

to transliterate into

```
p(I, Result) :-
     (    otherwise → Result = 1
     ;    I =:= 1 → Result = 0
     ;    I =:= 2 → Result = -1
     ).
```

and in some Prolog-like languages, this would work. But it doesn't work here,
because our 'otherwise' is absolutely identical to 'true' in every respect except
spelling. Write instead

```
p(I, Result) :-
     (    I =:= 1 → Result = 0
     ;    I =:= 2 → Result = -1
     ;    /* else */ Result = 1
     ).
```

The simplest way of avoiding the confusion is to avoid the confuser. Very often it is much clearer if you use an if→ then;else rather than a choice point. In some Prolog systems, it may also be considerably cheaper. In others, regrettably, it may be more costly.

4 Methods of Programming

The question before us is: "How does one *write* a Prolog program?"

4.1   The Problem of the Dutch National Flag

We are given a proper list of items, each of which is either red, white, or blue. The task is to construct a new list which contains the elements of the first list, first the red ones, then the white ones, and finally the blue ones.

Let's start by writing this specification down.

```
dutch_national_flag(Input, Output) :-
        permutation(Input, Output),
        red_white_blue(Output, []).

red_white_blue ⟶ reds, whites, blues.


reds    ⟶ [Item], {red(Item)},    reds    | [].

whites  ⟶ [Item], {white(Item)}, whites | [].

blues   ⟶ [Item], {blue(Item)},   blues   | [].
```

This is an absolutely correct translation of the problem into Prolog. It works. Why not stop here? Well, the trouble is that a non-trivial list has a *lot* of permutations. Suppose that there are 8 red elements, 8 white elements, and 8 blue elements. Then there are 6.2×10^{23} permutations to consider, and we have to consider all of them, because they might all be solutions. At first sight, there are only 6.6×10^{13} solutions, but nothing in the specification says that an item can't have more than one colour!

This is one of the things which distinguishes "relational" programming from "functional" programming. We have to worry about the number of solutions (actually, we have to worry about the number of proofs, but that is described in the section on cuts and choice points). If there are too many solutions, we may be able to write a program, but it will be of little practical use.

> A Prolog program may be correct, but to be useful it must also be *feasible*.

Let's refine the specification so that there is a single solution. For any items X and Y of the same colour, if X precedes Y in the Input, X is to precede Y in the Output. Now the paradigm is not sorting, but selecting a subset.

dutch_national_flag(Input, Output) :-
        red_items(Input, Output, Output1),
        white_items(Input, Output1, Output2),
        blue_items(Input, Output2, []).

red_items([], Rest, Rest).
red_items([Item|Items], [Item|SubSet], Rest) :-
        red(Item),
        red_items(Items, SubSet, Rest).
red_items([Item|Items], SubSet, Rest) :-
        white(Item),
        red_items(Items, SubSet, Rest).
red_items([Item|Items], SubSet, Rest) :-
        blue(Item),
        red_items(Items, SubSet, Rest).

white_items([], Rest, Rest).
white_items([Item|Items], SubSet, Rest) :-
        red(Item),
        white_items(Items, SubSet, Rest).
white_items([Item|Items], [Item|SubSet], Rest) :-
        white(Item),
        white_items(Items, SubSet, Rest).
white_items([Item|Items], SubSet, Rest) :-
        blue(Item),
        white_items(Items, SubSet, Rest).

blue_items([], Rest, Rest).
blue_items([Item|Items], SubSet, Rest) :-
        red(Item),
        blue_items(Items, SubSet, Rest).
blue_items([Item|Items], SubSet, Rest) :-
        white(Item),
        blue_items(Items, SubSet, Rest).
blue_items([Item|Items], [Item|SubSet], Rest) :-
        blue(Item),
        blue_items(Items, SubSet, Rest).

This is logically correct. It is much more efficient than the previous version. How did we get there?

Suppose we have a predicate *desirable*(Item) which recognises or generates desirable items, and this predicate has an opposite *undesirable*(Item), which recognises or generates items which are not desirable, and we want to write a predicate *subset*(Items,Subset) which selects the subset of desirable items out of the set of items. The general scheme for this is

subset([], []).
subset([Item|Items], [Item|SubSet]) :-
          desirable(Item),
          subset(Items, SubSet).
subset([Item|Items], SubSet) :-
          undesirable(Item),
          subset(Items, SubSet).

Let's take the case of finding the blue items. There is one way that an item can be desirable: it can be blue. There are two ways it can be undesirable: it can be red or it can be white. So we obtain

blue_items([], []).
blue_items([Item|Items], [Item|SubSet]) :-
          blue(Item), % *desirable*
          blue_items(Items, SubSet).
blue_items([Item|Items], SubSet) :-
          (red(Item) ; white(Item)), % *undesirable*
          blue_items(Items, SubSet).

Appealing to distributivity, we turn the last clause into two:

blue_items([Item|Items], SubSet) :-
          red(Item),
          blue_items(Items, SubSet).
blue_items([Item|Items], SubSet) :-
          white(Item),
          blue_items(Items, SubSet).

There is an important thing to notice about this method of selecting a subset: in a conventional Prolog system it can only be used to compute the subset given a proper list of items. If you try to compute the full list of items given a subset, you are in trouble. There are infinitely many lists containing any given subset. Prolog cannot be expected to enumerate infinitely many solutions in a finite time. Logic programming systems such as MU Prolog, NU Prolog, Prolog II, or David Warren's coroutining package for DEC-10 Prolog can do something sensible with such a query: they will put it to one side and hope that someone else will work out the input. But even those systems do not solve the problem of guessing which of infinitely many lists is the correct answer.

As a generalisation of the previous scheme, suppose we have predicates $p_1/1$, ..., $p_n/1$ which are mutually exclusive, and we want to split a list of items into a list of items satisfying p_1, ..., and a list of items satisfying p_n. That is, we want to *partition* the list. The scheme is

partition([], [], ..., []).
partition([Item|Items], [Item|Set1], ..., Setn) :-
        p_1(Item),
        partition(Items, Set1, ..., Setn).

$\vdots$

partition([Item|Items], Set1, ..., [Item|Setn]) :-
        p_n(Item),
        partition(Items, Set1, ..., Setn).

In this case we would have

dutch_national_flag(Input, Output) :-
        partition(Input, Reds, Whites, Blues),
        append(Reds, Output0, Output),
        append(Whites, Blues, Output0).

partition([], [], [], []).
partition([Item|Items], [Item|Reds], Whites, Blues) :-
        red(Item),
        partition(Items, Reds, Whites, Blues).
partition([Item|Items], Reds, [Item|Whites], Blues) :-
        white(Item),
        partition(Items, Reds, Whites, Blues).
partition([Item|Items], Reds, Whites, [Item|Blues]) :-
        blue(Item),
        partition(Items, Reds, Whites, Blues).

The next stage in the development of this program was to note that we want to append the lists of items. There is a general method for avoiding calls to append/3, and that is to use difference lists. That is, instead of having a single argument which stands for an entire list, have two arguments which stand for positions within a list. Here is how the output is divided:

0.2in[r1,r2,r3,r4,w1,w2,w3,b1,b2,b3,b4,b5]
        ⇑Output   ⇑Output1 ⇑Output2   ⇑[]

When you are developing a predicate like this, it is very helpful to draw such diagrams. They are very like the diagrams that J. C. Reynolds developed to describe arrays and their subscripts.

The general scheme for constructing a subset as a difference list is

subset([], List, List).
subset([Item|Items], [Item|List1], List) :-
        desirable(Item),
        subset(Items, List1, List).
subset([Item|Items], List0, List) :-
        undesirable(Item),
        subset(Items, List0, List).

Any predicate which constructs a list can be adapted to construct a difference list. Here we have a predicate which constructs three lists, so there are three pairs of arguments.

dutch_national_flag(Input, Output) :-
        dutch_national_flag(Input, Output, Output1,
                            Output1, Output2,
                            Output2, []).

dutch_national_flag([], R, R, W, W, B, B).
dutch_national_flag([Item|Items], [Item|R1], R, W0, W, B0, B) :-
        red(Item),
        dutch_national_flag(Items, R1, R, W0, W, B0, B).
dutch_national_flag([Item|Items], R0, R, [Item|W1], W, B0, B) :-
        white(Item),
        dutch_national_flag(Items, R0, R, W1, W, B0, B).
dutch_national_flag([Item|Items], R0, R, W0, W, [Item|B1], B) :-
        blue(Item),
        dutch_national_flag(Items, R0, R, W0, W, B1, B).

There is one more step to be taken before we have an efficient solution to the Dutch National Flag problem.

As far as I know, there are no commercially available Prolog compilers which can be told that red(X), white(X), and blue(X) are mutually exclusive. As soon as red(Item) has succeeded, *you* may know that there isn't any point in considering the other two clauses, but *Prolog* doesn't know that, so it will leave a choice point. Letting N_R, N_W, and N_B be the number of red, white, and blue items respectively, when Prolog finds its first solution, there will be N_R choice points left around from the "red" clause, and N_W choice points left around from the "white" clause. Some

Prolog systems may even leave N_B choice points behind from the "blue" clause just in case someone adds another clause later. If this solution is rejected, each of the choice points will go on to try the other clauses and fail, so the cost is linear, but (a) these choice points take up space proportional to the length of the proof, and (b) they will inhibit determinacy detection in the caller. So we would like to prevent these choice points being left.

There are three things we could do. Perhaps the most obvious is to add a cut in the single clause for dutch_national_flag/2:

```
dutch_national_flag(Input, Output) :-
        dutch_national_flag(Input, Output, Output1,
                            Output1, Output2,
                            Output2, []),
    !.
```

This would be wrong.

Why would it be wrong? Because dutch_national_flag/7 is supposed to be determinate, and the way to ensure that is to correct the culprit, not its callers.

The second most obvious thing would be to add cuts to the clauses which are responsible for creating the choice points.

```
dutch_national_flag([], R, R, W, W, B, B).
dutch_national_flag([Item|Items], [Item|R1], R, W0, W, B0, B) :-
        red(Item),
        !,
        dutch_national_flag(Items, R1, R, W0, W, B0, B).
dutch_national_flag([Item|Items], R0, R, [Item|W1], W, B0, B) :-
        white(Item),
        !,
        dutch_national_flag(Items, R0, R, W1, W, B0, B).
dutch_national_flag([Item|Items], R0, R, W0, W, [Item|B1], B) :-
        blue(Item),
        !,
        dutch_national_flag(Items, R0, R, W0, W, B1, B).
```

The cut in the last clause is an interesting matter of taste. It is quite redundant (unless, of course, blue/1 leaves choice points behind). In a case like this, where the order of the clauses is not supposed to matter, I like to make all the clauses alike.

The third solution is to reformulate the problem so that the choice points never arise. Since we expect each item to have precisely one colour, we introduce, in place of the three colour predicates, a single colour function colour(+Item, -Colour)

which returns the colour of a given item. It is up to the implementor of colour/2 to ensure that it is determinate, if indeed it should be determinate. We now write

dutch_national_flag(Input, Output) :-
        dnf(Input, Output, X, X, Y, Y, []).

dnf([], R, R, W, W, B, B).
dnf([Item|Items], R0, R, W0, W, B0, B) :-
        colour(Item, Colour),
        dnf(Colour, R0, R, W0, W, B0, B, Item, Items).

dnf(red, [Item|R1], R, W0, W, B0, B, Item, Items) :-
        dnf(Items, R1, R, W0, W, B0, B).
dnf(white, R0, R, [Item|W1], W, B0, B, Item, Items) :-
        dnf(Items, R0, R, W1, W, B0, B).
dnf(blue, R0, R, W0, W, [Item|B1], B, Item, Items) :-
        dnf(Items, R0, R, W0, W, B1, B).

If the Prolog system you use indexes predicates on their first argument (as DEC-10 Prolog, Quintus Prolog, ALS Prolog, SB Prolog, and many others do), this will never create any choice points, and is the most efficient way of solving this problem. (Begin aside.) In an earlier chapter I strongly recommended a particular argument ordering convention. dutch_national_flag/2 and dnf/7 follow it, but dnf/9 doesn't. That's fine; the argument ordering convention applies to predicates that are used elsewhere in the program, or to exported predicates, but dnf/9 is strictly local. By switching Item and Items to the end of dnf/9's argument sequence, I was able to leave the other arguments in a fixed order, which is particularly efficient in WAM-based systems, and harmless elsewhere. (End aside.)

4.2   The Problem of Merging Two Ordered Lists

This problem occurs again and again in various guises. Adding polynomials, finding the union or intersection of two sets, and sorting are just some of the variants of this problem.

We are given two ordered lists L1 and L2, where

ordered_list([]).
ordered_list([_]).
ordered_list([X1,X2|Rest]) :-
        X1 @$\leq$ X2,
        ordered_list([X2|Rest]).

The task is to compute the merge M, where M is an ordered list containing the elements of both L1 and L2.

```
merge(L1, L2, M) :-
        append(L1, L2, L),
        permutation(L, M),
        ordered_list(M).
```

Before doing that, let me point out a problem with the definition of ordered_list/1 I've given above. Suppose the list has 3 elements.

```
ordered_list([a,b,c]) ?
ordered_list([a,b|Rest]) :- % Rest = [c]
    a @< b,
    ordered_list([b|Rest]). % New cons cell
    ordered_list([b,c|Rest]) :- % Rest = []
        b @< c,
        ordered_list([c|Rest]). % New cons cell
        ordered_list([c]) :- true.
```

By induction, applying ordered_list/1 to a list which contains N elements will create $N - 1$ new cons cells, which is utterly pointless. The logic is fine, the problem is just that most compilers aren't smart enough to notice that the term [X2|Rest] already exists and doesn't need to be rebuilt. It is interesting to note that this improvement is not applicable in structure-sharing Prologs. The list cell must be inspected somewhere, so a global frame and a molecule will be created then, and the call to ordered_list([X2|Rest]) will share the global frame that was created to unify [X1,X2|Rest] against the argument.

There is another problem, which is that when we reach a list with one element, the second clause will match, but most compilers do not index deeply enough to notice that the third clause won't, so a choice point will be left behind. We could handle this by adding a cut, but since we want to recode anyway to avoid the redundant construction, we might as well try to avoid this choice point as well.

```
ordered_list([]).
ordered_list([Head|Tail]) :-
        ordered_list(Tail, Head).

ordered_list([], _).
ordered_list([Head|Tail], Prev) :-
        Prev @< Head,
        ordered_list(Tail, Head).
```

In Quintus Prolog, the second version takes about 65% of the time that the first takes, and there are no redundant choice points.

Representing a list known to have at least N elements by $N + 1$ arguments, one each for the first N elements and one for the remaining elements, is a common technique called *lagging*. It is discussed further in the chapter on Sequences.

Returning to merge(L1, L2, M), let's work backwards. There are two cases: M = [], or M = [X|M1] for some X and M1. In the former case, the other two arguments must also have been empty. So we have

merge([], [], []).

In the latter case, X must have come either from L1 or L2, and M1 must be the merge of whatever was left. So we have two cases

merge([X|L1], L2, [X|M1]) :-
    some test,
    merge(L1, L2, M1).
merge(L1, [X|L2], [X|M1]) :-
    some other test,
    merge(L1, L2, M1).

Let's examine these two cases. We would like to use the first clause unless the second clause must be used. The second clause must be used if X is less than the head of L1. So we write

merge(L1, [X|L2], [X|M1]) :- % *use*
    less_than_head(X, L1),
    !,
    merge(L1, L2, M1).
merge([X|L1], L2, [X|M1]) :- % *this*
    merge(L1, L2, M1).
merge([], L2, L2). % *version*

less_than_head(X, $[H|\_]$) :-
    X @< H.

We could expand less_than_head/2 in-line, producing

merge($[H_1|T_1]$, $[X|L_2]$, $[X|M_1]$) :-
    X @< H_1,
    !,
    merge($[H_1|T_1]$, L_2, M_1). % NEW CONS CELL
merge($[X|L_1]$, L_2, $[X|M_1]$) :-
    merge(L_1, L_2, M_1).
merge([], L_2, L_2).

but as you can see, this could create up to length(L1) pointless cons cells. Once again, structure-sharing systems are different. On a structure-sharing system such as DEC-10 Prolog or C Prolog, we might as well unfold less_than_head/2: we are going to create a global frame anyway, and we'll save a procedure call.

The implementors of one Prolog system implemented sort/2 by copying the code out of C Prolog. But their system uses structure copying, like Quintus Prolog, not structure sharing. When I replaced their version of merge/3 by one like the first version above, sort/2 speeded up by 25%.

The interesting point about this is that we arrived at a fairly reasonable implementation of merge/3 by induction on the output. I have coded several versions of merge/3 before, and this was the first time that it hasn't been any trouble. These days I would use the scheme described in section 5.2 which doesn't even need any cuts.

4.3   Computing the size of a tree

The Dutch National Flag problem was solved by induction on the input. The merging problem was solved by induction on the output.

A predicate often has the form of an induction over one of its arguments. In relational programming, we try to minimise the differences between inputs and outputs, so a predicate whose form is an induction on an "output" is just as natural as one whose form is an induction on an "input".

We can often develop a predicate by enriching a recognition predicate for the data type of interest.

For example, suppose we have

```
:- type tree(K,V) ⟶ []
                  | node(K,V,tree(K,V),tree(K,V)).
```

A recognition predicate for this would look like

```
is_tree([]).
is_tree(node(_,_,Lson,Rson)) :-
        is_tree(Lson),
        is_tree(Rson).
```

(The names of recognition predicates usually begin with "is_", but this is just a convention.) Suppose we want to compute the number of nodes in a tree. The obvious definition is

```
size_of_tree([], 0).
```

```
size_of_tree(node(_,_,Lson,Rson), Size) :-
        size_of_tree(Lson, Lsize),
        size_of_tree(Rson, Rsize),
        Size is Lsize+Rsize+1.
```

There is nothing wrong with this definition. But if the Prolog system you are using exploits last call optimisation (often called TRO), it is more efficient to write

```
size_of_tree(Tree, Size) :-
        size_of_tree(Tree, 0, Size).
```

```
%   size_of_tree(Tree, Size0, Size1)
%   is true when Size1-Size0 is the number of nodes in Tree.
```

```
size_of_tree([], Size, Size).
size_of_tree(node(_,_,Lson,Rson), Size0, Size) :-
        Size1 is Size0+1,
        size_of_tree(Lson, Size1, Size2),
        size_of_tree(Rson, Size2, Size).
```

This is still obviously an enrichment of is_tree/1.

Suppose that the Keys in a tree are 'yes', 'no', or 'maybe', and that we want to collect all the 'maybe' Values in a list.

```
maybes(Tree, Maybes) :-
        maybes(Tree, Maybes, []).
```

```
maybes([], Maybes, Maybes).
maybes(node(Key,Value,Lson,Rson), Maybes0, Maybes) :-
        maybe(Key, Value, Maybes0, Maybes1),
        maybes(Lson, Maybes1, Maybes2),
        maybes(Rson, Maybes2, Maybes).
```

```
maybe(yes, _, Maybes, Maybes).
maybe(no, _, Maybes, Maybes).
maybe(maybe, Value, [Value|Maybes], Maybes).
```

4.4   The Search for the Small Superset

This is a general design principle due to Dijkstra.

When a program has to generate the elements of a set A, there are two cases at design time:

1. we have a simple successor function which can be used to compute the "next"
   element of A.

   Suppose, for example, we have

   first_element(+SetDescription, -Element)
   next_element(+SetDescription, +ThisElement, -NextElement)

   Then we can write

   elements(SetDescription, [First|Rest]) :-
           first_element(SetDescription, First),
           !,
           elements(SetDescription, First, Rest).
   elements(_, []).

   elements(SetDescription, Element, [Next|Rest]) :-
           next_element(SetDescription, Element, Next),
           !,
           elements(SetDescription, Next, Rest).
   elements(_, _, []).

   to obtain the set as a list, or we can enumerate the elements thus

   element(SetDescription, Element) :-
           first_element(First),
           element(SetDescription, First, Element).

   element(_, Element, Element).
   element(SetDescription, This, Element) :-
           next_element(SetDescription, This, Next),
           element(SetDescription, Next, Element).

2. we do not have such a function. In this case, the usual approach is to generate
   the elements of a larger set B, where

   (a) Every A is a B

   (b) There is a way of generating B

   (c) There is a test which determines whether a given B is an A.

   Suppose, for example, we have

elements_of_superset(+SetDescription, -Elements)
in_set_of_interest(+SetDescription, +Element)

Then we can appeal to the *subset* scheme and write

elements(SetDescription, Elements) :-
       elements_of_superset(SetDescription, SuperSet),
       filter(SuperSet, SetDescription, Elements).

filter([], _, []).
filter([A|Bs], D, [A|As]) :-
       in_set_of_interest(D, A),
       !,
       filter(Bs, D, As).
filter([_|Bs], D, As) :-
       filter(Bs, D, As).

to obtain the set as a list. Alternatively, if we have

element_of_superset(+SetDescription, -Element)
in_set_of_interest(+SetDescription, +Element)

we can write

element(SetDescription, Element) :-
       element_of_superset(SetDescription, Element),
       in_set_of_interest(SetDescription, Element).

to enumerate the elements. This is, of course, just the familiar "generate and test" scheme.

Dijkstra's observation is that for this approach to be useful

1. B should not be too much larger than A

2. the generator of the superset B should be efficient

3. the test whether a given B is an A should be efficient, especially when the given B is *not* an A.

"The Search for the Small Superset" is the conscious decision of the programmer to look for a smaller superset B than whatever happens to be the obvious one.

Several people are suggesting that the proper approach for logic programming is to move away from conventional Prolog systems. It is often pointed out that coroutining systems like NU Prolog can interleave the execution of an enumerator and a test, thus making the generate-and-test (by enumeration) paradigm more efficient. Indeed, a NU-Prolog programmer will tend to write

```
element(Set, Element) :-
        in_set_of_interest(Set, Element), % test
        element_of_superset(Set, Element). % generator
```

precisely to obtain this interleaving. There is much in this point of view. But not quite as much as might appear. First, coroutining is not going to help unless the enumerator can quit part way through generating an element and go on to the next one. If the generator has to construct an element in its entirety before it can determine what the next element will be, coroutining will be of little benefit. Second, even if coroutining does move part of the test into the generator, it will still be helpful to have the set that gets to the rest of the test as small as possible.

So "smarter" Prolog systems will not relieve the programmer of the responsibility for searching for a small superset.

The next problem we shall look at is this:

D_1, D_2, ..., D_9 are distinct decimal digits, none of them zero, such that for each $1 \le n \le 9$ the n digits $D_1 \ldots D_n$ form a number which is divisible by n.

This problem has a unique answer: 381654729.

The standard method of encoding "X, ..., Z are distinct elements of S" in Prolog is

        perm(S, [X,...,Z|_])

So we can encode this specification in Prolog as

```
answer(Solution) :-
        Solution = [D1,D2,D3,D4,D5,D6,D7,D8,D9],
        perm([1,2,3,4,5,6,7,8,9], Solution),
        forall(append(D1_to_N, _, Solution), (
            length(D1_to_N, N),
            divisible(N, D1_to_N)
        )).
```

```
divisible(N, Ds) :-
        divisible(Ds, 0, N).

divisible([], 0, _).
divisible([D|Ds], R0, N) :-
        R1 is (R0*10 + D) mod N,
        divisible(Ds, R1, N).
```

so here perm/2 is generating trial Solutions, and the 'forall' is testing them.

The snag with this is that we generate each permutation blindly and only test any part of it after the whole thing has been made. For example, when we reach a guess which starts out "21", we'll try all $7! = 5,040$ permutations of the remaining elements despite the fact that 21 is not divisible by 2.

One improvement would be to test each D_n as soon as it is generated. We can unpack 'perm' and 'forall' thus:

```
answer(Solution) :-
        Solution = [D1,D2,D3,D4,D5,D6,D7,D8,D9],
        select(D1, [1,2,3,4,5,6,7,8,9], R1),
        select(D2, R1, R2),
        select(D3, R2, R3),
        select(D4, R3, R4),
        select(D5, R4, R5),
        select(D6, R5, R6),
        select(D7, R6, R7),
        select(D8, R7, R8),
        select(D9, R8, []),
        divisible(1, [D1]),
        divisible(2, [D1,D2]),
        divisible(3, [D1,D2,D3]),
        divisible(4, [D1,D2,D3,D4]),
        divisible(5, [D1,D2,D3,D4,D5]),
        divisible(6, [D1,D2,D3,D4,D5,D6]),
        divisible(7, [D1,D2,D3,D4,D5,D6,D7]),
        divisible(8, [D1,D2,D3,D4,D5,D6,D7,D8]),
        divisible(9, [D1,D2,D3,D4,D5,D6,D7,D8,D9]).
```

Testing each digit as soon as it is generated is merely re-ordering the conjuncts to

```
ans1([D1,D2,D3,D4,D5,D6,D7,D8,D9]) :-
        select(D1, [1,2,3,4,5,6,7,8,9], R1),
            divisible(1, [D1]),
```

```
select(D2, R1, R2),
      divisible(2, [D1,D2]),
select(D3, R2, R3),
      divisible(3, [D1,D2,D3]),
select(D4, R3, R4),
      divisible(4, [D1,D2,D3,D4]),
select(D5, R4, R5),
      divisible(5, [D1,D2,D3,D4,D5]),
select(D6, R5, R6),
      divisible(6, [D1,D2,D3,D4,D5,D6]),
select(D7, R6, R7),
      divisible(7, [D1,D2,D3,D4,D5,D6,D7]),
select(D8, R7, R8),
      divisible(8, [D1,D2,D3,D4,D5,D6,D7,D8]),
select(D9, R8, []),
      divisible(9, [D1,D2,D3,D4,D5,D6,D7,D8,D9]).
```

This change alone makes a big difference: it takes C Prolog only 3.9 seconds to find the answer, whereas it would have taken 100 times longer just to enumerate the permutations in the original specification, never mind checking them. Applying the rule:

```
Apply constraints early
```

has given us at least a 100-fold speedup.

As it stands, each of the D_i variables might be bound to any of the digits. We can easily reduce the ranges of the variables.

divisible(2, $[D_1, D_2]$) $\Rightarrow D_2$ is even
divisible(4, $[D_1, \ldots, D_4]$) $\Rightarrow D_4$ is even
divisible(6, $[D_1, \ldots, D_6]$) $\Rightarrow D_6$ is even
divisible(8, $[D_1, \ldots, D_8]$) $\Rightarrow D_8$ is even
divisible(5, $[D_1, \ldots, D_5]$) $\Rightarrow D_5$ is 5

So the even variables $[D_2, D_4, D_6, D_8]$ range over the even digits [2,4,6,8] and the odd variables $[D_1, D_3, D_7, D_9]$ range over the odd digits [1,3,7,9].

```
answer([D1,D2,D3,D4,D5,D6,D7,D8,D9]) :-
      select(D1, [1,3,7,9], R1),
            divisible(1, [D1]),
      select(D2, [2,4,6,8], R2),
            divisible(2, [D2]),
```

```
    select(D3, R1, R3),
        divisible(3, [D1,D2,D3]),
    select(D4, R2, R4),
        divisible(4, [D1,D2,D3,D4]),
    D5 = 5,
        divisible(5, [D1,D2,D3,D4,D5]),
    select(D6, R4, R8),
        divisible(6, [D1,D2,D3,D4,D5,D6]),
    select(D7, R3, R7),
        divisible(7, [D1,D2,D3,D4,D5,D6,D7]),
    select(D8, R8, []),
        divisible(8, [D1,D2,D3,D4,D5,D6,D7,D8]),
    select(D9, R7, []),
        divisible(9, [D1,D2,D3,D4,D5,D6,D7,D8,D9]).
```

This takes 0.9 seconds in C Prolog, so applying the rule

```
Reduce the ranges
```

has given us a 4.3 times speedup.

There are three obvious improvements to be made here. The first is that

```
    select(X, L, [])
```

is equivalent to

```
    L = [X]
```

so we don't need to call select/3 to find D_8 and D_9. The second is that some of the divisibility tests are not needed.

Some of the divisibility goals must succeed, so we don't need to test them:

divisible(1, [D1])	since 1 divides everything
divisible(2, [D1,D2])	since D2 is 2, 4, 6, or 8
divisible(5, [D1,D2,D3,D4,D5])	since D5 is 5
divisible(9, [D1,...,D9])	by casting out nines.

The idea of "casting out nines" is that since $9 = 10 - 1$,

$$(X * 10 + Y) \bmod 9 = (X * 9 + X + Y) \bmod 9 = (X + Y) \bmod 9,$$

so an integer is divisible by 9 if and only if the sum of the digits in its decimal representation is divisible by 9. Clearly,

$$(9 + (1 + 8) + (2 + 7) + (3 + 6) + (4 + 5)) \bmod 9 = 0$$

so we don't need to test that at run time.

We can simplify the calls to divisible/2:

divisible(4, [D1,D2,D3,D4])
$\Rightarrow$ divisible(4, [D3,D4])
because 4 divides 100.

divisible(8, [D1,D2,D3,D4,D5,D6,D7,D8])
$\Rightarrow$ divisible(8, [D6,D7,D8])
because 8 divides 1000.

divisible(6, [D1,D2,D3,D4,D5,D6])
$\Rightarrow$ divisible(6, [D4,D5,D6])
because 2 divides 1000 and 3 divides [D1,D2,D3].

We obtain

answer([D1,D2,D3,D4,5,D6,D7,D8,D9]) :-
        select(D1, [1,3,7,9], R1),
        select(D2, [2,4,6,8], R2),
        select(D3, R1, R3),
            divisible(3, [D1,D2,D3]),
        select(D4, R2, R4),
            divisible(4, [D3,D4]),
        select(D6, R4, [D8]),
            divisible(6, [D4,5,D6]),
        select(D7, R3, [D9]),
            divisible(7, [D1,D2,D3,D4,5,D6,D7]),
            divisible(8, [D6,D7,D8]).

These improvements reduce the time from 0.90 seconds to 0.53 seconds in C Prolog, a speedup of 1.7 times. Note that this is the least of the speedups we have seen so far, which is quite typical.

It is possible to improve this still further, but if we push it far enough we end up with

answer([3,8,1,6,5,4,7,2,9]).

which doesn't illustrate many general points.

Another problem like this is N-queens. Given an NxN chess-board, the N-queens problem is to find an assignment of N queens (chess-pieces) to the squares of the board so that no two queens are in the same row, the same column, or the same diagonal. To be specific, the task is to write a predicate

$$queens(N, Queens)$$

which is given an integer N and returns a list Queens of Row-Col pairs. We can specify this directly in Prolog like so:

```
queens(N, Queens) :-
        length(Queens, N),
        assign_all(Queens, 0, N),
        noattack(Queens).

assign_all([], _, _).
assign_all([Row-Col|Queens], Row0, N) :-
        Row is Row0+1,
        between(1, N, Col),
        assign_all(Queens, Row, N).

noattack([]).
noattack([R-C|Queens]) :-
        noattack(Queens, R, C),
        noattack(Queens).

noattack([], _, _).
noattack([R_2 - C_2|Queens], R_1, C_1) :-
        R_2 ≠ R_1, % not in same row
        C_2 ≠ C_1, % not in same column
        R_2 + C_2 ≠ R_1 + C_1, % not in same diagonal
        R_2 - C_2 ≠ R_1 - C_1, % not in same diagonal
        noattack(Queens, R_1, C_1).
```

```
%    between(L, U, X) should be in your library

between(L, U, X) :-
        integer(L), integer(U),
        (    var(X) →
             L ≤ U,
             between1(L, U, X)
```

```
    ;    integer(X),
         L ≤ X, X ≤ U
    ).

between1(L, U, X) :-
    (    X = L
    ;    M is L + 1, M ≤ U,
         between1(M, U, X)
    ).
```

%   perm/2 and select/3 should be in your library

```
perm([], []).
perm([H|T], Perm) :-
        select(H, Perm, Rest),
        perm(T, Rest).

select(X, [X|R], R).
select(X, [H|T], [H|R]) :-
        select(X, T, R).
```

For each queen, we guess one of N columns, and there are N queens, so the search space has N^N elements. To get some idea of this,

N	N^N	$N!$
1	1	1
2	4	2
3	27	6
4	256	24
5	3125	120

If there are N columns, N queens, and no two queens in the same column, it follows that there must be one queen in each column, and instead of guessing each column separately, we can guess a permutation. Thus we get

```
queens(N, Queens) :-
        length(Queens, N),
        rows_and_columns(Queens, Rows, Cols, 0),
        perm(Rows, Cols),
        noattack(Queens).
```

```
%    rows_and_columns([R_1 - C_1, ..., R_n - C_n], [R_1, ..., R_n], [C_1, ..., C_n], R_0)
%    is true when the first three arguments are a list of R - C
%    pairs, a list of Rs, and a list of Cs as pictured, and
%    R_i = R_0 + i for 1 ≤ i ≤ n.
%    That is, the first argument is a Queens list, where the
%    Cols have yet to be assigned values.
```

```
rows_and_columns([], [], [], _).
rows_and_columns([Row-Col|Queens], [Row|Rows], [Col|Cols], Row0) :-
        Row is Row0+1,
        rows_and_columns(Queens, Rows, Cols, Row).
```

where, since we have removed the possibility of two queens being in the same row or the same column by construction,

```
noattack([], _, _).
noattack([R_2 - C_2|Queens], R_1, C_1) :-
        R_2 + C_2 ≠ R_1 + C_1, % not in same diagonal
        R_2 - C_2 ≠ R_1 - C_1, % not in same diagonal
        noattack(Queens, R_1, C_1).
```

We have seen a technique for dealing with predicates of this shape before: interleave the 'noattack' test with the 'perm' generator.

```
queens(N, Queens) :-
        length(Queens, N),
        columns(N, Cols),
        queens(N, Cols, [], Queens).
```

```
columns(0, []) :- !.
columns(Col0, [Col0|Cols]) :-
        Col1 is Col0+1,
        columns(Col1, Cols).
```

```
queens(0, [], Queens, Queens) :- !.
queens(Row0, Cols0, Queens0, Queens) :-
        Row1 is Row0+1,
        select(Col0, Cols0, Cols1),
        noattack(Queens0, Row0, Col0),
        queens(Row1, Cols1, [Row0-Col0|Queens0], Queens).
```

At each iteration of queens/4, it tries to place the queen in row Row0 in a column Col0 such that square Row0-Col0 is not attacked by any of the queens in rows Row0+1...N which have already been placed in Queens0.

So far, this example has not used Prolog in any essential way. We could transliterate this into Lisp without inordinate pain. Another method represents the constraints in the board. A common device for ensuring that "no two things can be in the same location" in a Prolog program is to have a variable "the name of the thing in this location", and when a thing is assigned to that location, to bind the variable to the name of the thing. Since a variable cannot be bound to two different names, this will ensure that there are never two things assigned to the same location. In the N-queens program, the "locations" are the N rows, the N columns, the $2N - 1$ ∕ diagonals, and the $2N - 1$ ∖ diagonals. Our program never tries to put two queens in the same row or the same column, so the only "locations" we have to worry about are the diagonals. Here's a picture of a 5-by-5 board:

A V	B U	C T	D S	E R
B W	C V	D U	E T	F S
C X	D W	E V	F U	G T
D Y	E X	F W	G V	H U
E Z	F Y	G X	H W	I V

The letters A–I are used for the ∕ diagonals and the letters R–Z are used for the ∖ diagonals. If we place a queen in the 2nd row and 3rd column (the square) labelled (D U), we would bind these variables to 3 to indicate that queen 3 occupied diagonal D and diagonal U. This instantly "tells" the other squares in these diagonals that they cannot be used. That means that when we try to place the 5th queen, we just have to try assigning 5 to both variables in each square, and if that succeeds the square is not under attack.

```
queens(N, Queens) :-
        length(Queens, N),
        board(Queens, Board, 0, N, _, _),
        queens(Board, 0, Queens).

board([], [], N, N, _, _).
board([_|Queens], [Col-Vars|Board], Col0, N, [_|VR], VC) :-
        Col is Col0+1,
        functor(Vars, f, N),
        constraints(N, Vars, VR, VC),
        board(Queens, Board, Col, N, VR, [_|VC]).
```

```
constraints(0, _, _, _) :- !.
constraints(N, Row, [R|Rs], [C|Cs]) :-
        arg(N, Row, R-C),
        M is N-1,
        constraints(M, Row, Rs, Cs).

queens([], _, []).
queens([C|Cs], Row0, [Row-Col|Solution]) :-
        Row is Row0+1,
        select(Col-Vars, [C|Cs], Board),
        arg(Row, Vars, Row-Row),
        queens(Board, Row1, Solution).
```

I obtained the following times in seconds using C Prolog version 1.6.edai on a Sun-3/50 running SunOS 3.2.

N	Worst	Usual	Better	Best
1	<0.01	<0.01	<0.01	<0.01
2	0.05	0.02	0.02	0.05
3	0.21	0.05	0.03	0.03
4	2.10	0.23	0.13	0.08
5	28.70	1.40	0.52	0.25
6		9.28	2.12	0.70
7		74.30	9.20	2.53
8			42.20	9.58
9			204.00	39.60

The time in the right-hand column is approx 0.15×4^N milliseconds.
Here are some heuristics that we have used:

- Apply constraints early

- Reduce the ranges

- Propagate constraints forward

- Prefer the most constrained subgoal

and some reminders:

- Optimise at the Right Level!

- The compiler can't compensate for clumsy choices!

4.5   Rem's Algorithm for the Recording of Equivalence Classes

This section has two purposes:

- to show how an algorithm can be translated into Prolog

- to show why it is inadvisable to hack the data base

Chapter 23 of Dijkstra's "A Discipline of Programming" presents a beautiful algorithm for recording equivalence classes. If you have not already read that book, I strongly recommend it to you. What I want to show you here is how we can take such an algorithm and recast in in Prolog.

In Dijkstra's presentation of the algorithm, we are concerned with a graph over N nodes, numbered 0 to $N - 1$. Here, I shall use the numbering 1–N. The basic idea is that as edges are added to this graph, we maintain a function f(node) which maps each node to a representative of its equivalence class, such that f(p) = f(q) if and only if p and q are in the same equivalence class. Initially, each node is in its own equivalence class.

The non-Prolog code here is written in Dijkstra's notation (more or less) to make comparison with the original source easier. The main thing you may be unfamiliar with is "if" and "do" statements:

- if $C_1 \rightarrow S_1$ [] $\cdots$ [] $C_n \rightarrow S_n$ fi means "if every C_i is false, abort the program, otherwise execute an S_i which corresponds to a true C_i". This is an if statement where the order of the tests doesn't matter.

- do $C_1 \rightarrow S_1$ [] $\cdots$ [] $C_n \rightarrow S_n$ od means "while there is at least one true C_i, pick an S_i which corresponds to a true C_i, execute it, and try the whole loop again". This is a while statement with multiple continuation conditions, the order of which doesn't matter.

```
#    f:rem_create(n)
#    makes a new representative function for a graph with nodes 1–n

proc f:rem_create(n)
|[   arg var f : array(int);
     arg con n: int;
     pri var i: int;
```

```
    f := (); # an empty array with lower bound 1
    i := 1;
    do i ≤ n →
        f:hiext(i); # push i at the high end of f
        i := i+1;
    od # now f is (1,...,i)
]|
```

To map this into Prolog, I shall use the "trees" package from the public-domain DEC-10 Prolog library. The operations we shall need from that package are

```
    list_to_tree(+List, -Tree)
    get_label(+Index, +Tree, -Value)
    put_label(+Index, +OldTree, +NewValue, -NewTree)
```

:- ensure_loaded(library(trees)).

```
%    rem_create(+N, -F)
%    unifies F with a REM structure for a graph with N nodes.

rem_create(N, F) :-
        one_to_N(N, [], List),
        list_to_tree(List, F).


one_to_N(N, List0, List) :-
    (   N =:= 0 → List = List0
    ;   M is N-1,
        one_to_N(M, [N|List0], List)
    ).
```

What is happening here is that we create a list [1,2,...,N] (you will remark that the first argument is a counter being counted down to 0, and that the second and third arguments form an accumulator pair), and then we call list_to_tree/2 to make a binary tree out of the list. As soon as I had written this, I tested it by calling rem_create(5,F).

```
#    f.rem_head(p)
#    returns the representative in f of the equivalence class of p

proc f.rem_head(p)
|[   arg con f: array(int);
     arg con p: int;
     pri var h: int;
```

```
        h := p;
        do h ≠ f(h) → h := f(h) od;
        return h
]|
```

```
%   rem_head(+P, +F, ?Head)
%   is true when Head represents the equivalence class that P
%   belongs to in the graph whose REM structure is F.
```

```
rem_head(P, F, Head) :-
        get_label(P, F, H),
        (     H =:= P → Head = P
        ;     rem_head(H, F, Head)
        ).
```

The 1st and 3rd arguments form an accumulator pair for "h". Note that F is passed around unchanged. I tested this by calling

```
?- rem_create(5, F), rem_head(3, F, Head).
```

```
#   f.rem_equivalent(p, q)
#   is true when p and q belong to the same equivalence class in f
```

```
proc f.rem_equivalent(p, q)
|[   arg con f: array(int);
     arg con p, q: int;

     return f.rem_head(p) = f.rem_head(q)
]|
```

```
%   rem_equivalent(+P, +Q, +F)
%   is true when P and Q belong to the same equivalence class
%   in the graph whose REM structure is F.
```

```
rem_equivalent(P, Q, F) :-
        rem_head(P, F, Head),
        rem_head(Q, F, Head).
```

```
#    f:rem_add_link(p, q)
#    updates f so that p and q belong to the same equivalence class.

proc f:rem_add_link(p, q)
|[    arg var f: array(int);
      arg con p, q: int;
      pri var p0, q0, p1, q1: int;

      p0, q0 := p, q;
      p1, q1 := f(p0), f(q0);
      do q1 < p1 → f:(p0) := q1; p0, p1 := p1, f(p1)
      [] p1 < q1 → f:(q0) := p1; q0, q1 := q1, f(q1)
      od
]|
```

```
%    rem_add_link(+P, +Q, +F0, -F)
%    unifies F with a REM structure which represents the same
%    graph as F0 does, except that P and Q are equivalent.

rem_add_link(P0, Q0, F0, F) :-
        get_label(P0, F0, P1),
        get_label(Q0, F0, Q1),
        rem_add_link(P0, P1, Q0, Q1, F0, F).

rem_add_link(P0, P1, Q0, Q1, F0, F) :-
        (     Q1 < P1 →
              put_label(P0, F0, Q1, F1),
              get_label(P1, F0, P2),
              rem_add_link(P1, P2, Q0, Q1, F1, F)
        ;     P1 < Q1 →
              put_label(Q0, F0, P1, F1),
              get_label(Q1, F0, Q2),
              rem_add_link(P0, P1, Q1, Q2, F1, F)
        ; /*P1 = Q1*/
              F = F0
        ).
```

I postponed testing this until I had written something to print "F" trees more clearly.

```
rem_dump(F) :-
        tree_size(F, N),
        rem_heads(N, F, [], Heads),
        keysort(Heads, Sorted),
        format('Class-Node pairs: ~w~n', [Sorted]).

rem_heads(N, F, List0, List) :-
    (   N =:= 0 → List = List0
    ;   M is N-1,
        rem_head(N, F, Head),
        rem_heads(M, F, [Head-N|List0], List)
    ).
```

At this point, I checked that rem_create(5, F), rem_dump(F) did something sensible. The next thing was to test rem_add_link. A simple little test was

```
test1 :-
        rem_create(6, F),
        test([1-2,3-4,5-6,3-6,1-4], F).

test([], _).
test([X-Y|R], F) :-
        rem_add_link(X, Y, F, G),
        format('~nAfter adding ~w<=>~w,~n', [X,Y]),
        rem_dump(G),
        test(R, G).


?- test.

After adding 1<=>2,
Class-Node pairs: [1-1,1-2,3-3,4-4,5-5,6-6]

After adding 3<=>4,
Class-Node pairs: [1-1,1-2,3-3,3-4,5-5,6-6]

After adding 5<=>6,
Class-Node pairs: [1-1,1-2,3-3,3-4,5-5,5-6]

After adding 3<=>6,
Class-Node pairs: [1-1,1-2,3-3,3-4,3-5,3-6]
```

```
After adding 1<=>4,
Class-Node pairs: [1-1,1-2,1-3,1-4,1-5,1-6]
```

Now suppose we decide not to use the binary tree data type here, but to store the current state of the graph in the data base. We shall end up with a collection of

    f(Index, Value).

clauses in the data base. Here is what we get.

```
:- dynamic
        f/2.

rem_create(N) :-
        retractall(f(_,_)),
        rem_create_1(N).

rem_create_1(0) :- !. rem_create_1(N) :-
        asserta(f(N, N)),
        M is N-1,
        rem_create_1(M).

rem_head(P, Head) :-
        f(P, FofP),
        (    FofP =:= P → Head = P
        ;        rem_head(FofP, Head)
        ).

rem_equivalent(P, Q) :-
        rem_head(P, Head),
        rem_head(Q, Head).

change(OldClause, NewClause) :-
        clause(OldClause, true, Ref),
        !,
        asserta(NewClause),
        erase(Ref).

rem_add_link(P0, Q0) :-
        f(P0, P1),
        f(Q0, Q1),
        rem_add_link(P0, P1, Q0, Q1).
```

```
rem_add_link(P0, P1, Q0, Q1) :-
        (    Q1 < P1 →
             change(f(P0,P1), f(P0,Q1)),
             f(P1, P2),
             rem_add_link(P1, P2, Q0, Q1)
        ;    P1 < Q1 →
             change(f(Q0,Q1), f(Q0,P1)),
             f(Q1, Q2),
             rem_add_link(P0, P1, Q1, Q2)
        ; /*P1 = Q1*/
             true
        ).
```

I timed these two versions in both Quintus Prolog release 1.6 and Quintus Prolog release 2.0, both running on a Sun-3/50. The times (in milliseconds) to process L calls to rem_add_links given a set of N nodes were

Prolog	Trees	Data Base
QP 1.6	$1.21\ L \lg N$	$0.27\ L.N$
QP 2.0	$1.13\ L \lg N$	$16\ L$

The difference is that, starting at release 2.0, Quintus Prolog indexes dynamic code just like static code. These days, each call to change(f(X,Old), f(X,New)) takes a small amount of time because the index lets it find the unique f(X,Old) clause and lets it notice that this clause *is* unique. Old releases up to 1.6 did not index dynamic code, so that each call to change/2 scanned an average of $N/2$ clauses to find the unique f(X,Old) clause and still doesn't notice that the clause is unique. You should check the manual for your Prolog system to find out whether it indexes dynamic code or not.

I didn't much like the constant factor in the "trees" case, so I decided to rip out the binary trees (one data element and two branches at each node) and replace them by "3+4" trees, which have three data elements and four branches at each node. A node in such a tree has the form

$$\text{node}(V_1, V_2, V_3,\ S_0, S_1, S_2, S_3)$$

Indices 1, 2, and 3 select the first three elements, while indices $4 * k + j$ select the kth element of the S_j. The operations we need are

rem_create(0, _) :- !. rem_create(N, Tree) :-
        put_label(N, Tree, N, Tree),
        M is N-1,
        rem_create(M, Tree).

get_label(Index, Tree, Value) :-
        (Index < 4 →
                arg(Index, Tree, Value)
        ;   K is (Index∧3)+4,
                J is Index ≫ 2,
                arg(K, Tree, Son),
                get_label(J, Son, Value)
).

put_label(Index, OldTree, Value, NewTree) :-
        (Index < 4 →
                replace_arg(Index, OldTree, _, NewTree, Value)
        ;   K is (Index∧3)+4,
                J is Index ≫ 2,
                replace_arg(K, OldTree, OldSon, NewTree, NewSon),
                put_label(J, OldSon, Value, NewSon)
).

replace_arg(1, node(A,B,C,D,E,F,G), A, node(X,B,C,D,E,F,G), X).
replace_arg(2, node(A,B,C,D,E,F,G), B, node(A,X,C,D,E,F,G), X).
replace_arg(3, node(A,B,C,D,E,F,G), C, node(A,B,X,D,E,F,G), X).
replace_arg(4, node(A,B,C,D,E,F,G), D, node(A,B,C,X,E,F,G), X).
replace_arg(5, node(A,B,C,D,E,F,G), E, node(A,B,C,D,X,F,G), X).
replace_arg(6, node(A,B,C,D,E,F,G), F, node(A,B,C,D,E,X,G), X).
replace_arg(7, node(A,B,C,D,E,F,G), G, node(A,B,C,D,E,F,X), X).

With this change, the constant factor dropped from 1.13 to 0.65.

You will rightly object that I have not shown that changing the data base is to be avoided. On the contrary, in Quintus Prolog release 2.0, it is asymptotically more efficient than using even a 3+4 tree. True, but for practical purposes you have to consider the constant factor as well. For what value of N would changing the data base be at least as fast as using a 3+4 tree?

$$16L \leq 0.65L \lg N$$

if and only if

$$16 \leq 0.65 \lg N$$

if and only if

$$N \geq 25,000,000$$

I think we are safe in concluding that 3+4 trees are a more efficient approach for most practical purposes.

Of course this comparison is influenced by the speed of change/2 and the speed of calls to dynamic predicates. If these operations were twice as fast, the cross-over point would be about 5,000.

Are there any other reasons for preferring not to change the data base? Yes, there are several.

1. You do not have to invent all sorts of names for the "scratch" predicates. You can just pass a tree around as a parameter.

2. You can easily maintain any number of equivalence relations with the same predicates.

3. You can even do this in a parallel or distributed Prolog system.

4. If you want to abort a computation, you will have to clean up after the version which hacks the data base (note the call to retractall/1 in rem_create/1), but the tree automagically vanishes.

5. A tree made by rem_add_link/4 will be discarded on backtracking, and the original OldF will be available for other attempts, but changes made by change/2 will not be undone by backtracking.

6. You can keep copies of intermediate states using the "tree" version, but you can't do that so easily with the "data base" version.

A point that I would like to stress is that the version which uses a tree is *much* easier to debug. You can if you wish define a pretty-printer for the trees using portray/1. You can easily move around the proof tree with "f"ail and "r"etry.

4.6 Efficient Data Structures

There have been attempts to provide mutable arrays and hash tables and the like in Prolog. I shall not be talking about those.

Every data structure in Prolog has to be represented as some sort of tree. Prolog has two resources which you can exploit.

The first is the meta-logical operations functor/3 and arg/3, particularly the latter. A word of warning here: it is almost always a bad idea to use '=..'/2.

Do not use '=..'/2 to locate a particular argument of some term. For example, instead of

Term =.. [_F,_,ArgTwo|_]

you should write

arg(2, Term, ArgTwo)

You will find it easier to get the explicit number "2" right than to write the correct number of "don't care" variables in the call to '=..'/2. Other people reading your program will find the call to arg/3 a much clearer expression of your intent. Your program will also be more efficient. Even if you need to locate several arguments of a term, it is clearer and more efficient to write

arg(1, Term, First),
arg(3, Term, Third),
arg(4, Term, Fourth)

than to write

Term =.. [_,First,_,Third,Fourth|_]

Do not use '=..'/2 when you know the functor. (That is, when you know both the function symbol and the arity.) For example, one Prolog programmer actually wrote the following code:

```
add_date(OldItem, Date, NewItem) :-
        OldItem =.. [item,Type,Ship,Serial],
        NewItem =.. [item,Type,Ship,Serial,Date].
```

This could have been expressed more clearly and more efficiently as

```
add_date(OldItem, Date, NewItem) :-
        OldItem = item(Type,Ship,Serial),
        NewItem = item(Type,Ship,Serial,Date).
```

or, even better, as

```
add_date(item(Type,Ship,Serial), Date,
        item(Type,Ship,Serial,Date)).
```

Suppose you want to represent a collection of several thousand items, but you will need fast access to any one of them. A list is a good way of representing a sequence; it it is not a good way of getting at a particular item. Provided you don't want to replace elements, it is sufficient to use a tree of terms, with the terms being as wide as your system will permit. A general hack is the $N + K$-tree, where each node of the tree contains slots for N elements and K subtrees.

In this code, where N and K appear you should substitute the actual numbers.

access_N_plus_K(Index, Tree, Value) :-
        integer(Index),
        Index > 0,
        access_N_K(Index, Tree, Value).

access_N_K(Index, Tree, Value) :-
        functor(Tree, n_plus_k, $N + K$),
        (Index $\leq N$ →
              arg(Index, Tree, Value)
        ;   SonIndex is (Index $- N - 1$) mod $K + N + 1$,
              NewIndex is (Index $- N - 1$)$//K + 1$,
              arg(SonIndex, Tree, Son),
              access_N_K(NewIndex, Son, Value)
).

The trees we used in the equivalence class example above were 3+4 trees. You can adjust the numbers to suit your needs. If Prolog systems did not limit the maximum arity of a term, you wouldn't need to muck around with nested trees and could just use arg/3 directly.

Suppose you have a collection of 10,000 items to represent. Using a list, this will take 20,000 words of memory. Using a compound term, if your Prolog system will let you, it will take 10,000+x words for memory, for x something like 1, 2, or 3. Using 100+100 trees, it will take 20,301 words of memory, which is about the same as a list, and you'll get fairly rapid access to any element as the depth of the tree will be 2. Using 100+10 trees, the depth of the tree will be 3, but the storage cost will be 12,321 words.

I typed this and a similar predicate for accessing the Nth element of a list into Quintus Prolog. The speedup was

Index =	10	tree/list =	4 times faster
Index =	400	tree/list =	40 times faster
Index =	2000	tree/list =	120 times faster

Of course, a list is itself a 1+1 tree.

The second resource that Prolog offers is term comparison. It is difficult to over-estimate the importance of term comparison for practical programming.

The basic importance of term comparison is that it lets us sort. And the importance of sorting is that it lets us bring similar things together. Without term comparison, we would not have bagof/3 or setof/3. Actually, as a matter of history, term comparison was added to Prolog precisely to make these operations possible.

An elementary example of the practical utility of term comparison is calculating the union of two lists. The obvious definition, which has appeared in books, is

```
union([], Union, Union).
union([Element|Elements], Set, Union) :-
        memberchk(Element, Set),
        !,
        union(Elements, Set, Union).
union([Element|Elements], Set, [Element|Union]) :-
        union(Elements, Set, Union).
```

This is another instance of the "subset" scheme we saw before. The trouble with it is that if the first and second arguments have L and N elements respectively, the time is proportional to $L.(N + L)$, though the space cost is proportional to L.

If we represent sets by *ordered* lists with no duplicates, we can merge the lists in $L + N$ time and space. We saw above how merge/3 works.

Testing union/3 and merge/3 in Quintus Prolog,

L+N =	3	merge/union =	1.1 times faster
L+N =	10	merge/union =	1.4 times faster
L+N =	30	merge/union =	3.4 times faster
L+N =	100	merge/union =	9.2 times faster
L+N =	300	merge/union =	32.0 times faster

What this means is that even for small sets, it is worth using an ordered representation.

Finally, let's consider the problem of maintaining a priority queue. Many AI programs maintain an "agenda" (which literally means "the things which are to be done") of tasks with some sort of attached heuristic value, and we'd like to add tasks to the set and pick the most promising task efficiently.

The obvious way to do this is

```
add_task_to_queue(Task, Cost) :-
        assert(task(Task,Cost)).

draw_best_task_from_queue(Task) :-
        clause(task(Task,Cost), true, Ref),
        ¬ (task(_,C), C < Cost),
        !,
        erase(Ref).
```

Adding something to the set is easy, but when picking the best one, we have to scan all the tasks. This means quadratic cost!

If there is a small number of priority levels, say 1–10, we can improve this.

```
add_task_to_queue(Task, Cost) :-
        assert(task(Cost, Task)).

draw_best_task_from_queue(Task) :-
        between(1, 10, Cost),
        retract(task(Cost, Task)),
        !.
```

This is only an improvement if the Prolog system indexes dynamic predicates. Even with indexing, you don't want to have too many priority levels.

The answer, as so often, is to turn to the ordinary literature, such as "The Art of Programming", "Information Processing Letters", CACM, JACM, JCAM, Knuth, Sedgewick's "Algorithms", and so on. We find that there is a known data structure called a priority queue, also called a "heap". The public-domain DEC-10 Prolog library from Edinburgh contains a file HEAPS.PL which implements this data structure as a binary tree. Letting M be the maximum number of elements which have ever been in the heap at the same time, this implementation takes $O(N.\lg M)$ time to process N insertions and deletions, regardless of the number of priority levels involved.

Prolog has no hash-table data type, but you can obtain logarithmic time equivalents.

```
list_to_assoc(RawPairs, Assoc) :-
        keysort(RawPairs, OrdPairs),
        length(OrdPairs, N),
        list_to_assoc(N, OrdPairs, [], Assoc).

list_to_assoc(0, List, List, *) :- !.
list_to_assoc(N, List0, List, t(Key,Val,Lson,Rson)) :-
        A is (N-1) >> 1,
        Z is (N-1) - A,
        list_to_assoc(A, List0, [Key-Val|List1], Lson),
        list_to_assoc(Z, List1, List, Rson).

get_assoc(Key, t(K,V,L,R), Value) :-
        compare(Rel, Key, K),
        get_assoc(Rel, Key, V, L, R, Value).

get_assoc(=, _, Value, _, _, Value).
get_assoc(<, Key, _, Assoc, _, Value) :-
        get_assoc(Key, Assoc, Value).
```

```
get_assoc(>, Key, _, _, Assoc, Value) :-
        get_assoc(Key, Assoc, Value).
```

Note that since the set of keys is fixed, we don't have to worry about balancing the tree: list_to_assoc/2 will automatically construct a balanced tree.

Some Prolog systems will let you manipulate cyclic terms, where a term can be a subset of itself. Most Prolog systems will let you create such terms, but don't work with them very well. If you want to represent a cyclic graph, it is tempting to use cyclic terms. But instead of doing tricky (and risky) things with cyclic terms, you should think about keeping a forest of terms, using a tree like this to map from labels to nodes, and using explicit node labels rather than circular bindings.

To summarise, you can do a lot with functor/3, arg/3, N+K trees, and term comparison.

4.7 Keep it Clean!

The golden rule of Prolog programming is *Keep it Clean*. By that I mean that you should make your programs as pure and declarative as you can. Naturally, this is true in every programming language: if you want to write an efficient program, the first step is to write a program that is easy to understand. If you need to make your program faster, you will have to understand it so that your changes don't introduce mistakes. If you need to make your program faster, it is much simpler when you can work with your program the same kind of way that you would work with a mathematical formula. Best of all, if you want to write an efficient program in Prolog, you will very often find that a pure and declarative program is *more* efficient than one which has been hacked the way you would hack a Pascal program.

Three things you should avoid are

data base changes (asserts and retracts). It is quite common for a program which simulates the imperative style by using data base changes to run twenty or thirty times faster when rewritten to use pure data structures.

cuts often can't be avoided, because Prolog really isn't very smart about noticing when a query is determinate (and some Prologs are less clever than others). If you have a lot of "red" cuts in your program, the chances are that this is a symptom of underlying design problems which also lead to inefficiency. Try to design your data structures so that the right decision is usually obvious.

var tests which are there to check that it is safe for a goal to proceed are regrettable but sometimes needed. Using the bound/unbound of a variable—as tested by var/1—as part of the definition of a data structure is generally a bad idea. If you're a card-carrying wizard, you can sometimes get away with

it, especially if you are using the device to implement an abstraction which
behaves logically as far as the rest of the world is concerned. (I have an implementation of simple inequality constraints which does this.) Even so, you
should feel guilty and anxious about it (I do) because there is likely to be a
cleaner and faster way of doing the same thing.

I would like to illustrate the point about data structures using var/1 with an
example taken from a recent Prolog textbook. I don't name the book in this
section, because there is much in that book which is excellent, and I don't want
this one bad program to put you off that book in general.

The task is to write a predicate which will match a pattern with a sentence, where
a sentence is represented as a list of atoms, and the representation of a pattern is
up to us, but it is to be a sequence of items each of which can match either a single
word or a segment of one or more words. For example, we might be writing an
ELIZA-like program, and we might want this predicate to match the pattern "i X
my Y" with the sentence "i like my job".

The other author went straight from the visual appearance of a pattern to a
Prolog data structure. He chose to represent a pattern as a list of items, where an
item was either a Prolog atom, which would match the same atom appearing as a
word in the sentence, or a Prolog variable, which would match one or more words
in the sentence. With this representation, we would call

?-   match([i,X,my,Y], [i,like,my,job]).

for the example.

Here is the program as written by the other author.

```
match([], []).
match([Head|Tail], [First|Rest]) :- % "word" case
        nonvar(Head),
        !,
        Head = First,
        match1(Tail, Rest).
match1([Var|Tail], [First|Rest]) :- % "segment" case
        /* var(Head) */
        match1(Tail, Rest),
        Var = [First].
```

```
match1([Var|Tail], [First|Rest]) :- % "segment" case
        /* var Head */
        match1([NewVar|Tail], Rest),
        Var = [First|NewVar].
```

I am sorry to tell you that I found it very hard to understand. In particular, for about a quarter of an hour I was convinced that it couldn't possibly handle any pattern where a variable was repeated. I was wrong: it can handle such patterns. The trick is to notice that the "word" clause is tail recursive but the "segment" clauses aren't. If that puzzles you, don't worry, it puzzled me.

I chose a representation for patterns which is rather different. I started off by accepting the idea of a sequence of items, and asked "what are the possibilities for an item?" The answer is: it may be a single-word item (with associated information the word to be matched) or a segment item (with associated information the variable to be bound to the matching segment). I did not make the mistake of confounding the instantiation state of an item with the type of the item. Instead, I assigned names to each case. I used w(Word) to represent a single-word item, and s(SegmentVar) to represent a segment item. With this representation, we would call

```
?-    match([w(i),s(X),w(my),s(Y)], [i,like,my,job]).
```

for the example.

Here is the program I wrote for this representation.

```
match([], []).
match(([Item|Items], [Word|Words]) :-
        match(Item, Items, Word, Words).

match(w(Word), Items, Word, Words) :-
        match(Items, Words).
match(s([Word|Seg]), Items, Word, Words0) :-
        append(Seg, Words1, Words0),
        match(Items, Words1).
```

There are no cuts and no var/1 tests in my version of the program. All the decisions are made by unification in the clause heads. In order to see that the second clause of match/4 applies to segment items, we only need to look at that clause itself, while in the other author's programs we had to look back at the call to nonvar/1 and the cut in order to tell when the segment clauses applied. My program isn't half as clever as the other author's, I just followed a very mechanical rule for data structure design and the usual list mapping and case analysis schemes.

The pure program can be used to generate lists as well as match them. For example, we can do

?-   match([w(i),s(X),w(my),s(Y)], [i,like,my,job]),
      match([w(your),s(Y),s([?,why,do,you]),s(X),w(it),w(?)], Ans),
      write(Ans).
Ans = [your,job,?,why,do,you,like,it,?]

which is something that the vars-and-cuts version cannot do.

The pure program runs over twice as fast.

5 Data Structure Design

5.1 Introduction

In this chapter, I present several examples to show that the choice of one's data structures can make a big difference to the efficiency of one's program. In the last section, I present some general principles for representing data as Prolog terms.

5.2 Writing a Set-Union Predicate

A common problem is finding the union of two sets.

The obvious way to represent sets in Prolog is as lists. If we say that a list L represents the set S if and only if the members of L are the elements of the set, then we are using the *unordered* representation. This is the way that nearly everyone represents sets in Prolog.

So, we want to write a predicate

union(Set1, Set2, Union)

which is to be true when the set represented by the list Union is the union of the sets represented by Set1 and Set2. That is,

$(\forall X)$ member(X, Union) if and only if
            member(X, Set1) or
            member(X, Set2).

One of the first questions to ask ourselves is how closely we can expect our program to approximate the logical definition. To start with, suppose that Set1 and Set2 are ground, and that the union of the sets they represent has $N > 0$ members. Then there are infinitely many values of Union which would represent the union. For example, if Set1=[a], Set2=[a], then Union=[a], Union=[a,a], Union=[a,a,a] would all be solutions. If we decided to disallow duplicates, there would still be $N!$ values of Union which would represent the union. For example, if Set1=[a], Set2=[b], then Union=[a,b] and Union=[b,a] would both be solutions.

We should make our predicates fully relational when we can, but $N!$ is just too large to be considered feasible. We want a definition of union/3 which has a a small number of solutions. One would be ideal. So we shall have to specify *which* representative of the union you get.

Continuing with the question of how well we can approximate the ideal definition, could we expect union/3 to solve for its first two arguments? Again, duplicates are a problem. If Union=[a], Set2=[], then Set1=[a], Set1=[a,a], Set1=[a,a,a] are all solutions. If we rule out duplicates, we still have problems. If Union has N elements, there are 2^N distinct subsets of Union, so there are more than 2^N distinct solutions for Set1 and Set2. This is too many to enumerate.

Oddly enough, provided that we are happy to accept duplicates, we can easily find a definition of union/3 which has a unique solution. Just use append/3.

Suppose we want to ensure that if Set1 and Set2 do not contain duplicate elements, then neither will Union. We can design a union/3 with this property quite easily by considering cases.

- Set1 may be empty.

- Set1 may be non-empty. In this case, Set1=[Head|Tail]. There are two further cases.

    - Head may be a member of Set2. In this case, the union of [Head|Tail] and Set2 is the same as the union of Tail and Set2, and we can discard Head.

    - Head may not be a member of Set. In this case, Head must be transferred to Union. We could put it anywhere, but putting it at the beginning is easiest.

Given the predicate member/2 in library(basics), it is straightforward to turn this into Prolog code:

```
union([], Union, Union).
union([Head|Tail], Set2, Union) :-
        member(Head, Set2),
        union(Tail, Set2, Union).
union([Head|Tail], Set2, [Head|Union]) :-
        ¬ member(Head, Set2),
        union(Tail, Set2, Union).
```

The call to ¬ member(Head, Set2) is only sound when Head and Set2 are ground, and in that case, member/2 is determinate. So we can improve the code to

```
%   union(+Set1, +Set2, ?Union)
%   is true when Set1, Set2, and Union are lists, and the elements
%   of Union are the elements of Set1 not in Set2 followed by the
%   elements of Set2. Union represents the union of the sets
%   represented by Set1 and Set2. Set1 and Set2 should already be
%   ground when union/3 is called, but Union can be anything.

union([], Union, Union).   % C1
```

```
union([Head|Tail], Set2, Union) :- % C2
        member(Head, Set2),
        !,
        union(Tail, Set2, Union).
union([Head|Tail], Set2, [Head|Union]) :- % C3
        /* ¬ member(Head, Set2) */
        union(Tail, Set2, Union).
```

This is as restrictive as Lisp. But the restrictions are not due to Prolog as such, but simply due to the fact that there are too many solutions to enumerate.

What is the cost of union/3? Suppose Set1 has N_1 elements, of which P are present in Set2 and A are absent from Set2, and Set2 has N_2 elements. If we call the unification of a goal with a clause head one logical inference (LI), and take indexing into account,

- C1 will be executed once.

- C2 will get as far as the call to member/2 N_1 times. P times the call to member/2 will succeed after doing $o(N_2/2)$ LI. A times the call to member/2 will fail after doing N_2 LI.

- C3 will be executed A times.

So a total of $1 + (P + A) + P \times N_2/2 + A \times N_2 + A$ logical inferences will be executed, or $(N_1 + A) \times N_2/2$, and A cons cells will be created. The two extremes are $A = 0$ (Set1 is a subset of Set2), in which case the time cost is $N_1 \times N_2/2$ LI and the space cost is 0, and $P = 0$ (Set1 and Set2 are disjoint), in which case the time cost is $N_1 \times N_2$ LI and the space cost is N_1.

This is not good. Doubling the size of the inputs quadruples the time.

In order to do better, we have to change the representation of sets. A good representation to use is the one that the built-in predicate setof/3 returns, namely a list of elements in standard order (as defined by compare/3) with no duplicates. This is called the *ordered* representation.

So, we now want to write a predicate

    ord_union(Set1, Set2, Union)

which returns the union of two sets in ordered representation.

The same considerations as before show that we can only hope to calculate Union from given Set1 and Set2; we cannot expect to solve for Set1 or Set2 because there are too many solutions.

As before, we proceed by case analysis. But now when the list representing a set has the form [Head|Tail] we know that Head precedes every element of Tail in the standard order.

There are two cases for Set1: either it is empty or it is not. If Set1 is not empty, there are two further cases: Set2 is empty or it is not. If Set2 is not empty, the first element of the union is to be the smaller of the heads of Set1 and Set2, so we have to do a term comparison. Whenever we do a term comparison, there are three cases to consider.

The code below was derived directly from these cases, using two Prolog-specific implementation rules:

- The best was to do a case analysis is to dispatch on the first argument, so we keep moving the thing to be tested to the first argument position.

- Having decomposed a data structure, it is a good idea to pass the pieces on rather than rebuilding the structure only to dismantle it again later.

```
%    Case analysis on Set1.
%    Note Set2 being moved to the front, pieces H1, T1 passed on.

ord_union([], Set2, Set2).
ord_union([H1|T1], Set2, Union) :-
        ord_union_2(Set2, H1, T1, Union).


%    Case analysis on Set2.
%    Note the Order being moved to the front.

ord_union_2([], H1, T1, [H1|T1]).
ord_union_2([H2|T2], H1, T1, Union) :-
        compare(Order, H1, H2),
        ord_union_3(Order, H1, T1, H2, T2, Union).


%    Case analysis on the order of head(Set1), head(Set2)
%    The cases are H1 @< H2, H1 ≡ H2, H1 @> H2.

ord_union_3(<, H1, T1, H2, T2, [H1|Union]) :-
        ord_union(T1, [H2|T2], Union).
ord_union_3(=, H1, T1, _, T2, [H1|Union]) :-
        ord_union(T1, T2, Union).
ord_union_3(>, H1, T1, H2, T2, [H2|Union]) :-
        ord_union([H1|T1], T2, Union).
```

We can improve this. Look at the last clause of ord_union_3/6. It is obvious that the goal will match the second clause of ord_union/3, so we might as well unfold it, and call ord_union_2/4 directly. Since set union is symmetric in Set1 and Set2, we can do the same in the first clause of ord_union3/6. So the improved code is

```
ord_union_3(<, H1, T1, H2, T2, [H1|Union]) :-
        ord_union_2(T1, H2, T2, Union).
ord_union_3(=, H1, T1, _, T2, [H1|Union]) :-
        ord_union(T1, T2, Union).
ord_union_3(>, H1, T1, H2, T2, [H2|Union]) :-
        ord_union_2(T2, H1, T1, Union).
```

We have thus arrived straightforwardly at the following.

```
%    ord_union(+Set1, +Set2, ?Union)
%    if Set1 and Set2 are the ordered representations of two sets,
%    Union is unified with the ordered representation of their union.
%    ord_union/3 is not defined if Set1 or Set2 is insufficiently
%    instantiated or not in standard order.
ord_union([], Set2, Set2).          /* C1.1 */
ord_union([H1|T1], Set2, Union) :-  /* C1.2 */
        ord_union_2(Set2, H1, T1, Union).

ord_union_2([], H1, T1, [H1|T1]).      /* C2.1 */
ord_union_2([H2|T2], H1, T1, Union) :- /* C2.2 */
        compare(Order, H1, H2),
        ord_union_3(Order, H1, T1, H2, T2, Union).

ord_union_3(<, H1, T1, H2, T2, [H1|Union]) :- /* C3.1 */
        ord_union_2(T1, H2, T2, Union).
ord_union_3(=, H1, T1, _, T2, [H1|Union]) :-  /* C3.2 */
        ord_union(T1, T2, Union).
ord_union_3(>, H1, T1, H2, T2, [H2|Union]) :- /* C3.3 */
        ord_union_2(T2, H1, T1, Union).
```

What is the cost of ord_union/3? Suppose as before that Set1 and Set2 have N_1 and N_2 elements respectively, and that P of the elements are common to both lists.

- ord_union/3 will be called $P + 1$ times.

- ord_union_2/4 will be called about $N_1 + N_2 - P$ times, doing about $N_1 + N_2 - P$ comparisons.

- ord_union_3/6 will be called about $N_1 + N_2 - P$ times, constructing about $N_1 + N_2 - P$ list cells.

At worst, then, the cost is $2(N_1 + N_2)$ calls, $N_1 + N_2$ comparisons, and $N_1 + N_2$ list cells.

Exercise. *Implement set difference for ordered sets. Hint: $X \setminus Y$ and $Y \setminus X$ are not always equal, so you will need four predicates: neither set inspected, X inspected but not Y, Y inspected but not X, both inspected.*

Exercise. *Combine your solution to the previous exercise with your ord_union/3 code to implement ord_union/4, described elsewhere in this and the Searching chapter.*

There is indeed a predicate called ord_union/3 in the Quintus Prolog library, and it does use this pattern of code. Interestingly enough, the original version of ord_union/3 was different. It was coded by the light of nature rather than by working rigidly through a case analysis, and was propped up with several cuts. I have recently found many cases where rewriting code to make it cleaner made it faster, so I decided to overhaul the "set operations using the ordered representation" library package, library(ordsets). Most of the operations, including ord_union/3, speeded up by about 20% when I made them cleaner. Elegance is not optional!

We have seen that the cost of a set union is proportional to $N_1 \times N_2$ for union/3 and to $N_1 + N_2$ for ord_union/3. But what is the cross-over point? That depends on the implementation, particularly on the speed of term comparison. In Quintus Prolog version 2.4 on a Sun-3/50, the cross-over point is about $N_1 = N_2 = 6$ for lists of atoms and $N_1 = N_2 = 3$ for lists of integers. For most applications, then, using the ordered representation is likely to be much more efficient.

In fact, if you want to find the union of two unordered lists, it may be more efficient to convert to the ordered representation.

```
fast_union(Set1, Set2, Union) :-
        sort(Set1, Ord1),
        sort(Set2, Ord2),
        ord_union(Ord1, Ord2, Union).
```

Sorting a list costs $O(N \lg N)$ time. For $N_1 = N_2 = N$, the cost of taking a union this way is dominated by the cost of sorting, and $N \lg N$ beats N^2 for sufficiently large N.

What did we see in this section?

- A predicate should be as general as possible, but if there are exponentially many solutions for a particular "direction" there is no point trying to make it work that way around.

- A predicate may be further restricted by the need to make negation as failure or term comparison sound.

- Constructing a predicate by case analysis is worth a try.

- Term comparison is a powerful method for writing efficient Prolog.

5.3 The Importance of Data Structures

In this section, I examine a benchmark program that was originally designed by Art Fleck of the University of Iowa as part of a study of declarative languages.

The problem is this. We have a small algebra with three elements, 0, 1, and 2. There is a single operation, "m", with the following table:

m	Y=0	1	2
X=0	0	0	0
1	0	0	1
2	0	2	2

We can express this as

$$m(X,Y) = 0 \text{ if } X + Y < 3$$
$$m(X,Y) = X \text{ if } X + Y > 2$$

We are interested in the larger algebra of 27-element vectors of 0s, 1s, and 2s, with the obvious element-wise extension of m. More precisely, we are interested in the subalgebra of this larger algebra generated by the following elements:

g1 = 0 0 0 0 0 0 0 0 0 1 1 1 1 1 1 1 1 1 2 2 2 2 2 2 2 2 2
g2 = 0 0 0 1 1 1 2 2 2 0 0 0 1 1 1 2 2 2 0 0 0 1 1 1 2 2 2
g3 = 0 1 2 0 1 2 0 1 2 0 1 2 0 1 2 0 1 2 0 1 2 0 1 2 0 1 2

The way to find this algebra is to start with the set $[g1, g2, g3]$, then keep on forming all possible products of new elements with old (order matters, in this algebra), adding new ones to the set.

Before considering data structures, how are we to handle such a problem as this at all? As so often happens, it turns out to be an instance of a general problem which has already been studied. What we have is a "universe"

$$U = \{\langle x_1, \ldots, x_{27}\rangle | x_i \in \{0, 1, 2\}\},$$

an initial set

$$G = \{g_1, g_2, g_3\}$$

which is a subset of U, and a function

$$mt : U \times U \to U$$

What we want to find is the *smallest* set C such that

$$G \subseteq C \subseteq U$$

and

$$(\forall x, y \in C) mt(x, y) \in C$$

It turns out that this can be seen as finding a *least fixed point* of the function $\hat{mt}$ where

$$\hat{mt}(S) = S \cup \{mt(x,y) | x \in S, y \in S\}$$

An important thing about this function is that

$$\hat{mt}(S) \supseteq S$$

so that we can compute the closure we want by this simple method:

$C := G$
repeat $T := C;\ C := \hat{mt}(C)$
until $C = T$

This is essentially the same as Algorithm 3.3 in Ullman's "Principles of Database and Knowledge-base Systems" [5]. That algorithm is applied to finding the extension of a logical data base, but what it computes is a least fixed point.

Because finding least fixed points is so useful, people have worked out how to do better. In particular, Algorithm 3.4 of [5]—called the "semi-naïve method"—can be used on this problem. The idea is that we consider what happens when a small change is made to the current value. Since

$$\hat{mt}(S) = S \cup \{mt(x,y) | x \in S, y \in S\}$$

we can write

$$\hat{mt}(S) = S \cup \Delta S$$

where

$$\Delta S = \{mt(x,y) | x \in S, y \in S\} \setminus S$$

There is nothing very deep here, ΔS is just the new elements. What we do is maintain S and ΔS separately. The program then looks like

$S := \emptyset$
$\Delta S := G$
while $\Delta S \neq \emptyset$ **do**
$\quad T := \hat{mt}(S \cup \Delta S) \setminus (S \cup \Delta S)$
$\quad S := S \cup \Delta S$
$\quad \Delta S := T$
end while
$C := S$

This is more complicated than what we started with, but it turns out that although the definition of T looks complicated, it is cheaper to compute. Let's define

$$MT(S_1, S_2) = \{mt(x, y) | x \in S_1, y \in S_2\}$$

It's fairly obvious how to implement this by doing the multiplications and then sorting the result. It's also fairly obvious that we want to make S_1 and S_2 small when we do this. The definition of T is

$$T := (MT(S, S) \cup MT(S, \Delta S) \cup MT(\Delta S, S) \cup \\ MT(\Delta S, \Delta S)) \setminus (S \cup \Delta S)$$

But $MT(S, S)$ is precisely $S \cup \Delta S$, so we only have to compute

$$T := (MT(S, \Delta S) \cup MT(\Delta S, S \cup \Delta S)) \setminus (S \cup \Delta S)$$

This means that we can compute a closure like this with the following program:

```
S := ∅
ΔS := G
while ΔS ≠ ∅ do
    · O := S
    S := S ∪ ΔS
    ΔS := (MT(O, ΔS) ∪ MT(ΔS, S)) \ S
end while
C := S
```

To get some idea of the savings, suppose that at some stage S has 20 elements and ΔS has 5. Then computing

$$MT(S \cup \Delta S, S \cup \Delta S)$$

as the naïve algorithm would do, would cost $625c_1 + 5805c_2$ time units, where c_1 has to do with the cost of calling mt and c_2 has to do with the cost of sorting. However, computing

$$(MT(O, \Delta S) \cup MT(\Delta S, S)) \setminus S$$

as the semi-naïve algorithm would do, would cost roughly $225c_1 + 1758c_2$ time units. Whatever the values of c_1 and c_2, this is about a three-fold saving for this particular size of S and ΔS.

Enough about the algorithm.

When it comes to the data structures, the first choice we have is how to represent elements of the larger algebra. For most people, the obvious choice is a list of 27 integers. This makes the definition of the product easy.

```
%    mt(Xs, Ys, Zs)
%    is true when Xs, Ys, and Zs are lists of 0s, 1s, and 2s,
%    and m(X,Y,Z) is true for corresponding elements X of Xs,
%    Y of Ys, and Z of Zs.

mt([], [], []).
mt([X|Xs], [Y|Ys], [Z|Zs]) :-
        m(X, Y, Z),
        mt(Xs, Ys, Zs).

%    m(X, Y, Z)
%    is true when Z is the product of X and Y in Murski's algebra.
%    That is, Z = if X+Y < 3 then 0 else X. This has been coded
%    to be pure yet determinate.

m(0, _, 0).
m(1, X, Y) :- m1(X, Y).
m(2, X, Y) :- m2(X, Y).

m1(0, 0).
m1(1, 0).
m1(2, 1).

m2(0, 0).
m2(1, 2).
m2(2, 2).

g1([0,0,0,0,0,0,0,0,0,1,1,1,1,1,1,1,1,1,2,2,2,2,2,2,2,2,2]).
g2([0,0,0,1,1,1,2,2,2,0,0,0,1,1,1,2,2,2,0,0,0,1,1,1,2,2,2]).
g3([0,1,2,0,1,2,0,1,2,0,1,2,0,1,2,0,1,2,0,1,2,0,1,2,0,1,2]).
```

The second question is, how shall we represent a set of elements in the larger algebra? We've already seen in a previous section that the obvious choice of an unordered list may not be a good one. But for the moment, let's suppose that we didn't know that. We arrive at the following program.

```
:-    use_module(library(sets), [
            union/3,
            subtract/3
      ]).
```

```
solution(Solution) :-
        g1(G1),
        g2(G2),
        g3(G3),
        solution([], [G1,G2,G3], Solution).

solution(State, New, Solution) :-
        union(New, State, State1),    % add new elements to state
        subtract(New, State, New1),   % subtract old elements
        solution(New1, State, State1, Solution).

solution([], State, _, State).
solution([New|News], Old, State, Solution) :-
        products(Old, [New|News], Prods),
        solution(State, Prods, Solution).
```

```
%    products(Xs, Ys, Zs)
%    is true when Zs is the list of all the distinct products
%    of elements in Xs and elements in Ys. When Xs=S and Ys=ΔS,
%    it computes MT(S, ΔS) ∪ MT(ΔS, S) ∪ MT(ΔS, ΔS)
```

where the comment lines read: $MT(S, \Delta S) \cup MT(\Delta S, S) \cup MT(\Delta S, \Delta S)$

```
products(Old, New, Prods) :-
        products(Old, New, Prods0, Prods1),
        products(New, Old, Prods1, Prods2),
        products(New, New, Prods2, []),
        sort(Prods0, Prods).    % eliminate duplicates.
```

```
products([], _,P, P).
products([X|Xs], Ys, P0, P) :-
        products1(Ys, X, P0, P1),
        products(Xs, Ys, P1, P).
```

```
products1([], _, P, P).
products1([Y|Ys], X, [Z|P0], P) :-
        mt(X, Y, Z),
        products1(Ys, X, P0, P).
```

A program very like this took 26 seconds on a SUN-3/50 to find all 64 elements of the answer. Since this beat Fleck's program (which took seven minutes in C Prolog on a VAX-11/780) by a fairly large margin, and was equivalent to his Pascal program, I was pretty happy. But not entirely satisfied, because I had a C program which took 10 seconds on a SUN-3/50.

A rule of thumb for Prolog programs is that, other things being equal, the running time is proportional to the size of the data structures. So we have to have some idea of the size of the data structures we are dealing with here.

A list cell in Quintus Prolog costs 2 words of memory, one for each argument. For any other compound term with N arguments, the cost is $N + 1$ words, one for the functor and one for each argument. If we have a tuple with N elements, the cost is thus

$$
\begin{aligned}
2N & \quad \text{words using} \quad [X_1, \ldots, X_N] \\
N + 1 & \quad \text{words using} \quad f(X_1, \ldots, X_N)
\end{aligned}
$$

In this case, the elements of the larger algebra have 27 elements, so that space required to represent something like g1 is 54 words if we use a list, but only 28 words if we use a record. The ratio is 1.92 : 1. So if we avoid lists, we shall save nearly half the space.

Accordingly, I changed the representation to

```
g1(*(0,0,0,0,0,0,0,0,0,1,1,1,1,1,1,1,1,1,2,2,2,2,2,2,2,2,2)).
g2(*(0,0,0,1,1,1,2,2,2,0,0,0,1,1,1,2,2,2,0,0,0,1,1,1,2,2,2)).
g3(*(0,1,2,0,1,2,0,1,2,0,1,2,0,1,2,0,1,2,0,1,2,0,1,2,0,1,2)).

mt(*(Xa,Xb,Xc,Xd,Xe,Xf,Xg,Xh,Xi,Xj,Xk,Xl,Xm,
     Xn,Xo,Xp,Xq,Xr,Xs,Xt,Xu,Xv,Xw,Xx,Xy,Xz,X0),
   *(Ya,Yb,Yc,Yd,Ye,Yf,Yg,Yh,Yi,Yj,Yk,Yl,Ym,
     Yn,Yo,Yp,Yq,Yr,Ys,Yt,Yu,Yv,Yw,Yx,Yy,Yz,Y0),
   *(Za,Zb,Zc,Zd,Ze,Zf,Zg,Zh,Zi,Zj,Zk,Zl,Zm,
     Zn,Zo,Zp,Zq,Zr,Zs,Zt,Zu,Zv,Zw,Zx,Zy,Zz,Z0)) :-
        m(Xa, Ya, Za),
        :
        m(Xz, Yz, Zz),
        m(X0, Y0, X0).
```

Of course you do something like this by writing a program. Here is a way of generating something like this version of mt/3.

```
gen_mt(N) :-
        functor(X, *, N),
        functor(Y, *, N),
        functor(Z, *, N),
        gen_mt(N, X, Y, Z, true, Body),
        portray_clause(( mt(X,Y,Z) :- Body )).
```

```
gen_mt(0, _, _, _, Body, Body) :- !.
gen_mt(N, X, Y, Z, Body0, Body) :-
        arg(N, X, Xn),
        arg(N, Y, Yn),
        arg(N, Z, Zn),
        M is N-1,
        gen_mt(M, X, Y, Z, (m(Xn,Yn,Zn),Body0), Body).
```

There's no point in doing this at run time, is there?

You might like to measure this version of the program. If the speed up ratio of 54/28 were attained, the time would be about 13.5 seconds, which isn't too far from the speed of the C program (10.0 seconds).

The second problem with the program is the representation of sets. In order to eliminate duplicates, we are already sorting, so we might as well exploit the fact and use the ordered representation for sets. This changes the definition of solution/3 to

```
:-   use_module(library(ordsets), [
        ord_union/3,
        ord_subtract/3
     ]).
```

```
solution(State, New, Solution) :-
        ord_union(New, State, State1),
        ord_subtract(New, State, New1),
        solution(New1, State, State1, Solution).
```

Having written this program, I added two new predicates to the library:

```
/* in library(sets) */
    union(X, Y, Union, Difference) :-
            union(X, Y, Union),
            subtract(X, Y, Difference).
```

```
/* in library(ordsets) */
    ord_union(X, Y, Union, Difference) :-
            ord_union(X, Y, Union),
            ord_subtract(X, Y, Difference).
```

except that they accomplish this in a single pass. ord_union/4 is a particularly efficient way to merge new elements into a set and at the same time find out which of the elements were the new ones.

It turns out that the subalgebra generated by g1, g2, and g3 has only 64 elements, so that the biggest possible union or set difference could have only 64 elements in each set. The potential speedup is therefore at most a factor of 64 in each set operation, and we are already doing quadratic work in finding all the products. If you add a print command to solution/3:

```
solution(State, New, Solution) :-
        length(State, LS),
        length(New, LN),
        format('#State = ~d, #New = ~d~n', [LS,LN]),
        ... as before ...
```

you find that the sets are actually rather smaller than this. Even so, this change pays off. Using records instead of lists and the ordered instead of the unordered representation of sets, a version of the program took 10.3 seconds to find the solution, a speed-up of about 2.5. The result was a Prolog program that took little longer than a C program. Indeed, when I used a slightly more efficient sorting algorithm, the time dropped to 9.8 seconds, which actually beat the C program.

For the ultimate in speed, I decided to look for some problem-specific improvements. Using records instead of lists is always a good idea, and using the ordered set representation is always a good idea.

In this problem, $m(0,0) = 0$ and $m(2,2) = 2$, the first element of every '*'/27 record must be 0, and the last element must be 2, so we need not bother storing or computing those elements. This problem-specific improvement might save about 8% of the space (and so about 8% of the time).

But that's a rather small saving. I wanted a much bigger saving. I noticed that if we regard elements of the larger algebra as bit-strings, we can compute the product as

$$
\begin{aligned}
mt(X,Y) &= ((Y + \langle 01 \ldots 01 \rangle) \wedge X) \\
&- ((((\langle 10 \ldots 10 \rangle - Y) \gg 1) \wedge \langle 01 \ldots 01 \rangle \wedge X)
\end{aligned}
$$

Unfortunately, this takes 54 bits, so I had to represent algebra elements as pairs of integers. With this recoding, the space cost went down by a factor of 3.75, and the time went down by a factor of 3.

Now if we represent a pair of integers as [X|Y]—something I do *not* recommend as good practice—the space cost will be two words, rather than the 28 words taken by a record with 27 arguments. So why wasn't the saving a factor of 14? The answer is that each product that we calculate is incorporated in a list. In fact it may be incorporated in up to four lists: Prods0 always, Prods sometimes, then New1 and State1 sometimes. Just to be a member of Prods0 costs a list cell, so the space cost is at least 2+2 compared with 2+28. In fact there is worse: sorting a list of N elements turns over $N \lg N$ list cells, even though we never need all of them at once and the garbage collector can recover them. Prods0 typically has about 200 elements, so we're turning over about 3,000 words in sort/2. It turns out that the space saving is only about a factor of 2.3 in this case. Of course we are winning a lot of time by having smaller terms to compare.

What does this example show? It shows that using small data structures really does pay off, indeed that the design of one's data structures may have more effect (26 *vs* 10.3 seconds) than the choice of one's programming language (10.3 *vs* 10.0 seconds).

5.4 The Problem of Transitive Closure

One problem which Prolog programmers keep rediscovering is the problem of specifying a transitive closure.

Suppose we have a predicate base/2, and we want to express the fact that closure/2 is the transitive closure of base/2. The obvious thing to do is to write

```
/* Version 0 */
closure(X, Y) :- base(X, Y).
closure(X, Z) :- closure(X, Y), closure(Y, Z).
```

That is a beautiful piece of logic which expresses our intentions with admirable clarity. Unfortunately, it isn't so wonderful as a program. Suppose we have the table

```
base(1, 2). base(2, 3).
```

and pose the query

```
?- closure(1, 3).
```

Here is a trace from Quintus Prolog.

```
(1) 0 Call: closure(1,3) ?
(2) 1 Call: base(1,3) ?
(2) 1 Fail: base(1,3) ?
(3) 1 Call: closure(1,_970) ?
(4) 2 Call: base(1,_970) ?
(4) 2 Exit: base(1,2) ?
(3) 1 Exit: closure(1,2) ?
(5) 1 Call: closure(2,3) ?
(6) 2 Call: base(2,3) ?
```

```
    (6) 2 Exit: base(2,3) ?
    (5) 1 Exit: closure(2,3) ?
    (1) 0 Exit: closure(1,3) ?
yes
```

It worked. But suppose a subsequent goal were to fail? With the query

?- closure(1, 3), fail.

we obtain the trace

```
    (1) 0 Call: closure(1,3) ?
    (2) 1 Call: base(1,3) ?
    (2) 1 Fail: base(1,3) ?
    (3) 1 Call: closure(1,_983) ?
    (4) 2 Call: base(1,_983) ?
    (4) 2 Exit: base(1,2) ?
    (3) 1 Exit: closure(1,2) ?
    (5) 1 Call: closure(2,3) ?
    (6) 2 Call: base(2,3) ?
    (6) 2 Exit: base(2,3) ?
    (5) 1 Exit: closure(2,3) ?
    (1) 0 Exit: closure(1,3) ?
    (1) 0 Redo: closure(1,3) ?
    (5) 1 Redo: closure(2,3) ?
    (6) 2 Redo: base(2,3) ?
    (6) 2 Fail: base(2,3) ?
    (7) 2 Call: closure(2,_1067) ?
    (8) 3 Call: base(2,_1067) ?
    (8) 3 Exit: base(2,3) ?
    (7) 2 Exit: closure(2,3) ?
    (9) 2 Call: closure(3,3) ?
   (10) 3 Call: base(3,3) ?
   (10) 3 Fail: base(3,3) ?
   (11) 3 Call: closure(3,_1151) ?      --infinite loop
   (12) 4 Call: base(3,_1151) ?
   (12) 4 Fail: base(3,_1151) ?
   (13) 4 Call: closure(3,_1187) ?      --infinite loop
   (14) 5 Call: base(3,_1187) ?
   (14) 5 Fail: base(3,_1187) ?
   (15) 5 Call: closure(3,_1223) ?      --infinite loop
   (16) 6 Call: base(3,_1223) ? a
```

The interpreter goes into an infinite loop. This is not a bug in the Prolog system: there genuinely is an infinite failed branch in the proof tree. Readers familiar with grammars will recognise this as the problem of *left recursion*.

We might decide to block this by coding closure/2 thus:

```
/* Version 1 */
closure(X, Y) :- base(X, Y).
closure(X, Z) :- base(X, Y), closure(Y, Z).
```

Now the query

```
?- closure(1, 3), fail.
```

terminates. In fact the query will terminate even if either or both of the arguments of closure/2 is unbound.

It will terminate, that is, if the base/2 relation defines an *acyclic* graph. If there is a sequence

$$\text{base}(x_0, x_1), \ldots, \text{base}(x_n, x_0),$$

then the new version of closure/2 is perfectly happy to go around the loop x_0, x_1, ..., x_n, x_0 any number of times.

This is the same problem that we had in the Searching chapter. As we saw there, we can block these loops by keeping track of the nodes we have already visited (a Closed set):

```
/* Version 2 */
closure(X, Y) :-
        closure(X, Y, [X]).
```

```
%   closure(From, To, Avoiding)
%   is true when there is a path from From to To that
%   does not pass through any node in Avoiding.
```

```
closure(X, Y, _) :-
        base(X, Y).
closure(X, Z, Avoiding) :-
        base(X, Y),
        ¬ member(Y, Avoiding),
        closure(Y, Z, [Y|Avoiding]).
```

This has been coded to allow the query closure(X, X) to determine whether there
is a path from X to X. It should remind you of a depth-first search with an explicit
Closed set, because that's what it is.

However, even when the base/2 relation is acyclic, all of these versions of closure/2
are amazingly inefficient. To see this, suppose we have an "incestuous" graph:

```
----> a[2i+0] -----> a[2i+2] -----> a[2i+4] ---->
    /|          \  /|          \  /|          \
   /             \ /            \ /            \|
                  )              )
   \            / \            / \            /|
    \|         /  \|          /  \|          /
----> a[2i-1] -----> a[2i+1] -----> a[2i+3] ---->
```

For $N = 2k + 2$, this would correspond as a parent/child graph to k generations
of brother-sister incest, hence the name. It is fairly easy to see that there are 2^k
different paths from a_1 to a_N, so since closure/2 is able to explore all the paths,
even for known values of X and Y closure(X,Y) can be made to do $O(2^{N/2})$ work.

If we add one more node a_{N+1} to this graph, with a unique arc base(a_1,a_{N+1}),
the query

?- closure(a_1, Y), Y = a_{N+1}.

may yet chase down those 2^k blind alleys before noticing the answer.

The nice thing about declarative programming is that you can write a specification and run it as a program. The nasty thing about declarative programming is
that some clear specifications make incredibly bad programs. The hope of declarative programming is that you can move from a specification to a reasonable program
without leaving the language.

What is the best way to handle transitive closure problems like this? Well, a
logic programming system with a bottom-up component should be able to do a
reasonable job by computing the closure bottom-up. For ordinary Prolog systems,
it is possible to compute the transitive closure of a graph expressed as a list of
From-To arcs in cubic time. There is a predicate warshall/2 in the Quintus Prolog
library to do this: you will find it in library(graphs). The following version of
closure/2 will do the trick.

```
:-    use_module(library(graphs), [
           warshall/2
      ]),
      use_module(library(basics), [
           member/2
      ]).
```

```
/* Version 3 */
closure(Ancestor, Descendant) :-
        setof(Parent-Children,
              setof(Child, base(Parent, Child), Children),
              Graph),
        warshall(Graph, Closure),
        member(Ancestor-Descendants, Closure),
        member(Descendant, Descendants).
```

This doesn't have the direct clarity of the logical specification of closure/2 we started with. But it can be very much more efficient. If there are N nodes in the base/2 graph, the calls to setof/3 can cost $O(N^2 \lg N)$ time and turn over $O(N^2 \lg N)$ space, but this is dominated by the $O(N^3)$ cost of computing the transitive closure using Warshall's algorithm.

Here is the source code for warshall/2 (you will find it in library(graphs)). It is a direct translation into Prolog of Warshall's algorithm, which is a very well known standard algorithm for computing the transitive closure of graphs. Part of the point of this section is that there are many standard algorithms around, and it is generally very easy to transcribe them into Prolog.

Warshall's algorithm has no trouble at all with cyclic graphs, so even when there are cycles in the graph this version of transitive closure will not go into an infinite loop. The input is a graph represented as a list of FromNode-ToNodes pairs in standard order of FromNodes, where each ToNodes list is a list of node names in standard order. The output is the transitive closure in the same representation. We can obtain such a representation from a base/2 relation thus:

```
base_graph(Graph) :-
        setof(Parent-Children,
              setof(Child, base(Parent, Child), Children),
              Graph).
```

With that out of the way, here is Warshall's algorithm:

```
:-  use_module(library(basics), [
        memberchk/2
    ]),
    use_module(library(ordsets), [
        ord_union/3
    ]).
```

```
warshall(Graph, Closure) :-
        warshall(Graph, Graph, Closure).

warshall([], Closure, Closure).
warshall([V-_|G], E, Closure) :-
        memberchk(V-Y, E), % Y := E(v)
        warshall(E, V, Y, NewE),
        warshall(G, NewE, Closure).

warshall([], _, _, []).
warshall([X-Neibs|G], V, Y, [X-NewNeibs|NewG]) :-
        memberchk(V, Neibs),
        !,
        ord_union(Neibs, Y, NewNeibs),
        warshall(G, V, Y, NewG).
warshall([X-Neibs|G], V, Y, [X-Neibs|NewG]) :-
        warshall(G, V, Y, NewG).
```

Even cubic time is rather high. If base/2 is a dynamic predicate, we might prefer
to cache the transitive closure and only recompute it when necessary. Here is a
version of the program which does that.

```
:-    use_module(library(graphs), [
          warshall/2
      ]),
      use_module(library(basics), [
          member/2
      ]).

:- dynamic
          base/2,
          closure_cache/2,
          needs_recomputing/0.

c_assert(Fact) :-
          (    clause(Fact, true) → true
          ;    assert(Fact)
          ).
```

```
add_base(P, C) :-
        (    base(P, C) → true
        ;    assert(base(P, C)),
             c_assert(needs_recomputing)
        ).

del_base(P, C) :-
        (    retract(base(P, C)) →
             c_assert(needs_recomputing)
        ;    true
        ).

recompute_if_necessary :-
        (    needs_recomputing,
             retractall(closure_cache(_, _)),
             setof(Parent-Children,
                 setof(Child, base(Parent, Child), Children),
                 Graph),
             warshall(Graph, Closure),
             member(Ancestor-Descendants, Closure),
             member(Descendant, Descendants),
             assert(closure_cache(Ancestor, Descendant)),
             fail
        ;    retract(needs_recomputing)
        ).

/* Version 4 */
closure(X, Y) :-
        recompute_if_necessary,
        closure_cache(X, Y).
```

Now, while the base/2 relation isn't changing, a call to closure/2 takes at worst quadratic time, and when the graph does change, it takes cubic time to recompute it. A different data structure can be used to keep the closure cache up to date as new facts are added to the base/2 relation, and still take cubic time *total*, however many facts are added and in whatever order. I do not know whether it is possible to do this well as facts are deleted from the base/2 relation.

Now version 3 is not as pretty as version 0 or version 1, but it is enormously more efficient (and won't go into infinite loops) and is still declarative.

You might like to try the various versions of closure/2 on different graphs. I did some experiments using release 2.0 of Quintus Prolog and the latest versions of library(graphs) and library(ordsets). I found that the cross-over point for version

3 being faster than version 1 on an incestuous graph was N=10. For N=20, version 3 was 10 times faster than version 1, and version 4 was another 12 times faster still. That makes version 4 (using a standard algorithm and caching the result) a factor of 120 faster than the naive specification. Perhaps incestuous graphs are particularly bad? Apparently not. I generated some random acyclic graphs with N=20 nodes (using operations from library(random)). The lower ratio for version 1 over version 3 I obtained had version 3 being 6 times faster than version 1, and version 4 being another 70 times faster, for a total speedup of 420.

The moral of the story is that just because you can run a specification as a program, it doesn't mean that every specification you write is going to be efficient. Being a Prolog programmer doesn't exempt you from at least working out the asymptotic cost of your program, and doesn't exempt you from needing to know about standard algorithms like Warshall's. Very often you will be tempted to think that it is time to abandon Prolog for C. Often you will do better to replace a specification (in Prolog) by a program (in Prolog).

5.4.1 Beware of the General Case

The version of Warshall's algorithm presented above assumed that the nodes of the graph it was given to work on were ground terms. This seems an un-Prolog-like restriction. However, it does not reflect a peculiar feebleness of Prolog, but a peculiar difficulty of transitive closure.

Suppose we have a reflexive transitive closure problem stated as:

closure(X, X) ← node(X)
closure(X, Z) ← arc(X, Y) & closure(Y, Z)

If the arguments of node/1 and arc/2 are always ground, we can replace the ground terms by successive integers 1 to N (taking time and space proportional to the size of the problem) and compute the transitive closure in $O(N^3)$ time. The result takes $O(N^2)$ space.

If the arguments of node/1 and arc/2 can be arbitrary terms, *the problem may have no finite solution.* For example,

arc(X, s(X)).

Is there an intermediate case which is more general than the ground case but still feasible?

The simplest extension of the ground case involves *function-free* non-terminals. That is, the arguments of the non-terminals are allowed to be variables and constants, but not compound terms. It is straightforward to embed this version of the transitive closure problem in the *function-free* clausal calculus, which is known to have an (exponential) decision procedure. (The sketch below does not do that, but it could.)

Unfortunately, even this simple case is NP-hard. To show this, suppose we have an instance of SAT, namely a set of propositional clauses

$$(L_{11} \vee \cdots \vee L_{1n_1}) \quad \wedge$$

$$\vdots \quad \wedge$$

$$(L_{m1} \vee \cdots \vee L_{mn_m})$$

where each L_{ij} is either X_k or $\neg X_k$. We can convert this to a transitive closure problem thus. Suppose there are N variables. For each $i \in \{1, \ldots, m\}, j \in \{1, \ldots, n_i\}$, where L_{ij} is either X_k or $\neg X_k$, we have a clause

arc(p($i - 1$, U_1, ..., U_{k-1}, TV, U_{k+1}, ..., U_N),
    p(i, U_1, ..., U_{k-1}, TV, U_{k+1}, ..., U_N))

TV being 't' if L_{ij} is X_k or 'f' if L_{ij} is $\neg X_k$.

For example, the SAT instance

$$(X1 \vee \neg X3) \wedge (X2 \vee X3) \wedge (\neg X1 \vee X2)$$

would be translated to the clauses

arc(p(0,t,U2,U3), p(1,t,U2,U3)).
arc(p(0,U1,U2,f), p(1,U1,U2,f)).
arc(p(1,U1,t,U3), p(2,U1,t,U3)).
arc(p(1,U1,U2,t), p(2,U1,U2,t)).
arc(p(2,f,U2,U3), p(3,f,U2,U3)).
arc(p(2,U1,t,U3), p(3,U1,t,U3)).

After this translation, the query

?- closure(p(0,U_1, ..., U_N), p(m,U_1,...,U_N)).

(which asks about the transitive closure of the arcs), has a solution if and only if the SAT instance is satisfiable. So transitive closure, even in this restricted case, is NP-hard.

The fundamental problem is that if we have C constants, and the arity of a term is N, we have $O(C^N)$ nodes in the graph.

5.5 General Principles

- Use built-in data types whenever they are appropriate. In particular, if it makes sense to represent something as an integer, a floating point number, or an atom, you might as well do that. The "native" representation for characters in Edinburgh Prologs is as integer codes.

- Use library data-types whenever they are appropriate. The library currently offers representations for

  - sets [library(sets), library(ordsets)]
  - bags (multisets) [library(bags)],
  - finite functions [library(assoc), library(maps)]
  - arrays (as trees) [library(logarr), library(trees)]
  - balanced binary trees [library(avl)]
  - large chunks of text [library(big_text)]
  - date- and time-stamps [library(date)]
  - directed graphs [library(graphs), library(mst), library(rem)]
  - priority queues [library(heaps)]
  - queues [library(queues)]
  - strings (as atoms) [library(strings)]

  If you have a problem for which one of these data structures is suitable, it would be a good idea to look at the library before writing your own code. When the library hasn't got exactly what you want, you may be able to use a library file as a model. Some of the data structures listed above are only available in the Quintus version of the library, but most are in the DEC-10 Prolog library (hence are generally available).

- Don't use defaults.

- Don't use wrappers.

- Don't over-use lists.

- Think of trees.

What do I mean "don't use defaults?" Suppose you want a data structure to represent the following situations:

- a command can be a pair of commands C1 C2 to be executed one after another ("C1 ; C2" in the shell)

- a command can be a pair of commands C1 C2 to be executed with the output of C1 piped into C2 ("C1 | C2" in the shell)

- a command can be a simple command C

It is tempting to translate this directly into Prolog as

command form	Prolog coding
sequence "C1 ; C2"	(C1 ; C2)
pipe "C1 | C2"	(C1 | C2)
simple command C	C

If you try it, you'll run straight into the fact that (C1;C2) and (C1|C2) are mere syntactic variants, the two are read as exactly the same term. (Try it.) So you might be tempted to use a slightly different coding:

command form	Prolog coding
sequence "C1 ; C2"	(C1 , C2)
pipe "C1 | C2"	(C1 | C2)
simple command C	C

Don't do it! You will be making a rod for your own back. The only way you can recognise "anything else" will be by failing to recognise a sequence or a pipe, and you will end up with lots of code that looks like

```
process_command((C1 , C2)) :- !,
        /* do something */.
process_command((C1 | C2)) :- !,
        /* do something else */.
process_Command(Simplecommand) :-
        /* do yet a third thing */.
```

Suppose you want to represent one of N "situations" where

- in situation 1 you have data items $X_{11}, \ldots, X_{1k_1}$ available

- ...

- in situation N you have data items $X_{N1}, \ldots, X_{Nk_N}$ available

What you do is invent suitable symbolic names for the situations (if you must use an abbreviation, *always* abbreviate that word that way throughout your whole program). Then each situation is represented by a compound term with the situation name as the function symbol and with the associated data items as arguments.

If some of the situations have different numbers of arguments, you can give them the same name. But this is not a good idea, because if you ever add data items to one of the situations you may make two distinct situations conflict. I have failed to follow this rule in the past. When I used to design trees, I used to think it was clever to use the same function symbol to identify empty nodes, leaves, and internal nodes. I was wrong.

What would happen in our example of shell commands? There are three situations:

- a sequence, with associated data C1 and C2

- a pipe, with associated data C1 and C2

- a simple command, with associated data C

so we end up with the representation

command form	Prolog coding
sequence "C1 ; C2"	sequence(C1,C2)
pipe "C1 | C2"	pipe(C1,C2)
simple command C	simple(C)

Now we can write code with fewer cuts:

```
process_command(sequence(C1,C2)) :-
        /* do something */.
process_command(pipe(C1,C2)) :-
        /* do something else */.
process_command(simple(c)) :-
        /* do yet a third thing */.
```

and if we want to put these clauses in some other order, we can do that with no trouble at all. Each case says what it *is*, and you don't have to rely on context to tell you what it *isn't*.

Giving all of the situations names makes it easier to maintain code. Suppose that we want to know whether a command is a sequence of simple commands. Then we can write

simple_command_sequence(simple(_)). % version 2
simple_command_sequence(sequence(C1,C2)) :-
          simple_command_sequence(C1),
          simple_command_sequence(C2).

If we had been relying on "anything else" to tell us when something was simple,
we'd have had to code this as

simple_command_sequence((_ | _)) :- !, fail. % version 1
simple_command_sequence((C1,C2)) :- !,
          simple_command_sequence(C1),
          simple_command_sequence(C2).
simple_command_sequence(_).

Now suppose we add a new type of command, representing a pair of commands
which execute independently in parallel. Version 2, the pure one, is fine as it stands,
but version 1, with the cuts, needs another clause to reject parallel commands.

    Those of you familiar with polymorphic type-checking will recognise this as advice
to use sum-of-products types. For example, in the DEC-10 prolog type checker, we
could declare

:- type command(C) $\longrightarrow$
          sequence(command(C),command(C))
     | pipe(command(C),command(C))
     | simple(C).

:- pred
          simple_command_sequence(command(C)).

    Yet another advantage of giving each situation its own name is that we can then
tell portray/1 how to portray each situation. For example, we can write

portray(sequence(C1,C2)) :-
          format('(~p ; ~p)', [C1,C2]).
portray(pipe(C1,C2)) :-
          format('(~p $|$ ~p)', [C1,C2]).
portray(simple(C)) :-
          (var(C) → write(C)
          ;   functor(C, F, _), write(F)
).

With this definition, interactions like this are possible:

```
?- print(sequence(pipe(sequence(simple(wc([file1]))),
        simple(wc([file2]))),simple(sort)),pipe(simple(who),
        simple(egrep(fred)))))).
```
(((wc ; wc) | sort) ; (who | egrep))
yes

Without the distinctive record name on simple commands, portray/1 wouldn't be
able to tell simple commands (which we want it to print in abbreviated form) from
other terms (which are none of its business).

This seems to go contrary to advice I gave earlier in this section, where I said
that it is a good idea to make data structures small. It *is* a good idea to make
data structures small, but it is also a good idea to keep your code as free of cuts as
possible and as simple as possible. Code which never needed any cuts is likely to
run considerably faster than code with them.

Let's evaluate the savings in a particular instance from using the "defaulty" approach. Let's take the term we printed above, but let's make the simple commands
atoms rather than terms. Let's start by writing a meta-predicate to find the size
of a term in words.

```
term_size_in_words(Term, Size) :-
        term_size_in_words(Term, 0, Size).

term_size_in_words(Term, Size0, Size) :-
        var(Term),
        !,
        Size is Size0+1.
term_size_in_words(Term, Size0, Size) :-
        atomic(Term),
        !,
        Size is Size0+1.
term_size_in_words([Head|Tail], Size0, Size) :- !,
        Size1 is Size0+1,
        term_size_in_words(Head, Size1, Size2),
        term_size_in_words(Tail, Size2, Size).
term_size_in_words(Term, Size0, Size) :-
        functor(Term, _, Arity),
        Size1 is Size0+2,
        term_size_in_words(Arity, Term, Size1, Size).
```

```
term_size_in_words(n, term, size0, Size) :-
(    N =:= 0 → Size = Size0
;    arg(N, Term, Arg),
     term_size_in_words(Arg, Size0, Size1),
     M is N-1,
     term_size_in_words(M, Term, Size1, Size)
).
```

Now, what are the sizes of the example in clean and defaulty form?

```
?-    term_size_in_words(sequence(pipe(sequence(simple('wc file'),
          simple('we file2')),simple(sort)),pipe(simple(who),
          simple('egrep fred')))), CleanSize),
      term_size_in_words(sequence(pipe(sequence('wc file','wc file2'),
          sort),pipe(who,'egrep fred')), DefaultySize).
```

CleanSize = 23,
DefaultySize = 13

In general, if we have a set of N simple commands (each one an atom) connected by $N - 1$ pipe/2 or sequence/2 connectors, we'll have $5N - 2$ words in addition to the atoms in the clean representation, and $3N - 2$ words in addition to the atoms in the defaulty representation. That is enough of a difference to worry about, and *if* the extra space weren't buying us anything, it would be a good reason to adopt the defaulty representation. However, the speed, clarity, and maintainability advantages are compelling.

When the simple commands are themselves represented by non-trivial terms, the space advantage of the defaulty form is smaller. For the original version of this example, the clean representation costs 33 words, while the defaulty version costs 23.

What do I mean "don't use wrappers"? I mean that when you are using this sum-of-products approach, and there is only one situation to be represented, and it has only one associated datum, don't bother wrapping a record around it. You need a record name *either* to group together several associated data, *or* to distinguish between several cases.

For example, suppose we want to represent dates involving years, months, and days. A good data structure is

```
:- type date ⟶
          date(integer,integer,integer).
          /* year month day */
```

I have seen code where the programmer would consistently represent a date, not as

date(1987,10,11)

but as

date(year(1987),month(10),day(11))

In some programming languages that is a good idea, because it will help the type checker, and the compiler is able to generate code in which the wrapper does not appear. ML and Miranda do this. But in Prolog the wrapper will really be there. It will cost storage space (a date without wrappers costs 4 words; a date with wrappers costs 10 words), it will cost time (the unifier has to inspect the wrappers), and it doesn't buy you anything.

I have seen an even grosser misuse of wrappers for dates:

date([day = 11, month = 10, year = 1987])

A term $X = Y$ typically costs 3 cells, plus the 2 cells for appearing in a list, and the date(_) record costs 2 cells, so the total cost for a wrapped list of pairs like this is $2 + 5N$ cells where a straightforward compound term would cost $1 + N$ cells. A five-fold waste of space. A list like this makes it very hard to get at any one of the elements. For example, to get at the Year field, we would just do

Date = date(Year,_,_)

using the compact sum-of-products representation. This would typically compile to three WAM instructions, checking one structure and accessing one field. With the list representation, we would do

Date = date([_, _, year=Year])

which would compile into about ten WAM instructions, checking four structures and one constant before picking up the field we really want. Worse still, the program I got this from used member/2:

member(year=Year, Date)

It is indeed good to get at fields by name rather than position, but all it takes is one little special-purpose predicate with a clause for each field:

```
date(year,  date(Y,_,_),  Y).
date(month, date(_,M,_),  M).
date(day,   date(_,_,D),  D).
```

Why would anyone use wrappers? In many programming languages, records come with field names, and the programmer I have in mind was thinking in terms of an Ada-like language where you would write something like

date_var := date[year=1987, month=10, day=11]

or

date[year=yvar, month=mvar, day=dvar] := date_var

In Prolog (and some other declarative languages, such as ML and Miranda) the fields of a record are identified by position, not by name. Yes, this does mean you have to remember which field goes where, but then you always have to write all of the fields.

Time-stamps illustrate a minor point of data structure design. you may have wondered why my example used 10 for the month, rather than october or 'October'. The answer is that if we use month numbers, the standard order on (ground) time-stamps considered as terms coincides with the usual order on dates, whereas if we use month names we do not obtain this benefit. If you can easily arrange the fields of a record so that the standard order means something useful, it is a good idea to do that. If it would be too awkward, don't bother.

What do I mean "don't over-use lists"? Precisely that. There are very many applications where lists are exactly the right data structure. but there are many more where they aren't. To continue with time-stamps, you could represent a date by a list [Year,Month,Day], but there is so much against it that it would be fair to call it a mistake.

When should you use lists? To represent a collection of similar things. You should ask yourself

- would the empty list make sense here?

- are all of the elements of the list members of a single conceptual class?

- will anything other than a list ever appear here?

- if another element were added to the list, would that make sense?

Remember the algebra example? It did make sense to represent an element of the algebra by a list, because all the elements of the list were the same sort of thing (elements of the 3-element algebra), and every predicate or constructor that took such a list as an argument *only* accepted such lists as arguments. (For example,

mt/3 never accepted a number as an argument: all of its arguments had to be lists.)
But it wasn't the best choice, because the length of the list was fixed.

Here is an example where it is inappropriate to use lists. The task is to represent finite functions. There are two operations: pairup/3 constructs a function representation from a pair of lists, and lookup/3 evaluates a function at a given point.

```
/* BAD VERSION */
pairup([], [], []).
pairup([Key|Keys], [Val|Vals], [[Key,Val]|Pairs]) :-
        pairup(Keys, Vals, Pairs).

lookup(Key, [[Key,Val]|_], Val).
lookup(Key, [_|Pairs], Val) :-
        lookup(Key, Pairs, Val).
```

Using a list to represent the collection of pairs is a good idea. It passes all our tests. But using a two-element list to represent a pair is a bad idea: the empty list doesn't make sense, adding or deleting an element doesn't make sense, and the two elements of a [Key,Val] pair belong to different conceptual classes (the domain and range of the function).

What would the general sum-of-products approach tell us here? There is one situation (a pair) with two associated data (a Key and a Val). So we should pick a record name (constructor function). What constructor should we use? A popular choice is ','/2. There is a problem with that, and a missed opportunity. The problem is that comma is already used for enough things in Prolog that adding one more is asking for trouble. The missed opportunity is that the built-in predicate keysort/2 uses the constructor (-)/2: if we build pairs with that constructor, they will be the kind of thing that keysort/2 can sort. So I almost always use (-)/2 for pairs. We thus arrive at the code

```
/* GOOD VERSION */
pairup([], [], []).
pairup([Key|Keys], [Val|Vals], [Key-Val|Pairs]) :-
        pairup(Keys, Vals, Pairs).

lookup(Key, [Key-Val|_], Val).
lookup(Key, [_|Pairs], Val) :-
        lookup(Key, Pairs, Val).
```

This example has something else to teach us. Suppose we apply sum-of-products thinking to the entire data structure? A finite map can be

- empty, or

- it can map a Key to a Val, or map anything else as given by another finite Map.

If we took this approach, we would obtain

pairup([], [], empty_map).
pairup([Key|Keys], [Val|Vals], map(Key,Val,Rest)) :-
       pairup(Keys, Vals, Rest).

lookup(Key, map(Key,Val,_), Val).
lookup(Key, map(_,_,Rest), Val) :-
       lookup(Key, Rest, Val).

How can we decide between the two?

First, let's consider space. A finite function with N elements in its domain costs $6N$ words of copy stack as a list of 2-element lists, $5N$ words as a list of Key-Val pairs, and only $4N$ words if built out of map/3 triples.

Second, let's consider time. Most Prolog compilers generate something like this:

[[Key,Val]|_]	[Key-Val|_]	map(Key,Val,_)
match_list	match_list	match_cons(map)/3
match_list	match_cons(-)/2	unify_var Key
unify_var Key	unify_var Key	unify_var Val
match_list	unify_var Val	unify_void
unify_var Val	unify_void	
unify_nil		
unify_void		

All things considered, it is not unreasonable to expect the times for these code sequences to be in the same 6:5:4 ratio as the space costs. In fact measurements in Quintus Prolog show that the version using the map/3 constructor *is* noticeably faster.

So should we avoid the use of lists at all here? It depends on what else you want to do with these things. If you represent them as lists of (Key-Val) pairs, there are literally hundreds of library predicates which are potentially applicable, whereas if you use a problem-specific data structure you'll have to roll your own. If you want to find the size of a finite function, for example, it is useful to be able to call length/2 on it. It is useful to be able to put them into a canonical form by calling keysort/2. It is useful to be able to remove an element by calling select/3. But if there are only a few things that you want to do with your finite functions,

you would be well advised to avoid lists here too. In fact, it is advantageous to
do so, because then there is less risk of confusing things which you meant to be
finite functions with things which just happen to look like them (the empty list is
particularly good at masquerading as all sorts of things).

If you are prepared to consider using something other than a list, you are freed
to follow the last piece \of advice: think of trees. Accessing an arbitrary member
of a list takes time proportional to the length of the list, and deleting or replacing
it takes new space proportional to the length of the list. By using trees, you can
reduce this (N) factor to $O(\lg N)$. You will find many examples in the library.

5.5.1   Round Lists

If it is unwise to use lists too much, how much worse it is to over-use the comma!
Yet I have recently seen one Prolog text-book which makes much of so-called "round
lists", and another which (ab-)uses them frequently without making any fuss about
it.

There is one defaulty data structure which Prolog programmers always have to
deal with, and that is Prolog clauses. In a clause body like

   p, (q ; r), s

we can only tell that p, q, r, and s are simple goals by discovering that they are
not any of the built in control structures. This is a continuing nuisance when you
are writing macros or programs that manipulate programs: *your* code has to know
about *every* control structure, and too bad if a Prolog implementor adds a new one
without telling you (this does happen).

Taking one of the more cathedralgic[1] aspects of Prolog and making a policy of
imitating it is really not a good idea. If you want binary trees, make up your own
name for them, and make sure that the leaves have an explicit functor of their own.

Another mistake is to use commas for constructing tuples. For example, when
you want to represent the X-coördinate of a cell on a board, its Y-coördinate, and
the cost of moving there, it is tempting to write (X,Y,Cost). But this is infix syntax
for ','(X,','(Y,Cost)). It is clearer and cheaper to write move(X,Y,Cost).

I'm sorry to insult your intelligence with these warnings, but there really are
Prolog books that do it badly.

---

[1] *cathedra* = something you sit on, *algia* = pain

6 Sequences

6.1 Introduction and Notation

List processing is very important in Prolog. You don't want to use lists for *everything*, indeed one mark of a good Prolog programmer is knowing when to avoid lists. But there are many applications for collections of various kinds.

To be a good Prolog programmer, you need to know a reasonable number of coding "schemes", so that you can look at a problem and say to yourself, "Oh, I've seen that before, all I have to do is fill in the blanks in this scheme and I'll have something that works." Some schemes are built into programming languages: Fortran has DO loops and Pascal has **while** loops and Lisp has (map --). But there are always more schemes to know than there are special forms in the language you are using.

This chapter has two purposes. One is to exhibit some useful coding schemes. The other is to show how thinking at the level of coding schemes (rather than specific programs) gives us a lot of leverage: we can transfer whole schemes from one representation for sequences to another, so we instantly transfer a whole body of coding knowledge without having to figure it out all over again.

The aim of the chapter is very practical: when you master this material you will be a much more effective Prolog programmer than before. (Many of my readers will already know this material even better than I do. Reading familiar material can be a pleasure too.) But the practical point is that abstraction is a very powerful tool. So some of the material is rather more abstract than you may be used to.

According to a dictionary I checked, a sequence is "a number of things following one another considered collectively". That is, we have a collection of things—the *elements* of the sequence—which are in a definite order. If there are any elements at all, one of them is the first, and the remainder are the rest, and themselves form a sequence. The usual mathematical definition is that a sequence is a function which is defined on the integers 1 to N for some integer N, which is the length of the sequence.

The following notation is taken from '*Understanding* **Z**' by J. M. Spivey, and is pretty much standard.

$\#s$	Length of s
$\langle \rangle$	Empty sequence
$\langle x_1, \ldots, x_n \rangle$	The sequence containing x_1 then $\ldots x_n$ $\{1 \mapsto x_1, \ldots, n \mapsto x_n\}$
$s \frown t$	t appended to s $\langle x_1, \ldots, x_n \rangle \frown \langle y_1, \ldots, y_m \rangle = \langle x_1, \ldots, x_n, y_1, \ldots, y_m \rangle$

Many of the Prolog code fragments in this chapter contain meta-variables, which are written in italics. You should regard them as standing for entities in (the specification of) your program. A common one is *Variety*, which stands for your name for some type. Some other common meta-variables are

f	functions
p	(determinate) predicates
s	sequences
ϵ	enumerators (nondeterminate predicates)
σ	states (of generators)

The following notations are nonstandard but clear.

s suchthat p	the subsequence of s containing all x_i such that $p(x_i)$.
s while p	the prefix of s stopping just before the first x_i such that $\neg p(x_i)$

6.2 Representing sequences

Most programming languages have at least two ways of representing a sequence:

- *explicitly*, as a data structure. I call this a "spatial" representation, because the sequence occupies storage.

- *implicitly*, as the course of values of some variable. I call this a "temporal" representation.

Prolog offers two other kinds of representation:

- *explicitly,* as facts stored in the data base. This is Kowalski's "relational" representation.

- *implicitly,* as the sequence of solutions offered by a goal on backtracking.

Each of these representations has advantages and disadvantages.

- The "relational" representation (each element of the sequence is a separate fact in the data base) is a wonderful representation for sequences which do not change. However, it is an appallingly bad representation for sequences which are to be modified or dynamically calculated, as the cost of a single data base change is extremely high.

- If we have a sequence physically present as a data structure, it is bounded. We can write recursive and backtracking operations to examine it without fear of non-termination. We can rearrange the elements of the sequence and combine them with elements of other sequences without difficulty.

  The disadvantage of spatial (stored) representations is that they have to be stored. They occupy space whether we are examining them or not.

- If we have a sequence represented implicitly, we don't need to store the whole thing. This is especially useful when the sequence is not finite!

  There are two disadvantages of temporal sequences. If we want to examine a particular sequence more than once, we have to recompute the elements. And if we want to combine several sequences, they may not have compatible "clocks".

- The sequence of solutions returned by a goal is a very natural representation in Prolog. Selection and transformation are easy to do with this representation. But computing functions of such sequences, or combining two such sequences, can be very awkward, because the only way of obtaining the next element of such a sequence is to forget everything you have done with the current one.

Each of these methods has its uses; none of them is always better than the others. So it is important to be able to change representations.

The usual way of representing a sequence in Prolog is to use a *list*. We might as well call this the *standard* representation of sequences. If you don't know what lists look like by now, there's no point in my telling you. It's worth pointing out, though, that there is nothing sacred about that representation. Suppose we want a spatial representation for the sequence $\langle x_1, \ldots, x_n \rangle$. The general rule for designing a Prolog data structure is "decide what the possible situations are, and assign a distinct constructor to each situation." We obtain the usual representation by thinking of the situations as being

- $n = 0$. The sequence is empty. Use $[]$.

- $n > 0$. The first element of the sequence is x_1 and the rest of the sequence is $\langle x_2, \ldots, x_n \rangle$. Use $\bullet(x_1, R)$ where R represents the rest of the sequence.

That's not the only possible decomposition. We could have decided to distinguish the *last* element of the sequence, and then we might have had $<>$ for an empty sequence and $\langle x_1, \ldots, x_{k-1} \rangle + x_k$ as our sequence representation. Another possibility, which might occur to someone whose native language had a 'dual' number as well as 'singular' and 'plural', would be to distinguish three situations:

- $n = 0$. Use 'z'.

- $n = 1$. Use 'o'(x_1).

- $n > 1$. Use 't'$(x_1, x_2, \langle x_3, \ldots, x_n \rangle)$.

Exercise. *Write a version of append/3 suitable for this representation.*

Lists are particularly convenient because so many built-in and library predicates already exist using that representation. But if you find that you want to access the elements of a logical sequence in a way which is awkward with lists, you need to really understand that lists are just *one* representation so that you will be free to think of others which may be better suited to your problem.

It is often useful to remember that bit-patterns are not the only possible representation of numbers. For example, we can use a list as if it were a number: $[]$ represents 0, and $[H|T]$ represents one more than the number T represents. For example, if we want to select the Nth element of a list called Source, where N is the length of a list called Where, we could certainly write

```
list_nth0(Where, Source, Element) :-
        length(Where, N),
        nth0(N, Source, Element).
```

But instead of making the number N and then counting it down to 0, we could count Where down to "0":

```
list_nth0([], [Element|_], Element). % "0"
list_nth0([_—Where], [_—Source], Element) :- % "N+1"
        list_nth0(Where, Source, Element).
```

So we see that a list can be used to represent its own length.

If something as simple as a number can usefully be given another representation, how much more is that true for sequences!

Another representation for sequences I shall call *generators*. There is an unfortunate confusion of terminology here. I learned about generators from Interlisp, where a generator is basically a coroutine which can deliver new elements of a sequence on request. Generators in conventional languages don't have to be fully-fledged coroutines, a simple 'state vector' and 'next element function' suffice. Smalltalk often uses generators. My use of the word "generators" is standard terminology. The problem is that Prolog programmers tend to talk about the "generate and test" paradigm. So do other programmers, but in other languages, lacking backtracking, a sequence of trials is generated in ordinary *forward* computation. Prolog programmers tend to think that generate and test necessarily involves backtracking, which simply isn't true. I'm going to call the 'generate' part of a backtracking generate and test an *enumerator*.

The idea is that a generator is a data structure which represents the state of a process, and there is an operation which returns a value and a new state. To qualify as a generator, a data structure should support three operations:

make_*variety*(+*Arguments*, −*State*) Given some *Arguments* describing which sequence is wanted, this operation returns the *State* of a process which generates the elements of that sequence.

*variety_* **next**(?*Element*, +*State0*, −*State*) given an initial state *State0*, this operation returns an *Element* appropriate to that state and a new *State* which describes a process which generates the elements following this *Element*. This operation may have several solutions for a given *State0*, though that isn't often useful.

*variety_***done**(+*State0*) is to be true when *State0* describes the state of a process which can generate no further elements.

If we call

$$\text{make\_x}(\ldots, S_0),$$
$$\text{x\_next}(X_1, S_0, S_1),$$
$$\vdots$$
$$\text{x\_next}(X_n, S_m, S_n)$$

then each S_i represents the state of a process which has generated i elements, and those elements are $X_1, \ldots, X_i$.

For example, suppose we want to represent an interval of integers. Such an interval might be very large indeed, and we don't want to store parts of it which we haven't looked at yet.

```
make_interval(Low, High, i(Low,High)) :-
        integer(Low), integer(High).

interval_done(i(Low,High)) :-
        Low > High.

interval_next(Low, i(Low,High), i(Low1,High)) :-
        plus(Low, 1, Low1),
        Low ≤ High.
```

Now every time we advance an interval generator, we're going to construct a new i(_,_) pair, which is more expensive than a list element would have been. But there is nothing to stop you simplifying a program which uses such a generator, by passing two arguments to represent the state rather than one, and in that case no compound terms will be built. You should take everything in this chapter as a starting point for your own improvements, not as something to be followed slavishly.

The third way of representing a sequence I call *enumeration*. We can identify a logical set with a predicate which recognises and/or generates the elements of that set. But Prolog predicates work in a definite order, and may repeat a solution, so we can identify a sequence with the sequence of solutions enumerated by a Prolog predicate. There is a parallel between generators and enumerators:

make a generator	call an enumerator
the generator is done	the enumerator fails
find the next element	fail back into the goal

For example, we can represent an interval of integers as a predicate. In fact the Quintus Prolog library already contains such a predicate, inherited from DEC-10 Prolog: between/3.

```
between(Low, High, X) :-
        integer(Low), integer(High),
        (    var(X) →
             Low ≤ High,
             between1(Low, High, X)
        ;    integer(X) →
             Low ≤ X, X ≤ High
        ).

between1(L, U, L).
```

between1(L, U, X) :-
      L < U,
      M is L + 1,
      between1(M, U, X).

The query $\text{between}(1, N, X)$ *enumerates* the integers $1-N$ just as the generator $i(1, N)$ *generates* those integers, and the list $[1, \ldots, N]$ *lists* them.

6.3 Conversion

Sometimes one representation is useful, sometimes another. So we want to know how to convert from any representation to the others.

6.3.1 List to generator

This one is easy. We just need three trivial definitions:

make_list(List, List).

list_done([]).

list_next(Head, [Head|Tail], Tail).

6.3.2 List to enumerator

This one is easy too: just use member/2.

6.3.3 List to relation

One way of storing a sequence as facts is to store x_i as a pair element(i, x_i). Here's how:

store_sequence(List, Name) :-
      Skel =.. [Name,I,XI],
      retractall(Skel),
      forall(nth1(I, List, XI), assert(Skel)).

This is rather ugly. If your program first computes some large and costly sequences, and thereafter never changes them, it can be a good idea to store them. The stored form then gives you fast access to the element at a known index, but it is awkward to do anything *but* fetch an element.

6.3.4   Generator to list

There is a parallel between generators and lists:

list	generator
$X_0 = []$	$variety\_done(X_0)$
$X_0 = [E|X_1]$	$variety\_next(E, X_0, X_1)$

Accordingly, we can adapt append/3 thus:

$variety\_append(X_0, L, L)$:-
            $variety\_done(X_0)$.
$variety\_append(X_0, L, [E|R])$:-
            $variety\_next(E, X_0, X_1)$,
            $variety\_append(X_1, L, R)$.

$variety\_to\_list(X, L)$:-
            $variety\_append(X, [], L)$.

This simplifies to

$variety\_to\_list(X0, [])$:-
            $variety\_done(X0)$.
$variety\_to\_list(X0, [E|L])$:-
            $variety\_next(E, X0, X1)$,
            $variety\_to\_list(X1, L)$.

Of course, you will want to choose your generator data structure so that when you unfold the _done and _next operations in something like this you obtain a determinate predicate.

If you get into the habit of using grammar rule notation for operations on lists (when it is appropriate to do so), you will find that this carries over directly to generators. If you had intended to convert a generator to a list just so that you could parse it with some grammar rules, you needn't bother. Where you would have written

        [X]

in a grammar rule to work on lists, you just write

        $variety\_next(X)$

in a grammar rule to work on generators. Instead of calling

       phrase(NonTerminal, List)

to determine whether a List matches the NonTerminal, you call

       phrase(NonTerminal, State0, State),
       *variety*_done(State)

to determine whether State0 represents the state of a process that generates a sequence matching the NonTerminal.

For example, suppose we have a sequence of terms stored in text form on a file. (There had better not be any syntax errors, or this could go wrong.) We could use

```
make_reader(File, Stream, State) :-
        open(File, read, Stream),
        read(Stream, Term),
        reader_code(Term, Stream, State).

reader_code(end_of_file, _, end_of_file) :- !.
reader_code(Term, Stream, read(Term,Stream,Position)) :-
        stream_position(Stream, Position).

reader_done(end_of_file).

reader_next(Term, read(Term,Stream,Pos), State) :-
        stream_position(Stream, _, Pos),
        read(Stream, Next),
        reader_code(Next, Stream, State).

reader_phrase(NT, File) :-
        make_reader(File, Stream, State),
        (    phrase(NT, State, end_of_file) →
             close(Stream) /* and succeed */
        ;    close(Stream), fail
        ).
```

This example shows very clearly the advantage and disadvantage of generators: we only have to keep two terms in memory at once (the ones bound to Term and Next in reader_next/3) so we can parse enormous data files with this approach, but if the parser is not determinate we may read each term a great many times. With a little more work it is easy to allow several active queries directed at the same file, using just one stream.

I got the idea for this example from Frank McCabe.

6.3.5   Generator to enumerator

Using the parallel between generators and lists mentioned in the previous subsection, we can make a version of member/2 which applies to a generator.

*variety*_member(Element, X0) :-
        *variety*_next(E, X0, X1),
        (E = Element
        ;   *variety*_member(Element, X1)
).

6.3.6   Enumerator to list

This is the hairy one. The metaphor that I use to express the problem is that enumerators and generators are both temporal representations, but they correspond to orthogonal time axes. (If that doesn't help you, forget it.) Because backtracking is driven by failure, which undoes bindings, if we want to retain information between two states of an enumerator, we cannot keep it in variable bindings. There are three other ways of keeping information around:

- in files

- in the stored data base

- in C's world

The simplest method is to use one of the common "all solutions" predicates. They are described in a later chapter. For now, let it suffice that when $G(X)$ is a goal which enumerates bindings for X,

$$\text{findall}(X, G(X), L)$$

will unify L with a list of all the terms X that $G(X)$ enumerates. If you have bag_of_all/3, it is a good idea to use that instead.

A more beautiful, and thus more efficient, method is to rewrite the enumerator to construct a list in the first place. This can't always be done, but there is a lot of interest in doing this so that 'and-parallel' systems like Concurrent Prolog can simulate 'or-parallel'. Basically the idea is that you turn ors into ands.

A simple transformation which sometimes works goes like this. Suppose we have an enumeration predicate

$p(A, X)$:-
        $guard_1$,
        $q_1(A_1', X)$.

$\vdots$

$p(A, X)$:-
$$\quad guard_n,$$
$$\quad q_n(A'_n, X).$$

where each $q_i(A'_i, X)$ is either $X = term_i$ or a call to another such enumeration predicate. First we rename variables in the clauses so that only the arguments in the head are common, and then we convert the result to a single grammar rule thus:

$p(A, S1, S)$:-
$$\quad (\quad guard_1 \rightarrow q'_1(A'_1, S1, S2)$$
$$\quad ;\quad S1 = S2$$
$$\quad),$$
$$\quad \vdots$$
$$\quad (\quad guard_1 \rightarrow q'_n(A'1, Sn, S)$$
$$\quad ;\quad Sn = S$$
$$\quad).$$

where

Goal	$\rightarrow$	Nonterminal
$q_i(A'_i, X)$	$\rightarrow$	$q'_i(A'_i, S_i, S_j)$
$X = term_i$	$\rightarrow$	$S_i = [term_i \mid S_j]$
$enum(\alpha, X)$	$\rightarrow$	$nt(\alpha, S_i, S_j)$

where 'nt' is the nonterminal obtained by transforming the enumeration predicate 'enum' the same way.

For an example of this, consider between/3. The basic enumeration predicate in it is

between1(L, U, X) :-
$$\quad X = L.$$
between1(L, U, X) :-
$$\quad L < U,$$
$$\quad M \text{ is } L + 1,$$
$$\quad between1(M, U, X).$$

From this we derive the grammar rule

```
between1(L, U) ⟶
        [L],
        (     { L < U } →
              { M is L + 1 },
              between1(M, U)
        ;     []
        ).
```

and the analogue of between/3 is thus

```
between_list(Low, High, List) :-
        integer(Low), integer(High),
        Low ≤ High,
        between1(Low, High, List, []).
```

All done by kindness.

6.3.7   Enumerator to generator

In a Prolog system supporting program-visible parallel processes (note that coroutining, and-parallel, and or-parallel may be implemented using multiple processes,
but the processes are not visible to the program as objects) we would be able to
reify the state of an enumerator as a process, then perhaps we could treat an enumerator as a generator directly. In the absence of such a facility (which would take
us outside logic), the best we can do is to obtain a list holding the results of the
enumerator and treat that as a generator.

6.4   Computing Functions of Lists

In an earlier chapter, we looked at predicates that work on an interval of integers
$[L, U]$[1]. We found that there were at least three techniques we could use:

counting down Split the interval into $[L, U - 1]$ and $[U, U]$, process U first, and
   then process the remaining interval $[L, U - 1]$.

counting up Split the interval into $[L, L]$ and $[L + 1, U]$, process L first, and then
   process the remaining interval $[L + 1, U]$.

bisection If $L = U$, process that number, otherwise split the interval into $[L, \lfloor(L + U)/2\rfloor]$ and $[\lfloor(L + U)/2\rfloor + 1, U]$ and process each of the halves.

---

[1]Yes, interval brackets *do* look like list brackets, don't they?

Many computations on the elements of a sequence can be broken up in similar ways. In this section we are going to look at a generic problem whose instances are very common in practice. We're going to see several code schemes which can be used to solve this problem. These schemes are going to look a lot like the counting loops we looked at before.

Here are some instances of the generic problem. The methods we are going to develop can be used for all of them.

- finding the length of a list

- summing the elements of a list

- sorting a list

- concatenating all the elements of a list of lists

- taking the union of a set of sets

- finding the product of a sequence of matrices and scalars

- collecting all the elements of a set which satisfy a test

- for the Quintus Prolog "foreign code" interface, finding all the foreign functions said by a set of foreign_file/2 facts to be defined in a given set of foreign files

- your problem goes here...

Here is the generic problem in all its abstract glory:

There are three data types:

D are the Data items that we are given in the list.

R is the type of the Result.

W is the type of the intermediate or Working values.

We are given four functions:

$g : D \rightarrow W$ converts data elements to working values.

$f : W \times W \rightarrow W$ is associative with left identity e. It combines working values. It need not be commutative.

$e :\rightarrow W$ is the left identity of f

$h : W \rightarrow R$ converts working values to results.

We shall represent Nary functions by $(N+1)$ary relations. So the code fragments use

$e(E)$ E is the left identity of f.

$f(W_1, W_2, W)$ means that $W = f(W_1, W_2)$.

$g(D, W)$ means that $W = g(D)$.

$h(W, R)$ means that $R = h(W)$.

The task is to write a Prolog predicate p such that

$$p([X_1, \ldots, X_n], \text{ Answer}) :-$$
$$\text{Answer} = h(g(X_1)f \cdots fg(X_n)).$$

If you haven't seen problems described like this before, you may be feeling rather puzzled. The point is that we are looking for a general pattern (or rather for several such) that we can use over and over again whenever we come across a problem which can be fitted into this general mould. And to make a schema as useful as possible, we want it to be as general as possible.

To connect these two statements of the problem, here is how we can view these specific problems as instances of the general pattern.

- finding the length of a list

  $e = 0$

  $f(X, Y) = X + Y$

  $g(X) = 1$

  $h(X) = X$

- summing the elements of a list

  $e = 0$

  $f(X, Y) = X + Y$

  $g(X) = X$

  $h(X) = X$

- sorting a list

  $e = []$

  $f(X, Y) = \text{merge}(X, Y)$

  $g(X) = [X]$

  $h(X) = X$

- concatenating all the elements of a list of lists

  $e = []$

  $f(X, Y) = Z | \text{append}(X, Y, Z)$

  $g(X) = X$

  $h(X) = X$

- taking the union of a set of sets (here I assume that we are using the ordered set representation of library(ordsets))

  $e = []$

  $f(X, Y) = Z | \text{ord\_union}(X, Y, Z)$

  $g(X) = X$

  $h(X) = X$

- taking the product of a sequence of matrices and scalars, assuming that mat_times/3 has already a suitable definition

  $e = 1$ (the scalar 1)

  $f(X, Y) = Z | \text{mat\_times}(X, Y, Z)$

  $g(X) = X$

  $h(X) = X$

- collecting all the elements of a set which satisfy a test $\sigma(X)$.

  $e = []$

  $f(X, Y) = Z | \text{append}(X, Y, Z)$

  $g(X) = \text{if } \sigma(X) \text{ then } [X] \text{ else } []$

  $h(X) = X$

- the same example, using difference lists

  $e(L, L)$

  $f(L0, L1, \ L1, L, \ L0, L)$

  $g(X, [X|L], L){:}\text{-}\sigma(X)$

  $g(X, \ L, L){:}\text{-}\neg\sigma(X)$

  $h(L, [], \ L)$

- finding all the foreign functions said by a set of foreign_file/2 facts to be defined in a given set of foreign_files (assuming that each foreign file is attested to by exactly one foreign_file/2 fact)

$e = []$

$f(X, Y) = Z | \text{ord\_union}(X, Y, Z)$

$g(X) = S | \text{foreign\_file}(X, L), \text{sort}(L, S)$

$h(X) = X$

6.4.1 The "Tower" method

There is a very general approach to operations on recursively defined data structures (and the natural numbers are recursively defined too, don't forget). That is to try and mimic the structural definition of the data structure in the operation. Since lists are

empty [], or

non-empty [Head|Tail]

what could be more natural than to mimic this directly in p? We arrive almost at once at

```
p(List, Result) :-
        p'(List, Answer),
        h(Answer, Result).

p'([], Answer) :-
        e(Answer).
p'([Head|Tail], Answer) :-
        p'(Tail, Right),
        g(Head, Val),
        f(Val, Right, Answer).
```

If we apply this schema to the problem of summing the elements of a list, we get

```
list_sum([], 0).
list_sum([Head|Tail], Total) :-
        list_sum(Tail, Right),
        Total is Head+Right.
```

This works, so we could rest content with it. But if the list has N elements, we'll have a tower of N recursive calls waiting for the sum to the Right to be calculated, and we can do better than that.

6.4.2 The "Linear" method

Basically, we want to turn the body recursion into a tail recursion. There is a very simple way of doing so, which hinges on the fact that f is associative. We introduce an auxiliary predicate

$p'([X_{k+1}, \ldots, X_n]$, SoFar, Answer) :-
        Answer = SoFar f $g(X_{k+1})$ f $\cdots$ f $g(X_n)$.

When we fill in the details, we get

p(List, Result) :-
        e(E),
        p'(List, E, Answer),
        h(Answer, Result).

p'([], Answer, Answer).
p'([Head|Tail], SoFar, Answer) :-
        g(Head, Val),
        f(SoFar, Val, Next),
        p'(Tail, Next, Answer).

Applying this to the problem of sorting a list, we arrive at

sort(List, Sorted) :-
        sort(List, [], Sorted).

sort([], Sorted, Sorted).
sort([Head|Tail], SoFar, Sorted) :-
        insert(SoFar, Head, Next),
        sort(Tail, Next, Sorted).

insert([Head|Tail], Item, [Head|Rest]) :-
        Head @< Item,
        !,
        insert(Tail, Item, Rest).
insert([Head|Tail], Item, [Head|Tail]) :-
        Head == Item,
        !.
insert(List, Item, [Item|List]).

This is indeed a working sort, and it does run in bounded stack, but it is even worse than "Quick"sort (which sometimes takes $O(N^2)$ time): it *always* takes $O(N^2)$ time.

This approach is often very good. For example, to collect all the elements of a list satisfying a test, we might start with

sublist(Test, List, SubList) :-
        sublist(List, Test, [], SubList).

sublist([], _, SubList, SubList).
sublist([Head|Tail], Test, SoFar, SubList) :-
        filter(Test, Head, Val),
        append(SoFar, Val, Next),
        sublist(Tail, Test, Next, SubList).

filter(Test, Head, [Head]) :-
        call(Test, Head), % is Test true of Head?
        !.
filter(_, _, []).

As it stands, it is pretty appalling, but the problem is all those calls to append/3, not the structure of sublist/[3–4] itself. We can get rid of append/3 using difference lists, as usual, which I represent here by a pair of arguments.

sublist(Test, List, SubList) :-
        sublist(List, Test, X,X, SubList,[]).

sublist([], _, R0,R, R0,R).
sublist([Head|Tail], Test, L0,L, R0,R) :-
        filter(Test, Head, L0,L, M0,M),
        sublist(Tail, Test, M0,M, R0,R).

filter(Test, Head, M0,[Head|M], M0,M) :-
        call(Test, Head),
        !.
filter(_, _, M0,M, M0,M).

We observe that the 6th argument of sublist/6 is always [], and that since filter/6 always identifies its 3rd and 5th arguments, the 3rd argument of sublist/3 is always X, and is only carried along to be unified with SubList at the very end, the 5th argument of sublist/6 having no other purpose. Simplifying, we obtain

sublist(Test, List, SubList) :-
        sublist1(List, Test, SubList).

sublist1([], _, []).
sublist1([Head|Tail], Test, SubList0) :-
        filter(Test, Head, SubList0, SubList1),
        sublist1(Tail, Test, SubList1).

filter(Test, Head, [Head|M], M) :-
        call(Test, Head),
        !.
filter(_, _, M, M).

Finally, unfolding filter/4 into sublist1/3, we obtain

sublist(Test, List, SubList) :-
        sublist1(List, Test, SubList).

sublist1([], _, []).
sublist1([Head|Tail], Test, SubList) :-
        call(Test, Head),
        !,
        SubList = [Head|SubList1],
        sublist1(Tail, SubList1).
sublist1([_|Tail], Test, SubList) :-
        sublist1(Tail, Test, SubList).

There are some subtle details here, such as the need to postpone the unification until after the cut in the second clause of sublist1/3 to make it steadfast, which are not germane to the present topic.

  We seem to have gone all the way round Robin Hood's barn[2] to obtain what is after all a very simple operation. The point is that we got there by general methods.

6.4.3 When f has no left identity

What are we to do with a problem which is otherwise of this general form, but whose f has no left identity? An example of this would be obtaining the greatest element of a list: the "maximum" function over the numbers has no left identity ($-\infty$ is not a number). The answer is simple: we use the "Linear" method but move one step of the calculation back into the top predicate.

p([Head|Tail], Result) :-
        g(Head, Val),
        p(Tail, Val, Answer),
        h(Answer, Result).

---

[2]For Americans: Sherwood Forest.

$p([], \text{Answer}, \text{Answer})$.
$p([\text{Head}|\text{Tail}], \text{SoFar}, \text{Answer})$:-
        $g(\text{Head}, \text{Val})$,
        $f(\text{SoFar}, \text{Val}, \text{Next})$,
        $p(\text{Tail}, \text{Next}, \text{Answer})$.

In the specific case of the maximum, we obtain

maximum([Head|Tail], Max) :-
        maximum(Tail, Head, Max).

maximum([], Max, Max).
maximum([Head|Tail], Max0, Max) :-
        (Head > Max0 $\rightarrow$ maximum(Tail, Head, Max)
        ; /* Head $\leq$ Max0*/ maximum(Tail, Max0, Max)
).

A particularly interesting case is the average. We can define the average thus:

- $g(X) = /(X, 1)$

- $h(/(N, D)) = N/D$

- $f(/(N_1, D_1), /(N_2, D_2)) = /(N, D)$ where $N = N_1 + N_2$, $D = D_1 + D_2$.

As it happens, this f *does* have a left identity, namely $/(0, 0)$, but $h(e)$ is not defined, so we don't want to generate it. Working from this definition, and simplifying (so that we pass *two* accumulators and return *two* results from the auxiliary predicate) we obtain

average([Head|Tail], Average) :-
        average(Tail, Head, N, 1, D),
        Average is N/D.

average([], N, N, D, D).
average([Head|Tail], N0, N, D0, D) :-
        N1 is N0+Head,
        D1 is D0+1,
        average(Tail, N1, N, D1, D).

Now the "obvious" way of coding average/2 would be to write

```
average(List, Average) :-
        list_sum(List, Sum),
        length(List, Length),
        Average is Sum/Length.
```

By actual measurement, the "obvious" method is 28% slower, even with a Linear list_sum/2. And the less obvious method we obtained by instantiating this schema has no trouble with division by zero.

6.4.4   The "Logarithmic" method

The method I am about to describe is still based on "divide and conquer", but it divides the list in a different way. Instead of picking off one element at a time, we split the list in half. It is very similar to the "bisection" method for integer intervals. The schema uses an auxiliary predicate

```
p(N, List, Answer, Rest) :-
        length(N, Front),
        append(Front, Rest, List),
        p(Front, Answer).
```

that is, Answer is the result of applying g and f to the first N elements of List, and Rest is all but the first N elements of List. This way of splitting off N elements at a time completely avoids the construction of intermediate lists. To the best of my knowledge, David H. D. Warren was the first to use this device in Prolog.

```
p(List, Result) :-
        length(List, Length),
        p(Length, List, Answer, []),
        h(Answer, Result).
```

```
p(0, Rest, Answer, Rest) :- !,
        e(Answer).
p(1, [X|Rest], Answer, Rest) :- !,
        g(X, Answer).
p(N, List, Answer, Rest) :-
        /* N ≥ 2 */
        A is N // 2, p(A, List, X, Middle),
        Z is N - A,   p(Z, Middle, Y, Rest),
        f(X, Y, Answer).
```

The first thing you might notice about this schema is that it is not tail recursive. However, if the length of the list is N, the tower of recursive calls is only lg N deep.

Sometimes we can switch the last two goals of the last clause of $p/4$ around, but even so you still get a recursive tower lg N deep.

The second thing you might notice is that the first clause of $p/4$ is only used when $p([]$, Result) is called. So we can move that clause up:

p(List, Result) :-
        length(List, Length),
        (Length =:= 0, e(Answer)
        ;   Length > 0, p(Length, List, Answer, [])
        ),
        h(Answer, Result).

p(1, [X|Rest], Answer, Rest) :- !,
        g(X, Answer).
p(N, List, Answer, Rest) :-
        /* $N \geq 2$ */
        A is N // 2, p(A, List, X, Middle),
        Z is N - A, p(Z, Middle, Y, Rest),
        f(X, Y, Answer).

Another thing to notice is that predicates of this sort often work only one way around: List *must* be instantiated to a proper List or it won't work. In that case, since we have to look at the list anyway to discover its length, it is a really good idea to check that it is a proper list (length/2 does not do this). The auxiliary predicate is not affected. The top level predicate becomes

p(List, Result) :-
        length_of_proper_list(List, Length),
        !,
        (Length =:= 0 → e(Answer)
        ; p(Length, List, Answer, [])
        ),
        h(Answer, Result).
p(List, Result) :-
        format(user_error,
            ' N! First argument of $p/2$ is not\c
            a proper list. n! Goal: q n',
            [p(List,Result)]),
        fail.

where

```
length_of_proper_list(List, Length) :-
        nonvar(List),
        length_of_proper_list(List, 0, Length).
```

```
length_of_proper_list([], L, L).
length_of_proper_list([_|T], L0, L) :-
        nonvar(T),
        L1 is L0+1,
        length_of_proper_list(T, L1, L).
```

If there are other conditions which List must satisfy if $p/2$ is to work properly it might be a good idea to combine this check with the proper-list check.

To take the union of a list of sets, we do

```
ord_union(ListOfSets, Union) :-
        length(ListOfSets, Length),
        (    Length =:= 0 → Union = []
        ;    ord_union(Length, ListOfSets, Union, [])
        ).
```

```
ord_union(1, [Set|Sets], Set, Sets) :- !.
ord_union(N, Sets0, Union, Sets) :-
        A is N// 2, ord_union(A, Sets0, X, Sets1),
        Z is N-A,   ord_union(Z, Sets1, Y, Sets),
        ord_union(X, Y, Union). % in library(ordsets) already.
```

Now we see why the logarithmic method is useful. Taking the union of two disjoint sets of size A and B costs $O(A + B)$ time and space. So if we take the union of N disjoint sets, each having K members, the logarithmic method will take $O(K \times N \times \lg N)$ time and turn over a similar amount of space, whereas the linear method applied to this problem would take $O(K \times N \times (N + 1)/2)$ time and turn over a similar amount of space. This example is found in library(ordsets).

It is often a good idea to accelerate the auxiliary predicate by partially evaluating the N=2 case, when we get

```
p(2, [A,B|Rest], Answer, Rest) :- !,
        g(A, X),
        g(B, Y),
        f(X, Y, Answer).
```

to insert before the last clause. This is especially useful when g and f can be folded together, as we see in the case of sorting.

```
sort(List, Answer) :-
        length_of_proper_list(List, Length),
        (    Length =:= 0 → Answer = []
        ;    sort(Length, List, Answer, [])
        ).

sort(1, [X|Rest], [X], Rest) :- !.
sort(2, [X,Y|Rest], Answer, Rest) :- !,
        compare(R, X, Y),
        sort2(R, X, Y, Answer).
sort(N, List, Answer, Rest) :-
        /* N ≥ 3 */
        A is N // 2, sort(A, List, X, Middle),
        Z is N-A,    sort(Z, Middle, Y, Rest),
        merge(X, Y, Answer).

sort2(<, X, Y, [X,Y]).
sort2(>, X, Y, [Y,X]).
sort2(=, X, X, [X]).

merge(X, Y, Merged) :-
        /* covered elsewhere in the book */.
```

This gives us an $O(N \times \lg N)$ sorting routine, which after it been tidied up a bit is second best known sorting routine for Prolog. The best method is a variant of the natural merge. I have made a great many experiments, and no, "Quick"sort is *not* a good sorting routine for Prolog. It isn't a particularly good sorting routine for *anything* if the cost of a comparison is high relative to the cost of an exchange or of allocating a bit of workspace. Which is to say that "Quick"sort is ok for sorting telephone numbers, but not so good for sorting street addresses.

It is well known that if you want the sum of a sequence of floating point numbers to the highest accuracy you can get, the logarithmic method is the one to use. This is because there are at only $O(\lg N)$ steps between any of the inputs and the final result, so there are only $O(\lg N)$ opportunities for roundoff error, as opposed to the $O(N)$ opportunities in the linear method. But the logarithmic method has non-trivial overheads, so you would only use it if you really needed good results.

6.4.5 Odds and Evens

There is another way of dividing a list in two which is more natural in Prolog, and is useful when the function f that combines working values is commutative as well as associative. It can be used, for example, in forming the union of a list of sets, or the product of a list of polynomials. Instead of splitting a list into the first $\lfloor N/2 \rfloor$ and the last $\lceil N/2 \rceil$ elements, this method splits a list into odds and evens.

Splitting a list into odds and evens is easy enough, but falls foul of a subtlety of Prolog implementation:

```
%    split_odds_evens(?List, ?Odds, ?Evens)

split_odds_evens([], [], []).
split_odds_evens([O], [O], []).
split_odds_evens([O,E|L], [O|Os], [E|Es]) :-
        split_odds_evens(L, Os, Os).
```

The subtlety is that most Prolog systems index on the principal functor only. The principal functors of the first arguments in the three clauses are []/0, •/2, and •/2 respectively. This means that many Prolog systems will leave a choice point behind when this predicate reaches the end of a list with an odd number of elements. We could correct this by adding a cut to the second clause. Provided that either the first argument is proper or the last two arguments are both proper, we don't lose any solutions. Another approach works quite generally. That is to introduce a predicate for each level of indexing we need. As we need two levels of indexing here, we need two predicates.

```
split_odds_evens([], [], []).
split_odds_evens([O|L], [O|Os], Es) :-
        split_evens_odds(L, Os, Es).

split_evens_odds([], [], []).
split_evens_odds([E|L], Os, [E|Es]) :-
        split_odds_evens(L, Os, Es).
```

Now the pure version does one procedure call per element of the original list, while the version with one predicate and a cut does half as many procedure calls. Obviously the version with the cut must be faster. It may be obvious, but it isn't true. The pure version with the two predicates is consistently 30–40% faster in SICStus Prolog.

The generic scheme is easy to derive. Here is the result.

```
p([], Result) :-
        e(Answer),
        h(Answer, Result).
p([O|L], Result) :-
        p′(L, O, Answer),
        h(Answer, Result).
```

p'(L, O, Answer) :-
        split_evens_odds(L, Os, Es),
        p''(Es, O, Os, Answer).

p''([], O, [], Answer) :-
        g(O, Answer).
p''([E|Es], O, Os, Answer) :-
        p'(Es, E, EvenAnswer),
        p'(Os, O, OddAnswer),
        f(EvenAnswer, OddAnswer, Answer).

When we use this scheme to sum the elements of a list, we obtain

list_sum([], 0).
list_sum([O|L], Sum) :-
        list_sum_1(L, O, Sum).

list_sum_1(L, O, Sum) :-
        split_evens_odds(L, Os, Es),
        list_sum_2(Es, O, Os, Sum).

list_sum_2([], Sum, [], Sum).
list_sum_2([E|Es], O, Os, Sum) :-
        list_sum_1(Es, E, ESum),
        list_sum_1(Os, O, OSum),
        Sum is OSum+ESum.

You should *not* use the "Odds-and-Evens" technique for problems as simple as this. I timed Linear, Logarithmic, and Odds-and-Evens predicates for summing lists in SICStus Prolog, and the relative times were 1, 6, and 10 respectively. Now, the Odds-and-Evens method constructs N list cells when it splits a list of N elements, while the Logarithmic method constructs just $N/2$ list cells. As a rough guide, we expect a program that turns over twice as much memory to take twice as long, and this expectation is consistent with the observed ratio of 1.7. In this case, we expect the Linear method to be faster still, because it doesn't turn over any storage, and indeed it is the fastest method.

It is worth knowing that the Odds-and-Evens method exists, for three reasons.

- When the Logarithmic method is useful, so is Odds and Evens, and it doesn't need any cuts. So it provides an $N \lg N$ method in pure Horn clause logic.

- Odds and Evens combines the elements of the list in an order which is not left to right, so if you want to combine elements in some other order for debugging purposes you don't have to invent a new method.

- The Fast Fourier Transform is based on this method.

Exercise. *Write an FFT routine in Prolog. Assume that you are given a table* n_cos_sin/3 *such that*

$$n\_cos\_sin(N, C, S) \Leftrightarrow \exists K \ N = 2^K, C = \cos \frac{2\pi}{N}, S = \sin \frac{2\pi}{N}$$

Use the odds-and-evens method.

6.4.6   Summary

Four methods of producing a predicate with the desired behaviour were presented: the "Tower" method, the "Linear" method, the "Logarithmic" method, and the "Odds and Evens" method. The "Linear" method is the most generally useful of the three, but the "Logarithmic" method can sometimes be much more efficient.

6.5   Naming and Calculating Parts of Sequences

In this section we are going to define names for some parts of sequences, to develop generic predicates for computing these parts given suitable generators, and to develop instances of these predicates suitable for lists.

I claim that it is important to establish consistent naming conventions. This section shows what one such naming convention looks like. Most of the predicates will relate a Sequence of some *variety* with a Part of that sequence. All such predicates in this section look like

    variety_part(Sequence, Part)

except for the special case of lists, where we leave the variety 'list' implicit and just write

    part(List, Part)

This convention has several advantages.

First, by considering generic versions of the predicates, we ensure that we are using words like 'prefix' in the same sense.

Just by looking at such a predicate, we can tell exactly which data type it applies to (if no data type appears explicitly in the name, it applies to lists), and which part it computes. What is more, the order of the 'variety' and 'type' parts of the name is the same as the order of the corresponding arguments. When we see a goal interval_prefix(X, Y)

we know without having to read the code that X and Y are intervals and that X is the whole interval and Y is the prefix. An important part of this convention is that we always use the same name for the same type. For example, if some predicates in your program talk about 'integer's, it is sheer incompetence to have other predicates talking about 'int's.

You may, if you wish, invent a convention of your own which you like better. But it is difficult to underestimate the cognitive advantage of a consistent naming scheme. Here is an example drawn from the July 1989 draft of the ISO Prolog standard.

string(S) is true when S is bound to a string.

strlength(S, N) is true when N is the length of string S. It signals an error if S is not a string, which is a wee bit unfriendly.

concat(Sa, Sz, Saz) is the string version of 'append', but there is nothing in the name to indicate this. The Quintus library defines a similar predicate, but calls it string_append/3 to make its meaning obvious.

Str is a variable used in some of the predicate descriptions to refer to a *stream*, not a string!

This does not strike me as a consistent naming scheme. I for one find it very confusing. Is a 'str' a 'string' or is it a 'stream'?

When dealing with sequences, I find that it helps to keep a picture in mind of what goes where. The picture in this section is

```
Whole  =  Prefix  ⌢  Segment  ⌢  Suffix
       =  [Head]  ⌢  Tail
       =                _    ⌢  [Last]
```

6.5.1 Head

The *head* of a sequence $\langle x_1, \ldots, x_n \rangle$ is its first element x_1. In our generic representation of sequences, we have a predicate *variety*_done/1 which is true of empty sequences, and a predicate *variety*_next/3 which is true of non-empty sequences. Only non-empty sequences have a first element, so we'll have to use the 'next' predicate here. The generic code is just

```
variety_head(Sequence, Head) :-
        variety_next(Head, Sequence, _).
```

When we apply this scheme to lists, we get

head([Head|_], Head).

6.5.2   Tail

The *tail* of a sequence $\langle x_1, x_2, \ldots, x_n \rangle$ is the sequence $\langle x_2, \ldots, x_n \rangle$ of elements following the first. As with heads, only non-empty sequences have tails. The generic code is

*variety*_tail(Sequence, Tail) :-
        *variety*_next(_, Sequence, Tail).

When we apply this scheme to lists, we get

tail([_|Tail], Tail).

Note that the head and tail together give us all the information that the 'next' predicate provides. We could have based on sequence abstraction on three predicates

*variety*_done(S) S is an empty sequence

*variety*_head(S, H) S is a non-empty sequence whose first element is H

*variety*_tail(S, T) S is a non-empty sequence whose tail is T

instead of the two ('done' and 'next') that we are actually using. But the two-predicate approach is closer to the two-constructor model of lists, and often results in less recomputation.

6.5.3   Element

An *element* of a sequence $\langle x_1, \ldots, x_n \rangle$ is any one of the elements x_i. Elements of a sequence are often called members of it. However, we can't use 'member' as a generic sequence part name, because the common predicate member/2 does not follow the argument order convention that we have established for sequence parts. The generic code is

*variety*_element(Sequence, Element) :-
        *variety*_next(Head, Sequence, Tail),
        (Element = Head
        ;   *variety*_element(Tail, Element)
).

When we apply this scheme to lists, we get

```
element([Head|Tail], Element) :-
        (       Element = Head
        ;       element(Tail, Element)
        ).
```

This is just member/2 with the arguments switched, but that is no small change. Perhaps the most important thing about the change is that we obtained a "member" predicate which conformed to the generic sequence part interface by adding a new predicate, *not* by changing the interface of member/2 and breaking existing code. When I wrote this section, I discovered afterwards that I had already used "*variety_element*" in parts written several months before. The value of an interface convention can be seen in this fact: the old version had *exactly* the interface described here, so I didn't need to change the old text.

6.5.4   Prefix

A sequence P is a *prefix* of a sequence PS if there is another sequence S such that $PS = P \frown S$. Of course this is just a special case of 'append':

```
variety_prefix(Sequence, Prefix) :-
        variety_append(Prefix, _, Sequence).
```

We can expand this out by unfolding 'append':

```
variety_prefix(Sequence, Prefix) :-
        variety_done(Prefix).
variety_prefix(Sequence0, Prefix0) :-
        variety_next(Head, Sequence0, Sequence1),
        variety_next(Head, Prefix0,   Prefix1),
        variety_prefix(Sequence1, Prefix1).
```

Applied to lists, with the prefix argument switched to the front to exploit first-argument indexing, this scheme yields

```
prefix(List, Prefix) :-
        prefix_1(Prefix, List).

prefix_1([], List).
prefix_1([Head|Prefix], [Head|List]) :-
        prefix_1(Prefix, List).
```

If Prefix is a proper list, prefix/2 has at most one solution. If Prefix is a variable, and List is a proper list with N elements, prefix/2 has $N + 1$ solutions, and after finding them is sure to terminate. If both arguments are partial lists, prefix/2 will keep on guessing increasingly long answers.

A sequence P is a *proper prefix* of a sequence PS if there is a non-empty sequence S such that $PS = P \frown S$. That is, P is a prefix of PS, but it is not the whole of PS.

It is unfortunate that we are using the word 'proper' in two senses. When we speak of a "proper $\mathcal{T}hing$", we are talking about a recursively defined term which is sufficiently instantiated that a predicate which walks over it according to its type is sure to terminate. When we speak of a "proper $\mathcal{P}art$ of" something, we are talking about a $\mathcal{P}art$ of the thing which is smaller than the thing it is part of. The context always makes it clear which sense is intended: we speak of "a proper list" but "a proper prefix *of* X".

As before this is just a special case of 'append', except that we have to check that S is not empty, which is true precisely when 'next' accepts it.

*variety*_proper_prefix(Sequence, Prefix) :-
        *variety*_append(Prefix, Suffix, Sequence),
        *variety*_next(_, Suffix, _).

We can expand this out by unfolding 'append':

*variety*_proper_prefix(Sequence, Prefix) :-
        *variety*_done(Prefix),
        *variety*_next(_, Sequence, _).
*variety*_proper_prefix(Sequence, Prefix) :-
        *variety*_next(Head, Sequence0, Sequence1),
        *variety*_next(Head, Prefix0,   Prefix1),
        *variety*_proper_prefix(Sequence1, Prefix1).

When this scheme is applied to lists, it yields

proper_prefix(List, Prefix) :-
        proper_prefix_1(Prefix, List).

proper_prefix_1([], [_|_]).
proper_prefix_1([Head|Prefix], [Head|List]) :-
        proper_prefix_1(Prefix, List).

Noting that *variety*_next/3 is being called in several places, we might consider moving it.

*variety*_proper_prefix(Sequence, Prefix) :-
          *variety*_next(Head, Sequence, Sequence1),
          *variety*_proper_prefix_1(Prefix, Head, Sequence1).

*variety*_proper_prefix_1(Prefix, _, _) :-
          *variety*_done(Prefix).
*variety*_proper_prefix_1(Prefix0, Head, Sequence0) :-
          *variety*_next(Head, Prefix0, Prefix1),
          *variety*_next(Next, Sequence0, Sequence1),
          *variety*_proper_prefix_1(Prefix1, Next, Sequence1).

When this scheme is applied to lists, it yields

proper_prefix([Head|Tail], Prefix) :-
          proper_prefix_1(Prefix, Head, Tail).

proper_prefix_1([], _, _).
proper_prefix_1([Head|Prefix], Head, [Next|Tail]) :-
          proper_prefix_1(Prefix, Next, Tail).

I call the technique I have used here *lagging*. The idea is that you represent a
sequence $\langle x_1, x_2, \ldots, x_n \rangle$ by a pair of arguments representing x_1 and $\langle x_2, \ldots, x_n \rangle$.
We can lag by any fixed degree; for example we could pass around 4 arguments
representing x_1, x_2, x_3, and $\langle x_4, \ldots, x_n \rangle$, and that would be lagging by 3. One
reason for using lagging is that you want an induction to stop when a list has k
elements left; in that case lagging by k elements lets you write an induction which
stops when the lagged list has 0 elements left. As an example, consider the problem
of finding the last element of a list. That is, we want the induction to stop when
the list has 1 element. We could write

last(Last, [Last]).
last(Last, [X1,X2|Xs]) :-
          last(Last, [X2|Xs]).

but many Prolog systems would not execute that efficiently, as their indexing sys-
tems, if they checked the second argument at all, would put [_] and [_,_|_] in the
same "bucket" because they have the same principal functor. Instead, we can lag
by 1, writing

last(Last, [Head|Tail]) :-
          last_1(Tail, Head, Last).

last_1([], Last, Last).
last_1([Head|Tail], _, Last) :-
      last_1(Tail, Head, Last).

6.5.5 Suffix

A sequence S is a *suffix* of a sequence PS if there is a sequence P such that
$PS = P \frown S$. This is just the opposite of a prefix: if $PS = P \frown S$ then P must be
a prefix of PS and S must be a suffix of PS. The generic code is

*variety*_suffix(Sequence, Sequence).
*variety*_suffix(Sequence0, Suffix) :-
      *variety*_next(_, Sequence0, Sequence1),
      *variety*_suffix(Sequence1, Suffix).

When this scheme is applied to lists, it yields

suffix(List, List).
suffix([_|List], Suffix) :-
      suffix(List, Suffix).

    The 'prefix' predicates would terminate if either argument was proper. The 'suf-
fix' predicates, however, require that the first (whole sequence) argument must be
proper. That is because, for any fixed suffix S, there are infinitely many sequences
PS having S as a suffix, and the sequence manipulation predicates we have are
biassed in a left-to-right direction. We can easily represent a sequence with an as
yet undetermined suffix (just leave a variable there), but we cannot represent a
sequence with an as yet undetermined prefix.
    A sequence S is a *proper suffix* of a sequence PS if there is a non-empty sequence
P such that $PS = P \frown S$. That is, S is a suffix of PS and it is not the whole of
PS.
    This one is easy. All we have to do is throw away the first element of PS and
then S is a proper suffix of PS if it is a suffix of the tail of PS.

*variety*_proper_suffix(Sequence0, Suffix) :-
      *variety*_next(_, Sequence0, Sequence1),
      *variety*_suffix(Sequence1, Suffix).

When applied to lists, this scheme yields

proper_suffix([_|List], Suffix) :-
      suffix(List, Suffix).

6.5.6   Segment

Unfortunately, terminology here is rather confusing. The usual definition of "sub-sequence" is that a sequence $S = \langle S_1, \ldots, S_k \rangle$ is a subsequence of a sequence $B = \langle B_1, \ldots, B_n \rangle$ if $n \geq k$ and there is a strictly increasing function f such that

$$\forall_{i=1}^{k} S_i = B_{f(i)}$$

For example, [1,3,4,9] is a subsequence of [1,2,3,4,5,6,7,8,9].

The DEC-10 Prolog and Quintus Prolog libraries contain predicates which recognise or generate subsequences in this sense. For example, subseq/3 splits a list into two complementary subsequences:

```
subseq([], [], []).
subseq([Head|Tail], Sbsq, [Head|Cmpl]) :-
        subseq(Tail, Sbsq, Cmpl).
subseq([Head|Tail], [Head|Sbsq], Cmpl) :-
        subseq(Tail, Sbsq, Cmpl).
```

This can obviously be generalised to other kinds of sequences, but is just as obviously very costly, because a sequence of length N has 2^N subsequences.

Another way that a sequence can be part of another is to be a prefix of a suffix of it. We say that a sequence M is a *segment* of a sequence PMS if there are (possibly empty) sequences P and S such that $PMS = P \frown M \frown S$. This is just another variation on 'append':

```
variety_segment(Sequence, Segment) :-
        variety_append(_, Suffix, Sequence),
        variety_append(Segment, _, Suffix).
```

We can expand this out and use the earlier definition of 'prefix' to obtain

```
variety_segment(Sequence, Segment) :-
        variety_prefix(Sequence, Segment).
variety_segment(Sequence0, Segment) :-
        variety_next(_, Sequence0, Sequence1),
        variety_segment(Sequence1, Segment).
```

When applied to lists, this scheme yields

```
segment(List, Segment) :-
        prefix_1(Segment, List).
segment([_|List], Segment) :-
        segment(List, Segment).
```

This code has the same shape as 'suffix', so requires that the List argument be proper. It has one rather unpleasant property: the solution Segment=[] is found $N + 1$ times, where List has N elements. It turns out to be possible to avoid that. What we have to do is to ensure that non-empty prefixes of non-empty lists are not generated. The code for lists is

```
segment([], []).
segment([Head|Tail], [Head|Segment]) :-
        prefix_1(Segment, Tail).
segment([_|Tail], Segment) :-
        segment(Tail, Segment).
```

which generalises to

```
variety_segment(Sequence, Segment) :-
        variety_done(Sequence),
        variety_done(Segment).
variety_segment(Sequence0, Segment0) :-
        variety_next(Head, Sequence0, Sequence1),
        variety_next(Head, Segment0, Segment1),
        variety_prefix(Sequence1, Segment1).
variety_segment(Sequence0, Segment) :-
        variety_next(_, Sequence0, Sequence1),
        variety_segment(Sequence1, Segment).
```

I actually wrote this version of 'segment' as I was writing this section of the text. It's important to realise what abstraction has bought me: I solved the "too many []s" problem at the level of lists (the trick which finally worked was to concentrate on when I *did* want to yield the Segment=[] solution; in earlier unsuccessful attempts I had concentrated on when I *didn't* want it). That immediately generalised to other sequences. I now know, for example, how to enumerate all the closed intervals contained in a given interval of integers, enumerating each interval precisely once. I have never written that predicate, but when I need it I won't have to think about it.

A *proper segment* of a sequence is a segment of it which is not the whole sequence. The generic code for that is

```
variety_proper_segment(Sequence, Segment) :-
        variety_proper_prefix(Sequence, Segment).
variety_proper_segment(Sequence0, Segment) :-
        variety_next(_, Sequence0, Sequence1),
        variety_segment(Sequence1, Segment).
```

When applied to lists, this scheme yields

proper_segment(List, Segment) :-
       proper_prefix(List, Segment).
proper_segment([_|Tail], Segment) :-
       segment(Tail, Segment).

    Getting the names of predicates like these right can be hard. The Quintus Prolog library calls 'segment' sublist, which is a very good name for segments of lists, but unfortunately it doesn't generalise to other types of sequences, as it suggests that the segment is returned as a list. There is no reason why we couldn't have two families of predicates: a 'segment' family where the sequence and segment were the same type, and a 'sublist' family where the segment was always a list. The generic code for that would be

*variety*_sublist(Sequence, []) :-
       *variety*_done(Sequence).
*variety*_sublist(Sequence0, [Head|Sublist]) :-
       *variety*_next(Head, Sequence0, Sequence1),
       *variety*_prefix_1(Sublist, Sequence1).
*variety*_sublist(Sequence0, Sublist) :-
       *variety*_next(_,   Sequence0, Sequence1),
       *variety*_sublist(Sequence1, Sublist).

*variety*_prefix_1([], Sequence).
*variety*_prefix_1([Head—Prefix], Sequence0) :-
       *variety*_next(Head, Sequence0, Sequence1),
       *variety*_prefix_1(Prefix, Sequence1).

6.5.7 Summary

In this section we settled on names for parts of sequences: heads, tails, elements, last elements, prefixes, suffixes, segments, proper prefixes, proper suffixes, and proper segments, and saw how they could be defined for any sequence type. It is useful to design interface conventions like this so that you can use predicates that conform to your conventions (or write additional predicates that conform to them) without having to remember or invent the argument order for individual predicates.

    In the Quintus Prolog library, some other consistent names are used:

- is_*variety*; recognise a member of a data type

- *variety*_size; report the number of elements or associations

- *variety_fetch*; select a stored value according to a Key

- *variety_store*; create a new thing with an additional or changed association

- portray_*variety*; pretty-print a member of a data type

- *variety_to_other*; unidirectional conversion

- *variety_other*; bidirectional conversion

When you have over 900 predicates in your library, you *have* to structure it somehow!

6.6 Tree traversal

Suppose that we have a binary tree data structure:

```
:- type tree(Label) ⟶
        empty
    |   node(Label,tree(Label),tree(Label)).
```

and that we want to enumerate the labels of such a tree.

Following [Knuth, 2.3.1], we define preorder, inorder, and postorder traversal. All of them are left-to-right traversals; the question is whether a node's label is visited before, between, or after the traversals of its subtrees. In Prolog:

```
preorder_list(empty) ⟶ [].
preorder_list(node(Label,Left,Right)) ⟶
        [Label],
        preorder_list(Left),
        preorder_list(Right).

inorder_list(empty) ⟶ [].
inorder_list(node(Label,Left,Right)) ⟶
        inorder_list(Left),
        [Label],
        inorder_list(Right).

postorder_list(empty) ⟶ [].
postorder_list(node(Label,Left,Right)) ⟶
        postorder_list(Left),
        postorder_list(Right),
        [Label].
```

When we have a set of grammar rules which converts a data structure to a list, it is very easy to turn them into a set of clauses which provide a backtracking traversal of the data structure. Consider each grammar rule in turn. Let it have the form

$variety$_list(Args) $\longrightarrow$
       { $Guard$ },
       $B_1, \ldots, B_n$.

This turns into a clause with an n-way disjunction:

$variety$_element(Args, X) :-
    $Guard$,
    ($B_1'(X)$
    ; $\ldots$
    ; $B_n'(X)$
).

if B_i is	then $B_i'(X)$ is
[]	fail
[T]	$X = T$
$nt(\alpha)$	$nt(\alpha, X)$

where, in the last rule, nt is to be translated the same way. Applying this transformation to inorder_list//1, we obtain

inorder_element(empty, X) :-
    (fail
).
inorder_element(node(Label,Left,Right), X) :-
    (inorder_element(Left, X)
    ;   X = Label
    ;   inorder_element(Right, X)
).

where the first clause simplifies away.

   To illustrate what we do when there is a guard, suppose that the labels of a tree are integers, and that when the label is negative we want preorder, when it is positive, we want postorder, and when it is zero, we do not want the label at all.

funny_list(empty) $\longrightarrow$ [].

```
funny_list(node(Label,Left,Right)) ⟶
        { Label < 0, ! },
        [Label],
        funny_list(Left),
        funny_list(Right).
funny_list(node(Label,Left,Right)) ⟶
        { Label > 0, ! },
        funny_list(Left),
        funny_list(Right),
        [Label].
funny_list(node(0,Left,Right)) ⟶
        funny_list(Left),
        funny_list(Right).
```

This transforms to

```
funny_element(node(Label,Left,Right), X) :-
        Label < 0, !,
        (    X = Label
        ;    funny_element(Left, X)
        ;    funny_element(Right, X)
        ).
funny_element(node(Label,Left,Right), X) :-
        Label > 0, !,
        (    funny_element(Left, X)
        ;    funny_element(Right, X)
        ;    X = Label
        ).
funny_element(node(0,Left,Right), X) :-
        (    funny_element(Left, X)
        ;    funny_element(Right, X)
        ).
```

This is not a general transformation. If the original set of grammar rules bind anything other than the list segment they are to construct, it obviously *can't* work: such a binding will not be preserved by the transformed version. Further, if the original set of rules is not logically determinate, the enumerator obtained by writing

```
        variety_list(Structure, List),
        member(Element, List)
```

will first pick one of the alternatives for the entire List, and then enumerate the
elements of that List in order, while the

> *variety*_element(Structure, Element)

version will mix up guessing the List with enumerating the Elements. Let's look at
a particular example.

```
some_list(empty) ⟶ [].
some_list(node(Label,Left,Right)) ⟶
        [Label],
        some_list(Left).
some_list(node(Label,Left,Right)) ⟶
            some_list(Right),
            [Label].
```

Consider the goal

```
?- some_list(node(4,node(2,node(1,empty,empty),
                         node(3,empty,empty)),
                    node(6,node(5,empty,empty),
                         node(7,empty,empty))), List, []),
     member(X, List).
```

There are 8 solutions for List (really 4, each reported twice) each having 3 elements,
so the solutions we get for X are

4; 2; 1; 4; 2; 1; 4; 3; 2; 4; 3; 2;
6; 5; 4; 6; 5; 4; 7; 6; 4; 7; 6; 4.

Now suppose we ask

```
?- some_element(node(4,node(2,node(1,empty,empty),
                           node(3,empty,empty)),
                      node(6,node(5,empty,empty),
                           node(7,empty,empty))), X).
```

where

```
some_element(node(Label,Left,Right), X) :-
    (    X = Label
    ;    some_element(Left, X)
    ).
some_element(node(Label,Left,Right), X) :-
    (    some_element(Right, X)
    ;    X = Label
    ).
```

This time the answers are

(4; (2; (1; 1); (3; 3); 2); (6; (5; 5); (7; 7); 6); 4).

where the parentheses have been added to make the pattern clearer. We haven't even the same number of solutions as the original (14 instead of 24), let alone the same order. The transformed backtracking version is only equivalent to the original list version when the list version is logically determinate. We *have* preserved logical equivalence:

> some_list(Structure, List),
> member(Element, List)

is to be read as "there is a List such that Structure is mapped to List and Element occurs in List", and this is indeed true of each Element reported by

> some_element(Structure, Element)

6.7 Selecting a subsequence

The Quintus Prolog library includes some "higher-order" predicates for selecting subsets from lists, in the file library(more_maps). Two of them are include/3 and exclude/3:

```
%    include(+P:void(T), +Xs:list(T), ?Ys:list(T))
%    true when Ys is [X in Xs such that P(X) is true]

include(P, Xs, Ys) :-
        include1(Xs, Ys, P).

include1([], [], _).
include1([X|Xs], Ys, P) :-
        ¬ call(P, X),
        !,
        include(Xs, Ys, P).
include1([X|Xs], [X|Ys], P) :-
        /* P(X) is true */
        include1(Xs, Ys, P).

%    exclude(+P:void(T), +Xs:list(T), ?Zs:list(T))
%    true when Zs is [X in Xs such that P(X) is false]
```

```
exclude(P, Xs, Zs) :-
        exclude1(Xs, Zs, P).

exclude1([], [], P).
exclude1([X|Xs], Zs, P) :-
        ¬ call(P, X),
        !,
        Zs = [X|Zs1],
        exclude1(Xs, Zs1, P).
exclude1([X|Xs], Zs, P) :-
        /* P(X) is true */
        exclude1(Xs, Zs, P).
```

You may be curious about the form of these predicates. Each has an interface predicate where the meta-argument P comes first. This is a convention that the library generally follows. It's actually an historical accident, but it is a good convention none the less. We want to get P out of the way in order to use first-argument indexing, something we wouldn't need to do if we were allowed to index on other arguments. It would also be a good idea to validate P at this point; the latest version of the library doesn't do that, but a later version may.

Since we need to know whether P(X) is definitely true or definitely false, we need negation as failure to be sound, so each P(X) should be ground. (Well, there might be existentially quantified variables.) That being the case, no call(P,X) has a right to make any bindings, so it shouldn't make any *logical* difference whether we write what we did for exclude1/3 or whether we write instead

```
exclude1([], [], P).
exclude1([X|Xs], Zs, P) :-
        call(P, X),
        !,
        exclude1(Xs, Zs, P).
exclude1([X|Xs], [X|Zs1], P) :-
        exclude1(Xs, Zs1, P).
```

However, there *is* an implementation-level difference: some of the calls to P(X) may succeed, and may leave large amounts of garbage lying around on the stacks having done so. The latter version will leave that garbage there, while the actual code will reclaim it at once. There is a psychological difference too: with the latter version you might be tempted to exploit the fact that P(X) might sometimes bind variables, while in the actual code both include/3 and exclude/3 are consistent in making this impossible.

Finally, some of the unifications have been made explicit and moved down below the cuts in order to make these predicates steadfast: if you predict what Ys or Zs will be and guess wrong, you can't trick them into accepting an incorrect answer.

This is rather ugly. If you know definitely whether P(X) is true or false, you can instead write a function f(X,T) which classifies X. Suppose you have a function f(X,T) which classifies an X into one of k classes $c_1, \ldots, c_k$. Then you can write

```
partition([], [], ..., []).
partition([X|Xs], L₁, ..., Lₖ) :-
        f(X, T),
        partition1(T, L₁, ..., Lₖ, X, Xs).

partition1(c₁, [X|L₁], ..., Lₖ, X, Xs) :-
        partition(Xs, L₁, ..., Lₖ).
⋮
partition1(cₖ, L₁, ..., [X|Lₖ], X, Xs) :-
        partition(Xs, L₁, ..., Lₖ).
```

Suppose we have a generator

```
make_variety(+Args, -State)
variety_done(+State)
variety_next(?Element, +State0, ?State)
```

As we saw, we can turn this into a list by doing

```
variety_to_list(State0, []) :-
        variety_done(State0).
variety_to_list(State0, [X|Xs]) :-
        variety_next(X, State0, State1),
        variety_to_list(State1, Xs).
```

and we can turn it into an enumerator by doing

```
variety_element(State0, Element) :-
        variety_next(X, State0, State1),
        (    Element = X
        ;    variety_element(State1, Element)
        ).
```

Now suppose we have a predicate p, and we want the subsequence of elements satisfying p. We can easily adapt the list version:

```
variety_to_p_list(State0, []) :-
        variety_done(State0).
variety_to_p_list(State0, Xs) :-
        variety_next(X, State0, State1),
        (    p(X) → Xs = [X|Xs1]
        ;    /* ¬p(X) */ Xs = Xs1
        ),
        variety_to_p_list(State1, Xs1).
```

Here, every time that the basic version would include X in the result, the subsequence version checks whether $p(X)$ and includes X only if that test succeeds. The enumerator version is even easier to adapt:

```
variety_p_element(State0, Element) :-
        variety_next(X, State0, State1),
        (    p(X), Element = X
        ;    variety_p_element(State1, Element)
        ).
```

But can we make a generator version? Yes.

```
make_p_variety(Args, State) :-
        make_variety(Args, S),
        find_p_element(S, State).
```

```
find_p_element(S, done) :-
        variety_done(S),
        !.
find_p_element(S0, State) :-
        next_variety(X, S0, S1),
        (    p(X) → State = next(X,S1)
        ;    find_p_element(S1, State)
        ).
```

```
p_variety_done(done).
```

```
p_variety_next(X, next(X,S0), S1) :-
        find_p_element(S0, S1).
```

Let's see how this works in a particular case. Recall the example of an integer interval:

make_interval(Low, High, i(Low,High)) :-
      integer(Low), integer(High).

interval_done(i(Low,High)) :-
      Low > High.

interval_next(Low, i(Low,High), i(Low1,High)) :-
      plus(Low, 1, Low1),
      Low ≤ High.

Suppose we want to select the even elements of an interval. Following the scheme above, and simplifying, we get

make_even_interval(Low, High, State) :-
      integer(Low), integer(High),
      find_even_element(Low, High, State).

find_even_element(Low, High, State) :-
      (Low > High → State = done
      ;   plus(Low, 1, Low1),
         (Low mod 2 =:= 0 →
            State = next(Low,Low1,High)
         ;   find_even_element(Low1, High, State)
)
).

even_interval_done(done).

even_interval_next(X, next(X,Low,High), State) :-
      find_even_element(Low, High, State).

This obviously isn't an ideal way of generating even integers in an interval. For simple cases like this you can do quite well by the light of nature. The point is that this approach works even when the underlying generator is much more complicated.

    This isn't the only way of defining generators. If you read chapter 8 of Timothy Budd's *A Little SmallTalk*, you'll find another approach. If you read the CLU or Alphard manuals, you'll find others again. They are all much the same in concept, and I don't claim that the version here has any advantage other than looking as much like a list as possible. In particular, we can regard a list as a state of a generator, and define

list_done([]).

list_next(Head, [Head|Tail], Tail).

The arguments of the 'next' operation were ordered to make it as easy as possible to use generators in grammar rules as if they were lists.

6.8   Prefixes

If we are given a sequence $s = \langle x_1, \ldots, x_n \rangle$ and a predicate $p(x)$, we define

$$s \ \textbf{while} \ p = \langle x_1, \ldots, x_m \rangle$$

where

$$(\forall 1 \leq i \leq m) \ p(x_i) \text{ and } (i = n \text{ or } \neg p(x_{i+1}))$$

That is, keep accepting elements of s as long as they satisfy p and then stop, whether any later elements satisfy p or not.

6.8.1   Prefixes of lists

We can calculate $Ys = Xs$ while p by calling

$$p\_prefix(Xs, Ys)$$

where

p_prefix([], []).
p_prefix([$X|$_], P) :-
          $\neg p(X)$,
          !,
          $P = []$.
p_prefix([$X|Xs$], [$Y|Ys$]) :-
          p_prefix(Xs, Ys).

The obvious code would have been

$*p$_prefix([$X|Xs$], [$X|Ys$]) :-
          $p(X)$,
          !,
          $*p$_prefix(Xs, Ys).
$*p$_prefix(_, []).

That, however, has the disadvantage that it is not steadfast. The version recommended before works rather like include/3.

   If you have a function $f(X, T)$ which classifies Xs into two classes (for argument's sake '+' and '-') you can compute a prefix with pure code:

$f\_\text{prefix}([],[]).$
$f\_\text{prefix}([X|Xs],Ys) :-$
    $f(X,T),$
    $f\_\text{prefix}(T,Ys,X,Xs).$

$f\_\text{prefix}(-,[],\_,\_)$
$f\_\text{prefix}(+,[X|Ys],X,Xs) :-$
    $f\_\text{prefix}(Xs,Ys).$

For example, suppose we have a list of terms known to be in ascending order (perhaps they are the result of sort/2 or setof/3), and we want to select all the elements x @< T.

smaller_prefix$([],\_,[]).$
smaller_prefix$([X|Xs],T,Ys) :-$
    compare$(R,X,T),$
    smaller_prefix$(R,T,Ys,X,Xs).$

smaller_prefix$(>,\_,[],\_,\_).$
smaller_prefix$(=,\_,[],\_,\_).$
smaller_prefix$(<,T,[X|Ys],X,Xs) :-$
    smaller_prefix$(Xs,T,Ys).$

6.8.2   Generators

We can stop a generator early by making its termination condition true. We have

make_prefix(Args, State) :-
    make_sequence(Args, State).

prefix_done(State) :-
    sequence_done(State).
prefix_done(State) :-
    sequence_next(X, State, _),
    $\neg p(X).$

prefix_next(X, State0, State) :-
    sequence_next(X, State0, State),
    $p(X).$

6.8.3 Enumerators

Suppose we have a goal $\epsilon(x)$ which enumerates the elements of a sequence, and we want the p-prefix of that sequence. In a correctly implemented Prolog system, it is just possible to do this. We introduce a new predicate p_ϵ thus:

$p\_\epsilon(X)$:-
$\qquad \epsilon(X)$,
$\qquad (\quad p(X) \rightarrow$ true
$\qquad ; \qquad$!, fail
$\qquad)$.

The point is that disjunctions are transparent to cuts, so that we have here a *conditional* cut which is executed as soon as an X is found for which $p(X)$ fails. If disjunctions were not transparent to cuts, this would not work.

6.8.4 Prefixes determined by length

In the Quintus Prolog library, you will find a predicate

append_length(A, Z, AZ, N) $\Longleftrightarrow$
$\qquad$ append(A, Z, AZ) &
$\qquad$ length(A, N).

The actual definition goes to some trouble to ensure that it works in as many modes as possible. For example, if you call it with all arguments unbound, it will enumerate the solutions

$$A = [], AZ = Z, N = 0 ;$$
$$A = [\_1], AZ = [\_1|Z], N = 1 ;$$
$$A = [\_1, \_2], AZ = [\_1, \_2|Z], N = 2 ;$$
$$\vdots$$

In particular, if A is proper or N is known, it is determinate.

Exercise. *Write your own version of this predicate without looking at the version in the library.*

Abstractly, the predicate is $AZ = A \frown Z$ & $\#A = N$. Note that the test is $\#A = N$, not $\#A \leq N$.

We cannot tell whether a sequence represented by a generator has enough elements to satisfy a test like this unless we actually try to generate the first N elements. We can convert a generator into one which generates *at most* N elements easily enough:

make_bounded_*variety*(Args, N, b(N,State)) :-
    integer(N), $N \geq 0$,
    make_*variety*(Args, State).

bounded_*variety*_done(b(0,_)).
bounded_*variety*_done(b(N,State)) :-
    $N > 0$,
    *variety*_done(State).

bounded_*variety*_next(X, b(N0,State0), b(N,State)) :-
    succ(N, N0), % $N0 \geq 1$
    *variety*_next(X, State0, State).

We cannot place either an exact limit or an upper bound on an enumerator. Not in general, that is. Some Prolog systems (such as IBM's VM/Prolog) have a version of 'call' with an additional argument which reports the number of times it has succeeded. If you have a Prolog system embedded in some other language such as Lisp or Pop, you can probably implement that yourself. Assume that the host language can be made to provide the following functions:

    consref(N)   make a box and put N in it
    inccont(B)   increment and return the contents of B

Then you can write

counted_call(Goal, Count) :-
    consref(0, Box),
    call(Goal),
    inccont(Box, Count).

Similarly, you can put a bound on the number of solutions:

bounded_call(Goal, Bound) :-
    consref(0, Box),
    call(Goal),
    inccont(Box, Count),
    (Count < Bound $\rightarrow$ true
    ;   /* Bound reached, so */ !
).

Of course, this relies on the host language having a garbage collector. You could do something like this with C as the host language, using `malloc()` to allocate a box, but there is no place to put a call to `free()`. (Don't forget the effect of a cut in the caller!)

Warning. *Don't do this, even if your host language lets you.*

If you have an application where you think you have a use for something like this, consider using a bounded generator, and basing an enumerator on that if necessary.

6.9 Concatenation

Concatenation is an associative (but not commutative) operation with identity the empty sequence. Technically, the algebra $(T^*, \frown, \langle\rangle)$ is a *monoid*. It is useful to bear this in mind, because very often it pays to rearrange concatenations. For example, suppose we want to compute $s_1 \frown \cdots \frown s_n$. Two obvious ways of arranging this computation are

$$s_1 \frown (s_2 \frown \cdots s_n)$$

and

$$(s_1 \frown \cdots s_{n-1}) \frown s_n$$

If the sequences are represented as lists and we use append/3, the first arrangement will cost $\sum_{i=1}^{n-1} \#s_i$ cons cells, while the second arrangement will turn over $\sum_{i=1}^{n-1} (n-i).\#s_i$ cons cells. Clearly the first arrangement is much better, for lists. If we used strings, however, the first arrangement would turn over $\sum_{i=1}^{n} i.\#s_i$ bytes, while the second arrangement would turn over $\sum_{i=1}^{n} (n+1-i).\#s_i$ bytes. We see that lists admit a much more efficient implementation of concatenation. As is well known, if we are content to generate list *differences* and then paste them together, we can concatenate sequences with no wasted storage turnover at all. (So much for strings!)

Suppose we want to append $n > 2$ lists together. We see from the previous paragraph that the most economical way to do this is

```
append_n(Xs_1, ..., Xs_n, Ys_1) :-
      Ys_n = Xs_n,
      append(Xs_{n-1}, Ys_n, Ys_{n-1}),
      ⋮
      append(Xs_i, Ys_{i+1}, Ys_i),
      ⋮
      append(Xs_1, Ys_2, Ys_1).
```

However, that is not the best way to order the conjuncts. If Ys_1 is a proper list, there are obviously only finitely many solutions for the other arguments. But if any Xs_i is a partial list, the code as written above will try ever longer guesses for Xs_i. The right order is

$$\text{append\_}n(Xs_1, \ldots, Xs_n, Ys_1) :-$$
$$\text{append}(Xs_1, Ys_2, Ys_1),$$
$$\vdots$$
$$\text{append}(Xs_i, Ys_{i+1}, Ys_i),$$
$$\vdots$$
$$\text{append}(Xs_{n-1}, Xs_n, Ys_{n-1}).$$

This version is sure to terminate if either all of the Xs_i are proper lists or Ys_1 is a proper list. For example, the query

?- append3(A, B, C, [1,2]).

where

append3(A, B, C, ABC) :-
        append(A, BC, ABC),
        append(B, C, BC).

has the solutions

```
A = [],      B = [],      C = [1,2]  ;
A = [],      B = [1],     C = [2]    ;
A = [],      B = [1,2],   C = []     ;
A = [1],     B = [],      C = [2]    ;
A = [1],     B = [1,2],   C = []     ;
A = [1,2],   B = [],      C = []     .
```

Note that to append n lists together like this, the first $n-1$ of them have to be proper. If they are not proper before you call append$n/(n+1)$ they will be afterwards. This method does not let you concatenate sequences whose length is still unknown.

Sometimes, instead of computing something, it is just as good to return a promise to compute it. For example, instead of appending two lists A and B, you might construct a data structure $+(A, B)$. For example, suppose you use the following predicates to access sequences:

tree_done([]).
tree_done($A + B$) :-
        tree_done(A), tree_done(B).

tree_next(Head, Tree0, Tree) :-
        tree_cons(Tree0, Head, Tree).

tree_cons($[H|T], H, T$).
tree_cons($A + B, H, T$) :-
        tree_cons(A, H, T, B).

tree_cons($[], H, T, B$) :-
        tree_cons(B, H, T).
tree_cons($[H|R], H, R + B, B$).
tree_cons($X + Y, H, T, B$) :-
        tree_cons($X, H, T, Y + B$).

Then as far as your program is concerned, $A + B$ is just as good as $A \frown B$; it represents exactly the same sequence.

If you push this technique much further, your data structures start looking like a miniature programming language. Fine! In another chapter we discuss the use of miniature interpreters.

Concatenation is a particularly good operation to avoid. I have seen a program written in Prolog which generated assembly code. Assembly code allows expressions like "FRED+1" as operands. The program I have in mind used an internal data structure where such operands were represented as atoms, e.g., 'FRED+1'. This was a bad idea for several reasons. One is that the program tried to warn you when a label had been used but not defined, so it would warn you about 'FRED+1' even when 'FRED' had been defined. Another was that it made fairly strong assumptions about the syntax accepted by the target assembler, and made them far too early. But what was particularly silly about this was that the only time that a character representation was needed was at the instant that output was generated. How much better to let the abstract syntax tree represent its output form, and write a special purpose "output interpreter". That is, instead of doing

mklabel(Base+Offset, Label) :-
        name(Base, BaseChars),
        name(Offset, OffsetChars),
        append(BaseChars, OffsetChars, LabelChars),
        atom_chars(Label, LabelChars).

$\vdots$

it would have been faster and cheaper to do

mklabel(Base+Offset, Base+Offset).

$\vdots$

```
prlabel(Base+Offset) :-
        prlabel(Base), write(+), prlabel(Offset).
```
$\vdots$

6.9.1   Concatenating Generators

When $s_1, \ldots, s_n$ are represented as generators, we can use the "return a promise" idea of the previous section to construct a generator representing their concatenation. For each $1 \le i \le n$ let σ_i represent the state in which the first $i - 1$ sequences have been exhausted. (So state σ_i has $n + 1 - i$ arguments.) Then

$$\text{make\_concatenation}(X_1, \ldots, X_n, \sigma_1(X_1, \ldots, X_n)).$$

$\vdots$

```
concatenation_done(σᵢ(Xᵢ, ..., Xₙ)) :-
        doneᵢ(Xᵢ),
        concatenation_done(σᵢ₊₁(Xᵢ₊₁, ..., Xₙ)).
concatenation_done(σₙ(Xₙ)) :-
        done(Xₙ).
```

$$\text{concatenation\_done}(\sigma_i(X_i, \ldots, X_n)) \text{ :-}$$
$$\text{done}_i(X_i),$$
$$\text{concatenation\_done}(\sigma_{i+1}(X_{i+1}, \ldots, X_n)).$$
$$\text{concatenation\_done}(\sigma_n(X_n)) \text{ :-}$$
$$\text{done}(X_n).$$

$\vdots$

$$\text{concatenation\_next}(E, \sigma_i(X_i, \ldots, X_n), \sigma_i(Y_i, \ldots, X_n)) \text{ :-}$$
$$\text{next}_i(E, X_i, Y_i).$$
$$\text{concatenation\_next}(E, \sigma_i(X_i, \ldots, X_n), \text{State}) \text{ :-}$$
$$\text{done}_i(X_i),$$
$$\text{concatenation\_next}(E, \sigma_{i+1}(X_{i+1}, \ldots, X_n), \text{State}).$$

$\vdots$

6.9.2   Concatenating Enumerators

Let $\epsilon_1(X), \ldots, \epsilon_n(X)$ be enumerators. Constructing an enumerator which represents the concatenation of the sequences they represent is trivial:

$$\epsilon(x) \text{ :-}$$
$$(\quad \epsilon_1(x)$$
$$\vdots$$
$$; \quad \epsilon_n(x)$$
$$).$$

For example, suppose we have two lists A and C, and we want an enumerator $\text{abc}(A, C, X)$ which represents $A \frown \langle b \rangle \frown C$. All we have to write is

abc(A, C, X) :-
       (member(X, A)
        ; $X = b$
        ;   member(X, C)
).

6.10   Mapping

We often want to derive a new sequence by applying a function to the elements of an existing sequence. The usual way to code a function f which takes n inputs and yields m results in Prolog is as a predicate with $n + m$ arguments, thus:

$$f(I_1, \ldots, I_n, O_1, \ldots, O_m)$$

In the case of a list, we have the well-known maplist/3.

```
maplist(P, Is, Os) :-
        maplist1(Is, Os, P).
```

```
maplist1([], [], _).
maplist1([I|Is], [O|Os], P) :-
        call(P, I, O),
        maplist1(Is, Os, P).
```

When we want to construct a list of results (or, if the function we are applying yields more than one result, several lists of results) we can generalise this pattern.

```
map_f(Is_1, ..., Is_n, [], ..., []) :-
        variety_1_done(Is_1),
        .
        .
        .
        variety_n_done(Is_n).
map_f(Is_1, ..., Is_n, [O_1|Os_1], ..., [O_m|Os_m]) :-
        variety_1_next(I_1, Is_1, Js_1),
        .
        .
        .
        variety_n_next(I_n, Is_n, Js_n),
        f(I_1, ..., I_n, O_1, ..., O_m),
        map_f(Js_1, ..., Js_n, O_1, ..., O_m).
```

The library predicate keys_and_values/3 is an instance of this pattern:

keys_and_values([], [], []).
keys_and_values([$K|Ks$], [$V|Vs$], [$K - V|KVs$]) :-
        keys_and_values(Ks, Vs, KVs).

and of course such a predicate can have context arguments as well. For example, if
you want a obtain the quotients Qs and remainders Rs when some numbers Ns are
divided by a fixed divisor D, you would write

quotients_and_remainders([], _, [], []).
quotients_and_remainders([$N|Ns$], D, [$Q|Qs$], [$R|Rs$]) :-
        Q is $N//D$,
        R is N mod D,
        quotients_and_remainders(Ns, D, Qs, Rs).

Producing a generator is only a little harder. All we have to do is carry around
the (current state of the) generators and lists that the result is made from. Because
a generator represents precisely one sequence, we're only interested in functions
having one result. Suppose then that we have sequences $Is_1, \ldots, Is_n$ defined by
generators, and context parameters $C_1, \ldots C_k$, and a function

$$f(I_1, \ldots, I_n, C_1, \ldots, C_k, O)$$

make_$f(Is_1, \ldots, Is_n, C_1, \ldots, C_n, \text{state}(Is_1, \ldots, Is_n, C_1, \ldots, C_n))$.

done_$f(\text{state}(Is_1, \ldots, Is_n, C_1, \ldots, C_n))$:-
        $variety_1$_done(Is_1),
        $\vdots$
        $variety_n$_done(Is_n).

next_$f(O,\quad \text{state}(Is_1, \ldots, Is_n, C_1, \ldots, C_n),$
$\quad\quad\quad\quad \text{state}(Js_1, \ldots, Js_n, C_1, \ldots, C_n))$:-
        $variety_1$_next(I_1, Is_1, Js_1),
        $\vdots$
        $variety_n$_next(I_n, Is_n, Js_n),
        $f(I_1, \ldots, I_n, C_1, \ldots, C_k, O)$.

You may be wondering what will or should happen when the sequences haven't
got the same length. What *will* happen is that as soon as one of the sequences runs
out, neither done_f nor next_f will succeed. Whether that is what *should* happen
depends on what you want it to do. If you know that one particular sequence is

the shortest, you can just check whether that one is 'done', but it is up to you to explain in the comments of your program why this is so. One common reason is that some of the sequences are unbounded.

As an example, let's consider a generator which pairs the elements of a list L with the integers 1–∞. Only one of these sequences is bounded, so that's the only one we need to check. We get

make_counted_generator(List, state(List,1)).

counted_generator_done(state([],_)).

counted_generator_next($X - M$, state($[X|Xs], M$), state(Xs, N)) :-
    plus($M, 1, N$).

When you have several input sequences represented as lists or generators, it is easy to enumerate elements of the results.

enum_$f(Is_1, \ldots, Is_n, C_1, \ldots, C_k, O_1, \ldots, O_m)$:-
    $variety_1$_next(I_1, Is_1, Js_1),

    $\vdots$

    $variety_n$_next(I_n, Is_n, Js_n),
    ($f(I_1, \ldots, I_n, C_1, \ldots, C_k, O_1, \ldots, O_m)$
    ;   enum_$f(Js_1, \ldots, Js_n, C_1, \ldots, C_k, O_1, \ldots, O_m)$
).

Thus, for example, to enumerate corresponding elements X and Y from two lists Xs and Ys, one would write

corresponding($[X|_], [Y|_], X, Y$).
corresponding($[_|Xs], [_|Ys], X, Y$) :-
    corresponding(Xs, Ys, X, Y).

Enumerators are tricky. If there is just one input sequence, that is straightforward. We merely write

        enum(I),
        f(I, O)

For example, if we want to enumerate the squares S of the elements of a list L, we write

        member(X, L),
        S is $X * X$

Now consider the case of one enumerator enum(X) which enumerates the sequence $\langle x_1, \ldots, x_n \rangle$ and one list L representing the sequence $\langle y_1, \ldots, y_n \rangle$. To keep the example simple, suppose we just want to enumerate the pairs (x_i, y_i). The obvious thing to try is

> enum(X),
> member(Y, L),
> Answer = (X, Y)

Unfortunately, that won't work. It enumerates all pairs (x_i, y_j). The trouble is that every time enum/1 reports another x_i, member/2 starts again from the beginning. The simplest way around the problem is to use findall/3 to eliminate the enumerator.

6.11 Cross-products

By a cross-product of sequences $\langle x_1, \ldots, x_m \rangle$ and $\langle y_1, \ldots, y_n \rangle$ we mean a sequence

$$\langle f(x_i, y_j) \rangle \text{ for } 1 \leq i \leq m \text{ and } 1 \leq j \leq n$$

As we saw in the previous section, it is easy to enumerate a cross-product of enumerated sequences, even if you don't really want to. Cross-products of lists and generators follow this pattern:

```
product(P, Xs, Ys, PXYs) :-
        product1(Xs, Ys, PXYs, P).

product1([], _, [], _).
product1([X|Xs], Ys, PXYs0, P) :-
        product1(Ys, X, P, PXYs0, PXYs1),
        product1(Xs, Ys, PXYs1, P).

product1([], _, _) ⟶ [].
product1([Y|Ys], X, P) ⟶
        { call(P, X, Y, PXY) },
        [PXY],
        product1(Ys, X, P).
```

6.12   Recurrences

Suppose we have a sequence defined by the following rules:

$$f_1 = e_1$$

$$\vdots$$

$$f_k = e_k$$

$$f_n = g(n, f_{n-1}, \ldots, f_{n-k}) \text{ for } n > k$$

A familiar example is the Fibonacci numbers:

$$f_1 = 1$$

$$f_2 = 1$$

$$f_n = f_{n-1} + f_{n-2} \text{ for } n > 2$$

The naïve way of coding something like this in Prolog is

f$(1, X)$:- !, $e_1(X)$.

$\vdots$

f(k, X) :- !, $e_k(X)$.
f(N, X) :-

        $N > k$,

        N_1 is $N - 1$, f(N_1, X_1),

        $\vdots$

        N_k is $N - k$, f(N_k, X_k),

        g$(N, X_1, \ldots, X_k, X)$.

For example, the Fibonacci numbers might be computed thus:

fib$(1, X_1)$:- !, $X = 1$.
fib$(2, X_2)$:- !, $X = 1$.
fib(N, X) :- $N > 2$,

        N_1 is $N - 1$, fib(N_1, X_1),

        N_2 is $N - 2$, fib(N_2, X_2),

        X is $X_1 + X_2$.

Perhaps it is unfair to call this code naïve. There are several things that *could* be wrong with it that aren't. But it is far from efficient. You should already know the general method for coding such recurrences in Prolog:

f(1, X_1) :- !, $e_1(X_1)$.

$\vdots$

f(k, X_k) :- !, $e_k(X_k)$.
f(N, X) :- $N > k$,
$\qquad$ $e_1(X_1), \ldots, e_k(X_k)$,
$\qquad$ f(k, N, $X_k, \ldots, X_1, X$).

f(N, N, $X_k, \ldots, X_1, X$) :- !, $X = X_k$.
f(N_0, N, $X_k, \ldots, X_1, X$) :-
$\qquad$ /* $X_k = f_{N_0}, \ldots, X_1 = f_{N_0-k+1}$ */
$\qquad$ N_1 is $N_0 + 1$,
$\qquad$ $g(N_1, X_k, \ldots, X_1, X_{new})$,
$\qquad$ f(N_1, N, $X_{new}, X_k, \ldots, X_2, X$).

For example, a more efficient way of calculating Fibonacci numbers is

fib(1, X) :- !, $X = 1$.
fib(2, X) :- !, $X = 1$.
fib(N, X) :- $N > 2$,
$\qquad$ fib(2, N, 1, 1, X).

fib(N, N, X2, _, X) :- !, $X = X2$.
fib(N_0, N, X2, X1, X) :-
$\qquad$ N_1 is $N_0 + 1$,
$\qquad$ $X3$ is $X2 + X1$,
$\qquad$ fib(N_1, N, X3, X2, X).

The original version did an exponential amount of work each time. This tail-recursive version does $O(n)$ work each time it is called, which is a big improvement. But if we want to examine the first n elements of the sequence, we'll do $O(m)$ work for the mth element, for a total of $O(n^2)$ work. It is possible to do better.

The better way is to use a generator. For each $0 \leq i < k$, we have a state where the first i elements of the sequence have been computed. In such a state there are i associated data: the elements which have been computed so far. There is also a kth state, where at least the first k elements have been computed, and in that state the associated data are the latest k elements to have been computed and the index n of the most recent of them.

make_recurrence(σ_0).

recurrence_next(X_1, σ_0, $\sigma_1(X_1)$) :-
    $e_1(X_1)$.

$\vdots$

recurrence_next(X_{k-1}, $\sigma_{k-2}(X_{k-2}, \ldots, X_1)$, $\sigma_{k-1}(X_{k-1}, X_{k-2}, \ldots, X_1)$) :-
    $e_{k-1}(X_{k-1})$.
recurrence_next(X_k, $\sigma_{k-1}(X_{k-1}, \ldots, X_1)$, $\sigma_k(k, X_k, X_{k-1}, \ldots, X_1)$) :-
    $e_k(X_k)$.
recurrence_next(X_{k+1}, $\sigma_k(N_0, X_k, \ldots, X_1)$, $\sigma_k(N_1, X_{k+1}, X_k, \ldots, X_2)$) :-
    N_1 is $N_0 + 1$,
    $g(N_1, X_k, \ldots, X_1, X_{k+1})$.

When applied to the Fibonacci numbers, this yields

make_fibonacci(s0).

fibonacci_next(Fib, State0, State) :-
    next_fibonacci(State0, Fib, State).

next_fibonacci(s0, 1, s1(1)).
next_fibonacci(s1(X1), 1, s2(1,X1)).
next_fibonacci(s2(X2,X1), X3, s2(X3,X2)) :-
    X3 is X2+X1.

It goes without saying that a recurrence need not be numeric.

Exercise. *Find the first N Fibonacci numbers using each of these three methods. Time them for $N = 10, 20, 50$.*

6.13 Meta-programs and Object-Oriented Programming

We have seen how to code some operations on sequences. It would be pleasant if we could do this once for all, instead of writing everything from scratch whenever we think of a new way to represent sequences. Two approaches we can use are *meta-programming* and *object-oriented programming*. We shall see that both are similar.

6.13.1 Meta-programming

The idea of meta-programming is best shown by example. Consider maplist/2, defined thus:

```
%    maplist(+Pred, +Xs)
%    is true when Pred(X) is true for each X in Xs.
```

maplist(_, []).
maplist(P, [$X|Xs$]) :-
        call(P, X),
        maplist(P, Xs).

Thanks to `library(call)`, this will work as it stands, but it is inefficient. Suppose we want a predicate which is true when all the elements of a list are atoms. We could define

all_atoms(L) :-
        maplist(atom, L).

This is correct, but if L has n elements, call(atom, X) will be executed n times. In an interpreter, the overhead of call/2 may seem slight, but a good compiler will make it seem high. We would rather *not* go through call/2. The answer is simple. We use elementary program transformation to eliminate maplist/2.

1. Unfold maplist/2 in all_atoms/1, obtaining

   all_atoms([]).
   all_atoms([$X|Xs$]) :-
           call(atom, X),
           maplist(atom, Xs).

2. Simplify call(atom, X) to atom(X).

3. Fold the call to maplist/2 with the original definition of all_atoms/1, obtaining

   all_atoms([]).
   all_atoms([$X|Xs$]) :-
           atom(X),
           all_atoms(Xs).

With the right tools, this can be done in seconds.

The basic idea is that we write a predicate which is not complete: it needs one or more operations (or terms) specified to complete it. Those missing operations are specified as additional arguments of the meta-code. Conventionally they are

placed ahead of the normal arguments, as they are very strict inputs. Meta-code
can be executed, thanks to the built-in predicate call/1 which lets you use a term as
a name of a predicate. The most efficient use of meta-code is to instantiate it and
use basic program transformation methods to produce ordinary first-order code.
You might have one meta-argument for each missing operation or term, or you
might use fewer meta-arguments, giving them additional arguments to say which
operation or term is wanted.

As another example, suppose that we have a generic version of append/3 coded
thus:

```
generic_append(Class, State0, R, R) :-
        call(Class, done(State0)).
generic_append(Class, State0, L, [H|R]) :-
        call(Class, next(H, State0, State)),
        generic_append(Class, State, L, R).
```

We might have a 'pairing' generator defined like this:

```
pairing(make(Xs, Ys, Xs + Ys)).
pairing(done([] + [])).
pairing(next(X − Y, [X|Xs] + [Y|Ys], Xs + Ys)).
```

We could define keys_and_values/3 like this:

```
keys_and_values(Ks, Vs, KVs) :-
        pairing(make(Ks, Vs, S0)),
        generic_append(pairing, S0, [], KVs).
```

Unfolding pairing/1 gives us

```
keys_and_values(Ks, Vs, KVs) :-
        generic_append(pairing, Ks + Vs, [], KVs).
```

Unfolding generic_append/4 gives us

```
keys_and_values(Ks, Vs, []) :-
        call(pairing, done(Ks,Vs)).
keys_and_values(Ks, Vs, [H|R]) :-
        call(pairing, next(H, Ks + Vs, S1)),
        generic_append(pairing, S1, [], R).
```

Simplifying call/2, unfolding the resulting calls to pairing/1, and folding with the
original definition, yields

keys_and_values([], [], []).
    /* from generic_append clause 1 */
    /* and pairing(done(_)). */
keys_and_values([$K|Ks$], [$V|Vs$], [$K - V|KVs$]) :-
        keys_and_values(Ks, Vs, KVs).
    /* from generic_append clause 2 */
    /* and pairing(next(_,_,_)). */

This approach really deserves to be illustrated by a larger example. But if I used realistic examples, this would be a much bigger book!

You should start your own collections of meta-code. I hope that the `generic` handout will be a good seed for your collection. When you get the feeling "haven't I done this before?" you're often right, and what you are repeating may be a good thing to add to your collection. When you discover a new generic operation, look for ways to improve it, prove it correct, combine it with other operations, and so on. That effort will pay off every time you use it. Conversely, when parts of a program are derived from meta-code, keep a record of the high level version in case you later discover a way of improving the meta-code.

6.13.2 Object-oriented programming

Object-oriented programming was invented by the designers of Simula 67. The fundamental idea is to divide the state space of an imperative program into little loosely connected chunks, each chunk representing the state of an "object". *If it hasn't got mutable state, it isn't an "object".* Following on from this key idea one provides limited access to the state of an object by equipping each object with its own set of operations for inspecting and altering its state. How this set of operations is defined is a separate question: 'inheritance' in a type hierarchy does *not* make a system object-oriented, nor does the absence of inheritance mean that a system is not object-oriented.

Prolog being a declarative language, we cannot represents objects in Prolog. (Well, we could hack around with the data base, but that would be inefficient and a Bad Thing in general.) What we *can* do is represent the *states* of objects. This is not in general sufficient: if two objects A and B know the name of a third object C, it is easy in a true object-oriented system for A to tell C to change, whereupon B will observe that C has changed. Using as we shall (copies of) states of objects, A can obtain a revised version C' of C, but B will still have (a copy of) C. But this approach is often good enough. It is the technique used in Concurrent Prolog, for example.

We want to represent (a state of) an object by a single data structure. This data structure must thus incorporate both the data associated with the object (or enough information to locate those data), and the 'script' or set of operations which

the object currently supports. (By the way, there is no reason why the script should
not change. It can't in Simula 67 or Smalltalk 80, but what of that?) We'll use
send/2 to inspect the state of an object, and send/3 to alter it, and we'll use new/2
to make objects, where

```
new(Template, Self) :-
        call(Template, Self).
```

```
send(Property, Self) :-
        call(Self, Property, Self).
```

```
send(Message, Self0, Self) :-
        call(Self0, Message, Self0, Self).
```

For example, we could implement an "integer interval" object class like this:

```
/*   ii(L, U, X) is the state vector of an "integer interval"
     "object" with lower bound L and upper bound U, integers.
     X is the "current position" in the interval.
*/
```

interval(L, U, ii(L, U, L)) :-
        integer(L), integer(U),
        $L \leq U$.

```
%   ii(L, U, X, Message, Self) handles 'get' messages
%   for the"integer interval" class. We switch the
%   arguments around so as to index on the Message.
```

ii(L, U, X, Message, Self) :-
        ii_1(Message, L, U, X, Self).

ii_1(done, _, _, _, Self) :-
        ¬ send(more, Self).
ii_1(more, L, U, X, _) :-
        $L \leq X, X \leq U$.
ii_1(first(L), L, U, X, _).
ii_1(last(U), L, U, X, _).
ii_1(this(X), L, U, X, _).

```
%    ii(L, U, X, Message, Self0, Self) handles 'send' messages
%    for the "integer interval" class. We switch the
%    arguments around so as to index on the Message.
```

ii(L, U, X, Message, Self0, Self) :-
        ii_1(Message, L, U, X, Self0, Self).

ii_1(next, L, U, X, _, ii(L, U, Y)) :-
        plus($X, 1, Y$).
ii_1(prev, L, U, X, _, ii(L, U, Y)) :-
        plus($Y, 1, X$).
ii_1(reset, L, U, X, _, ii(L, U, L)).

We can define 'length' on (states of) objects supporting 'done' and 'next' like this:

object_length(S, N) :-
        object_length($S, 0, N$).

object_length($S0, N_0, N$) :-
        (send(done, $S0$) $\rightarrow$ $N = N_0$
        ;   send(next, $S0, S1$),
             N_1 is $N_0 + 1$,
             object_length($S1, N_1, N$)
).

We can then find out how wide the interval $[1, 10]$ is by asking

?- new(interval(1,10), I), object_length(I, Length).

By adding a new clause at the front of send/2:

send(length(L), Self) :- !,
        object_length(Self, 0, L).

we could arrange for length(L) to be available as a derived property of every object supporting 'done' and 'next'. (Remember, inheritance is *not* a defining property of 'object orientation'.)

One thing we can arrange easily this way is to have an object turn itself into something else. For example,

```
concretise(S, L) :-
    (   send(done, S) → L = []
    ;   send(this(X), S),
        send(next, S, S1),
        L = [X|L₁],
        concretise(S1, L₁)
    ).


list(L, ll(L, L)).


ll([], _, done, _).
ll([_|_], _, more, _).
ll(_, [X|_], first(X), _).
ll([X|_], _, this(X), _).
ll(L, _, last(X), _) :-
        last(L, X).
ll([_|Xs], L, next, _, ll(Xs, L)).
ll(_, L, reset, _, ll(L, L)).


ii_1(concretise, _, _, _, Self, List) :-
        concretise(Self, List).
```

With these definitions, **sending** the message `concretise` to an integer interval doesn't yield an updated interval, but another kind of object entirely, which represents a position in a list.

As you can see from these examples, the 'states of objects' approach isn't very different from the 'meta-predicates' approach. The main difference is that meta-programming is a technique which is used to derive programs in which meta-code no longer appears, while object-orientation encourages run-time discrimination. Both approaches require more support than plain Prolog gives you. For meta-programming, you want the unfolder. (No you don't, you want something *better*.) For object-oriented programming, you want a library which lets you add operations to the repertoires of existing objects, and would like some kind of inheritance. Meta-programming leads to efficient object programs, where special cases (such as mapping down the same list more than once) are exploited (yielding a single loop, for example). But each instance leads to a new set of object predicates, so there is little code-sharing. Object-oriented programming lets you use the same object code directly, but at the price of increased run time. There are two run-time costs: the overhead of call/N and wrapping up the associated data instead of passing them around as separate arguments.

If you want to write simulation programs in Prolog, that is what object-oriented programming was invented for. Get it right first, and then worry about the cost.

One trick which is useful is to separate out the parts of an object's state which do change from the parts which don't. For example, suppose you are simulating traffic in a network of computers. Then most of the characteristics of a node (capacity, type, connections, and so on) will not change, so may reasonably be stored in the data base. Similarly, the characteristics of a message (size, destination) will not change. So you might represent a node by

> node(Which,Queue)

where Queue is a queue of message names and Which is a name that can be used to query the data base for the static properties of the node, e.g.,

```
node(    /* Which =*/ 57,
         /* Capacity =*/ 100 /* megabytes */,
         /* Neighbours =*/ [50,84]).
```

6.14 Quantification

Here we examine briefly the following forms:

$$\text{some}(\sigma;p) \quad \exists i \in \text{dom}\,\sigma \mid p(\sigma_i)$$
$$\text{each}(\sigma;p) \quad \forall i \in \text{dom}\,\sigma \mid p(\sigma_i)$$
$$\text{first}(\sigma;p) \quad \sigma_j, \text{ where}$$
$$\qquad\qquad j = \min i \in \text{dom}\,\sigma \mid p(\sigma_i)$$
$$\text{count}(\sigma;p) \quad \sum_{i\in\text{dom}\,\sigma} \chi_p(\sigma_i)$$
$$\qquad\qquad \text{where } \chi_p(x) = 1 \text{ if } p(x), 0 \text{ otherwise}$$

This means that

$$\text{some}(\langle\rangle;p) = \text{false}$$
$$\text{some}(\langle x\rangle;p) = p(x)$$
$$\text{some}(\alpha \frown \beta;p) = \text{some}(\alpha;p) \vee \text{some}(\beta;p)$$

$$\text{each}(\langle\rangle;p) = \text{true}$$
$$\text{each}(\langle x\rangle;p) = p(x)$$
$$\text{each}(\alpha \frown \beta;p) = \text{each}(\alpha;p) \wedge \text{each}(\beta;p)$$

$$\begin{aligned}
\text{count}(\langle\rangle; p) &= 0 \\
\text{count}(\langle x \rangle; p) &= \chi_p(x) \\
\text{count}(\alpha \frown \beta; p) &= \text{count}(\alpha; p) + \text{count}(\beta; p)
\end{aligned}$$

$$\begin{aligned}
\text{first}(\langle\rangle; p) &= \text{undefined} \\
\text{first}(\langle x \rangle; p) &= x \text{ provided } p(x) \\
\text{first}(\alpha \frown \beta; p) &= \text{first}(\alpha; p) \text{ if some}(\alpha; p) \\
&= \text{first}(\beta; p) \text{ otherwise}
\end{aligned}$$

We note that *any* way of breaking a sequence into two parts will serve to drive the induction. In the next chapter we'll see how this can be useful. We note here that it can be used to eliminate a sequence entirely. For example, suppose we want to test whether

   each(preorder(Tree), atom)

is true for some tree. We could, of course, write

all_atoms_tree(Tree) :-
         preorder_list(Tree, List, []),
         maplist(List, atom).

but this is inefficient in two ways:

- it constructs a List we have no other use for. (Of course, if we *did* have other uses for the List, it might be a good idea to compute it.)

- it traverses the whole Tree even when there is no need to, For example, suppose the Label of the root of the Tree is an integer. In that case we could stop as soon as we had checked the root, but the code above will still build the whole List.

If we observe that preorder_list/3 constructs its result by the equivalent of $\langle\rangle$ ([]), $\langle x \rangle$ ([X]), and $\alpha \frown \beta$ (α',β'), we see that "each" can be moved inside it, and we can define

each_p_tree(empty).
each_p_tree(node(Label,Left,Right)) :-
         p(Label),
         each_p_tree(Left),
         each_p_tree(Right).

6.14.1 Lists and Generators

some_*variety*_satisfies_*p*(State0) :-
        *variety*_next(X, State0, State1),
        ($p(X)$ → true
        ;   some_*variety*_satisfies_*p*(State1)
).

first_*variety*_satisfies_*p*(State0, X) :-
        *variety*_next(Y, State0, State1),
        ($p(Y)$ → $X = Y$
        ;   first_*variety*_satisfies_*p*(State1)
).

each_*variety*_satisfies_*p*(State0) :-
        *variety*_done(State0).
each_*variety*_satisfies_*p*(State0) :-
        *variety*_next(X, State0, State1),
        p(X),
        each_*variety*_satisfies_*p*(State1).

count_*variety*_such_that_*p*(State0, N) :-
        count_*variety*_such_that_*p*(State0, 0, N).

count_*variety*_such_that_*p*(State0, N, N) :-
        *variety*_done(State0).
count_*variety*_such_that_*p*(State0, N_0, N) :-
        *variety*_next(X, State0, State1),
        ($p(X)$ → N_1 is $N_0 + 1$; N_1 is N_0),
        count_*variety*_such_that_*p*(State1, N_1, N).

Note the parallels between 'some' and 'first' on one hand and 'each' and 'count' on the other. The difference is the 'each' and 'count' must examine the whole sequence, whereas 'some' and 'first' can stop as soon as they find an element satisfying p. In fact the only real difference between 'some' and 'first' is whether they return this first element or not.

All of these cuts and arrows are rather distressing. It is cleaner—and in current versions of Quintus Prolog, it is often faster—to have a function f returning 'true' or 'false' rather than a predicate which succeeds or fails. Here's how 'first' and 'count' would look with such an f; you can figure 'some' and 'each' out for yourself.

```
first(State0, X) :-
        next(Y, State0, State1),
        f(Y, Flag),
        first1(Flag, X, Y, State1).
```

```
first1(true, X, X, _).
first1(false, X, _, State) :-
        first(State, X).
```

```
count(State0, N, N) :-
        done(State0).
count(State0, N0, N) :-
        next(X, State0, State1),
        f(X, Flag),
        count1(Flag, N0, N, State1).
```

```
count1(true, N0, N, State) :-
        N1 is N0 + 1,
        count(State, N1, N).
count1(false, N0, N, State) :-
        count(State, N0, N).
```

6.14.2   Enumerators

```
some_ε_satisfies_p :-
        ( ε(X), p(X) → true ).
```

```
each_ε_satisfies_p :-
        ¬ ( ε(X), ¬p(X) ).
```

```
first_ε_such_that_p(X) :-
        ( ε(Y), p(Y) → X = Y ).
```

```
count_ε_such_that_p(N) :-
        findall('.', (ε(X), p(X)), L),
        length(L, N).
```

In NU Prolog you can write these more clearly as

```
some_ε_satisfies_p :-
        some X ( ε(X), p(X) ).
```

each_ε_satisfies_p :-
        all X ($\epsilon(X) \Rightarrow p(X)$).

first_ε_such_that_p(X) :-
        ($\epsilon(Y), p(Y) \rightarrow X = Y$
        ;   fail % → is broken in NU prolog
).

count_ε_such_that_p(N) :-
        count(X, ($\epsilon(X), p(X)$), N).

'count' cannot be implemented directly in Prolog, but must use some sort of all-solutions predicate. Note that each of these forms contains negation as failure, implicitly if not explicitly. We need to know definitely whether or not $p(X)$. To make the conclusion $\neg p(X)$ sound, X must be ground at the time of the call. Further, we must definitely have all and only the elements of the sequence represented by ϵ, so any variables in $\epsilon(X)$ other than X must be sufficiently instantiated to uniquely determine the abstract sequence in full.

As noted in the section defining **some_element**, enumerators derived from non-determinate predicates mix things up and may yield elements from trial sequences which the underlying predicate would eventually reject. So make *very* sure of your enumerator!

As we shall see in the chapter on "all-solutions predicates", findall/3 really is *not* a satisfactory way of handling *sets*. Here, however, we are using it to handle a *sequence* represented by an enumerator. Suppose we have a list L and want to know how many of its elements are integer.

        findall('.', (member(X,L),integer(X)), Is),
        length(Is, N)

will correctly compute count(L;integer), albeit inefficiently. But that is not the same as

$$\#\{x \in L \mid \text{integer}(x)\}$$

6.15   The importance of Algebra

By *algebra*, I do not mean all that stuff about cubic equations and matrices you studied in high-school, but abstract algebra. The idea of abstract algebra is to study the properties of a set of functions while remaining as noncommittal as possible about the values the functions operate on. While it is abstract, it is very practical. A well-chosen set of basic functions and axioms will give you a rich mathematical structure, which provides many opportunities for rearranging and simplifying. Sequences are particularly rich. They are a monoid with a natural homomorphism to the natural numbers. When we add additional structure, we find that many operations distribute over concatenation in useful ways. We haven't touched on regular expressions yet (see the Dragon Book). All sorts of useful results are already to hand.

It isn't just the possibility of rearranging and simplifying programs working with sequences which makes abstraction so useful: if some handy result is true of sequences, it is true of every representation of sequences. For example, we have to prove

$$\text{some}(\sigma; p) \wedge \text{some}(\sigma; q) \equiv \text{some}(\sigma; p \wedge q)$$

once, and then we can use the result for lists, enumerators, and any sort of generator. Apart from the sheer economy of not having to prove the same kind of result over and over, this means that we can shuffle a program around according to the laws of sequences before we decide how to represent the sequences. The result may not be realisable in a particular representation (enumerators are the wasps in the jam-pot), but if it is realisable it is correct.

Another way in which the abstract approach may be helpful is that an algorithm coded for one representation of an abstract data type can serve as a model for a version using another representation.

6.16   Summary

In this chapter, we have examined three ways of representing sequences in Prolog programs:

- as lists

- as generators (data structures together with operations to get the next element and test whether a sequence is finished)

- as enumerators (goals which enumerate the elements of a sequence, the next element being obtained by backtracking).

We saw how sequences could be converted from one representation to another, and some of the things that could be done with sequences.

This has been a fairly abstract chapter. Why have I included it in a book called "The Craft of Prolog"? Because this is some of the knowledge about sequences that I *use*. I hope that the techniques illustrated in this chapter will be useful to you too. But the most important lesson is that by thinking in terms of an abstract notion (sequences) rather than a built in data type (lists) we are free to consider other, perhaps implicit, implementations. We can often transform a program fragment using one representation into an abstractly equivalent fragment using another representation. You should be as ready to rearrange predicates as you are to rearrange arithmetic expressions.

7 Writing Interpreters

7.1 Introduction

An important programming technique in Prolog (and in Lisp) is the creation of special-purpose interpreters. That is, instead of writing a program to perform some task directly, you invent a high-level notation for that task and write an interpreter for that notation in Prolog. In Lisp, it is easy to write interpreters for languages that resemble Lisp. In Prolog, it is easy to write interpreters for languages that resemble Prolog (or pure Lisp). We shall illustrate this technique by showing how you can write an interpreter for Prolog in Prolog. (An interpreter for a language L which is written in L can be used to interpret (a copy of) itself; such interpreters are therefore called *meta-circular* interpreters. In the Prolog world, this term seems to be abbreviated to "meta-interpreters", even when it is applied to languages which are not Prolog. Don't bother; just call the whole lot interpreters.)

7.2 But first, an easy case

Let's suppose we want to write a good Noughts and Crosses[1] program. One component of such a program might be a pattern language for recognising interesting configurations (such as a fork). One pattern language looks like this:

line(L, P, N)	— L is a line containing N of P's marks
blank(L, R, C)	— cell (R,C) lies on line L and is empty
Pat1 , Pat2	— both patterns succeed
Pat1 ; Pat2	— at least one pattern succeeds
Term1 \== Term2	— the two terms are not the same
call(Head)	— if there is a rule pattern(Head, Pattern)
	— call(Head) succeeds if Pattern does.

P is 'x' or 'o', R and C are integers 1–3, and L is r1,r2,r3, c1,c2,c3, md (main diagonal) or cd (cross diagonal). Here is a little rule set for Noughts and Crosses written in this language. It is not supposed to be a particularly brilliant Noughts and Crosses program, just an example.

```
pattern(won(P), % The game is won by player P if
    (    line(_, P, 3) % P has a line of 3 marks in a row.
    )).
```

---

[1] For American readers: "Tick-Tack-Toe"

```
pattern(win(P, R, C), % (R,C) is a winning move for player P if
    (   line(Line, P, 2), % there is a line containing two of P's marks
        blank(Line, R, C) % and (R,C) is a blank on that line
    )).
pattern(fork(P, R, C), % (R,C) creates a fork for player P if
    (   line(Line_1, P, 1), % there are two lines each containing one
        blank(Line_1, R, C), % of P's marks and none of the other player's,
        line(Line_2, P, 1), % and (R,C) is a blank cell on each of them.
        blank(Line_2, R, C),
        Line_2 \== Line_1
    )).
pattern(pre_fork(P, R, C), % (R,C) prepares for a fork by player P if
    (   line(Line_1, P, 1), % there is a line Line1 with one mark of P's
        blank(Line_1, X, Y),
        line(Line_2, P, 0), % there is a line Line2 with no marks
        blank(Line_2, X, Y), % Line1 and Line2 intersect at (X,Y)
        blank(Line_2, R, C), % (R,C) is a point on Line2 other than
        (R \== X ; C \== Y) % the future fork (X,Y)
    )).
pattern(x_move(R, C),
    (   call(win(x, R, C))
    ;   call(win(o, R, C))
    ;   call(fork(x, R, C))
    ;   call(fork(o, R, C))
    ;   call(pre_fork(x, R, C))
    ;   call(pre_fork(o, R, C))
    ;   blank(_, R, C), R \== 2, C \== 2 % R,C is a corner
    ;   blank(_, R, C)
    )).
```

It is easy to write an interpreter which checks whether a given board matches such a pattern or not:

```
match(call(Head), Board) :-
        pattern(Head, Pattern),
        match(Pattern, Board).
match(Term1 \== Term2, _) :-
        Term1 \== Term2.
match((Pat1 ; _), Board) :-
        match(Pat1, Board).
match((_ ; Pat2), Board) :-
        match(Pat2, Board).
```

```
match((Pat1 , Pat2), Board) :-
        match(Pat1, Board),
        match(Pat2, Board).
match(blank(Line,Row,Col), Board) :-
        blank(Line, Board, Row, Col).
match(line(Line,Player,Count), Board) :-
        line(Line, Board, A, B, C),
        count(Count, Player, A, B, C).

count(0, _, b, b, b).
count(1, X, X, b, b).
count(1, X, b, X, b).
count(1, X, b, b, X).
count(2, X, X, X, b).
count(2, X, X, b, X).
count(2, X, b, X, X).
count(3, X, X, X, X).

line(r1, b(A,B,C, _,_,_, _,_,_), A, B, C).
line(r2, b(_,_,_, A,B,C, _,_,_), A, B, C).
line(r3, b(_,_,_, _,_,_, A,B,C), A, B, C).
line(c1, b(A,_,_, B,_,_, C,_,_), A, B, C).
line(c2, b(_,A,_, _,B,_, _,C,_), A, B, C).
line(c3, b(_,_,A, _,_,B, _,_,C), A, B, C).
line(md, b(A,_,_, _,B,_, _,_,C), A, B, C).
line(cd, b(_,_,C, _,B,_, A,_,_), A, B, C).

blank(r1, b(A,B,C, _,_,_, _,_,_), 1, Col) :- blank_1(Col, A, B, C).
blank(r2, b(_,_,_, A,B,C, _,_,_), 2, Col) :- blank_1(Col, A, B, C).
blank(r3, b(_,_,_, _,_,_, A,B,C), 3, Col) :- blank_1(Col, A, B, C).
blank(c1, b(A,_,_, B,_,_, C,_,_), Row, 1) :- blank_1(Row, A, B, C).
blank(c2, b(_,A,_, _,B,_, _,C,_), Row, 2) :- blank_1(Row, A, B, C).
blank(c3, b(_,_,A, _,_,B, _,_,C), Row, 3) :- blank_1(Row, A, B, C).
blank(md, b(A,_,_, _,B,_, _,_,C), RC, RC) :- blank_1(RC, A, B, C).
blank(cd, b(_,_,C, _,B,_, A,_,_), R, Col) :-
        blank_1(Col, A, B, C),
        R is 4-Col.

blank_1(1, b, _, _).
blank_1(2, _, b, _).
blank_1(3, _, _, b).
```

Since the Noughts and Crosses language has a unique principal functor for each construct, the interpreter was easy to write without any cuts.

7.3   Compiling the Interpreter away

For any given rule-set, we are only really interested in interpreting that rule-set. So we would like to compile the rule-set into Prolog. The method for doing this is very simple, and involves no special magic. An interpreter is just another program that walks over a data structure, and all we have to do is unfold. Suppose that we are interested in two specific cases:

```
won(X, Board) :-
        match(call(won(X)), Board).

x_move(R, C, Board) :-
        match(call(x_move(R,C)), Board).
```

Let's take the simple one first: won/2. Which clauses of match/2 could possibly apply to it? Only the first. So we can replace the call of match/2 by the appropriate instance of the matching clause, and get

```
won(X, Board) :-
        /* after unfolding the 'call' clause of match/2 */
        pattern(won(X), Pattern),
        match(Pattern, Board).
```

We don't yet know enough about the second goal to replace it, but we do know enough about the first goal to see that there is a unique clause of pattern/2 which could match. So we unfold that clause, and get

```
won(X, Board) :-
        /* after unfolding the 'won' clause of pattern/2 */
        match(line(_,X,3), Board).
```

Now we have enough information to determine which clause of match/2 will apply, and we can unfold that. We get

```
won(X, Board) :-
        /* after unfolding the 'line' clause of match/2 */
        line(Line, Board, A, B, C),
        count(3, X, A, B, C).
```

We don't know anything about the line, but only one clause matches for count/5, so we end up with

```
won(X, Board) :-
        /* after unfolding the '3' clause of count/5 */
        line(_, Board, X, X, X).
```

We can unfold x_move/3 similarly, though it is rather harder work. Expanding all calls to match/2, then expanding count/5 when we can, yields

```
x_move(R, C, Board) :-
    (   line(Line, Board, A1, B1, C1),
        count(2, x, A1, B1, C1),
        blank(Line, Board, R, C)
    ;   line(Line, Board, A1, B1, C1),
        count(2, o, A1, B1, C1),
        blank(Line, Board, R, C)
    ;   line(Line_1, Board, A1, B1, C1),
        count(1, x, A1, B1, C1),
        blank(Line_1, Board, R, C),
        line(Line_2, Board, A2, B2, C2),
        count(1, x, A2, B2, C2),
        blank(Line_2, Board, R, C),
        Line_2 \== Line_1
    ;   line(Line_1, Board, A1, B1, C1),
        count(1, o, A1, B1, C1),
        blank(Line_1, Board, R, C),
        line(Line_2, Board, A2, B2, C2),
        count(1, o, A2, B2, C2),
        blank(Line_2, Board, R, C),
        Line_2 \== Line_1
    ;   line(Line_1, Board, A1, B1, C1),
        count(1, x, A1, B1, C1),
        blank(Line_1, Board, X, Y),
        line(Line_2, Board, b, b, b),
        blank(Line_2, Board, X, Y),
        blank(Line_2, Board, R, C),
        ( R \== X ; C \== Y )
```

```
;     line(Line_1, Board, A1, B1, C1),
      count(1, o, A1, B1, C1),
      blank(Line_1, Board, X, Y),
      line(Line_2, Board, b, b, b),
      blank(Line_2, Board, X, Y),
      blank(Line_2, Board, R, C),
      ( R \== X ; C \== Y )
;     blank(Line, Board, R, C), R \== 2, C \== 2
;     blank(Line, Board, R, C)
).
```

When this version was compiled, and compared with a compiled version of match/2 and pattern/2, it was found to run about 25% faster. For most purposes such a speed-up is not worth the effort, unless of course the translation can be done automatically. But this particular example does a lot of work in the "primitives" (blank/4 and line/5). As an illustration, a different version of count/5 was plugged in, which could be unfolded still further.

	This count/5	"fast" count/5
"Interpreted"	100%	91%
"Compiled"	76%	59%

(The entries in this table are the time taken for a particular test, as a percentage of the time taken by the original interpreted version.)

7.3.1 Summary

- Compiling away an interpreter is just unfolding.

- Special-purpose interpreters can make it easier to write complex rule-based systems.

- Sometimes there isn't much point in compiling an interpreter away.

- The benefits of unfolding depend on how much you can unfold away, which depends on how you have written your code. Pure code with lots of case analysis unfolds away nicely.

7.4 Multiple Interpretations

The pattern language for Noughts and Crosses made it easy to write concise rules for moves in that game. But brevity is not the only reason for using interpreters. It is often the case that a single language can be interpreted in multiple ways. The different interpretations might be no more than variant control strategies (e.g., iterative deepening -vs- naïve depth-first), or they might extract different information.

In the chapter on Searching, we saw several ways of searching a tree. All of those searching methods can be regarded as interpreters for a language defined by start/1, solution/1, and child/2 or children/2: the same language each time but different interpreters yielding different behaviour.

As an example of extracting multiple meanings from a single text, let's consider a mini-language for simple plans:

Act1 // Act2	— do Act1 and Act2 in parallel
Act1 , Act2	— do Act1 then Act2
do(BasicAct)	— do a primitive action
execute(Plan)	— same as Body, where plan(Plan, Body)

where we are given two sorts of information about BasicActs:

precond(BA1, BA2)	— before doing BA1, BA2 must have been done
cost(BasicAct, Cost)	— the cost of doing BasicAct

We can find out the cost of executing a plan thus:

```
plan_cost(Plan, Cost) :-
        plan_cost(Plan, 0, Cost).

plan_cost(Act1 // Act2, C0, C) :-
        plan_cost(Act1, C0, C1),
        plan_cost(Act2, C1, C).
plan_cost((Act1, Act2), C0, C) :-
        plan_cost(Act1, C0, C1),
        plan_cost(Act2, C1, C).
plan_cost(do(BasicAct), C0, C) :-
        cost(BasicAct, Cost),
        C is C0+Cost.
plan_cost(execute(Name), C0, C) :-
        plan(Name, Plan),
        plan_cost(Plan, C0, C).
```

But a more interesting question is whether a plan is certain to be valid. A plan is certain to be valid unless there might be a basic action attempted when one of its preconditions has not been done.

```
valid_plan(Plan) :-
        check_plan(Plan, [], _).

check_plan(Act1 // Act2, Before, After) :-
        check_plan(Act1, Before, After1),
        check_plan(Act2, Before, After2),
        union(After1, After2, After).
check_plan((Act1 , Act2), Before, After) :-
        check_plan(Act1, Before, InBetween),
        check_plan(Act2, InBetween, After).
check_plan(do(BasicAct), Before, [BasicAct|Before]) :-
        ¬ unprepared(BasicAct, Before).
check_plan(execute(Name), Before, After) :-
        plan(Name, Plan),
        check_plan(Plan, Before, After).

unprepared(BasicAct, Before) :-
        precond(BasicAct, PreCond),
        nonmember(PreCond, Before).
```

Both of these interpreters yield information about a plan, rather than actually executing it. In just the same way, if you were drawing pictures, it would be useful to be able to ask for a rough estimate of the size of a picture before deciding where on the screen to draw it, or you might like to determine what scale of the picture will permit the smaller details to be resolved. A "procedural" representation of pictures is just *too* restricted.

7.5   Writing Simple Prolog Interpreters

One Prolog textbook offers the following code as a meta-circular interpreter for (pure) Prolog:

```
prove(true).
prove((A,B)) :-
        prove(A),
        prove(B).
prove(Goal) :-
        clause(Goal, Body),
        prove(Body).
```

This relies for its correctness on the assumption that no clause in the clause/2 table matches the goals 'true' or 'A,B'. There is, as far as I know, no reason why a Prolog system might not contain the fact clause(true,true). Worse, some Prolog systems report an attempt to look at clauses for built-in predicates as errors, so the following interaction might take place:

```
?-    findall(., prove(true), L),
      length(L, N). % how many proofs of 'true' are found?

! The clauses of true/0 are inaccessible because it is (built_in)
! Goal: clause(true,_1159)
```

No, we can't tolerate something "defaulty" like that. The third clause should say exactly when it is to be used. I'll use an operation which is specific to Quintus Prolog, but the idea is generally applicable.

```
prove(true).
prove((A, B)) :-
        prove(A),
        prove(B).
prove(Goal) :-
        predicate_property(Goal, interpreted ),
        clause(Goal, Body),
        prove(Body).
```

Inserting this test does stop clause/2 being called inappropriately, but it doesn't stop that clause of prove/1 being tried. We had better either fix our representation, or add some cuts. Just for now, we'll add the cuts. We'll also add a case for built-in operations like clause/2 and predicate_property/2:

```
prove(true) :- !.
prove((A,B)) :- !,
        prove(A),
        prove(B).
prove(Goal) :-
        predicate_property(Goal, built_in),
        !,
        call(Goal).
prove(Goal) :-
        predicate_property(Goal, interpreted),
        clause(Goal, Body),
        prove(Body).
```

Oops. This interpreter sort-of works now, but it can't interpret itself, because of those cuts. We had better either (a) fix the representation of Prolog code so that the cuts aren't needed, or (b) write an interpreter which *can* handle cuts.

The cleanest thing to do is to change the representation, and if you want to embed a logic programming language other than Prolog into Prolog, this is the way to do it. Note that the representation which is used by the interpreter doesn't have to be exactly the same as what the programmer originally wrote. To stress that, let's use as our input notation

$$\text{Head} \leftarrow \text{Goal \& } \ldots \text{\& Goal.}$$
or   Head $\leftarrow$ true.

and as our internal representation facts of the form

$$\text{rule(Head, } [G_1, \ldots, G_n]).$$

where each G_i is either system(Goal) or user(Goal). We can accomplish this translation with term_expansion/2:

```
:- op(1200, xfx, (←)).
:- op(1000, xfy, (&)).

term_expansion((Head ← Goals), rule(Head,List)) :-
        flatten_goals(Goals, List, []).

flatten_goals((G1 & G2)) ⟶ !,
        flatten_goals(G1),
        flatten_goals(G2).
flatten_goals(true) ⟶ !, [].
flatten_goals(system(G)) ⟶ !,
        [system(G)].
flatten_goals(user(G)) ⟶ !,
        [user(G)].
flatten_goals(G) ⟶
        { predicate_property(G, built_in) },
        !,
        [system(G)].
flatten_goals(G) ⟶
        [user(G)].
```

An interpreter for rules so represented looks like this:

```
prove(system(Goal)) :-
        call(Goal).
prove(user(Goal)) :-
        rule(Goal, Body),
        prove_body(Body).

prove_body([]).
prove_body([Goal|Goals]) :-
        prove(Goal),
        prove_body(Goals).
```

Now this interpreter is not yet a meta-circular interpreter, but

```
prove(system(G)) ← call(G).
prove(user(G)) ← system(rule(G,B)) & prove_body(B).

prove_body([]) ← true.
prove_body([G|Gs]) ← prove(G) & prove_body(Gs).
```

is meta-circular.

Let's compare some of these interpreters on the infamous "naïve reverse" benchmark. The versions we'll try are

- the one-predicate version with a compiled table of claws/2 facts

- the two-predicate version with a compiled rule/2 table

- the two-predicate version interpreting itself.

The figures I obtained on a Sun-3/50 with Quintus Prolog 2.4 were

- 4.6 kLI/s,

- 4.4 kLI/s, and

- 0.5 kLI/s respectively.

This was an unpleasant surprise, because I dislike the one-predicate version, and hoped that it would be slower. Back to the drawing board.

The reason for the two-predicate version being so slow is that it has all those system(_) and user(_) wrappers, which are justified because they distinguish distinct cases, but which cost a fair bit of space. If we only had to deal with the user(_) case, the interpreter could be simplified. Instead of catching built-in predicates at the top, we can build them in at the bottom: for each $p(X_1, \ldots, X_N)$ for which we want p/N to be built-in (as far as the interpreter is concerned) we have only to ensure that there is a clause

$$\text{rule}(p(X_1, \ldots, X_n), []) :-$$
$$\quad p(X_1, \ldots, X_n).$$

This change exploits the lack of any distinction between code and data in Prolog: the caller of rule/2 has no way of telling whether it works by pattern matching in a table or what. With this change, we obtain

term_expansion((Head ← Goals), rule(Head,List)) :-
        flatten_goals(Goals, List, []).

flatten_goals((G1 & G2)) ⟶ !,
        flatten_goals(G1),
        flatten_goals(G2).
flatten_goals(true) ⟶ !, [].
flatten_goals(G) ⟶
        [G].

prove(Goal) :-
        rule(Goal, Body),
        prove_body(Body).

prove_body([]).
prove_body([Goal|Goals]) :-
        rule(Goal, Body), % body of prove/1
        prove_body(Body), % unfolded here
        prove_body(Goals).

rule(rule(H,B), []) :- % build rule/2 in
        rule(H, B). % add a similar clause for each built-in

prove(G) ← rule(G, B) & prove_body(B).

prove_body([]) ← true.
prove_body([G|Gs]) ← prove(G) & prove_body(Gs).

The speeds obtained with this code were

- 5.2 kLI/s interpreting naïve reverse

- 1.4 kLI/s interpreting itself interpreting naïve reverse

Now the Prolog proof procedure is often described as operating on an entire conjunction, and the connexion between that and what prove_body/1 is up to should be clear. What if we explicitly construct the entire conjunction as a list? The changes to the current interpreter are small:

```
term_expansion((Head ← Goals), rule(Head,List,Tail)) :-
        flatten_goals(Goals, List, Tail).

prove(Goal) :-
        prove_conjunction([Goal]).

prove_conjunction([]).
prove_conjunction([Goal|Goals]) :-
        rule(Goal, Goals1, Goals),
        prove_conjunction(Goals1).

rule(rule(H,B0,B), Goals, Goals) :- % build rule/3 in
        rule(H, B0, B). % and similar built-ins
```

This pushed the speed up to 5.5 kLI/s plain, 2.3 kLI/s interpreting itself. We thus have the following table:

	defaulty	wrapped	rule/2	rule/3	Quintus	
plain	4.6	4.4	5.2	5.5	67.0	(compiled)
iterated	1.3	0.5	1.4	2.3	1.9	(interpreted)

where the last column gives the speed of the version of Quintus Prolog used, for comparison. All figures are speed for naïve reverse, in kLI/s. Yes, 1.9 kLI/s is rather slower than 5.5 kLI/s, but the Quintus Prolog interpreter has to carry around a lot of information just in case the debugger might want it.

We see from this that by careful coding, it is possible to write a meta-circular interpreter for a pure variant of Prolog which goes quite fast. Making an interpreter go fast is just like making any other piece of Prolog code go fast:

- make decisions obvious (exploit indexing),

- keep the size of data structures down,

- exploit tail recursion,

- and use difference structures.

7.6   Conditional Cuts

We had two alternatives in the previous section: (a) fix the representation of Prolog code so that the cuts aren't needed, or (b) write an interpreter which *can* handle cuts. There we explored (a). Here we explore (b).

Cuts are notoriously tricky to deal with in Prolog interpreters (although a paper of mine showed how it could be done without requiring any new features in the language) and the usual response to this is to claim that *stronger* features should be added to Prolog, generally some sort of ancestral cut. Now that isn't a very good idea. In order to get the most benefit from compiling interpreters away, we want the interpreter itself to use simple, *local*, techniques. We can cover a large amount of sensible Prolog code by (a) rewriting, and (b) introducing a new construct which is *weaker* than ordinary cuts.

The basic idea is that we are going to store clauses as quadruples

   rule(Head, Before, Cut, After)

where Head is the usual head of the clause, and Before and After represent the code before and after the first cut in the clause body. If a clause has several cuts, e.g.,

p(...) :- q(...), !, r(...), !, s(...), !, t(...).

it can be transformed to

p(...) :-
            q(...),
            !,
            (r(...) → (s(...) → t(...) ; fail) ; fail).

without changing its behaviour, so only the first cut really needs special treatment. However, some clauses won't have any cuts at all. So we represent a clause

   p(...) :- q(...), !, r(...).
as
   rule(p(...), [q(...)], 1, [r(...)]).

and a clause

   p(...) :- q(...).
as
   rule(p(...), [], 0, [q(...)]).

The interpreter is a straightforward variation of what we have seen before:

```
prove(Goal) :-
        rule(Goal, Before, Cut, After),
        prove_body(Before),
        ( Cut =:= 1 → ! ; true ),
        prove_body(After).

prove_body([]).
prove_body([Goal|Goals]) :-
        prove(Goal),
        prove_body(Goals).
```

The form (Cut=:=1→!;true) is the operation which I want to call "conditional cut", and write !(Cut). It does a cut if its argument is 1, does nothing if its argument is 0, and is undefined otherwise. We can implement this operation in the translation phase, representing

$$p(\dots) :\text{-} q(\dots), !(Cut), r(\dots).$$

as

$$rule(p(\dots), [q(\dots)], Cut, [r(\dots)]).$$

Translating a clause is now somewhat more complex:

```
term_expansion((Head ← Body), Translation) :-
        flatten_goals(Body, List, []),
        (       append(Before, [!(Cut)|After], List) → true
        ;       append(Before, [!|After], List) → Cut = 1
        ;       Before = [], Cut = 0, After = List
        ),
        (       member(!, After) → Translation = (
                :-      write('! More than one cut in clause (clause discarded):'), nl,
                        write((Head ← Body)), nl
                )
        ;       Translation = rule(Head,Before,Cut,After)
        ).

flatten_goals((G1 & G2)) ⟶ !,
        flatten_goals(G1),
        flatten_goals(G2).
flatten_goals(true) ⟶ !, [].
flatten_goals(G) ⟶
        [G].
```

Built-in operations are hooked in underneath rule/4, as before:

```
rule(rule(H,B,C,A), [], 0, []) :-
        rule(H, B, C, A).
```

A meta-circular version of this interpreter is written thus:

```
prove(Goal) ←
        rule(Goal, Before, Cut, After) &
        prove_body(Before) &
        !(Cut) &
        prove_body(After).
```

```
prove_body([]) ← true.
prove_body([Goal|Goals]) ←
        prove(Goal) &
        prove_body(Goals).
```

We can extend this to support the if→ then;else and disjunction constructs, provided that they are not allowed to contain cuts, by adding some more clauses to rule/4 and augmenting the translator:

```
rule(or(A,_), [], 0, A). % (A|B) :- A.
rule(or(_,B), [], 0, B). % (A|B) :- B.
rule(if(A,B,_), A, 1, B). % (A→B;C) :- A, !, B.
rule(if(_,_,C), [], 0, C). % (A→B;C) :- C.
```

```
flatten_goals((G1 & G2), L0, L) :- !,
        flatten_goals(G1, L0, L1),
        flatten_goals(G2, L1, L).
flatten_goals(true, L, L) ⟶ !.
flatten_goals((G1 | G2), [or(A,B)|L], L) :- !,
        flatten_goals(G1, A, []),
        flatten_goals(G2, B, []).
flatten_goals((If → Then ; Else), [if(A,B,C)|L], L) :- !,
        flatten_goals(If, A, []),
        flatten_goals(Then, B, []),
        flatten_goals(Else, C, []).
flatten_goals(G, [G|L], L).
```

This version runs naïve reverse at only 3.7 kLI/s, and interprets itself at 0.8 kLI/s.

7.6.1   In Broken Prologs

The interpreter presented above exploits a feature of Edinburgh Prologs: not only can cuts cut their way through conjunctions (_,_), they can cut through the other control structures too. In particular, cuts are not supposed to be blocked by disjunctions (_;_) or (if→ then;else)s. If a Prolog system allows cuts in not-provables ¬(_), cuts aren't supposed to be blocked by them either. Cuts *are* blocked by call/N, setof/3, bagof/3, findall/3, and the like. A mnemonic you may find useful is that *letters* block cuts: the control structures which are transparent to cuts have no letters in their names. (The library predicate not/1, which checks that the goal is sufficiently instantiated for negation as failure to be sound, *does* block cuts, which is consistent with this mnemonic.)

If you want to write a Prolog-like interpreter in Prolog that handles cuts, the Prolog system you are using must supply one of two things: either a correct implementation of ordinary cuts, or some form of "ancestral cuts". I have shown above what you can do when the Prolog system implements cuts correctly. This section tells you what to do when the Prolog system does not implement cuts correctly, but does provide ancestral cuts.

There are three ways that ancestral cuts may be implemented.

- pattern match for ancestor

- user-provided label

- system-provided label

When the method is "pattern match for ancestor", you write cut(Goal) where Goal is a term, and the Prolog system searches down the ancestor list (that is, it looks at the current goal, the goal that called it, the goal that called that one, and so on) until it finds a goal which unifies with Goal. Then it cuts back to that point. (Note that this means that last call optimisation cannot be done, or at any rate not to predicates which might be looked for this way.)

```
prove(Goal) :- % this is the grandparent of the cut
        rule(Goal, Before, Cut, After),
        prove_body(Before),
        prove(Cut, After).

prove(1, After) :- % this is the parent of the cut
        cut(prove(_)), % the cut smashes back to the grandparent
        prove_body(After).
prove(0, After) :-
        prove_body(After).
```

When the method is "user-provided label", you write label(MagicMarker) to indicate an interesting place, and cut(MagicMarker) to cut back to the most recent instance of MagicMarker. In this method, MagicMarker is a term that *you* have to choose. In some Prologs, it can be any term. In at least one commercial Prolog, it has to be an integer.

```
prove(Goal) :-
        label(649865), % you name the choice point
        rule(Goal, Before, Cut, After),
        prove_body(Before),
        (    Cut =:= 1 → % when a cut is needed
             cut(649869) % you supply your name again
        ;    true
        ),
        prove_body(After).
```

Both of these kinds of ancestral cut have the extremely nasty property that if you don't know what you are doing, you can cut to the wrong place. That isn't a problem with these particular fragments, but if the caller tries to use the same magic marker you are in *trouble*.

When the method is "system-provided label", you write label(MagicMarker) where MagicMarker is a *variable*, and the system will bind the variable to a special value which uniquely identifies the current stack state. Apart from that, it looks like the "user-provided label" method.

```
prove(Goal) :-
        label(MagicMarker), % the system invents this name
        rule(Goal, Before, Cut, After),
        prove_body(Before),
        (    Cut =:= 1 → % when a cut is needed
             cut(MagicMarker) % you cite the system's name
        ;    true
        ),
        prove_body(After).
```

This method is much safer than the other two. (Which is like saying that polio is safer than smallpox. Even so, it can kill you.) Quintus Prolog, SICStus Prolog, and NU Prolog all have this method internally, but do not document or promise to retain it. LPA Prolog Professional for the PC has a rather curious variant of it: the same predicate is used for both label(_) and cut(_). In LPA Prolog we could write this as

```
prove(Goal) :-
        \(MagicMarker), % bound here
        rule(Goal, Before, Cut, After),
        prove_body(Before),
        (    Cut =:= 1 →
             \(MagicMarker) % used here
        ;    true
        ),
        prove_body(After).
```

Please, if you value the portability, clarity, and maintainability of your programs, *avoid* ancestral cuts if you possibly can. It is now (in 1989) about four years since I issued a challenge on the net asking for examples of problems which could be solved with the aid of ancestral cuts which could not be solved with the aid of ordinary cuts correctly implemented, and I have yet to receive any suggestions. If the Prolog system you have to use doesn't do something right, by all means do whatever you have to do to make your programs work, but using ancestral cuts without dire necessity is *begging* for trouble.

7.7 Augmenting Prolog

Augmenting a Prolog interpreter is just like enriching any other predicate which walks over a data structure. Let's consider an easy case first: counting the number of resolution steps in a proof.

```
count(Goal, Count) :-
        count_conjunction([Goal], 0, Count).

count_conjunction([], Count, Count).
count_conjunction([Goal|Goals], Count0, Count) :-
        Count1 is Count0+1,
        rule(Goal, Goals1, Goals),
        count_conjunction(Goals1, Count1, Count).
```

This runs naïve reverse at about 4.7 kLI/s. (Incidentally, calling

```
?- length(L, 30), count(reverse(L,_), Count).
```

will show you where the magic number 496 comes from in that benchmark.)

Another interpreter is rather more interesting. Instead of picking off the first goal on the left, we'll pick off the first "ready" goal.

```
sidetrack(Goal) :-
          sidetrack([Goal], Residue),
          report(Residue, Goal).

report([], Goal) :-
          write(Goal), nl.
report([G|Gs], Goal) :-
          write(Goal), write(' :-'), nl,
          write_goals(Gs, G).

write_goals([], G) :-
          put(9), write(G), put("."), nl.
write_goals([H|Gs], G) :-
          put(9), write(G), put(","), nl,
          write_goals(Gs, H).

sidetrack([Goal|Goals], Residue) :-
          select(Ready, [Goal|Goals], Goals1),
          ready(Ready),
          !,
          rule(Ready, Goals2, Goals1),
          sidetrack(Goals2, Residue).
sidetrack(Goals, Goals).
```

This interpreter needs to be told when each goal is ready to run. Let's illustrate it with append/3, as usual.

```
ready(append(X,Y,Z)) :- nonvar(X) ; nonvar(Z).
ready(reverse(X,Y)) :- nonvar(X) ; nonvar(Y).
```

With the usual definition of naïve reverse, the query

```
?- sidetrack(reverse([a,b,c|L], R)).
```

yields the output

```
reverse([a,b,c|A], B) :-
          reverse(A, C),
          append(C, [c], D),
          append(D, [b], E),
          append(E, [a], B).
```

More to the point, if we call

?- prove(reverse(X, [a,b])). % or
?- count(reverse(X, [a,b]), N).

and reject the answer X=[b,a] that we are offered, those interpreters will go into a
loop looking for another answer, but

?- sidetrack(reverse(X, [a,b])).

terminates. As a further example, the query

?- sidetrack(append(X, Y, [1,2|L])).

finds the solutions

append([], [1,2|A], [1,2|A]).
append([1], [2|A], [1,2|A]).
append([1,2|A], B, [1,2|C]) :-
        append(A, B, C).

Suppose we want to produce a proof tree. We might represent the proof of a fact
F as

   since(F, R, Ps)

where R identifies the rule which was used, and Ps is a list of proofs of the the
hypotheses of R, or as

   given(F, R)

to indicate that F is an instance of given fact R.
   To obtain such proofs, we represent given facts by pairs

   axiom(Head, Rule)

and other clauses by triples

   rule(Head, Rule, Body)

where Body is a list of goals, and use the following interpreter:

```
proof(Fact, given(Fact,Rule)) :-
        axiom(Fact, Rule).
proof(Fact, since(Fact,Rule,Proofs)) :-
        rule(Fact, Rule, Body),
        proofs(Body, Proofs).

proofs([], []).
proofs([H|Hs], [P|Ps]) :-
        proof(H, P),
        proofs(Hs, Ps).

print_proof(Proof) :-
        print_proof(Proof, 0).

print_proof(check(Fact), Depth) :- % to be defined shortly
        print_node(Depth, Fact, '(to be checked)').
print_proof(given(Fact,Rule), Depth) :-
        print_node(Depth, Fact, 'instance of '(Rule)).
print_proof(since(Fact,Rule,Proofs), Depth) :-
        print_node(Depth, Fact, 'by '(Rule)),
        Depth1 is Depth+2,
        print_proofs(Proofs, Depth1),
        tab(Depth), write('--'), nl.

print_node(Depth, Term, Label) :-
        tab(Depth), write(Term), put(" "), write(Label), nl.

print_proofs([], _).
print_proofs([P|Ps], D) :-
        print_proof(P, D),
        print_proofs(Ps, D).
```

An example we shall return to is

```
rule(kill(A,B), 'Killing',
    [ hate(A,B), possess(A,C), weapon(C) ]).
rule(hate(A,A), 'Self-hatred',
    [ depressed(A) ]).
rule(possess(U,V), 'Purchase',
    [ buy(U,V) ]).
rule(weapon(X), 'Is-a-gun',
    [ gun(X) ]).
```

axiom(depressed(john), 'Fact 1').
axiom(buy(john,gun1), 'Fact 2').
axiom(gun(gun1),   'Fact 3').

With this rule base, the query

?- proof(kill(X,X), Proof), print_proof(Proof).

prints

```
kill(john, john) by (Killing)
  hate(john, john) by (Self-hatred)
    depressed(john) instance of (Fact 1)
  --
  possess(john,gun1) by (Purchase)
    buy(john,gun1) instance of (Fact 2)
  --
  weapon(gun1) by (Is-a-gun)
    gun(gun1) instance of (Fact 3)
  --
--
```

This example comes from the paper "Explanation-Based Generalization as Resolution Theorem Proving", by Kedar-Cabelli and McCarty [21]. Their idea is to run two proofs in parallel, using the same clauses.

```
proof(Goal, given(Goal,Rule), G_Goal, check(G_Goal)) :-
        given(Goal, Rule).
proof(Goal, since(Goal,Rule,Proofs), G_Goal, since(G_Goal,Rule,G_Proofs)) :-
        rule(Goal, Rule, Body),
        rule(G_Goal, Rule, G_Body),
        proofs(Body, Proofs, G_Body, G_Proofs).

proofs([], [], [], []).
proofs([G|Gs], [P|Ps], [G_G|G_Gs], [G_P|G_Ps]) :-
        proof(G, P, G_G, G_P),
        proofs(Gs, Ps, G_Gs, G_Ps).
```

Running the query

```
?-   proof(kill(john, john), _, Gen, GP),
     numbervars(GP, 0, _),
     print_proof(GP).
```

through this interpreter produces the result

```
kill(A,A) by (Killing)
  hate(A,A) by (Self-hatred)
    depressed(A) (to be checked)
  --
  possess(A,B) by (Purchase)
    buy(A,B) (to be checked)
  --
  weapon(B) by (Is-a-gun)
    gun(B) (to be checked)
  --
--
```

That is to say, in the course of solving a *specific* problem (namely, kill(john, john))
the interpreter has noticed a *general* rule. This general rule is a consequence of
the interpreter's existing rule base, so it doesn't add anything in principle to our
knowledge, but it may be useful in simplifying future questions.

We can simplify this interpreter to just return the subgoals to be checked.

```
proof(Goal, rule(GenGoal,Body)) :-
        functor(Goal, F, N),
        functor(GenGoal, F, N),
        proof([Goal], [GenGoal], Body).


proof([], [], []).
proof([G|Gs], [GenG|GenGs], [GenG|Body]) :-
        given(G),
        proof(Gs, GenGs, Body).
proof([G|Gs], [GenG|GenGs], Body) :-
        rule(R, G, Gs1, Gs),
        rule(R, GenG, GenGs1, GenGs),
        proof(Gs1, GenGs1, Body).


rule(1, kill(A,B),      [hate(A,B),possess(A,C),weapon(C)|Gs], Gs).
rule(2, hate(A,A),      [depressed(A)|Gs], Gs).
rule(3, possess(U,V), [buy(U,V)|Gs], Gs).
rule(4, weapon(X),    [gun(X)|Gs], Gs).


given(depressed(john)).
```

given(buy(john,gun1)).
given(gun(gun1)).

The query

?- proof(kill(john, john), Rule).

has the solution

Rule = rule(kill(A,A),[depressed(A),buy(A,B),gun(B)])

which means that kill(john, john) follows from the Rule shown, and that the Rule follows from the existing rules.

7.8 Summary

- Writing special-purpose interpreters in Prolog is easy.

- Interpreters are just programs that do things with trees, and can be improved and combined just like other programs.

- Unfolding can be used to "compile away" an interpreter.

- It is useful to transform the "program" that an interpreter interprets so that it is better behaved as a data structure (e.g., is not "defaulty"); this means that the code which executes often can be clean. The built-in predicate term_expansion/2 is a good place to do such transformations.

- A single "language" may have more than one interpreter.

8 Some Notes on Grammar Rules

8.1   Introduction

One of the less conventional, and one of the most useful, aspects of Prolog is the ease with which it can be used for parsing. Parsers can be written in Prolog at least as easily as by using "parser generators" like YACC, and they have the inestimable advantage that all the Prolog support tools such as the cross-referencer and the debugger can be applied to them. Indeed, it is the "grammar rule" component of Prolog which makes any special string data type not only superfluous but positively disadvantageous; one can do pattern matching and rewriting in Prolog as easily as in SNOBOL (or, for UNIX hackers, more easily than in 'ed'). What may be more surprising is that measurements indicate that this is often *faster* than using packed arrays of bytes.

8.2   A Brief Description of Grammar Rules

The grammars that Prolog understands are called *Definite Clause Grammars*, so called because they can be translated directly into Horn clauses, also called *definite clauses*. This is not an introduction to grammar rules or their use; you should read Chapter 9 of Clocksin & Mellish for that. Briefly,

grammar_rule ⟶
      grammar_head,
      [⟶],
      grammar_body.

grammar_head ⟶
      non_terminal,
      ([','], terminal | []).

grammar_body ⟶
      grammar_arm,
      ([';'], grammar_body | []).

grammar_arm ⟶
      grammar_and,
      (['⟶'], grammar_and | []).

grammar_and ⟶
      grammar_item,
      ([','], grammar_and | []).

grammar_item $\longrightarrow$
>   variable
> | non_terminal
> | terminal
> | ['!']
> | ['(', grammar_body, ')']
> | ['{', prolog_body, ['}'].

non_terminal $\longrightarrow$
>   – a Prolog callable term –.

terminal $\longrightarrow$
>   ['[',']']
> | ['[', terminals, ']'].

terminals $\longrightarrow$
>   any_prolog_term,
>   ([','], terminals | []).

There are several points to note here. The first is that you can use if$\rightarrow$ then;else in a grammar rule, and it works exactly as you would expect. You can also use a variable as a non-terminal, though it had better be bound by the time you try to call it! We shall see below how variables are handled.

A mistake I make fairly often is to write a recursive definition like this:

terminals $\longrightarrow$
>   ['[',
>   ([']']
> | terminal, more_terminals, ']']
>   ).

more_terminals $\longrightarrow$
>   [','], terminal,
>   more_terminals.
more_terminals.

See the mistake? (Actually, there is a better way to write the whole thing. This is just an illustration.) The mistake is in the last clause; it is an ordinary clause, not a grammar rule.

Beware! **There is no analogue of a unit clause in grammar rules.** If you want a rule which matches the empty string, you have to say so *explicitly*. The last clause should have read more_terminals ⟶ [].

The obvious translation of grammar rules into Prolog is the one used in the Clocksin & Mellish book (after correcting a mistake). For example, here is a non-terminal taken from page 231 of the 2nd edition:

```
rel_clause(X, P1, P1&P2) ⟶
        [that],
        verb_phrase(X, P2).
rel_clause(_, P, P) ⟶
        [].
```

and here is its translation:

```
rel_clause(X, P1, P1&P2, [that|S1], S) :-
        verb_phrase(X, P2, S1, S).
rel_clause(_, P, P, S, S).
```

Now that translation, which moves the terminals into the other goals, is a very pretty one, and the code which results is efficient. But there is a nasty problem. It's a very general problem: if we have cuts or if→ then;elses in our rules, pattern matching can force us down the "wrong" alternative. (We say that the incorrect predicate is not *steadfast*.) Here is an example of the problem:

```
rel_phrase(X, P1, P1&P2) ⟶
        { must_be_relativised(X, P1) },
        !,
        [that],
        verb_phrase(X, P2).
rel_phrase(X, P1, P1&P2) ⟶
        { may_be_relativised(X, P1) },
        [that],
        verb_phrase(X, P2).
rel_phrase(_, P, P) ⟶
        [].
```

Here the idea is that the X,P contexts fall into three groups: those which must have a relative clause, those which may, and those which must not. Now the obvious translation is

```
rel_phrase(X, P1, P1&P2, [that|S1], S) :-
        must_be_relativised(X, P1),
        !,
        verb_phrase(X, P2).
```

rel_phrase(X, P1, P1&P2, [that|S1], S) :-
        may_be_relativised(X, P1),
        verb_phrase(X, P2).
rel_phrase(_, P, P, S, S).

Do you see the problem? The check for [that] has been moved into the head of the clause; that is to say, it has been moved *before* the cut. Now suppose we have a sentence in which the X,P context says that there must be a relative clause, but there is no [that]. Then the pattern match in the head will fail *before* we ever get as far as the cut, and after checking again in the second clause, the third clause will be tried, and it will *succeed*. This is not at all what we intended!

In any kind of Prolog source-level transformations, this problem crops up again and again: you must *never* move anything back over a cut! We don't yet have a general tool available to work around the problem; though we do know how to get rid of cuts in favour of if→ then;elses, which have the same problem. There *is*, however, a work-around for grammar rules, which has sufficient merit that it is worth using anyway.

The method which Dec-10 Prolog, C Prolog, and Quintus Prolog use is this. We rewrite a terminal [a,b,c] as a sequence of calls to 'C'/3, viz

            'C'(S0, a, S1),
            'C'(S1, b, S2),
            'C'(S2, c, S3)

where 'C'/3 is defined by the single clause

'C'([Token|Tokens], Token, Tokens).

Apart from the fact that this entirely eliminates the problem with cuts, this approach has another merit: the *only* part of the Prolog system which knows or cares that grammar rules work on lists is the predicate 'C'/3. If a Prolog implementor chooses to add another clause

'C'(Stream/Offset, Char, Stream/Next) :-
        input_stream(Stream),
        succ(Offset, Next),
        stream_seek(Stream, Offset),
        get0(Stream, Char).

he is at liberty to do so. Then grammar rules could be used to match patterns in files. Why not?

A moderately common mistake is forgetting to put the curly braces around a piece of ordinary Prolog code, e.g., writing

[Char], Char ≥ "A", Char ≤ "Z"

when one meant to write

[Char],
{Char ≥ "A", Char ≤ "Z"}

Very often these tests are comparisons, or the Prolog code may be constructing a result with '=', or calling name/2 to pack a list of character codes into a symbol. If you use the cross-referencer on your source code, because it uses the same expand_term/2 facility, it will see these as calls to predicates with two extra arguments, and you will see this built-in predicates listed as UNDEFINED.

8.3 Phrase/[2,3]

Dec-10 Prolog, C Prolog, and Quintus Prolog all provide a predicate called phrase/2. To quote Clocksin & Mellish:

phrase(P, L) is true iff list L can be parsed as a phrase of type P.

Calling phrase(P, L) is very like calling P(L,[]), except that the first argument of phrase/2 can be *any* term which would be accepted as a grammar rule body. This is exactly like call(X), which allows X to be *any* term which would be accepted as a clause body.

Quintus Prolog adds a predicate phrase(P,L0,L) which is true if the segment between the positions L0 and L in some list can be parsed as a phrase of type P. If a variable X appears in a grammar rule body, it is treated as though phrase(X) appeared instead, so this turns into a call to phrase(X,L0,L) for some L0,L. So phrase/3 is the analogue of call/1 for grammar rule bodies. The Quintus implementation of phrase/2 and phrase/3 makes a special case of lists, so that calling phrase("abc") is not too much more expensive than doing an append.

As an example, we might use the following definitions:

:- op(400, yf, [*,?]).

(X?) ⟶ [] | X.

(X*) ⟶ [] | X, X* . % space needed!

X*Sep ⟶ X, ([] | Sep, X*Sep).

With the aid of those definitions, we could write rules like

declaration $\longrightarrow$
        [id]*[','], [:], type, ([:=],expr)? .

In fact, you would not do this in a real program, because you almost always
need to pass inherited attributes down to the arguments and combine synthesised
attributes in special ways. But it's pretty...

8.4 Examples

There are several examples of DCG notation in the chapter on Sequences. Grammar rules are such a handy tool for constructing sequences that I have used them
all through this book without comment. They are an optional part of Prolog in
precisely the same sense that **for** statements are optional in C or Pascal.

8.4.1 Append

As a really trivial example, we'll use grammar rules to define a version of append/3,
except that the arguments will be the other way around.

literal([]) $\longrightarrow$ [].
literal([X|Xs]) $\longrightarrow$ [X], literal(Xs).

We read this, as a grammar, as

- the segment between S0 and S can be parsed as a phrase of type literal([]) if
  there is *nothing* ([]) between S0 and S.

- the segment between S0 and S can be parsed as a phrase of type literal([X|Xs])
  if there is an S1 such that there is an X between S0 and S1 and the segment
  between S1 and S can be parsed as a phrase of type literal(Xs).

As Prolog code, this is

literal([], S, S).
literal([X|Xs], S0, S) :-
        'C'(S0, X, S1),
        literal(Xs, S1, S).

Since there are no cuts around, we can safely unfold the call to 'C'/3, and obtain

literal([], S, S).
literal([X|Xs], [X|S1], S) :-
        literal(Xs, S1, S).

as the logical equivalent of the grammar, and we recognise this as append/3 with
the second and third arguments swapped.

Now, if we write a grammar rule

date(YearCs, MonthCs, DayCs) $\longrightarrow$
        literal(DayCs), "/", literal(MonthCs), "/", literal(YearCs).

we see that this is *logically* equivalent to

date(YearCs, MonthCs, DayCs, S0, S) :-
        append(DayCs, [0'/|S2], S0),
        append(MonthCs, [0'/|S4], S2),
        append(YearCs, S, S4).

If we call

?- phrase(date("87","11","17"), Result).

or directly call

?- date("87", "11", "17", Result, []).

we are told that the answer is

Result = "17/11/87"

If we ask

?- phrase(date(Y,M,D), "17/11/87").

or directly call

?- date(Y, M, D, "17/11/87", []).

we are told that the answer is

Y = "87", M = "11", D = "17"

The advantage of the grammar rule notation is that the last two arguments of
the predicates, which are being used in a very rigid and predictable manner, don't
appear in the text, so it is easier to see the interesting part. Prolog has no special
parser: grammar rules *are* ordinary Prolog clauses and they are executed *exactly*
the same way that all Prolog clauses are executed.

8.4.2 Flattening a Tree

Suppose we have a tree which is either a node(Label,Lson,Rson) where the Lson and Rson are trees, or the empty tree 'empty', and we want to collect the Labels as a list. We can write

labels(Tree, S) :-
        labels(Tree, S, []).

labels(empty) ⟶ [].
labels(node(Label,L,R)) ⟶ labels(L), [Label], labels(R).

   Earlier in the book we saw this as

labels(Tree, S) :-
        labels(Tree, S, []).

labels(empty, S, S).
labels(node(Label,L,R), S0, S) :-
        labels(L, S0, [Label|S1]),
        labels(R, S1, S).

There is no substantive difference between these two presentations of the routine. It is rather more obvious that the grammar rule version is building a list, but that's about it. As far as efficiency is concerned, don't worry, the two versions are much the same code, so neither is more efficient than the other.

8.4.3 Replacing One Sublist by Another

Suppose we want to express the following relation:

replace(OldSub, /*by*/NewSub, /*in*/OldStr, /*giving*/NewStr) is to be true when all four arguments are lists, and there exist lists Before and After such that

$$OldStr = Before \frown OldSub \frown After$$
$$NewStr = Before \frown NewSub \frown After$$

   How might we code it? Well, a good thing to try is *directly*.

replace(OldSub, NewSub, OldStr, NewStr) :-
        divide3(Before, OldSub, After, OldStr, []),
        divide3(Before, NewSub, After, NewStr, []).

divide3(Before, Middle, After) ⟶
        literal(Before), literal(Middle), literal(After).

Try it; it will work. It has some performance flaws, but they have nothing to do with whether we code it using grammar rule notation or not.

8.4.4   Finding a Pattern in a String

Now let's consider a more general problem: finding the Index where a Pattern occurs in a given Sequence. All we do is

```
index(Pattern, Sequence, Index) :-
        index(Pattern, 0, Index, Sequence, _).
```

```
index(Pattern, Index, Index) ⟶
        Pattern.
index(Pattern, Index0, Index) ⟶
        [_], % skip a character
        {Index1 is Index0+1},
        index(Pattern, Index1, Index).
```

That truly is all there is to it. If Pattern is a string (i.e., a list of character codes), this is somewhat slower than the code would could have written for that special case. But Pattern could be any term acceptable as a grammar rule body. For example, supposing we had a non-terminal which matched file names, we could ask, "where does a file name occur in this string, and what is it?" by writing

```
    index(file_name(FileName), String, Index)
```

8.4.5   library(morelists)

The Quintus library contains a file library(morelists) defining predicates specially intended for use in grammar rules. Some of these operations were inspired by SNOBOL. Most of them exist in pairs: a version which constructs or matches a plain list, and a version which constructs or matches a difference list and so can be used in a grammar rule.

For example, suppose we are given a list of characters looking like

    month/day/year spaces customer spaces $amount spaces

and want to turn this into

    YearMonthDay amount customer

This is all it takes:

translate(InputLine, OutputLine) :-
        input_line(M, D, Y, C, A, InputLine, []),
        output_line(Y, M, D, A, C, OutputLine, []).

input_line(M, D, Y, C, A) ⟶
        lit(M), "/", lit(D), "/", lit(Y), spaces,
        lit(C), spaces, lit("$"), lit(A), spaces.

output_line(Y, M, D, A, C) ⟶
        adjust(right, 2, 0'0, Y), % pad Y on the left with 0
        adjust(right, 2, 0'0, M), % to 2 digits, similarly M
        adjust(right, 2, 0'0, D), % and D
        " ", lit(A), " ", lit(C).

8.5   A Notational Convention

When we want to refer to a predicate of N arguments whose predicate symbol is
P, we write P/N. When we want to indicate the module as well, we write $M{:}P/N$.
For example, to talk about the predicate which the goal append(X,Y,Z) calls, we
write append/3, or to highlight the fact that it comes from the "basics" module,
we write basics:append/3. There are built-in Prolog commands such as listing/1
which understand this notation.

A non-terminal Q with N arguments (such as output_line above with 5 arguments) has two more arguments added by the grammar rule translator, so it really
is the predicate $Q/(N+2)$. I find it useful to write about non-terminals as $Q//N$ or
$M{:}Q//N$. You may find this useful too, but be warned that Prolog systems don't
understand it (yet).

8.6   Perspective on a Problem

You have probably met compiler-writing tools such as UNIX's YACC. There are
many others, based on LL(1), SLR(1), LALR(1), or WP(1,2) methods. They are
generally based on the idea that the programs they are used to construct will
be given very long strings to parse (entire programs containing many thousands
of tokens), but that the grammars are unambiguous and a unique parse is to be
found.

That is not what Definite Clause Grammars were originally intended for. Prolog
was originally designed for parsing sentences in human languages such as French,
where the sentences are short (at most a few dozen words) and the (context-free

skeletons of the) grammars are thoroughly ambiguous, and several different parses
may need to be tried before one is found which is acceptable to semantic analysis.

Prolog grammar rules, then, are supposed to be

- clear

- parametric

- integrated with the rest of the system (debugger, compiler, &c)

- well-suited to ambiguous languages.

That's the perspective: what's the problem?

The problem is that in most implementations, the sequence being parsed con-
tributes nothing to indexing. Suppose we have the following grammar:

```
command(delete(File))        ⟶ [rm], file(File).
command(copy(From,To))       ⟶ [cp], file(From), file(To).
command(print(File))         ⟶ [lpr], file(File).
```

This will be translated to

```
command(delete(File), S0, S) :-
        'C'(S0, rm, S1),
        file(File, S1, S).
command(copy(From,To), S0, S) :-
        'C'(S0, cp, S1),
        file(From, S1, S2),
        file(To, S2, S).
command(print(File), S0, S) :-
        'C'(S0, lpr, S1),
        file(File, S1, S).
```

The form of the parse tree appears in the heads of these clauses, so if you are
using these rules to *generate* UNIX commands from given parse trees, you will get
indexing. But the tokens (rm, cp, lpr) which select a unique appropriate rule when
you are *parsing* given commands don't appear in the heads, but appear in goals in
the body. You can hardly expect Prolog to index on something which doesn't even
appear in the head! So if you call

```
?- phrase(command(X), [rm,example]).
```

or, equivalently,

?- phrase(command(X), [rm,example], []).

Prolog scratches its (clause-)head for a bit and decides that since it doesn't know
what X is, and the clause heads don't restrict S0 or S at all, *any* of the rules might
apply. In this case, the first rule will succeed, but Prolog doesn't realise that none
of the other rules can succeed, so it will leave a choice point behind.

A technique that some people use to get around this problem is to add cuts to
the rules. In this example, we'd get

command(delete(File)) $\longrightarrow$ [rm], !, file(File).
command(copy(From,To)) $\longrightarrow$ [cp], !, file(From), file(To).
command(print(File)) $\longrightarrow$ [lpr], !, file(File).

This is as regrettable as adding cuts always is, but if either the first argument of
command//1 or the sequence to be parsed is known, the cuts are blue.

A cleaner technique is to *promote* the first token into the head.

command(Interpretation) $\longrightarrow$
        [Token],
        command(Token, Interpretation).

command(rm, delete(File)) $\longrightarrow$ file(File).
command(cp, copy(From,To)) $\longrightarrow$ file(From), file(To).
command(lpr, print(File)) $\longrightarrow$ file(File).

Suppose we have a non-terminal where the first token does disambiguate which
rule to use, but some of its rules do not start by consuming the token. For example,

sexpr(A) $\longrightarrow$ [number(A)].
sexpr(A) $\longrightarrow$ [atom(A)].
sexpr(A) $\longrightarrow$ ['('], list(A).

list([]) $\longrightarrow$ [')'].
list(A) $\longrightarrow$ ['.'], sexpr(A), [')'].
list([X|Xs]) $\longrightarrow$ sexpr(X), list(Xs).

In this example, an sexpr cannot begin with ')' or '.', so the first token does disambiguate list//1, but the third rule doesn't consume that token. One approach is to
introduce a look_ahead//1 non-terminal:

look_ahead(Token),[Token] $\longrightarrow$ [Token].

list(Xs) $\longrightarrow$ look_ahead(Token), list(Token, Xs).

list(')',   [])   ⟶ [')'].
list('.',   A)   ⟶ ['.'], sexpr(A), [')'].
list(number(_), [X|Xs]) ⟶ sexpr(X), list(Xs).
list(atom(_),   [X|Xs]) ⟶ sexpr(X), list(Xs).
list('(',   [X|Xs]) ⟶ sexpr(X), list(Xs).

look_ahead/1 can be simplified (when 'C'/3 is list traversal) to

look_ahead(Token, [Token|S], [Token|S]).

Let's return to the UNIX command example, to see why the lack of indexing may not be a problem in practice. Suppose we have many commands, some of which take one argument, some of which take two, some of which take none, and some of which take any number.

command(Interpretation) ⟶
        [Command],
        {command_table(Command, Interpretation)},
        command_1(Interpretation).

command_table(rm, cmd_1(delete,_)).
command_table(cp, cmd_2(copy,_,_)).
command_table(lpr, cmd_L(print,_)).
command_table(logout, cmd_0(logout)).

command_1(cmd_0(_))   ⟶ [].
command_1(cmd_1(_,F))   ⟶ file(F).
command_1(cmd_2(_,F,G)) ⟶ file(F), file(G).
command_1(cmd_L(_,L))   ⟶ files(L).

files([]) ⟶ [].
files([F|Fs]) ⟶ file(F), files(Fs).

Here we have looked the command name up in a dictionary, and then dispatched (in command_1//1) on the interpretation found therein. Natural-language parsers often do this. Indeed, it is not uncommon for natural-language dictionary entries to be miniature programs.

For example, suppose we wanted to parse an extensible programming language[1]. Suppose that we have non-terminals variable//1, expression//1, and statement//1 available. We might have a table like

---

[1]Something like the WonderPop "forms" facility.

keyword(set, [variable(V),{to},expression(E)], assign(V,E)).
keyword(increment, [variable(V)], assign(V,plus(V,number(1)))).
keyword(decrement, [variable(V)], assign(V,plus(V,number(-1)))).
keyword(while, [expression(E),{do},statement(S)], while_do(E,S)).
keyword(do, [statement(S),{while},expression(E)], do_while(E,S)).
keyword(call, [variable(V)], call(V)).

which could be extended in obvious ways, and we would then define statement//1
thus:

statement(Meaning) $\longrightarrow$
            [Keyword],
            {keyword(Keyword, Items, Meaning)},
            items(Items).

items([]) $\longrightarrow$ [].
items([Item|Items]) $\longrightarrow$
            item(item),
            items(Items).

item(variable(V)) $\longrightarrow$ variable(V).
item(expression(E)) $\longrightarrow$ expression(E).
item(statement(S)) $\longrightarrow$ statement(S).
item({Keyword}) $\longrightarrow$ [Keyword].

In effect, the second argument of the keyword/3 table is a miniature program,
and items//1 is an interpreter for such programs. Apart from the sheer declarative
beauty of stuffing things into tables (:-), this technique makes it easy to dynamically extend the language being parsed. Note that this grammar *does* benefit from
ordinary Prolog indexing, though if we had written it as

statement(assign(V,E)) $\longrightarrow$
            [set], variable(V), [to], expression(E).

$\vdots$

it would not have benefited from indexing.

The moral is not "write interpreters", but "make grammar rules general and put
specific information in tables". Another example concerns operator precedence.
Suppose that the tokeniser delivers to the parser

number(X)	for numbers
identifier(X)	for plain identifiers
operator(X)	for operators

and reports keywords and punctuation marks as atoms, so that

(X+1)/(X-1)

would be reported to the parser as

... '(',identifier('X'),operator(+),number(1),')',operator(/),
    '(',identifier('X'),operator(-),number(1),')',...

With the aid of three tables:

max_prio(*greatest infix operator priority + 1*).

prefix_operator(*operator, argument, translation*).

infix_operator(*operator, priority, left arg, right arg, translation*).

we can write a general expression grammar thus:

expression(Expr) ⟶
        { max_prio(MaxPrio) },
        expression(MaxPrio, Expr).

expression(MaxPrio, Expr) ⟶
        primary(Primary),
        rest_expression(Primary, 0, MaxPrio, Expr).

primary(Primary) ⟶
        [Token],
        primary(Token, Primary).

primary(identifier(X), variable(V)) ⟶
        rest_variable(X, V).
primary(number(X), number(X)) ⟶ [].
primary('(', Expr) ⟶
        expression(Expr), [')'].
primary(operator(Op), Expr) ⟶
        { prefix_operator(Op, Arg, Expr) },
        primary(Arg).

rest_expression(Lhs, CurPrio, MaxPrio, Expr) $\longrightarrow$
       [operator(Op)],
       { infix_operator(Op, OpPrio, Lhs, Rhs, This) },
       { OpPrio $\geq$ CurPrio, OpPrio $<$ MaxPrio },
       !,
       expression(OpPrio, Rhs),
       rest_expression(This, OpPrio, MaxPrio, Expr).
rest_expression(Expr, _, _, Expr) $\longrightarrow$ [].

The particulars of the language then appear in tables, and the whole thing can be done cleanly without the clumsy subterfuges of YACC.

9 Prolog Macros

This section introduces you to the user-definable predicate term_expansion/2 and its uses.

The basic top-level loop of a Prolog system looks something like this:

```
handle(File) :-
        open(File, read, Stream),
        repeat,
                read(Stream, Term),
                expand_term(Term, Clause),
                process(Clause),
        !,
        close(Stream).
```

Note that the cut is needed to shut down the "repeat" loop. All "repeat" loops are variations on the scheme

```
        repeat,
                obtain_next_datum(Datum),
                do_something_with_the_datum(Datum),
                fail_unless_this_is_the_last_datum(Datum),
        !,
```

Any repeat loop which isn't terminated by a cut in the same clause probably has something wrong with it. You should always bear in mind that the code which *follows* a call to your predicate might fail and backtrack into your code.

Typically the "process" predicate for a file loop looks like this:

```
process(end_of_file) :- !.
process(:-(Command)) :- !,
        call(Command),
        fail.
process(?-(Query)) :- !,
        (    call(Query),
             format(user_output, '~NProved: ~q~n', Query),
             ¬ yesno('More?'),
             !
        ;    format(user_output, '~NNo (more) answers~n', [])
        ),
        fail.
process(Clause) :-
        "assert"(Clause),
        fail.
```

This style was formed in the very early days of Prolog, before tail recursion optimisation and garbage collectors were available. In systems like the later DEC-10 Prolog and Quintus Prolog, it is more natural to write loops like this:

```
handle(File) :-
        open(File, read, Stream),
        read_clause(Stream, Clause),
        handle(Clause, Stream).

read_clause(Stream, Clause) :-
        read(Stream, Term),
        expand_term(Term, Clause).

handle(end_of_file, Stream) :- !,
        close(Stream).
handle(Clause, Stream) :-
        process(Clause),
        fail.
handle(_, Stream) :-
        read_clause(Stream, Clause),
        handle(Clause, Stream).
```

In either case, a very important thing happens in between reading a term and processing a command, query, or clause: the built in predicate expand_term/2 is called. This predicate was introduced in DEC-10 Prolog to handle grammar rules. The point is that a grammar rule such as

```
s ⟶ np(Subj), vp(Subj).
```

is treated by the system as if not was not only *equivalent* to the clause

```
s(S0, S) :- np(Subj, S0, S1), vp(Subj, S1, S).
```

but in fact actually *identical* to it. compile/1 and consult/1 do not have to treat grammar rules specially, because they never *see* them, and they can treat grammar rules similarly, because they always see the same translation. The fact that expand_term/2 is available as a built-in predicate means that you can write programs to analyse Prolog source code without having to know anything at all about the translation of grammar rules, or even that there are such things as grammar rules.

But why not build this translation into read/1 itself? For a very simple reason: read/1 may be used to read data which have the syntax of Prolog terms but are not Prolog code. For example, you could very easily write an interpreter for production rules in Prolog, and these rules might look like

Condition —→ *Action.*

When you read such rules, the last thing you'd want would be to have them translated as if they were grammar rules! Indeed, several other formalisms resembling DCGs have been used in Prolog, including XGs (eXtraposition Grammars), MSGs (Modifier Structure Grammars), and DCSGs (Definite Clause Slash Grammars) among others.

There is at least one commercial Prolog system where the equivalent of expand_term/2 is built into assert/1. While that does work for the special case of loading a file containing grammar rules, it means that if you want to read a program (perhaps to check whether it is determinate) without asserting it into the data base, you are stuck: you have to implement your own term expansion. If you want a version of assert/1 which does term expansion, you can easily make one using expand_term/2:

```
assert_expanded_term(Term) :-
        expand_term(Term, Clause),
        assert(Clause).
```

9.1   A digression about print/1

The point of expand_term//2 is not just to handle grammar rules, but to provide a "hook" which you can use to define your own translations. Prolog has another such "hook" in the print/1 predicate.

Once upon a time, DEC-10 Prolog provided display/1, which writes terms to the standard output stream without quoting atoms or using operators, write/1, and writeq/1, and that was it. display/1 had been written in MACRO-10 assembly code to help in debugging the system itself. It was expected that programmers would use write/1—analogous to (PRINC) in Lisp—and writeq/1—analogous to (PRIN1) in Lisp—and if they needed anything fancy they would write it themselves.

The trouble with "if you need something fancy you can write it yourself" is that the Prolog system itself writes things out. There are at least two places where this happens:

- answers to top-level queries

- showing goals during debugging

Chris Mellish was a student at Edinburgh. The semantic analyser he was working on generated very large terms, so that when he used the debugger he couldn't even see the current goal because it overflows the screen. The DEC-10 Prolog team responded to this problem by adding a new predicate:

```
print(Term) :- % OLD definition
        nonvar(Term),
        current_predicate(portray, portray(Term)),
        portray(Term),
        !.
print(Term) :- % OLD definition
        write(Term).
```

The top level and the debugger were changed to use print/1 instead of write/1.
This meant that you could specify how a goal was to be abbreviated by writing,
for example,

```
portray(append(A,Z,AZ)) :-
        write('append('), write_len(A),
        write(','), write_len(Z),
        write(','), write_len(AZ),
        write(')').
```

```
write_len(L) :-
        write('|'),
        write_len(L, 0).
```

```
write_len(V, N) :- var(V), !,
        write(N), write(..+).
write_len([], N) :- !,
        write(N). write_len([_—L], M) :- !,
        N is M+1,
        write_len(L, N).
write_len(_, N) :-
        write(N), write(..?).
```

Then if you had a goal like

```
    append("abc", "def", X)
```

the debugger might show it to you as

```
    append(|3,|4,|0..?)
```

There are some subtle points to this. For example, if the debugger calls print/1,
it must temporarily disable debugging so that you don't trace portray/1 while
printing a trace.

The next thing that happened was that the MECHO project needed a rational
number package for PRESS, the PRolog Equation Solving System. A rational
number like -42/33 was represented by a triple

        number(-,[42],[33])

and it really didn't make mathematical formulas look very readable if they were
printed with raw Prolog terms in them like that instead of the intended numeric
values. This time the focus was different: instead of saying how to abbreviate
specific *goals*, we wanted to say how to portray specific *terms*. It was easy enough
to write a predicate portray_number/1 so that

```
:-    eval(X is -42/33), portray_number(X), nl.
(-14/11)
```

What we did for a while was to use a version of portray/1 which essentially duplicated everything that write/1 did, except for calling another predicate to check
each term. That was rather a waste, because we already had code to do that in
write/1. So the next step was that print/1 was replaced. The current definition
works like this:

```
print(X) :- var(X), !,
        write(X).
print(X) :-
        current_predicate(portray, portray(X)),
        ¬¬ portray(X),
        !.
print(X) :- atomic(X), !,
        print a number or atom.
print([H|T]) :- !,
        write a list, calling print on its elements.
print(Compound) :-
        write a compound term, calling print on its arguments.
```

This works very nicely, except for one thing. How do you define portray/1? In
DEC-10 Prolog, there was no really satisfactory method. Because the compile/1
command acts like reconsult/1, putting a clause for portray/1 meant that if you
compiled that file you couldn't have clauses for portray/1 in any *other* files. The
work-around that I adopted was to put predicates *variety*_portray/1 in my files,
and then in the "root file" for my program write

```
:- op(op declaration).
:
:- op(op declaration).
```

```
:- compile([
      'file1', % comment
        ⋮
      'filen' % comment
 ]).
```

portray(X) :- *variety*₁-portray(X), !.
⋮
portray(X) :- *variety*ₘ-portray(X), !.

or something similar.

In Quintus Prolog, there is an additional problem: portray/1 lives in the module user:. If you write a module that defines some data structure, you would like to make a printing method for it available to portray/1, but a module file cannot contain clauses for any other module[1].

The method I finally settled on uses a pair of commands:

add_portray(P) ensures that there is a clause

> portray(X) :- P(X).

> somewhere in the clauses for portray/1, where P is an atom naming a predicate in the current module.

del_portray(P) ensures that there is *no* such clause.

This means that a module file can hook into portray/1 like this:

```
:- ensure_loaded(library(add_portray)).
:- del_portray(my_portray).

my_portray(X) :-
         is_one_of_my_things(X),
         print_it_my_way(X).

:- add_portray(my_portray).
```

The call to del_portray/1 ensures that if the file is reloaded, and print/1 is called before my_portray/1 is redefined, the incomplete definition will not be used. You

---

[1] This has changed in release 2.5

should put calls to add_portray/1 at the end of your file, to ensure that your por-
trayals are not called until their definitions are complete.

I discussed discussing portray/1 in this chapter because term_expansion/2 has
exactly the same problem; we do not want to get too many or too few clauses for
it when we consult or compile files, and we want to provide clauses for it in other
modules. Accordingly, the library provides two more commands:

add_expansion(P) ensures that there is a clause

> term_expansion(X, Y) :- P(X, Y).

> somewhere in the clauses for term_expansion/2, where P is an atom naming
> a predicate in the current module.

del_expansion(P) ensures that there is *no* such clause.

Some Prolog systems have other such hooks, and you may want to use this
method for predicates of your own. The basic commands are

```
add_linking_clause(Link, Pred, Arity) :-
        make_goal(Pred, Arity, Head),
        make_goal(Link, Arity, Body),
        (    user:clause(Head, Body) → true
        ;    user:assert((Head :- Body))
        ).

del_linking_clause(Link, Pred, Arity) :-
        make_goal(Pred, Arity, Head),
        make_goal(Link, Arity, Body),
        (    user:retract((Head :- Body)), fail
        ;    true
        ).
```

where the details of make_goal/3 and so on depend on your module system.

The bottom line is that defining term_expansion/2 directly is going to make
your life difficult (it will interfere with other library packages which try to add
expansions) so you should use the scheme

```
:- ensure_loaded(library(add_portray)).
:- del_expansion(my_expansion).

my_expansion(Term, Clause) :-
        ...

:- add_expansion(my_expansion).
```

9.2   How expand_term/2 works

DEC-10 Prolog introduced expand_term/2. C-Prolog went a stage further, and
introduced term_expansion/2. This is a predicate which *you* define, and the Prolog
system calls. Just as you can add clauses for portray/1 in order to extend the
built-in predicate print/1, you can add clauses for term_expansion/2 in order to
extend the translation done by the built-in predicate expand_term/2.

Basically, expand_term/2 does this:

```
expand_term(Term, Expansion) :-
        var(Term),
        !, % avoid false matches
        Expansion = Term.
expand_term(Term, Expansion) :-
        current_predicate(_, user:term_expansion(_,_)),
        user:term_expansion(Term, Mid),
        !,
        rest_expansion(Mid, Expansion).
expand_term(Term, Expansion) :-
        rest_expansion(Rest, Expansion).


rest_expansion((Lhs⟶Rhs), (Head:-Body)) :- !,
        dcg_expansion(Lhs, Rhs, Head, Body).
rest_expansion(Term, Term).
```

Note that this means that you can be sure that the Prolog system will never call
term_expansion/2 with a variable as first argument, just as you can be sure that
the Prolog system will never call portray/1 with a variable as first argument. Also,
your expansion can produce a DCG grammar rule as its result, and the system will
expand it. Thus you might have a rule

```
term_expansion(n(Word), (n(Word) ⟶ [Word])).
```

In this case,

```
    expand_term(n(example), Clause)
```

would call

```
    term_expansion(n(example), Mid)
```

which would bind

Mid = (n(example) $\longrightarrow$ example)

and then the built-in translation for DCG grammar rules would produce

Clause = (n(example,S0,S) :- 'C'(S0,example,S))

9.3 Conditional Reading

Suppose we wanted a way of including certain clauses in a program only if a particular condition was met. Just for argument's sake, let's make the syntax for this

{ *Clause* } when *Condition*

or   { *Clause* } unless *Condition*

Here's what we do.

First, we have to define 'when' and 'unless' as operators. So that the *Condition* can be a disjunction, the priority will have to be higher than 1100. We don't particularly want these operators to associate in either direction, so we'll select 'xfx' as their pictogram.

:- op(1150, xfx, [(when),(unless)]).

Now we need to define term_expansion/2.

```
conditional_expansion((Term when Condition), Clause) :-
        (    call(Condition) →
             expand_term(Term, Clause)
        ;    Clause = (:-true)
        ).
conditional_expansion((Term unless Condition), Clause) :-
        (    call(Condition) →
             Clause = (:-true)
        ;    expand_term(Term, Clause)
        ).
conditional_expansion({Term}, Clause) :-
        expand_term(Term, Clause).
```

:- add_expansion(conditional_expansion).

That is all it takes.

For an example of this, suppose you have the Quintus-invented library predicate environment/1 handy. One of the entries in that table is os(X), which says what sort of operating system the program is running under. This tells you what file names look like. Then we might write

```
data_file('[.FRED.JIM]FOO')  when environment(os(vms)).
data_file('fred/jim/foo')     when environment(os(unix)).
data_file('FOO')              unless environment(os(vms))
                              | environment(os(unix)).
```

There are three cases for environment(os(X)),

1. X = vms, and the input is seen as

```
data_file('[.FRED.JIM]FOO').
:- true.
:- true.
```

2. X = unix, and the input is seen as

```
:- true.
data_file('fred/jim/foo').
:- true.
```

3. X = something else, and the input is seen as

```
:- true.
:- true.
data_file('FOO').
```

This code, like all the concrete code in this text, has been tested in Quintus Prolog, and appeared to work.

9.4 Macros

We can even use term_expansion/2 to provide a simple macro facility.

```
:- dynamic
        macro/2.

expand_clause((Form → Replacement), (:- true)) :-
        asserta(macro(Form, Replacement)).
expand_clause((Head :- OldBody), (Head :- NewBody)) :-
        expand_body(OldBody, NewBody).
expand_clause((:- OldBody), (:- NewBody)) :-
        expand_body(OldBody, NewBody).
expand_clause((?- OldBody), (?- NewBody)) :-
        expand_body(OldBody, NewBody).

expand_body(Var, call(Var)) :-
        var(Var),
        !.
expand_body((OldA, OldB), Answer) :- !,
        expand_body(OldA, NewA),
        expand_body(OldB, NewB),
        get_rid_of_extra_true(NewA, NewB, Answer).
expand_body((OldA ; OldB), (NewA ; NewB)) :- !,
        expand_body(OldA, NewA),
        expand_body(OldB, NewB).
expand_body((OldA → OldB), (NewA → NewB)) :- !,
        expand_body(OldA, NewA),
        expand_body(OldB, NewB).
expand_body(¬(Old), ¬(New)) :- !,
        expand_body(Old, New).
expand_body(setof(T,Old,R), setof(T,New,R)) :- !,
        expand_body(Old, New).
expand_body(bagof(T,Old,R), bagof(T,New,R)) :- !,
        expand_body(Old, New).
expand_body(Old, New) :-
        macro(Old, New),
        !. % FORCE a unique expansion.
expand_body(Old, Old). % Not a macro
```

```
%    Macros very often turn into 'true', and clauses that come out
%    looking like ... :- true,true,true,true,true. would be silly.
%    So if one member of a conjunction is 'true' we discard it. A
%    final 'true' as in "p :- true" does no harm as Prolog will do
%    any removal necessary. We **can't** remove 'true' disjuncts,
%    though we could in logic, as that would change the behaviour
%    of the program by backtracking a different number of times.

get_rid_of_extra_true(true, X, X) :- !.
get_rid_of_extra_true(X, true, X) :- !.
get_rid_of_extra_true(X, Y, (X,Y))
```

```
%    Note that we cannot define term_expansion/2 until everything it
%    calls is defined, otherwise consult/1 will end up calling those
%    undefined predicates!

:- add_expansion(expand_clause).
```

When discussing context arguments in an early chapter, I promised to show you how the overhead of calling field access predicates could be reduced. We do it with macros:

```
context(Context, A, B, C, D) → Context = context(A,B,C,D).

context_a(Context, A) → Context = context(A,_,_,_).
context_b(Context, B) → Context = context(_,B,_,_).
context_c(Context, C) → Context = context(_,_,C,_).
context_d(Context, D) → Context = context(_,_,_,D).

c :-
        context(Context, 1, 2, 3, 4),
        p(Context).
p(Context) :-
        context_a(Context, *).
p(Context) :-
        context_b(Context, ?).
```

Having consulted this, the command

```
:- listing([c/0,p/1]).
```

produces the output

```
c :-
        A = context(1, 2, 3, 4),
        p(A).

p(A) :-
        A = context(*, B, C, D).
p(A) :-
        A = context(B, ?, C, D).
```

This macro facility is very crude. Nevertheless, it may be useful if some application has to be both fast and clear.

9.5 Problems

An extremely important thing about expand_term/2 and term_expansion/2 is that they do not tell you where to get the input or what to do with the output. For example, suppose that you would prefer to translate a file in "batch" mode, and later on compile the translated file. You could write a macro-expanding program by taking the previous definition of term_expansion/2 and combining it with

```
translate(InputFile, OutputFile) :-
        see(InputFile),
        tell(OutputFile),
        repeat,
            read(Term),
            expand_term(Term, Expansion),
            (   Expansion ≡ end_of_file
            ;   portray_clause(Expansion), fail
            ),
        !,
        told,
        seen.
```

There is an important difference between term_expansion/2 and portray/1. The built-in predicate print/1 works on arbitrary *terms*, not clauses as such (use portray_clause/1 for that). Every sub-term of a term is a term. So print/1 calls portray/1 for *every* sub-term of the term it is writing. But expand_term/2 is for translating *clauses* from one notation (DCG rules or whatever) to another (the basic :- notation), and sub-terms of clauses are not in general clauses. So expand_term/2 calls term_expansion/2 *once* with the entire term as its argument, and if term_expansion/2 fails, it will *not* be given a chance to look at any of the sub-terms of the term.

There are two problems with the expand_term/2 mechanism. The first is that it although it is easy to rewrite a clause to nothing (the :-true command), it is hard to rewrite a clause to more than one clause. What we really want for generality is a mechanism which will return a list of clauses.[2]

The second is that user-defined term expansion rules have to come in a definite order relative to DCG rule expansion:

- either user-defined term expansion rules are tried before DCG rule expansion, in which case the output of a user-defined expansion can be a DCG rule (which is more useful than you might think), and in which case a user-defined expansion can use the DCG syntax (the principal functor $(\longrightarrow)/2$) for its own purposes, but it is hard to do anything to the translations of DCG rules.

- or user-defined term expansion rules are tried after DCG rule expansion, in which case it is easy to macro-expand the clauses which result, but you cannot capture the DCG syntax for any other purpose, and you cannot have an expansion which is a DCG rule.

For example, you might want to have a macro

void(X,X) $\longrightarrow$ true.

for use in grammar rules such as

s $\longrightarrow$ np(Subj), void, vp(Subj).

But although 'void' will indeed be expanded to void(S1,S2), the macro expander illustrated here will never see the expansion of a DCG rule.

As another example, suppose that the :-multifile directive of Quintus Prolog did not exist. You could use term_expansion/2 to obtain much the same effect, except that each such predicate would also be :-dynamic. Here's how:

```
:- dynamic
        is_multifile/1.

declare_multifile((A,B)) :-
        declare_multifile(A),
        declare_multifile(B).
```

---

[2]This is provided in Quintus Prolog release 2.5

```
declare_multifile(Name/Arity) :-
        functor(Head, Name, Arity),
        (    is_multifile(Head) → true
        ;    abolish(Name, Arity),
             assert(Head, Ref),
             erase(Ref), % Name/Arity is now dynamic and empty
             assert(is_multifile(Head))
        ).

multifile_expansion(:-(multifile(Preds)), :-(true)) :- !,
        declare_multifile(Preds).
multifile_expansion(Clause, :-(assert(Clause))) :-
        prolog_clause(Clause, Head, _), % from library(decons)
        is_dynamic(Head),
        !.

:- add_expansion(multifile_expansion).
```

Again, this doesn't mesh well with grammar rules. You can actually hack around this. What we want to do is to have some rules applied *before* DCG expansion, and some applied *after*. The hack is to call expand_term/2 recursively, but to block any deeper recursion. How do we do that?

```
:- dynamic
        in_second_phase/0.

term_expansion(Term0, Term) :-
        (    retract(in_second_phase) →
             fail
        ;    before_dcg_expansion(Term0, Term1),
             assert(in_second_phase),
             expand_term(Term1, Term2),
             after_dcg_expansion(Term2, Term)
        ).
```

How does this work? Here is a trace:

```
expand_term(T0, T)
     retract(in_second_phase) FAILS
     before_dcg_expansion(T0, T1)
     assert(in_second_phase)
     expand_term(T1, T2)
```

retract(in_second_phase) SUCCEEDS
term_expansion FAILS
dcg_expansion is done if applicable
after_dcg_expansion(T2, T).

To test this code, it was applied with the definitions

before_dcg_expansion(n(X), (n(X) ⟶ [X])) :- !.
before_dcg_expansion(X, X).

after_dcg_expansion((H :- B), (call(H) :- B)) :- !.
after_dcg_expansion(:-(X), :-(X)) :- !.
after_dcg_expansion(?-(X), ?-(X)) :- !.
after_dcg_expansion(end_of_file, end_of_file) :- !.
after_dcg_expansion(H, call(H)).

go :-
        repeat,
            read(X),
            expand_term(X, Y),
            portray_clause(Y),
            Y = end_of_file,
    !.

For example, the input "n(fred)" was mapped to

call(n(fred,S0,S)) :- 'C'(S0, fred, S).

I'm very much afraid that this is a hack, but it *does* give you considerable freedom
in tailoring the Prolog language to your own taste.

10 Writing Tokenisers in Prolog

In this chapter, we address the problem of using Prolog character transput. One of the virtues of Prolog is that the embedded grammar rule formalism makes it easy to write parsers, but that wouldn't be much use if the user had to type each sentence in as a list. Transput does not fit well into the general spirit of Prolog, and we need to take unusual care with it. The point of this chapter is to show in some detail how one goes about doing it.

10.1 Reading a Sentence

A common use of character input is to read a sentence from the current input stream as a list of words. Saying that we want to read a list of words from the current input stream is a bit vague. What constitutes a word? And where do we stop? I shall actually consider two definitions, and develop two programs.

Definition 1. The input to be read is everything up to the end of the current line. Some words are punctuation marks: """ ' , ; : . ? !". Spaces and tabs are not included in words. Other words are made up of characters that aren't spaces, tabs, ends of lines, or punctuation marks.

Definition 2. There are three sorts of words: punctuation marks, as above, numbers, and letter sequences. Alphabetic case is ignored in letter sequences. Other characters are ignored except that they separate words. The input to be read is everything up to the first full stop, question mark, or exclamation mark, and any remaining characters on the last line of the input are to be ignored.

I prefer definition 2.

10.2 What Tools Already Exist?

The first thing to do is to go through a Prolog manual to see what we can use. What we would really like to find is something that does the entire job, or is close enough that we are happy to accept its definition in place of the one we first thought of. The public-domain DEC-10 Prolog library (available from the University of Edinburgh) contains two such commands:

```
read_in(Words)      — in READIN.PL
read_sent(Words)    — in RDSENT.PL
```

The Quintus Prolog supported library includes improved versions of these commands: they are even in the manual.

But let's suppose that nobody has told you about the library routines, or that you have been sold a version of Prolog without them, or that you like definition 1 and want to stick with it. There isn't anything available that implements definition 1. So we turn to the Prolog manual.

What we want to know is: how can we read a character at a time, what do characters look like when we have read them, what can we do with characters, and how can we combine characters into Prolog atoms and numbers?

The character transput primitives in Prolog represent characters as integers, just as C does, using whatever encoding method your system supports. So do the conversion predicates name/2, atom_chars/2, and number_chars/2. Some common codings are

- EBCDIC

- ASCII (the American variant of ISO 646)

- the IBM PC character set (an extension of ASCII)

- the Macintosh character set (an extension of ASCII)

- DEC's Multinational character set (an extension of ASCII)

- ISO 8859/1 (the standard extension of ASCII for Western Europe and the Americas)

- other versions of ISO 8859

Most Prolog systems have some way of representing character constants in source code:

$0'c$ Dec-10 Prolog, C Prolog, Quintus Prolog
`'c`   PopLog
$\tilde{}c$ ALS Prolog

Most Prologs also allow "c" in arithmetic expressions.

Anything we can do to integers we can do to characters. In particular, we can add and subtract other integers. Thus to find the decimal value of a digit, we can write

decimal_value(Digit, N) :-
            integer(Digit), Digit $\geq$ "0", Digit $\leq$ "9",
            % now we know that it *is* a digit
            N is Digit-"0".

and to convert a letter to lower case, we can write

lower_case(Letter, Letter) :-
       integer(Letter), Letter $\geq$ "a", Letter $\leq$ "z",
       %   it is the code of a lower case letter
       !.
lower_case(Letter, Lower) :-
       integer(Letter), Letter $\geq$ "A", Letter $\leq$ "Z",
       %   it is the code of an upper case letter
       !,
       Lower is Letter+("a"-"A").

Actually, this only works in ASCII. It doesn't work for accented or non-Roman letters in extensions of ASCII. Check your Prolog manual to see whether the public-domain library predicates is_lower/1 and to_lower/2 are available.

That suffices for characters. Now how do we read them? The manual describes three built in predicates.

get0(N) N is the ASCII code of the next character from the current input stream.

get(N) N is the ASCII code of the next non-blank printable character from the current input stream.

skip(N) Skips to just past the next ASCII character code N from the current input stream. N may be an integer expression.

Don't be misled by the phrasing of get0/1 and get/1. What they do is *read* the next suitable character from the current input stream and unify the character code with N. If you want to check whether the next character is a space, get0(32) will succeed if it is and fail if it isn't. But in either case the character is gone forever. You almost always want the argument of get0/1 or get/1 to be a variable.

Now definition 1 says that we want to read up to the end of the line and no further. But in Dec-10 Prolog the end of line character is NL (31), and in C-Prolog and Quintus Prolog the end of line character is Line Feed (LF, 10), and in Macintosh Prologs the end of line character is typically Carriage Return (CR, 13) and none of these characters is a "non-blank printable character". So get/1 is perfectly happy to throw away a character we want to see. skip/1 is there precisely to throw characters away. So the way we are going to read characters is get0(C) with C a variable.

The other thing we want to do with characters is to turn a sequence of characters into a Prolog atom or integer. There are several predicates to do that.

name(C, L) if C is a constant, unifies L with a list containing the ASCII codes
    of the printed representation of C. If C is a variable, L should be a list of
    ASCII codes. If that looks like a number, C will be unified with that number.
    Otherwise C will be unified with the atom having those characters as its name.

atom_chars(C, L) is like name/2 except that C must be an atom or a variable,
    and that even if C is a variable and L looks like a number, C will be unified
    with an atom.

number_chars(C, L) is like name/2 except that C must be a number or a vari-
    able, and that if C is a variable and L doesn't look like a number it will fail.
    It handles decimal integers and floats.

name/2 is exactly what we want here.

10.3   A Simplified Problem

Let's ignore words for the moment, and consider instead the problem of reading all
the characters up to the end of the line. The main problem we have to face is that
characters aren't *there* like elements of a data structure or facts in a data base,
we have to go out and read them with get0/1, and if we fail past a call to get0/1
the character is lost forever.   Backtracking does *not* undo any form of transput.
Transput programming in Prolog would be much simpler if it did. So the general
pattern of character input has to be something like

```
foo(Inputs, Outputs) :-
        get0(C),
        handle_foo_character(C, Inputs, Outputs).
```

An Important Analogy. *If you are familiar with finite state machines, predicates
like foo correspond to states, and predicates like handle_foo_character correspond
to arcs.*

We can use the correspondence to write Prolog character input routines by first
drawing a suitable finite state machine and then turning it directly into Prolog.
    Suppose we have a finite state machine which has a state that looks like

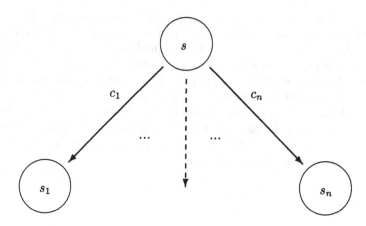

We would translate such a state as two Prolog predicates: one to represent the state itself and one to represent the arcs (or transitions) leading out of the state. The translation looks like this:

s :- get0(C), s(C).% state predicate

$s(c_1)$:- s_1. % transition clause

$\vdots$

$s(c_n)$:- s_n. % transition clause

You have only to ensure that each transition predicate will handle any possible input character and that it is tail recursive, and you are safe. It is of the utmost practical importance for this technique that get0/1 should signal reaching the end of a stream by returning an integer distinct from any character value.

If you are not familiar with finite state machines, don't worry.

Let's get started on the code then. First, let's think of a name. Since we are reading a line of characters, read_line/1 seems like a good name. So here is the first predicate.

```
%    read_line(Chars)
%    reads characters from the current input stream and returns them
%    as a list of ASCII codes. It is not steadfast unless var(Chars).

read_line(Chars) :-
        get0(C),
        read_line(C, Chars).
```

"Hang on a minute", I hear you cry in alarm, "you've made a mistake. You've got the same predicate with one argument and two arguments." No I haven't. read_line/1 and read_line/2 are completely different predicates. I happen to like using the same name for predicates which are very strongly related, as states and transitions are related. If you want to call the pair of predicates corresponding to a state *variety_state*/N and *variety_transition*/$(N + 1)$, do so.

Now we have to decide what read_line/2 should do. There are two cases to consider. Either C is the end of the line or it isn't. If C is the end of the line, there are no more characters to go in the list. If it isn't, C must go in the list, and we have to read the remaining characters in the line.

```
read_line(C, []) :-
        ends_line(C).
read_line(C, [C|Chars]) :-
        ¬ ends_line(C)),
        read_rest_of_line(Chars).
```

What does read_rest_of_line/1 have to do? It has to read all the characters that remain on the current line. But that is exactly what read_line/1 does! There is another simplification to make. If we have a predicate

```
p(...) :-
        test(...),
        rest_p_1(...).
p(...) :-
        ¬ test(...),
        rest_p_2(...).
```

where the test will either succeed once or fail, we can avoid making the test twice by writing

```
p(...) :-
        test(...),
        !,
        rest_p_1(...).
p(...) :-
        % ¬ test(...),
        rest_p_2(...).
```

This is called the "if-then-else" use of the cut. As you can see from this example, I think it is a good idea to leave the ¬test(...) in as a comment. It helps other people work out what you are doing, and if your program is correct, then ¬test(...) is indeed true at that point.

There is one predicate left to code, and that is ends_line/1. Different Prolog systems use different characters for that: DEC-10 Prolog used 31, C-Prolog uses 10 (LF), and Quintus Prolog uses 13 (CR) on the Xerox Lisp Machines, 10 (LF) on most other machines, and 21 (NL) on IBM mainframes. On MS-DOS systems, it would have been sensible to discard CRs and treat LFs as line terminators, except that the RETURN or ENTER key is likely to be mapped to CR rather than LF. So you may have to take CR as the line terminator and discard LFs.

There is another problem: what should the program do if there is *no* line terminator in the current input stream. When it hits the end of a file, get0/1 returns -1 (26 in DEC-10 Prolog). If you try to read another character from the same stream, Prolog will print an error message and return you to Prolog command level. We could just let that happen. Or we could accept -1 as a line terminator. To keep things simple, I suggest we take the first alternative.

Since there is only one line terminator character, ends_line(C) would be

```
ends_line(31).    % TOPS-10, TOPS-20
ends_line(10).    % UNIX, VMS, some MS-DOS
ends_line(13).    % INTERLISP-D, Macintosh, some MS-DOS
ends_line(21).    % MVS, VM/CMS
```

So we can substitute this test in line. We finally get two versions of the program:

```
%    Pure version.

read_line(Chars) :-
        get0(C),
        read_line(C, Chars).

read_line(C, []) :-
        ends_line(C).
read_line(C, [C|Chars]) :-
        ¬ ends_line(C),
        read_line(Chars).

ends_line(10). % or 31 or whatever

%    Improved version

read_line(Chars) :-
        get0(C),
        read_line(C, Chars).
```

read_line(10, []) :- % or 31 or whatever
       !.
read_line(C, [C|Chars]) :-
      % C =\= 10,
      read_line(Chars).

For LPA Prolog Professional, where we want to discard LF (10) characters and use CR (13) characters as line terminators, read_line/2 would be

read_line(10, Chars) :- !, % discard LF
      read_line(Chars).
read_line(13, []) :- !.% stop at CR
read_line(C, [C|Chars]) :-
      % $10 \neq C \neq 13$
      read_line(Chars).

To give the "pure" and "improved" methods a fair comparison, I used them to read a file containing 97 lines, 930 words, and 5616 characters. I used DEC-10 Prolog on a KL-10, Quintus Prolog 2.5 on a Sun-3/50, and SICStus Prolog 0.6 on a Sun-3/50. For the latter two, I also tried a version which was as fast as I could make it.

DEC-10	pure	2.30 sec =	0.41 ms/char
DEC-10	improved	0.34 sec =	0.06 ms/char
Quintus	pure	1.63 sec =	0.29 ms/char
Quintus	improved	1.13 sec =	0.20 ms/char
Quintus	fastest	0.88 sec =	0.16 ms/char
SICStus	pure	1.74 sec =	0.31 ms/char
SICStus	improved	1.06 sec =	0.19 ms/char
SICStus	fastest	1.00 sec =	0.18 ms/char

The disappointing performance of the "pure" version in DEC-10 Prolog is due to the fact that the DEC-10 Prolog compiler doesn't know what to do with '¬', so most of the characters end up doing an interpreted call to ends_line. Current Prolog compilers like Quintus Prolog and SICStus Prolog *do* know what to do with negation, and it is perfectly possible for a compiler to perform the cut introducing optimisation. The performance of the "fastest" version on the Sun-3/50 relative to the DEC-10 Prolog speed is due to Quintus and SICStus Prolog calling out to C 'stdio' routines rather than using their own assembler-level I/O code as DEC-10 Prolog did.

The moral of this example is that if you stick as close as you can to logic, you do have to pay for it, but not more than you can afford. One thing the world has learned from 40 years of programming is

make it *work* before you make it *fast*

We shall follow the same pattern in the next section.

10.4   Programming Definition 1

Definition 1 mentions four classes of characters.

- the end of the line

- spaces and tabs

- the punctuation marks " ' , ; : . ? !

- anything else

Let's start by defining predicates to recognise each of these classes. I'll use Edinburgh ($0'$) notation for character codes.

:- prolog_flag(character_escapes, _, on).

ends_line($0'$\n).

space_or_tab($0'$\s). % space
space_or_tab($0'$\t). % tab

How are we going to recognise the punctuation marks? The simplest way is to write a clause for each of them. So let's do that.

punctuation($0'$").
punctuation($0'$').
punctuation($0'$,).
punctuation($0'$;).
punctuation($0'$:).
punctuation($0'$.).
punctuation($0'$?).
punctuation($0'$!).

Finally, we have to recognise the other characters. There are 11 characters in the three classes defined so far, so there would be 117 clauses in this predicate. While the "pure" thing to do would be to write the clauses, we have to remember that we would be almost certain to make a mistake in that many clauses. So we define other characters by exclusion:

```
other(C) :-
        integer(C),
        C ≥ 0, C ≤ 127,
        ¬ ends_line(C),
        ¬ space_or_tab(C),
        ¬ punctuation(C).
```

Exercise. *Use this definition to generate a table. Compare the speed of the version using this code and the version using a table.*

To generate a table from this version of other/1, you might write

```
gen_other :-
        tell('other.pl'),
        between(0, 127, C),
        other(C),
        portray_clause(other(C)),
        fail
    ;   told.
```

Then you could drop 'other.pl' into your program using your favourite text editor. This is one of the nice things about Prolog: the rest of the program can't tell whether other/1 is a pure table or what.

We are now ready to start from the top down. Our first predicate is similar to read_line/1. Since it reads words I shall call it read_words/1.

```
%   read_words(Words)
%   reads characters from the current input stream up to the end
%   of the current line, and forms them into a list of words. It
%   follows definition 1. It is not steadfast unless var(Words).

read_words(Words) :-
        get0(C),
        read_words(C, Words).
```

Since we have four character classes to consider, read_words/2 will have four clauses. In general we might find that two or more of these clauses were much the same, in which case we might replace them by a single clause. But that is an improvement which can wait until we have something working.

If C is the end of the line, there are no more words, and we should stop. If C is a space or tab, we can ignore it. If C is a punctuation mark, we have a word right away, and want to read the rest of the words. If C is any other character, we have a bit of a problem. We have read the first character of the word, and want to read the rest. But the only way we can tell where a word ends is by reading one character too many. We can't put that character back once it has been read, and we can't afford to throw it away (it might be the end of the line, or a punctuation mark), so the predicate which reads a word has to return the extra character.

```
read_words(C, []) :-
        ends_line(C).
read_words(C, Words) :-
        space_or_tab(C),
        read_words(Words).
read_words(C, [Word|Words]) :-
        punctuation(C),
        name(Word, [C]),
        read_words(Words).
read_words(C, [Word|Words]) :-
        other(C),
        read_rest_of_word(Chars, LeftOver),
        name(Word, [C|Chars]),
        read_words(LeftOver, Words).
```

Notice that two of the clauses recur on read_words: "read rest of line", but that when we have a word made of "other" characters we want to do "read rest of line given that one character, this one, has already been read", and this is exactly what read_words/2 does. This is quite a common pattern: one of the sub-predicates reads one character (or token) too many and returns it, but we already have a predicate which takes a character (or token) that has been read. Carrying around one or more characters which have already been read is rather like the lagging technique in list processing.

read_rest_of_word/2 follows the same general pattern as read_line/1. The only difference is the stopping condition, and the fact that we are interested in the last character read.

```
%    read_rest_of_word(Chars, LeftOver)
%    reads as many "other" characters from the current input stream as
%    it can, stopping when it finds the first non-"other" character.
%    The "other" characters are returned as a list in Chars, and
%    the last character read is returned in LeftOver.
```

```
read_rest_of_word(Chars, LeftOver) :-
        get0(C),
        read_rest_of_word(C, Chars, LeftOver).
```

```
read_rest_of_word(C, [], C) :-
        ¬ other(C).
read_rest_of_word(C, [C|Chars], LeftOver) :-
        other(C),
        read_rest_of_word(Chars, LeftOver).
```

And now have have finished our program for Definition 1.

We can improve it exactly the same way that we improved read_line. The if-then-else pattern has a more general form. If we have

```
p(...) :-
        test1(...),
        rest_p_1(...).
p(...) :-
        test2(...),
        rest_p_2(...).
 .
 .
 .
p(...) :-
        ¬ test1(...),
        ¬ test2(...),
        ...
        rest_p_x(...).
```

where each of the tests will either succeed once or fail, and no two of the tests can both be true at once, we can improve the clauses to

```
p(...) :-
        test_1(...),
        !,
        rest_p_1(...).
```

```
p(...) :-
        test_2(...),
        !,
        rest_p_2(...).
    .
    .
    .
p(...) :-
        % ¬ test1(...),
        % ¬ test2(...),
        ...
        rest_p_x(...).
```

This saves repeating all the tests in the last clause. But it also saves us ever considering test_2 once we know that test_1 is true. By the way, though I have written the tests and rests as if they were single goals, I don't mean *only* that. The tests and rests can be any conjunctions, and indeed they needn't have any goals in them at all. It can happen that the pattern in the head of a clause is a sufficient test, and it can also happen that when a test succeeds that means there is nothing further to be done.

In this improved version, I have treated ends_line/1 as a macro just as I did in read_line/1. I have treated space_or_tab/1 the same way, but as there are two ways that space_or_tab(X) can be true we get two clauses in the improved version where there was one in the purer version.

```
%    Improved version

read_words(Words) :-
        get0(C),
        read_words(C, Words).

read_words(0'\n, []) :- !. % line terminator
read_words(0'\t, Words) :- !, % tab
        read_words(Words).
read_words(0'\s, Words) :- !, % space
        read_words(Words).
read_words(C, [Word|Words]) :-
        punctuation(C),
        !,
        name(Word, [C]),
        read_words(Words).
```

```
read_words(C, [Word|Words]) :-
        % C isn't NL space tab or a punctuation mark
        read_rest_of_word(Chars, LeftOver),
        name(Word, [C|Chars]),
        read_words(LeftOver, Words).

read_rest_of_word(Chars, LeftOver) :-
        get0(C),
        read_rest_of_word(C, Chars, LeftOver).

read_rest_of_word(C, [], C) :-
        not_other(C),
        !.
read_rest_of_word(C, [C|Chars], LeftOver) :-
        read_rest_of_word(Chars, LeftOver).

not_other(0'\n) :- !. % ends_line
not_other(0'\t) :- !. % space_or_tab
not_other(0'\s) :- !. % space_or_tab
not_other(C) :-
        punctuation(C),
        !.
```

I applied these programs to the same file as read_line/1. As before, the DEC-10 times were measured in DEC-10 Prolog on a KL-10, and the other times were measured on a Sun-3/50.

DEC-10	pure	2.18 sec =	0.39 ms/char
DEC-10	improved	1.30 sec =	0.23 ms/char
Quintus	pure	4.56 sec =	0.81 ms/char
Quintus	improved	2.88 sec =	0.51 ms/char
Quintus	fastest	1.27 sec =	0.23 ms/char
SICStus	pure	4.10 sec =	0.73 ms/char
SICStus	improved	2.44 sec =	0.43 ms/char
SICStus	fastest	1.23 sec =	0.22 ms/char

The "fastest" version was obtained by unfolding as much as I could, so that punctuation/1, not_other/1, and read_rest_of_word/2 disappeared, their bodies having replaced the calls to them, and read_words/2 called itself rather than read_words/1.

Once again, we conclude that the speed-up of the improved version is worth having, but that the ratio is tolerable. Given that we usually have to put in a lot of time stepping through a program when we are debugging it, efficiency is not our main concern in the first draft of a program. Once a program has been written and debugged, and you are sure that it does what you said you wanted it to, and that you still want something to do that, *then* is the time to worry about efficiency. In fact, it is precisely *because* we kept the original code clean that it was easy to apply the "unfolding" method to speed it up.

The careful use of cuts can save a lot of space as well as a lot of time, as discussed in 3. But the way to get these savings is *not* to ask yourself "where can I put the cuts to get the greatest efficiency", but to ask "where should the cuts go so that the program is still correct". If you stick to introducing cuts so as to force an if-then-else effect, you may not get the utmost efficiency out of the Prolog system, but you will usually get enough.

There is another way of programming definition 1. That is to use read_line/1 to read a line of characters and then to parse the characters using grammar rules.

Exercise. *Write a version of read_words/1 using that method and time it.*

10.5   Programming Definition 2

Definition 2 forces us to read in two steps. First we read words until we come to the end of the sentence, and then we skip characters until we come to the end of the line. So we have

```
read_sentence(Words) :-
        read_sent(Words),
        skip(0'\n).
```

skip(EndOfLineChar) skips all the characters to the end of the line. This is no accident. Indeed, it is about the only thing this predicate is ever used for. skip(-1) can be used to skip to the end of the file, but you might as well close it at once.

read_sent/1 is very like read_words/1, except that this time we have four kinds of words, not two:

- periods . ! ?
- punctuation marks " ' , ; :
- numbers
- words made of letters

and five classes of characters:

- periods . ! ?

- punctuation marks " ' , ; :

- digits

- letters

- anything else (like spaces and tabs)

The other thing we have to do, according to definition 2, is to force letters to lower case. We can do that as we read them, but we might as well write a predicate which converts a character list to its lower case equivalent, as some day we might want it in another program. The version I give here is for the ISO 8859/1 character set. In that character set, codes 192–214 and 216–221 represent upper case letters, 215 represents "×", codes 223–246 and 248–255 represent lower case letters, and 247 represents "÷".

```
lower_case_chars([], []).
lower_case_chars([Char—Chars], [Lower—Lowers]) :-
        (    Char ≥ 192, Char ≤ 222, Char =\= 215 →
             Lower is Char-32 % Upper case accented letter
        ;    Char ≥ "A", Char ≤ "Z" →
             Lower is Char-32 % Upper case plain letter
        ;    /* any other character */
             Lower is Char
        ),
        lower_case_chars(Chars, Lowers).
```

The rest of the code should be obvious from the preceding examples. For the special characters, instead of calling name/2 whenever we see one, I have provided the appropriate atom in the period/2 and punctuation/2 tables.

```
period(0'., '.').
period(0'?, '?').
period(0'!, '!').

punctuation(0'", '"').
punctuation(0'', ''').
punctuation(0',, ',').
punctuation(0';, ';').
punctuation(0':, ':').
```

```
digit(C) :-
        C ≥ "0", C ≤ "9".

letter(C) :-
    (   C ≥ 192 → C =\= 215, C =\= 247
    ;   C ≥ "a" → C ≤ "z"
    ;   C ≥ "A" → C ≤ "Z"
    ).

read_sent(Words) :-
        get0(C),
        read_sent(C, Words).

read_sent(C, [Word]) :-
        period(C, Word),
        !.
read_sent(C, [Word|Words]) :-
        punctuation(C, Word),
        !,
        read_sent(Words).
read_sent(C, [Word|Words]) :-
        letter(C),
        !,
        read_rest_letters(Chars, LeftOver),
        lower_case_string([C|Chars], Name),
        atom_chars(Word, Name),
        read_sent(LeftOver, Words).
read_sent(C, [Word|Words]) :-
        digit(C),
        !,
        read_rest_digits(Chars, LeftOver),
        number_chars(Word, [C|Chars]),
        read_sent(LeftOver, Words).
read_sent(C, Words) :-
        % C is not a letter, digit, or punctuation mark
        read_sent(Words).

read_rest_letters(Digits, LeftOver) :-
        get0(C),
        read_rest_letters(C, Digits, LeftOver).
```

```
read_rest_letters(C, [C|Chars], LeftOver) :-
        letter(C),
        !,
        read_rest_letters(Chars, LeftOver).
read_rest_letters(C, [], C).
        % C is not a letter

read_rest_digits(Digits, LeftOver) :-
        get0(C),
        read_rest_digits(C, Digits, LeftOver).

read_rest_digits(C, [C|Chars], LeftOver) :-
        digit(C),
        !,
        read_rest_digits(Chars, LeftOver).
read_rest_digits(C, [], C).
        % C is not a digit
```

Exercise. *Try to make read_sent/1 faster. Measure your version and this version on some moderately large files. Would it pay to combine reading the rest of a word and forcing it to lower case into one routine?*

10.6   Character output

The character output commands in Prolog are

put(C) write the character whose integer code is C to the current output stream. C may be an arithmetic expression, such as "0" + N. A character literal such as 0'x is an integer, hence an arithmetic expression.

nl terminate the line currently written to the current output stream.

tab(N) write N space characters to the current output stream.

You should bear in mind that nl/0 must be called at the *end* of a line, not at the beginning of a line. I'm sorry to insult your intelligence with this warning, but I've seen too many Prolog programs whose output started with a useless empty line and whose last line was not properly terminated (to the distress of not a few UNIX utilities) just because the programmer used nl/0 at the wrong end of his lines. The Prolog commands are similar to the Pascal commands

(* put(C) *) write(C);
(* nl *)   writeln;
(* tab(N) *) if N > 0 then write(' ':N);

If you want your programs to be portable, do not rely on put(0'\n) to terminate your lines, but use only nl/0.

It is often useful to have a command which will ensure that the current output stream is positioned at the beginning a line, by terminating the current line if and only if there something in it. Unfortunately, there is as yet no portable way of doing that. Some versions of C Prolog have a command sl/0. MProlog has opt_nl/0. Quintus Prolog has

format('~N', [])

and a library predicate tab_to(Column). Your Prolog is likely to have some way of doing it, but it's not portable.

10.7   Tokenising Prolog

In 1984 it was realised that the most painless way to encourage Prolog implementors to make their systems syntactically compatible with DEC-10 Prolog was to put a DEC-10 Prolog tokeniser and parser in the public domain. To my knowledge, three Prolog systems *have* started from the public-domain code, but many others haven't. This means that you may, unfortunately, have a use for the Prolog tokeniser presented in this section.

The Prolog tokeniser returns two lists: a list of tokens and a dictionary of variables. The encoding of tokens, which goes back to DEC-10 Prolog, is

var(Var,Name)	Var is a variable, Name is an atom.
	Name is the name of the variable.
atom(Atom)	Atom is an atom.
	It may or may not be an operator.
number(Number)	Number is a number.
	It may be an integer or a float.
string(Chars)	Chars is a list of character codes.

'{'   opening curly brace punctuation
'}'   closing curly brace punctuation
'['   opening square bracket punctuation
']'   closing square bracket punctuation
'␣('   opening round parenthesis punctuation
'('   "(" immediately after an atom
')'   closing round parenthesis punctuation
','   comma punctuation
'|'   vertical bar punctuation

Note that although ";" and "!" do not combine with other characters to make bigger tokens the way "+" or "$" do, they are atom characters, not punctuation marks. You can change the operator properties of the atom ';' just like you can change the operator properties of any other atom. But "," and "|" are punctuation marks, not atoms, and you cannot change the syntactic properties of punctuation marks. Just to confuse things, there *is* an atom ',' which is normally an operator, and you can change the operator properties of that atom, but the atom and the punctuation mark have nothing to do with each other. For example,

    ! ',' ; , "|".

is a legal sequence of tokens which will be returned as

    [atom(!),atom(','),atom(;),',',string([124])]

The dictionary of variables is a list of Name=Var pairs, suitable for printing out one per line in the response to a top-level query. There are more efficient ways of managing this dictionary than as a simple list with a hole at the end, but the variable dictionary is usually not the bottle-neck when reading terms.

This tokeniser does not accept the DEC-10 Prolog forms

- "%(" as a synonym for "{"

- "%)" as a synonym for "}"

- ", .." as a synonym for "|"

- NOLC (no lower case) mode

- large integers are not read as xwd(HI18,LO18)

Like Quintus Prolog, and unlike DEC-10 Prolog, it accepts floating-point numbers, and when the 'character_escapes' flag is on, it accepts escaped characters similar to those in C and PopLog, and it accepts the full ISO 8859/1 character set. That is one of the reasons why so many magic numbers appear in the code. Some of the other magic numbers are there so that this can be compiled by a Prolog system which does not support character escapes or by one which does. There are some minor differences between this tokeniser and Quintus Prolog, such as allowing underscores in numbers, like Ada.

As time has gone on, I have continued to revise this code. Always, making it purer has made it faster.

```
%    read_tokens(-TokenList, -Dictionary)
%    returns a list of tokens, and a dictionary of VarName=Variable pairs
%    in standard order, where the VarNames are atoms and the variables
%    are all the named variables among the tokens.
%    This predicate "primes" read_tokens/3 with the first non-layout
%    character, and checks for end of stream.
%    The way end of file is handled is that everything else FAILS when it
%    hits character -1, sometimes printing a warning. It might have been
%    an idea to return the atom 'end_of_file' instead of the same token list
%    that you'd have got from reading "end_of_file. ", but (1) this file is
%    for compatibility, and (2) there are good practical reasons for wanting
%    this behaviour.

read_tokens(TokenList, Dictionary) :-
        get(C1),
        read_tokens(C1, Dict, ListOfTokens),
        terminate_list(Dict), % fill in the "hole" at the end.
        !, % we have to unify explicitly so
        sort(Dict, Dictionary), % that we'll read and then check
        TokenList = ListOfTokens. % even with filled in arguments.
read_tokens([atom(end_of_file)], []). % End Of File is only problem.

%    terminate_list(?List)
%    finds the "hole" at the end of a partial list and fills it in with [].

terminate_list([]).
terminate_list([_|Tail]) :-
        terminate_list(Tail).
read_tokens(C1, Dict, Tokens) :-
    (   C1 ≤ " " → % layout: CR, LF, TAB, space, &c
        C1 ≥ 0, % FAIL at end of file
        get(C2),
        read_tokens(C2, Dict, Tokens)
```

```
    ;     C1 ≥ "a", C1 ≤ "z" → % plain identifier
          read_identifier(C1, Dict, Tokens)
    ;     C1 ≥ "A", C1 ≤ "Z" → % variable name
          read_variable(C1, Dict, Tokens)
    ;     C1 ≥ "0", C1 ≤ "9" →
          read_number(C1, Dict, Tokens)
    ;     C1 < 127 → % special character
          read_special(C1, Dict, Tokens)
    ;     C1 ≤ 160 → % DEL or unassigned control
          get(C2),
          read_tokens(C2, Dict, Tokens)
    ;     C1 ≥ 223, C1 =\= "÷" → % ISO 8859/1 lower case letter
          read_identifier(C1, Dict, Tokens)
    ;     C1 ≥ 192, C1 =\= "×" → % ISO 8859/1 upper case letter
          read_variable(C1, Dict, Tokens)
    ;     C1 =\= 170, C1 =\= 186 → % ISO 8859/1 symbol char
          read_symbol(C1, Dict, Tokens)
    ;           % _a_ or _o_ ordinal characters
          read_identifier(C1, Dict, Tokens)
    ).

read_special(0'_, Dict, Tokens) :- % underscore; starts variables
          read_variable(0'_, Dict, Tokens).
read_special(0'÷, Dict, Tokens) :- % code is 247
          read_symbol(0'÷, Dict, Tokens).
read_special(0'×, Dict, Tokens) :- % code is 215
          read_symbol(0'×, Dict, Tokens).
read_special(0'%, Dict, Tokens) :- % %comment
          repeat, % skip characters to any
                get0(Ch), % line terminator
                Ch < " ", Ch =\= 9 /*TAB*/, % control char, not tab
          !, % stop when we find one
          Ch =\= -1, % fail on EOF
          get0(NextCh),
          read_tokens(NextCh, Dict, Tokens).
read_special(0'/, Dict, Tokens) :- % /*comment?
          get0(C2),
          (     C2 =:= "*" → % is /*comment*/
                read_solidus(0'\s /*space*/, NextCh),
                read_tokens(NextCh, Dict, Tokens)
```

```
;/* C2 =\= "*" */ % begins symbol
        rest_symbol(C2, Chars, NextCh),
        read_after_atom(NextCh, Dict, Tokens, [0'/|Chars])
    ).
read_special(0'!, Dict, [atom(!)|Tokens]) :- % This is a special case so
        get0(NextCh), % that "!." is two tokens
        read_after_atom(NextCh, Dict, Tokens). % It could be cleverer.
read_special(0'(, Dict, ['␣('|Tokens]) :- % NB!!! "(" turns into
        get0(NextCh), % the token '␣('.
        read_tokens(NextCh, Dict, Tokens).
read_special(0'), Dict, [')'|Tokens]) :-
        get0(NextCh),
        read_tokens(NextCh, Dict, Tokens).
read_special(0',, Dict, [','|Tokens]) :-
        get0(NextCh),
        read_tokens(NextCh, Dict, Tokens).
read_special(0';, Dict, [atom(;)|Tokens]) :- % ; is not a punctuation
        get0(NextCh), % mark but an atom (e.g., you can :-op declare it).
        read_after_atom(NextCh, Dict, Tokens).
read_special(0'[, Dict, ['['|Tokens]) :-
        get0(NextCh),
        read_tokens(NextCh, Dict, Tokens).
read_special(0'], Dict, [']'|Tokens]) :-
        get0(NextCh),
        read_after_atom(NextCh, Dict, Tokens).
read_special(0'{, Dict, ['{'|Tokens]) :-
        get0(NextCh),
        read_tokens(NextCh, Dict, Tokens).
read_special(0'|, Dict, ['|'|Tokens]) :-
        get0(NextCh),
        read_tokens(NextCh, Dict, Tokens).
read_special(0'}, Dict, ['}'|Tokens]) :-
        get0(NextCh),
        read_after_atom(NextCh, Dict, Tokens).
read_special(0'., Dict, Tokens) :- % full stop
        get0(NextCh), % or possibly .=. &c
        read_fullstop(NextCh, Dict, Tokens).
read_special(0'", Dict, [string(Chars)|Tokens]) :- % "string"
        read_string(Chars, 0'", NextCh),
        read_tokens(NextCh, Dict, Tokens).
```

read_special(0'', Dict, Tokens) :- % 'atom'
          read_string(Chars, 0'', NextCh),
          read_after_atom(NextCh, Dict, Tokens, Chars).
read_special(0'#, Dict, Tokens) :-
          read_symbol(0'#, Dict, Tokens).
read_special(0'$, Dict, Tokens) :-
          read_symbol(0'$, Dict, Tokens).
read_special(0'&, Dict, Tokens) :-
          read_symbol(0'&, Dict, Tokens).
read_special(0'*, Dict, Tokens) :-
          read_symbol(0'*, Dict, Tokens).
read_special(0'+, Dict, Tokens) :-
          read_symbol(0'+, Dict, Tokens).
read_special(0'-, Dict, Tokens) :-
          read_symbol(0'-, Dict, Tokens).
read_special(0':, Dict, Tokens) :-
          read_symbol(0':, Dict, Tokens).
read_special(0'<, Dict, Tokens) :-
          read_symbol(0'<, Dict, Tokens).
read_special(0'=, Dict, Tokens) :-
          read_symbol(0'=, Dict, Tokens).
read_special(0'>, Dict, Tokens) :-
          read_symbol(0'>, Dict, Tokens).
read_special(0'?, Dict, Tokens) :-
          read_symbol(0'?, Dict, Tokens).
read_special(0'@, Dict, Tokens) :-
          read_symbol(0'@, Dict, Tokens).
read_special(92, Dict, Tokens) :- % 92 is "\\"
          read_symbol(92, Dict, Tokens).
read_special(0'^, Dict, Tokens) :-
          read_symbol(0'^, Dict, Tokens).
read_special(0'`, Dict, Tokens) :-
          read_symbol(0'`, Dict, Tokens).
read_special(0'~, Dict, Tokens) :-
          read_symbol(0'~, Dict, Tokens).

%   read_symbol(+C1, +Dict, -Tokens)
%   C1 is the first character of an atom made up of the following characters:
%   #$&*+-./:<=>?\^`~ (which are ASCII codes) and the ISO 8859/1
%   codes 215 (×) 247 (÷) 161-169, 171-185, 187-191

read_symbol(C1, Dict, Tokens) :-
        get0(C2),
        rest_symbol(C2, Chars, NextCh), % might read 0 chars
        read_after_atom(NextCh, Dict, Tokens, [C1|Chars]).

%   rest_symbol(+C2, -String, -NextCh)
%   reads the second and subsequence characters of an atom made up of
%   "symbol" characters. It returns those characters as the list
%   String, and the following character as NextCh. Note that it need
%   not read any characters at all, e.g., C2 might be " ".

rest_symbol(C2, [C2|Chars], NextCh) :-
        (C2 > 160 → C2 < 192, C2 =\= 186, C2 =\= 170
        ;   symbol_char(C2)
        ),
        !,
        get0(C3),
        rest_symbol(C3, Chars, NextCh).
rest_symbol(C2, [], C2).

symbol_char(0'#).
symbol_char(0'$).
symbol_char(0'&).
symbol_char(0'*).
symbol_char(0'+).
symbol_char(0'-).
symbol_char(0'.). % yes, +./* is a legal atom
symbol_char(0'/).
symbol_char(0':).
symbol_char(0'<).
symbol_char(0'=).
symbol_char(0'>).
symbol_char(0'?).
symbol_char(0'@).
symbol_char(92 /* \ */).
symbol_char(0'^).
symbol_char(0'`). % CHAT-80 uses ` as an atom.
symbol_char(0'~).
symbol_char(0'×). % ISO 8859/1 code is 215
symbol_char(0'÷). % ISO 8859/1 code is 247

read_after_atom(Ch, Dict, [atom(Atom)|Tokens], Chars) :-
        atom_chars(Atom, Chars),
        read_after_atom(Ch, Dict, Tokens).

%   The only difference between read_after_atom(Ch, Dict, Tokens) and
%   read_tokens/3 is what they do when Ch is "(". read_after_atom
%   finds the token to be '(', while read_tokens finds the token to be
%   '␣('. This is how the parser can tell whether *atom paren* must
%   be an operator application or an ordinary function symbol application.
%   See the public-domain library file READ.PL for details.

read_after_atom(0'(, Dict, ['('|Tokens]) :- !,
        get0(NextCh),
        read_tokens(NextCh, Dict, Tokens).
read_after_atom(Ch, Dict, Tokens) :-
        read_tokens(Ch, Dict, Tokens).

%   read_string(Chars, Quote, NextCh)
%   reads the body of a string delimited by Quote characters.
%   The result is a list of ASCII codes. There are two complications.
%   If we hit the end of the file inside the string this predicate FAILS.
%   It does not return any special structure. That is the only reason
%   it can ever fail. The other complication is that when we find a Quote
%   we have to look ahead one character in case it is doubled. Note that
%   if we find an end-of-file after the quote we *don't* fail, we return
%   a normal string and the end of file character is returned as NextCh.

read_string(Chars, Quote, NextCh) :-
        get0(Ch),
        read_char(Ch, Quote, Char, Next),
        rest_string(Char, Next, Chars, Quote, NextCh).

rest_string(-1, NextCh, [], _, NextCh) :- !. % string ended
rest_string(Char, Next, [Char|Chars], Quote, NextCh) :-
        read_char(Next, Quote, Char2, Next2),
        rest_string(Char2, Next2, Chars, Quote, NextCh).

%   read_char(C1, Quote, Char, C2)
%   reads a single 'character' from a string, quoted atom, or
%   character constant. C1 is the first character it is to look
%   at, and has been read already. Quote is the surrounding

% quotation mark, which is " for strings, ' for
% quoted atoms, and the radix character (also ') for
% character constants. If the 'character_escapes' flag is
% on, \ introduces C-like escape sequences and
% lines may not end in the middle of quoted constants; if the
% flag is off quoted constants are compatible with DEC-10
% Prolog. As reading an extended character would sometimes
% read one character too many, it is made to do so always, and
% to return the first character which does not belong in the
% character as C2. When we have hit the end of the string, we
% return Char = -1 (which does not necessarily mean that we
% have hit the end of the source file, look at C2 for that).

```
read_char(Char, Quote, Result, Next) :-
    (   Char =:= 92 /* \ */, % the escape character
        prolog_flag(character_escapes, on)
    →   get0(C1),
        (   C1 < 0 →
                format(user_error, '~N** end of file in ~cquoted~c~n',
                    [Quote,Quote]),
                Result = -1, Next = C1
        ;   C1 ≤ " " →
                /* \layout is skipped */
                get0(C2),
                read_char(C2, Quote, Result, Next)
        ;   C1\/32 =:= "c" →
                /* \c layout is skipped; to get a blank after this */
                /* do e.g., "..\c \␣" where the "\␣" ends */
                /* the skipping and the next blank is taken. */
                get(C2),
                read_char(C2, Quote, Result, Next)
        ;   C1 ≤ "7", C1 ≥ "0" →
                /* \1-3 octal digits */
                /* hairy bit: \1234 is S4 */
                get0(C2),
                (   C2 ≤ "7", C2 ≥ "0" →
                    get0(C3),
                    (   C3 ≤ "7", C3 ≥ "0" →
                        get0(Next),
                        Result is (C1*8+C2)*8+C3 - 73*"0"
```

```
                ;     Next = C3,
                      Result is (C1*8+C2) - 9*"0"
                )
           ;    Next = C2,
                Result is C1-"0"
           )
    ;    C1 =:= "^" →
             get0(C2),
             (    C2 < 0 →
                  format(user_error, '~N** end of file in ~c..~c^..~c~n',
                       [Quote,92 /* \ */,Quote]),
                  Result = -1, Next = C2
             ;    C2 =:= "?" →
                  Result = 127, % \^? = DEL
                  get0(Next)
             ;    Result is C2/\31, % \^X → control-X
                  get0(Next)
             )
    ;    escape_char(C1, Result) →
             get0(Next)
    ;    /* otherwise */
             Result = C1, % probably ", ', or \ itself
             get0(Next)
    )
;    Char =:= Quote →
     get0(Ch),
     (    Ch =:= Quote →
          Result = Quote,
          get0(Next)
     ;    Result = -1, Next = Ch
     )
;    Char < " ", Char =\= 9 /*TAB */,
     prolog_flag(character_escapes, on)
→    Result = -1, Next = Char,
     format(user_error,
          '~N** Strange character ~d ends ~ctoken~c~n',
          [Char, Quote, Quote])
;
     Result = Char,
     get0(Next)
).
```

% This table is for ASCII. On Xerox Lisp systems, \n maps to
% 13 (CR). The whole table needs replacing in EBCDIC systems,
% in which the assumption that A..Z and a..z are contiguous
% blocks also needs correcting. \z only makes sense as an
% isolated character; it shouldn't be in strings or atoms.

escape_char(0'a, 7). % \a = Audible Alarm = BEL = ^G
escape_char(0'A, 7). % \A = Audible Alarm = BEL = ^G
escape_char(0'b, 8). % \b = Backspace
escape_char(0'B, 8). % \B = Backspace
escape_char(0'd,127). % \d = Delete
escape_char(0'D,127). % \D = Delete
escape_char(0'e, 27). % \e = Escape
escape_char(0'E, 27). % \E = Escape
escape_char(0'f, 12). % \f = FormFeed
escape_char(0'F, 12). % \F = FormFeed
escape_char(0'n, 10). % \n = NewLine
escape_char(0'N, 10). % \N = NewLine
escape_char(0'r, 13). % \r = Return
escape_char(0'R, 13). % \R = Return
escape_char(0's, 32). % \s = visible Space
escape_char(0'S, 32). % \S = visible Space
escape_char(0't, 9). % \t = Tab
escape_char(0'T, 9). % \T = Tab
escape_char(0'v, 11). % \v = Vertical tab
escape_char(0'V, 11). % \V = Vertical tab
escape_char(0'z, -1). % \z = end of file
escape_char(0'Z, -1). % \Z = end of file

% read_variable(+C1, +Dict, -Tokens)
% C1 is the first character of a variable name. If the whole
% variable name is "_", this is an anonymous variable, not identical
% to any other variable. Otherwise, the variable and its name are
% looked up in (or added to) the dictionary, which is an improper list.
% This is the only place that read_lookup/2 is called.

```
read_variable(C1, Dict, [var(Var,Name)|Tokens]) :-
        read_name(C1, Chars, NextCh),
        atom_chars(Name, Chars),
        (   Name == '_' → true
        ;   read_lookup(Dict, Name, Var)
        ),
        read_after_atom(NextCh, Dict, Tokens).

read_lookup([N=V|L], Name, Var) :-
        (   N = Name → V = Var
        ;   read_lookup(L, Name, Var)
        ).
```

```
%   read_solidus(+Ch, -LastCh)
%   is called when we have read the "/" and "*" that open a PL/I-style
%   comment. It skips the rest of the comment. We have to take great
%   care to handle end of file inside a comment; if the end-of-file is
%   is reported, we return -1 as LastCh, while a space is returned if
%   the "*" and "/" that terminate the comment are found, and the next
%   character is left unread. That might be changed.
```

```
read_solidus(Ch, LastCh) :-
        (   Ch =:= 0'* → % maybe end of comment
            get0(NextCh),
            (   NextCh =:= 0'/ → % end of comment*/ found
                get(LastCh) % skip over any layout following
            ;   read_solidus(NextCh, LastCh)
            )
        ;   Ch =\= -1 → % ordinary comment character
            get0(NextCh),
            read_solidus(NextCh, LastCh)
        ;       % end of file
            LastCh = Ch,
            format(user_error, '~N** end of file in /*comment~n', [])
        ).
```

```
%   read_identifier(+C1, +Dict, -Tokens)
%   reads an atom which begins with a lower case letter C1 and
%   continues with letters, digits, and underscores.
```

```
read_identifier(C1, Dict, Tokens) :-
        read_name(C1, Chars, NextCh),
        read_after_atom(NextCh, Dict, Tokens, Chars).
```

```
%   read_name(+C1, -Chars, -LastCh)
%   reads a sequence of letters, digits, and underscores, where the
%   last character read was C1 and it is known that C1 is to be
%   included in the result. The desired characters are returned as
%   the list Chars, and the next character as LastCh.
%   This version has been tuned, oy, has it been tuned!
%   A table-driven version is nearly as fast in Prolog.
```

```
read_name(C1, [C1|Chars], LastCh) :-
    get0(C2),
    (   C2 ≥ "a" →
        (   C2 ≤ "z" → % ASCII lower case letter
            read_name(C2, Chars, LastCh)
        ;   C2 < 192, C2 \/ 16 =\= 186 → % {|}~, ISO 8859/1 symbols
            Chars = [], LastCh = C2
        ;   C2 \/ 32 =:= 247 → % times or divide-by chars
            Chars = [], LastCh = C2
        ;       % ISO 8859/1 top letters
            read_name(C2, Chars, LastCh)
        )
    ;   C2 ≥ "A" →
        (   C2 > "Z", C2 =\= "_" → % [\]^`
            Chars = [], LastCh = C2
        ;       % ASCII upper case or "_"
            read_name(C2, Chars, LastCh)
        )
    ;   ( C2 ≥ "0", C2 ≤ "9" → % ASCII digits
            read_name(C2, Chars, LastCh)
        ;       % other characters
            Chars = [], LastCh = C2
        )
    ).
```

```
%   read_fullstop(Char, Dict, Tokens)
%   looks at the next character after a full stop. There are
%   three cases:
%       (a) the next character is an end of file. We treat this
```

```
%              as an unexpected end of file. The reason for this is
%              that we HAVE to handle end of file characters in this
%              module or they are gone forever; if we failed to check
%              for end of file here and just accepted .EOF like .NL
%              the caller would have no way of detecting an end of file
%              and the next call would abort.
%        (b) the next character is a layout character. This is a
%              clause terminator.
%        (c) the next character is anything else. This is just an
%              ordinary symbol and we call read_symbol to process it.

read_fullstop(Ch, Dict, Tokens) :-
           (    Ch ≤ "9", Ch ≥ "0" →
                Tokens = [number(Number)|Tokens1],
                read_float(Number, Dict, Tokens1, "0", Ch)
           ;    Ch > " " → % ordinary token starting with "."
                rest_symbol(Ch, Chars, NextCh),
                read_after_atom(NextCh, Dict, Tokens, [0'.|Chars])
           ;    Ch ≥ 0 → % END OF CLAUSE
                Tokens = []
           ;        % END OF FILE
                format(user_error, '~N** end of file just after full stop~n', []),
                fail
           ).


% read_float(N, C, Dict, Tokens)
% is called when we have parsed digits.digit; N is the integer
% value of the characters preceding the decimal point, and C is the
% first digit after the decimal point.

read_float(Number, Dict, Tokens, Digits, Digit) :-
           prepend(Digits, Chars, Rest),
           read_float(Digit, Rest, NextCh, Chars),
           number_chars(Number, Chars),
           read_tokens(NextCh, Dict, Tokens).


prepend([]) ⟶ ".".
prepend([C|Cs]) ⟶ [C], prepend(Cs).
```

```
read_float(C1, [C1|Chars], NextCh, Total) :-
        get0(C2),
        (     C2 ≥ "0", C2 ≤ "9" →
              read_float(C2, Chars, NextCh, Total)
        ;     C2\/32 =:= "e" →
              get0(C3)
              (     C3 =:= "-" → get0(C4), Chars = [C2,0'-|More]
              ;     C3 =:= "+" → get0(C4), Chars = [C2|More]
              ;C4 = C3, Chars = [C2|More]
              ),
              (     C4 ≥ "0", C4 ≤ "9" →
                    read_exponent(C4, More, NextCh)
              ;     More = " ",
                    format(user_error, '^N** Missing exponent in ^s^n',[Total]),
                    fail
              ;     More = "0", NextCh = C4
              )
        ;     Chars = [], NextCh = C2
        ).

read_exponent(C1, [C1|Chars], NextCh) :-
        get0(C2),
        (     C2 ≥ "0", C2 ≤ "9" →
              read_exponent(C2, Chars, NextCh)
        ;     Chars = [], NextCh = C2
        ).

% read_number(+C1, +Dict, -Tokens)
% C1 is the digit which begins the number.

read_number(C1, Dict, [number(Number)|Tokens]) :-
        read_number(C1, C2, 0, N),
        (     C2 =:= 0' →
              (     N ≥ 2, N ≤ 36 →
                    read_based(N, 0, Number, C)
              ,     N =:= 0 →
                    get0(C3),
                    read_char(C3, -1, Number, C)
```

```
        ;    format(user_error, '^N** ^d'' read as^d ''^n',[N,N]),
             Number = N, C = C2
        ),
        read_tokens(C, Dict, Tokens)
   ;    C2 =:= 0' . →
        get0(C3),
        (    C3 ≥ "0", C3 ≤ "9" →
             number_chars(N, Digits),
             read_float(Number, Dict, Tokens, Digits, C3)
        ;    Number = N,
             read_fullstop(C3, Dict, Tokens)
        )
   ;    Number = N,
             read_tokens(C2, Dict, Tokens)
   ).
```

% read_number(+C0, -C, +N0, -N)
% read a decimal integer.

```
read_number(C0, C, N0, N) :-
   (    C0 ≥ "0", C0 ≤ "9" →
        N1 is N0*10 - "0" + C0,
        get0(C1),
        read_number(C1, C, N1, N)
   ;    C0 =:= 0' _ →
        get0(C1),
        read_number(C1, C, N0, N)
   ;    C = C0, N = N0
   ).
```

% read_based(+Base, +N0, -N, -LastCh)
% read an integer in base Base.

```
read_based(Base, N0, N, C) :-
        get0(C1),
        (    C1 ≥ "0", C1 ≤ "9" → Digit is C1-"0"
        ;    C1 ≥ "A", C1 ≤ "Z" → Digit is C1-("A"-10)
        ;    C1 ≥ "a", C1 ≤ "z" → Digit is C1-("a"-10)
        ;    Digit is 99
        ),
```

```
(     Digit < Base →
      N1 is N0*Base + Digit,
      read_based(Base, N1, N, C)
;     C1 =:= "_" →
      read_based(Base, N0, N, C)
;     N = N0, C = C1
).
```

I want to stress to you the importance of an idea and a fact. The fact is that get0/1 signals end-of-file by returning a special integer code (just like getchar() in C). The idea is the idea of writing tokenisers as finite-state machines and transliterating them into Prolog as predicates for states and clauses for arcs. Two years after I first heard of Prolog, I decided to write my own Prolog system, with as much of the system being in Prolog as possible. The attempt failed because I spent several days trying to write a tokeniser and failing. Indeed, when I needed a tokeniser later, I got one of the implementators of DEC-10 Prolog to make the actual DEC-10 Prolog tokeniser visible. But once I got the "finite state machine" idea, it really did take me a single evening to write the first draft of the tokeniser above, including everything except character escapes and floating-point numbers.

If you examine the code above, you will understand why some of the details of DEC-10 Prolog syntax are the way they are. For example, why is the "!" character not allowed to combine with other characters the way "?" is? The answer is that cuts are often followed by full stops, and full stops *are* allowed to combine with other characters. You cannot have both "!" and "." as combining characters, otherwise the rather common sequence "! ." will be misread. It would have made sense to make "." the character which doesn't combine with anything, but the symbols "= . ." and ", . ." were used in DEC-10 Prolog ("= . ." is still in use), and it would have made trouble for floating-point numbers.

11 All Solutions

11.1   Introduction

It is often useful in Prolog to collect all the solutions to a goal in a single data
structure. Doing so lets you convert backtracking to iteration, and gets around
the most serious problem with backtracking as a control structure: namely that
it is very difficult (and *should* be) to pass information from one "iteration" of a
backtracking control structure to the next.

11.2   Some Examples

The examples in this section are to show you that "all solutions" predicates can be
useful. The operation used, namely setof/3, is explained later in this chapter. For
the moment, a vague understanding that

setof(X, p(X), L)

unifies L with a set of all the instances of X for which Prolog was able to prove
p(X) will serve.

Suppose we have a small business data base held as a Prolog program, and we
want to print a report showing the names of all the people who owe us money. Let's
suppose that the data base contains a predicate

debt(Debtor, Invoice, AmountUnpaid)

meaning that Debtor is the name of a person, Invoice is the label of an invoice that
the Debtor sent to us for goods which we have supplied, and that AmountUnpaid
is the amount of money still owing for those goods. At the terminal, we could just
type the Prolog command

:-   debt(Debtor, _, _)
     write(Debtor), nl,
     fail.

This would enumerate the names of all the debtors in the data base.

That's rather crude. There are two problems:

- if someone owes us for two invoices, he will show up in the debtors report
  twice.

- if there are no debtors, nothing will be printed. As a general rule, a report
  that has nothing to say should be explicit about it rather than just printing
  nothing.

So what we do is ask Prolog to find the *set* of debtors. The setof/3 predicate fails when the set would be empty (this property is essential for correct behaviour in complex situations, and is almost always useful). This means that the one predicate solves both our problems.

```
print_debtor_report :-
        setof(Debtor, debtor(Debtor), Debtors),
        !, /* there is at least one Debtor */
        print_debtor_report_header
        print_debtor_lines(Debtors)
        print_debtor_report_footer.


print_debtor_report :-
        print_null_debtor_report

print_debtor_lines([]).
print_debtor_lines([Debtor | Debtors]) :-
        print_debtor_lines(Debtor)
        print_debtor_lines(Debtors).


debtor(Debtor) :-
        debt(Debtor, _, _).
```

As the next step in developing such a report, we might decide to print each debtor's total debt as well as his name. How can we obtain the total debt of a given Debtor? It is the sum of the AmountUnpaid for each Invoice which has not been paid in full. We can calculate this quite easily once we have the set of Invoice-AmountUnpaid pairs for the debtor, so that's what we do.

```
total_debt(Debtor, Debt) :-
        setof(Invoice-AmountUnpaid,
              debt(Debtor, Invoice, AmountUnpaid),
              InvoiceAmounts),
        total_sum(InvoiceAmounts, 0, Debt).


total_sum([], Sum, Sum).
total_sum([Invoice-Amount | InvoiceAmounts], Sum0, Sum) :-
        Sum1 is Sum0+Amount,
        total_sum(InvoiceAmounts, Sum1, Sum).
```

With the aid of this, we could define, for example,

```
print_debtor_line(Debtor) :-
        total_debt(Debtor, Debt)
        write(Debtor), write(' owes $'), write(Debt), nl.
```

If you already know about bagof/3, you may think that it should have been used in the definition of total_debt/2 and that we should not have bothered with the Invoice names. You would be wrong, unless you knew for sure that the same Invoice-Amount pair would never be reported more than once by debtor/3.

Basically, "all solutions" predicates let us convert a predicate which enumerates solutions by backtracking into a data structure (a list or set) which we can process recursively (that is, by conventional iteration).

11.3 Standard Predicates

The three "standard" all solutions predicates are

- findall/3, collects instances in the order in which they are found, but doesn't handle free variables right, and is hard to give a declarative reading to

- setof/3, returns a set of instances (a list in standard order with no duplicates), handles free variables right, and is almost logical

- bagof/3, a hybrid between findall/3 and setof/3.

The predicate findall/3, described by Clocksin & Mellish, has been around for many years. David H. D. Warren introduced the predicates bagof/3 and setof/3 in a paper entitled "Higher-Order Extensions to Prolog, Are They Needed?".

Every Prolog system should provide bagof/3 and setof/3. There is no difficulty in doing this, as source code for these operations was made public several years ago. It is not so important to provide findall/3, as bagof/3 can simulate it:

```
findall(Template, Enumerator, Solutions) :-
        bagof(Template, Enumerator^Enumerator, X),
        !,
        Solutions = X.
findall(_, _, []).
```

Each of these predicates has its uses and its subtleties. (Such as the fact that it would not make any kind of sense for setof/3 ever to yield an empty result.) We shall start by looking in some detail at the very simplest of them all, namely findall/3, as finding all the results has its own subtleties.

11.4 Clocksin & Mellish

Many new Prolog programmers learn about findall/3 in the book "Programming in Prolog" by Clocksin and Mellish. In the first edition, it appears at the end of section 7.8, on pages 152–153. The idea is that findall(Template, Enumerator, List)

finds all the instances of Template for which Enumerator is provable, collects them
into a list in the order in which it found them (that is, the first instance found is
the first element of the list, the last instance found is the last element of the list),
and unifies List with this list. Normally, List is a variable. Template is usually a
variable or a compound term whose arguments are variables, but it can be anything.

How can we implement this? The first thing which springs to mind is probably
something like

```
findall_1(Template, Enumerator, List) :-
        L := []
        (    call(Enumerator),
             L := [Template|L],
             fail
        ;    reverse(L, List)
        )
```

To find all the solutions of Enumerator, you have to put it inside a failure-driven
loop like this. But assignment is not a standard part of Prolog. [1]

The next step is to say, very well, we'll simulate assignment by using the data
base.

```
findall_2(Template, Enumerator, List) :-
        assert(ℓ([])),
        (    call(Enumerator),
             retract(ℓ(L)),
             assert(ℓ([Template|L])),
             fail
        ;    retract(ℓ(L)),
             reverse(L, List)
        ).
```

There are several problems with this. The first is that the Enumerator could quite
reasonably call findall/3 itself, so the calls to assert/1 should use asserta/1. The
second is that retract/1 backtracks over a predicate, and each time it finds a clause
which matches it retracts that clause. The third is that building the list this way
will take $O(N^2)$ time, where N is the number of solutions found. (Can you see
why?) Now, since we have to manage $ℓ(\_)$ as a stack so that findall/3 can call
findall/3, we might as well put individual elements on the stack. We finally arrive
at the version of findall/3 given in Clocksin & Mellish:

---

[1]Some Prolog systems use the assignment *symbol* := where Common Prolog uses **is**. That
is rather confusing, because the operation they provide under that name is *not* conventional
assignment.

```
findall_c_and_m(Template, Enumerator, _) :-
        asserta(found(mark)),  % push 'mark' on stack 'found'
        call(Enumerator),
        asserta(found(Template)),
        fail.
findall_c_and_m(_, _, List) :-
        collect_found([], L),
        !,                     % this cut is totally pointless
        List = L.

collect_found(S, L) :-
        getnext(X),            % while there is a non-mark on the stack
        !,                     % do cons that element on the front
        collect_found([X|S], L).
collect_found(L, L).           % return L when 'mark' is found

getnext(X) :-
        retract(found(X)),
        !,                     % stop retract backtracking
        X \== mark.            % check for end of list
```

11.5   Doing it Right

Apart from layout, spelling, and comments, that is what appears on page 152 of
C&M. What need is there for me to say more? Well, um, er, I'm afraid it has,
er, a *mistake*. In fact, DEC-10 Prolog has exactly the same mistake (involving a
different constant), and a right nuisance it was too. A recent book of Prolog utility
predicates *still* has the mistake! Can you see the mistake?

Perhaps not. The mistake is this: what if Template=mark? Here is a transcript
of an actual test of the Clocksin and Mellish code.

```
?- compile(library(basics)).
[/usr/ok/library.d/basics.pl compiled in module basics]
[1.550 sec 1232 bytes]
yes

?- findall_c_and_m(X, member(X,[tom,dick,harry]), L).
X = _732,
L = [tom,dick,harry]
```

?- findall_c_and_m(X, member(X,[matthew,mark,luke,john]), L).
X = _732,
L = [luke, john]

?- listing(found).
found(matthew).
found(mark).
yes

?- end_of_file.

This is a fairly major sort of mistake. How can we fix it?

There are two ways that we can tell clauses apart. One is by their *contents*. Here that means that a "marker" clause would have to look different from an "element" clause. The other is by their *names*. Every clause and data base record has a unique name, called a *data base reference*. If you don't already know about data base references, look them up in your Prolog manual.

There is one more problem with findall_c_and_m/3. found/1 is a pretty useful sort of predicate name, and we have no business taking it away from users. What's more, in using such a "likely" name for an internal predicate, we are running a serious risk that the user's program will clobber it. A convention I used to follow in DEC-10 Prolog and C Prolog is to use names with spaces in them for internal predicates. In Quintus Prolog, it is possible to use a module, so the problem doesn't exist. Beware, though: there are several other Prolog module systems around, and some of them are so incoherent that you are better off without them.

So now we are ready to make a version of findall/3 which distinguishes markers from elements. I have chosen to use {_} as the wrapper to distinguish elements from markers: this means exactly the same term as '{}'(_) and always has.

```
findall_4(Template, Enumerator, List) :-
        asserta('find all'([])),
        call(Enumerator),
        asserta('find all'({Template})),
        fail
    ;   'all found 4'([], List).

'all found 4'(SoFar, List) :-
        retract('find all'(Item)),
        !, % stop retract looking for more Items
        'all found 4'(Item, SoFar, List).
```

'all found 4'([], List, List).
'all found 4'({Template}, SoFar, List) :-
        'all found 4'([Template|SoFar], List).

The other approach uses data base references. So we have to remember the data base reference of the marker, and it doesn't much matter what goes inside it.

findall_5(Template, Enumerator, List) :-
        asserta('find all'([]), MarkRef),
        (call(Enumerator),
             asserta('find all'(Template)),
             fail
        ;   'all found 5'(MarkRef, [], List)
).

'all found 5'(MarkRef, SoFar, List) :-
        clause('find all'(Item), _, Ref),
        !, % stop clause/3 looking for more Items
        erase(Ref),
        (Ref = MarkRef → SoFar = List
        ;   'all found 5'(MarkRef,[Item|SoFar],List)
).

DEC-10 Prolog had two "data bases": the 'clause' data base where the clauses of dynamic predicates go, and the 'recorded' data base which is a sort of glorified "property list" area. C Prolog, Quintus Prolog, SICStus Prolog, NU Prolog, and some other compatible Prologs also support this extra, 'recorded', data base. Using that, we get another two choices for implementing findall. findall_6 is just like findall_4 except for using the 'recorded' data base, and findall_7 is just like findall_5 except for using the 'recorded' data base:

findall_7(Template, Enumerator, List) :-
        recorda('find all', [], MarkRef),
        (call(Enumerator),
             recorda('find all', Template, _),
             fail
        ;   'all found 7'(MarkRef, [], List)
).

```
'all found 7'(MarkRef, SoFar, List) :-
        recorded('find all', Item, Ref),
        !, % stop recorded/3 looking for more Items
        erase(Ref),
        (    Ref = MarkRef →
             SoFar = List
        ;    'all found 7'(MarkRef, [Item|SoFar], List)
        ).
```

How shall we choose between these methods? In a Prolog system which doesn't
support data base references, there is no choice. We'd have to use findall_4/3.
When we do have the choice, the answer is that we should check to see which is
fastest. At this point, I stopped to time the four variants, and received something
of a surprise. In Quintus Prolog release 2.4 on a Sun-3/50, the cost of obtaining
N solutions with findall/3, over and above the cost of finding the solutions to the
Enumerator, was

findall_4	const +	7.1N	milliseconds
findall_5	const +	7.4N	milliseconds
findall_6	const +	4.5N	milliseconds (as _4, but recorda)
findall_7	const +	4.3N	milliseconds (as _5, but recorda)
bagof/3	const +	1.5N	milliseconds (the built-in)

If it ever matters, *don't* rely on your intuition about how to make a Prolog
predicate go fast, *measure it*! Don't forget that the winner might be different in
another Prolog implementation: I repeated these measurements in SICStus Prolog,
and findall_6 was a little faster than findall_7.

So, if we wanted an efficient version of findall/3 in Quintus Prolog, the one to
pick would be findall_7.

11.6   findall/3 reconsidered

It is all very well knowing how findall/3 works. But what (if anything) does it
mean?

The plain answer is that it is impossible to give a first-order logical reading to
findall/3. We have to read

findall(Template, Enumerator, Instances)

as "Instances is the sequence of instances of Template which correspond to proofs
of Enumerator in the order in which they are found by the Prolog system." This is

meta-logical in two senses: the results depend on the instantiation state of Template and Enumerator, and on the proof strategy of the particular Prolog system.

Lee Naish has pointed out that findall/3 can be used to define all sorts of nasty things like not/1 and var/1.

¬(Goal) :-
        findall(., Goal, []).

var(Var) :-
        findall(., (Var=a ; Var=b), [_,_]).

It is well known that negation as failure (the "unprovable" operation ¬) is not a sound implementation of logical negation (not), but that it is sound when the goal is ground. Similarly, whatever findall/3 means, it is sound when the Enumerator has no free variables that are not captured by the Template.

The Template may be a single variable, or it may be any term at all containing any number of variables, even none.[2] Variables in the Template should be viewed as quantified variables. It is very bad style to use those variables anywhere else in the clause. Just as negation as failure leaves any variables in the goal unbound at the end of the day, so does findall/3 leave every variable in the Template or Enumerator unbound after it has finished.

Let's look at an example. With the data base

calendar(tom, algebra, monday).
calendar(tom, cooking, tuesday).
calendar(tom, english, wednesday).
calendar(sue, algebra, tuesday).
calendar(sue, history, wednesday).
calendar(sue, biology, thursday).

we obtain the following results from findall/3:

?- findall(Day, calendar(_,_,Day), Days).
Day = _33,
Days = [monday,tuesday,wednesday,tuesday,wednesday,thursday]

?- findall(Subject, calendar(Person,Subject,_), Subjects).
Subject = _33,
Person = _56,
Subjects = [algebra,cooking,english,algebra,history,biology]

---

[2]In early versions of Turbo Prolog the first argument of findall/3 had to be a single variable. I do not know whether that is still true.

In the first query, we get multiple copies of answers. This reminds us that although Prolog *reports* solutions, it is *looking for* proofs, and findall/3 is defined to return an instance of the Template for every *proof* of the Enumerator. setof/3 addresses this problem. We also see that the Day variable is left uninstantiated, as is appropriate.

In the second query, we see that the Subject is quantified over (by appearing in the Template), so it is no surprise that it is left unbound. But someone who has gone to the trouble of naming the Person argument of calendar is probably expecting to have it instantiated. bagof/3 addresses this problem.

11.7   bagof/3 and setof/3

bagof/3 and setof/3 have the same shape as findall/3:

bagof(Template, Enumerator, InstanceList)

setof(Template, Enumerator, InstanceSet)

There are two major differences. First, bagof/3 makes sense when the Enumerator contains unbound variables which are not captured by the Template. This means that it can enumerate bindings for those variables. There are thus three kinds of variables which may appear (at run-time) in the enumerator:

- variables captured by the Template

- variables you want to be bound by bagof/3 ("free" variables)

- variables whose values you do not want to know about ("existential" variables)

Let's look at that second query above. We had

    ...   calendar(Person,Subject,_) ...

where Subject is captured by the Template, Person we want bound, and the anonymous variable we want to ignore.

How are we to indicate which variables belong to which class? The Template already indicates which variables are quantified there, whose values are to appear in the list of instances. But we have at least three choices for distinguishing free from existentially quantified variables:

- We could forbid existentially quantified variables. This would mean that programmers would often have to define auxiliary predicates, such as

calendar_YYN(Person, Subject) :-
        calendar(Person, Subject, _Day).

and call those instead of writing the query directly. Actually, this is a pretty good idea, and whenever you find the setof/3 query you are writing unclear you should consider introducing an auxiliary predicate like this anyway. A benefit in DEC-10 Prolog, Quintus Prolog, and many other Prolog implementations is that the use of the interpreter will be reduced. A benefit all the time is that you will understand exactly what the query is.

• We could label the free variables in some way. This is what many data base query languages do, using a construct like "GROUP BY". For example, an SQL version of our query might look like

SELECT SUBJECT
    FROM CALENDAR
    GROUP BY PERSON

• We could label the existential variables in some way. This, of course, is precisely what is done in logic, so that's what Prolog does.

The notation for existential quantification in Prolog is rather odd. One writes

    X1^X2^X3^Goal

which, to be consistent with the usual idea of scope, has to be read as

    X1^(X2^(X3^Goal))

The Enumerator in a call to bagof/3 or setof/3 can have any number of existentially quantified variables.

Here is the Person/Subjects query written using bagof/3:

?- bagof(Subject, Day^calendar(Person,Subject,Day), Subjects).
Day = _51,
Person = sue,
Subject = _34,
Subjects = [algebra,history,biology] ;

Day = _51,
Person = tom,
Subject = _34,
Subjects = [algebra,cooking,english] ;

no more solutions

Beware! It is tempting to write

?- bagof(Subject, calendar(Person,Subject,_), Subjects).

But anonymous variables are *not* existentially quantified! To say that a variable is existentially quantified, you have to mention it twice—once where it normally appears and once in the quantifier—and that means that it cannot be anonymous. This version of the query gives completely different results:

```
/* _ = thursday, */
Person = sue,
Subject = _33,
Subjects = [biology] ;

/* _ = tuesday, */
Subject = _33,
Person = sue,
Subjects = [algebra] ;

/* _ = wednesday, */
Subject = _33,
Person = sue,
Subjects = [history] ;

/* _ = monday, */
Subject = _33,
Person = tom,
Subjects = [algebra] ;

/* _ = tuesday, */
Subject = _33,
Person = tom,
Subjects = [cooking] ;

/* _ = wednesday, */
Subject = _33,
Person = tom,
Subjects = [english] ;
```

no more solutions

I have added the bindings of the anonymous variable to this output so that you can see why these solutions are obtained.

setof/3 goes a step further. It takes the sequence of instances that bagof/3 would have found, and returns a *set* of instances. So we can ask questions like

?- setof(Person, S^D^calendar(Person,S,D), People).
Person = _33,
S = _50,
D = _67,
People = [sue,tom]

?- setof(Subject, P^D^calendar(P,Subject,D), Subjects).
Subject = _33,
P = _50,
D = _67,
Subjects = [algebra,biology,cooking,english,history]

?- setof(Day, P^S^calendar(P,S,Day), Days).
Day = _33,
P = _48,
S = _65,
Days = [monday,thursday,tuesday,wednesday]

We can *almost* give a logical reading to setof/3.

    setof(Template, Exvars^Enumerator, Solutions)

can be read as

Solutions = {Template|(∃Exvars)Enumerator} and Solutions is not the empty set

However, this still involves both a positive claim (that each of the members of Solutions is a solution) and a negative claim (that these are the *only* solutions).

The negative claim is the reason that bagof/3 and setof/3 must never yield the empty list. Consider the query

?- bagof(., calendar(X,Y,Z), []).

There are infinitely many terms X,Y,Z such that calendar(X,Y,Z) is not provable. We cannot hope to enumerate them. If bagof/3 or setof/3 were allowed to return the empty list when the Enumerator had no solutions, such queries would be unsound in exactly the same way that ¬calendar(X,Y,Z) would be an unsound attempt to find an X, Y, and Z such that calendar(X,Y,Z) was false.

As we saw in the 'debtors' example, the fact that the result of setof/3 can never be empty is sometimes a natural restriction. For example, suppose we have a "library" data base containing journal(Department, Title, YearlySubscription)

facts, and we want to know the yearly subscription of the most expensive journal
for each department:

most_expensive_subscription(Department, Amount) :-
        setof(Sub, T^journal(Department, T, Sub), Subs),
        maximum(Subs, Amount).

The maximum is not defined on an empty set, but since this predicate will never
call maximum with Subs=[] we don't need to worry about that when defining maxi-
mum/2. Similarly, to find the average subscription per journal for each department
(perhaps to see whether Cell Biology journals tend to be more expensive than
Computer Science ones) we could write

average_subscription(Department, Amount) :-
        setof(Title-Sub, journal(Department, Title, Sub), Subs),
        total_sum(Subs, 0, Total),
        length(Subs, Count),
        Amount is Total/Count.

We don't have to worry about division by zero, because setof/3 is never going to
return an empty set of Subs.
    It is easy to nest calls to setof/3. Just as simple calls to setof/3 are useful for
turning implicit *sets* into explicit lists, so nested calls to setof/3 are useful for
turning implicit *graphs* into explicit adjacency lists. For example, suppose we have
a data base of

precondition(Task1, Task2)

facts, meaning that Task1 must be completed before Task2 can begin. One thing
we might want to do with this information is to construct a list of tasks TaskList
such that if each of the tasks is done in the order it appears in the list, it will find
that all its preconditions have already been completed. The DEC-10 and Quintus
Prolog libraries contain a predicate called top_sort/2[3] to do this, but it wants an
adjacency list as input. No problem, just do

?-   setof(T1-T2s,
            setof(T2, precondition(T1,T2), T2s), [4]
            TaskGraph),
        top_sort(TaskGraph, TaskList).

_____
[3]for "topological sort".

In the discussion of transitive closure, we saw setof/3 serving as an interface between the data base and Warshall's algorithm in just this way.

For a more "commercial" example, suppose we have

employee_department(Name, Department)

facts in our data base, and want to know all the departments employing at least three people.

```
?-  setof(Dept,
        setof(Emp, employee_department(Emp,Dept), [_,_,_|_]),
        Depts).
```

will give us the answer.

11.8   How do bagof/3 and setof/3 work?

bagof(Template, Enumerator, Instances) and
  setof(Template, Enumerator, Solutions) basically work like this:

1. The Enumerator is checked for existentially quantified variables. This step produces two new terms: FreeVars and RealEnumerator.

2. findall(FreeVars-Template, RealEnumerator, VarTemplatePairs)

   is called to obtain all the proofs of RealEnumerator.

3. VarTemplatePairs is sorted using FreeVars as the key. This sort is stable, so that the relative order of Template instances associated with the same bindings for FreeVars is preserved. This is in fact the Prolog predicate keysort/2.

4. The sorted list is grouped into blocks FRinstance-TPinstances associating each distinct instance FRinstance of the FreeVars with a list of all the corresponding instances TPinstances of the Template.

5. bagof/3 then does

   member(FreeVars-Instances, ListOfBlocks)

   to enumerate the bindings of the free variables.

   setof/3 does instead

   member(FreeVars-Instances, ListOfBlocks), sort(Instances, Solutions)

This is the reason that the Prolog predicate sort/2 eliminates duplicate elements and keysort/2 does not.

A skilled Prolog programmer will exploit the standard ordering on terms, using sorting to group together similar terms. But this only works when the terms are sufficiently instantiated. Suppose, for example, that we have the data base

p(_, a).
p(b, _).

and the query

?- G = p(X,Y), setof(G, G^G, Gs).

We obtain the solution

Gs = [p(_100,a),p(b,_103)]

If later code binds _100=b, _103=a, the two solutions will be identical, and we will have Gs=[p(b,a),p(b,a)] when we would have expected Gs=[p(b,a)]. There is nothing that a conventional Prolog system can do to prevent this.

Ordering terms using term comparison is only sound when each pair of terms being compared is either already identical or already distinct. Since bagof/3 and setof/3 involve sorting, they are only sound when the free variables and template variables are bound to sufficiently instantiated terms, particularly ground terms or terms with distinct principal functors.

11.9   Doing it Differently

Some people prefer a style where the free variables are explicitly marked rather than the existential variables. What should be done about that?

Well, the answer is *not* to change the definition of bagof/3 or setof/3. The answer is to define new predicates with the desired properties. These new predicates will have to specify a template, a goal, an output parameter, and will have to specify the grouping (free) variables.

Here's a design question: what should the argument list of these operations look like? It will greatly reduce the burden on our memory if the arguments of these new operations which resemble the arguments of bagof/3 and setof/3 are in the same order as they are in those predicates. The simplest way of marking the grouping variables is to wrap them up in a term and pass them as an argument. Shall we put this at the front of the argument list or at the end? The rule is that you try to put inputs near the beginning of the argument list, and outputs near the end, and this is really an input. So we arrive at

grouped_bag_of(GroupVars, Template, Enumerator, Bag)
grouped_set_of(GroupVars, Template, Enumerator, Set)

where the arguments are exactly the same as the arguments of findall/3, bagof/3, or setof/3 except for the GroupVars at the front.

To over-simplify somewhat, here is how we would code them.

```
grouped_set_of(GroupVars, Template, Enumerator, Set) :-
        grouped_bag_of(GroupVars, Template, Enumerator, Bag),
        sort(Bag, Set).

grouped_bag_of(GroupVars, Template, Enumerator, Bag) :-
        findall(GroupVars-Template, Enumerator, RawPairs),
        keysort(RawPairs, OrdPairs),
        concordant_subset(OrdPairs, GroupVars, Answer),
        Bag = Answer.

%    concordant_subset([Key-Val list], Key, [Val list])
%    takes a list of Key-Val pairs which has been keysorted to bring
%    all the identical keys together, and enumerates each different
%    Key and the corresponding lists of values.

concordant_subset([Key-Val|Rest], Clavis, Answer) :-
        concordant_subset(Rest, Key, List, More),
        concordant_subset(More, Key, [Val|List], Clavis, Answer).

%    concordant_subset(Rest, Key, List, More)
%    strips off all the Key-Val pairs from the from of Rest,
%    putting the Val elements into List, and returning the
%    left-over pairs, if any, as More. Note the use of ==.

concordant_subset([Key-Val|Rest], Clavis, [Val|List], More) :-
        Key == Clavis,
        !,
        concordant_subset(Rest, Clavis, List, More).
concordant_subset(More, _, [], More).

%    concordant_subset/5 tries the current subset, and if that
%    doesn't work if backs up and tries the next subset. The
%    first clause is there to save a choice point when this is
%    the last possible subset.
```

concordant_subset([], Key, Subset, Key, Subset) :- !.
concordant_subset(_, Key, Subset, Key, Subset).
concordant_subset(More, _, _, Clavis, Answer) :-
        concordant_subset(More, Clavis, Answer).

What happens when we try this on the calendar example?

?- grouped_bag_of(Person, S, calendar(Person,S,_), Subjects).
Person = sue,
S = _50,
Subjects = [algebra,history,biology] ;

Person = tom,
S = _50,
Subjects = [algebra,cooking,english] ;

no more answers

We see that the anonymous variable was implicitly existentially quantified.

The hardest thing here was writing concordant_subset, but I was able to lift that from the DEC-10 Prolog public-domain library, which contains an implementation of bagof/3 and setof/3. But it isn't hard to put something like this together.

The moral of the story is that if findall/3, bagof/3, or setof/3 doesn't do exactly what you need, don't let that stop you. Go ahead and roll your own.

You might be worried about the (in-)efficiency of writing your own versions compared with using the built-in predicates. Suppose there are N solutions, each of size S cells. These predicates have two phases:

- phase 1 obtains all the solutions. This involves exploring the proof tree, which is going to happen no matter what, so we ignore that cost. It also involves storing a copy of all the solutions, which takes $O(S.N)$ time.

- phase 2 sorts the solutions. This takes $O(S.N.\lg N)$ time.

Now if the implementor has an especially clever way of sorting terms which goes blindingly fast, he ought to provide it to as sort/2 and keysort/2, so your phase 2 should be about the same speed as anything the system can do. A clever implementation of phase 1 can be *much* faster than anything you can write, but there again, if the implementor has been this clever, he really ought to provide you with findall/3 so you can take advantage of his cleverness. Even so, if N is big enough, the cost of sorting will eventually dominate the cost of copying.

Just to see what sort of difference it does make, I timed six versions of bagof/3 working on a task which had 145 solutions.

0.65s	bagof/3	Quintus Prolog built-in
0.70s	findall/3	one of the versions described here
1.10s	bag_of/3	Public domain version
1.10s	grouped_bag_of/4	Described here
1.00s	bag_of/3	with a faster keysort/2
1.00s	grouped_bag_of/4	with a faster keysort/2

This is enough to encourage one to use the built-in predicates when they are appropriate, but not enough to discourage one from using one's own routines when *they* are appropriate.

11.10   In NU Prolog

NU Prolog is an Edinburgh-compatible Prolog compiler written at the University of Melbourne. It is a "research" Prolog rather than an "industrial" one, although it is quite as solid as some commercial products. The main emphasis of NU Prolog is on providing a more declarative language than "standard" Prolog.

NU Prolog provides some "logical" all-solutions predicates, described by Lee Naish [23, 24]. These, provided in addition to the "standard" predicates findall/3, bagof/3, and setof/3, are:

solutions(Template, Enumerator, Set) This is exactly the same as setof/3 in concept: the solutions of Enumerator are found and the corresponding instances of Template sorted. However, solutions/3 will wait until the solutions are sufficiently instantiated for sorting to be sound. For example,

```
?-  setof(X, member(X, [A,B]), L),
    A = a, B = a.
```

yields the answer

L = [a, a], B = a, A = a

where L contains a duplicated value, despite having been sorted to eliminate duplicates. The reason for this is that setof/3 sorted the list while A and B were still (different) variables. In contrast,

```
?-  solutions(X, member(X, [A,B]), L),
    A = a, B = a.
```

yields the logically correct answer

L = [a], B = a, A = a.

count(Template, Enumerator, Count) binds Result to the number of distinct instances of Template corresponding to proofs of Enumerator. This means the same as

    solutions(Template, Enumerator, Set),
    length(Set, Count)

Like solutions/3, it will wait until the instances of Template are sufficiently instantiated to tell them apart.

max(Template, Enumerator, Max)

min(Template, Enumerator, Min) these return the greatest (max) or least (min) instances of Template corresponding to a proof of Enumerator, where the ordering used is the standard order on terms. They are almost the same as

    solutions(Template, Enumerator, Set),
    append(_, [Max], Set)

and

    solutions(Template, Enumerator, [Min|_])

respectively.

sum(Summand,Template,Enumerator,Sum) forms a set of the distinct pairs (Template, Summand) corresponding to solutions of Enumerator, and unifies Sum with the sum of the Summands. In essence, the Templates are carried along to prevent Summands which happen to have the same value being coalesced. In this chapter we have used this operation several times, in the form

    setof(Template-Summand, Enumerator, Set),
    total_sum(Set, 0, Sum)

The Quintus Prolog library contains an operation called aggregate/[3–4] which lets you ask for several "summary" values at once. The correspondence between NU Prolog and Quintus Prolog is

max(X, Enumerator, M)	aggregate(max(X), Enumerator, M)
min(X, Enumerator, M)	aggregate(min(X), Enumerator, M)
count(D, Enumerator, C)	aggregate(count, D, Enumerator, C)
sum(X, D, Enumerator, S)	aggregate(sum(X), D, Enumerator, S)
bagof(X, Enumerator, B)	aggregate(bag(X), Enumerator, B)
setof(X, Enumerator, B)	aggregate(set(X), X, Enumerator, B)

The first argument of aggregate/[3–4] may be a list containing several summary requests, so to find the average price of journals in the library we could ask

aggregate([sum(S),count], T, D^journal(D,T,S), [Tot,Cnt]),
Average is Tot/Cnt.

The NU Prolog equivalent would be

sum(S, T, some D journal(D,T,S), Tot),
count(T, some D.S journal(D,T,S), Cnt),
Average is Tot/Cnt

which enumerates all the journals twice.

Implementing your own version of aggregate/[3–4] is a good exercise. The simplest method I could think of was to build it on top of setof/3. For NU Prolog, you would want to build it on top of solutions/3.

Bibliography

[1] Edsger W. Dijkstra. *A Discipline of Programming*. Prentice-Hall, Englewood Cliffs NJ, 1979. ISBN 0-13-215871-X.

This is one of the classics of computer programming. Dijkstra's theme is a rigorous and methodical way of developing (small) programs. One of his ideas is that it pays to view a program text as a mathematical object rather than as a sort of machine. Some people dislike his approach because it is so "mathematical", but if you have trouble handling formulas you are in the wrong business, and if you don't like a logical view of programs Prolog is not for you.

Dijkstra's methods are developed for an imperative language with "dont'-care nondeterminism". The approach carries over very well indeed to Prolog.

[2] David Gries. *The Science of Programming*. Texts and Monographs in computer science, Springer-Verlag, New York, 1981. ISBN 0-387-90641-X.

This text-book is based on Dijkstra's approach, but it is bigger, with more examples and lots of exercises. If you want to master the "discipline of programming" approach, this is the text-book to get. The details of handling arrays don't carry over to Prolog, but the techniques of designing a loop (in Prolog, a recursive predicate) by generalising the condition the loop is supposed to establish do carry over nicely. I *strongly* recommend this book.

[3] H. Ledgard & J. Tauer. *Professional Software, volume 2: Programming Practice*. ISBN 0-201-12232-4.

Ledgard and Tauer introduce the term "P_A programmer". A P_A programmer is an amateur programmer who *thinks* he is a professional, or a professional who is acting like an amateur. Near enough is *not* good enough for a professional, and the two volumes discuss things such as user interface design (that's in volume 1) and naming conventions and layout (in volume 2). There is a lot of good stuff in these two volumes, though I'm afraid that their examples finally convinced me that Pascal-like languages are part of the problem. The layout style I use for Prolog is essentially the "comb" style that they recommend (nice to know they got it right (:-)).

[4] David Maier. *The Theory of Relational Databases*. Computer Science Press, 1983. ISBN 0-914894-42-0.

For the mathematical theory of relational data bases you would have a hard time finding a better book. I've left relational data bases out of this book on the grounds that (a) I've got to finish some time, and (b) Maier and Ullman do a better job than I can ever hope to. This may be too advanced for some.

[5] Jeffrey D. Ullman. *Principles of Database and Knowledge-Base Systems*. Computer Science Press. Volume 1, 1988; ISBN 0-7167-8069-0. Volume 2, 1989; ISBN 0-7167-8162-X.

This is the latest edition of Ullman's classic. If there is one data base book that every Prolog programmer should have and should study, this is it. The book covers network, hierarchical, relational, and deductive data bases. If you want to know what logic programming looks like when applied to data bases, these books will tell you. Some of the techniques (such as the "semi-naïve method", have applications in everyday Prolog programming.

[6] Robert Kowalski. *Logic for Problem Solving*. North-Holland, 1979. ISBN 0-444-00368-1.

From the preface: "This book investigates the application of logic to problem-solving and computer programming. It assumes no previous knowledge of these fields, and may be appropriate therefore as an introduction to logic, the theory of problem-solving, and computer programming." It is, it is. Basically, this is the kind of background every Prolog programmer should have. There is some good material in here about problem-solving. My book will help you become a better Prolog programmer; *this* book will help you become a better logic programmer.

[7] William F. Clocksin & Christopher S. Mellish. *Programming in Prolog, 3rd edition* Springer-Verlag, New York, 1987. ISBN 0-387-17539-3.

Bill Clocksin and Chris Mellish taught Prolog at Edinburgh while David Warren, Lawrence Byrd, and Fernando Pereira (the "DEC-10 Prolog team at Edinburgh") were still there. Chris Mellish wrote PDP-11 Prolog and played a major part in the development of Poplog. Bill Clocksin wrote the Prolog-X system (Lawrence Byrd was involved in that too). Unlike the authors of many Prolog books, these two people do actually understand the language. Despite the many Prolog books that have come out since the first edition of this one, it is still my choice for a *first* Prolog textbook. Follow it up with Sterling & Shapiro or Peter Ross's book.

[8] John Malpas. *Prolog: a Relational Language and its Applications*. Prentice-Hall, 1987.

This is another introductory Prolog textbook. It covers more material than Clocksin & Mellish. I have a hard time saying nice things about Prolog text-books, but this one isn't too bad.

[9] Leon Sterling & Ehud Shapiro. *The Art of Prolog*. MIT Press,Cambridge Mass, 1986.

Your second Prolog text-book should either be this one or Peter Ross's. There is a lot of valuable material in it.

[10] Peter Ross. *Advanced Prolog, techniques and examples*. Addison-Wesley, 1989. ISBN 0-201-17527-4.

Peter Ross has been at Edinburgh since the early DEC-10 Prolog days too. He has had a lot of experience teaching Prolog and using Prolog for AI. His book is full of excellent practical advice. It is one of the very few Prolog books whose description of setof/3 and bagof/3 is correct. His examples of code are nicely laid out, but could often be improved.

[11] Helder Coelho & José C. Cotta. *Prolog by Example*. Springer-Verlag, New York, 1988. ISBN 0-387-18313-2.

This is essentially a new edition of "How to Solve it with Prolog". There are some 175 examples. Some are tiny, some are several pages. The text explains the problems the examples are supposed to solve, but it does not explain why the sample programs have the forms they have. You will find larger examples whose structure *is* explained in Sterling & Shapiro and in Peter Ross's book, but you won't find this many. The earlier editions of "How to Solve it with Prolog" were an important part of the Prolog "culture".

[12] David Maier & David S. Warren. *Computing with Logic—Logic Programming with Prolog*. Benjamin/Cummings Publishing Company, Menlo Park CA, 1988. ISBN 0-8053-6681-4.

If you want to know how a Prolog system might work, this is the book for you. The book has three parts. The first part explains PropLog (pure Prolog where predicates can have no arguments) and how to write an interpreter for it. The second part explains DataLog (Prolog, where the arguments of predicates can be constants and variables but not compound terms) and how to write an interpreter for it. DataLog is of some interest as an intermediate stage between the relational calculus used in relational data base systems and the richer logics used in deductive databases. The third part discusses Prolog. It describes compilation to an abstract instruction set similar to David H. D. Warren's "New Engine". There is an extended example of Prolog used in a data base application.

[13] David H. D. Warren. *Applied logic—its use and implementation as a programming tool.* Technical Note 290, SRI International, Menlo Park CA, 1983.

This is David H. D. Warren's PhD thesis from Edinburgh. It explains how the DEC-10 Prolog system (the first Prolog compiler) works.

[14] David H. D. Warren. *An abstract Prolog instruction set.* Technical Note 309, SRI International, Menlo Park, CA, 1983.

This describes the "New Engine" or WAM, the basis of many of today's Prolog compilers (including Quintus Prolog and ALS Prolog, among others). There are several tutorials on the WAM instruction set around, but although the paper is rather terse, it is an improvement on its successors.

[15] D.L. Bowen, Lawrence Byrd, Fernando C.N. Pereira, Luis M. Pereira, & David H.D. Warren. *DECsystem-10 Prolog user's manual.* Occasional Paper 27, Department of Artificial Intelligence, University of Edinburgh, 1982.

This is the manual for DEC-10 Prolog. If you want to know what an "Edinburgh-compatible" or "DEC-10 compatible" Prolog should look like, this is it.

[16] Quintus Computer Systems, Ltd. *Quintus Prolog reference manual.* Quintus, Mountain View CA, 1988.

This is the manual for Quintus Prolog. I was working for Quintus when I wrote my book, so my opinion is not altogether unbiassed. The Quintus manual could stand a lot of improvement, but most Prolog manuals have a long way to go to match it.

[17] Mats Carlsson & Johan Widen. *SICStus Prolog user's manual.* Research Report 88007B, Swedish Institute of Computer Science, Kista, Sweden, 1988.

This is the manual for SICStus Prolog. SICStus Prolog is very similar to Quintus Prolog (which means that it is very similar to DEC-10 Prolog), it is rather efficient, it's quite reliable, and it has coroutining primitives as well. It's proof that you don't have to have come from Edinburgh to write a good DEC-10 compatible Prolog.

[18] James Thom & Justin Zobel. *NU-Prolog reference manual, version 1.3.* Technical Report 86/10, Department of Computer Science, University of Melbourne, Australia, 1988.

I have seen the future and it worked quite often. Think of an angel with warts. NU Prolog has many features which make it possible to write programs that are rather closer to logic than in conventional Prologs, and for the most part it is quite DEC-10 compatible as well. It has good indexing, including multikey indexing for predicates held on disc. I have never encountered a better set of debugging tools for Prolog than NU Prolog has. If I could have the expressiveness of NU Prolog combined with the reliability of Quintus Prolog I would be a very happy Prolog programmer, It's worth getting this report just to find out what the future may hold.

[19] Richard A. O'Keefe. *Prolog Compared With Lisp?* SIGPLAN Notices Vol. 18 No. 5, May 1983, pp 46–56.

This was a reply to a paper which attacked David Warren's claim that Prolog was close to Lisp in speed. I showed that it was possible to do substantially better in both Prolog and Lisp than the paper I was responding to, and gave some guidelines for when to use the dynamic data base (as seldom as you can) and when to use lists (often, but not *that* often).

[20] Mark Johnson. *Attribute-Value Logic and the Theory of Grammar.* CLSI Lecture Notes Series No 16, Chicago University Press, 1988.

The q(Counter,Front,Back) data structure for queues comes from this.

[21] S. T. Kedar-Cabelli & L. T. McCarty. *Explanation-Based Generalisation as Resolution Theorem Proving.* Proceedings of the Fourth International Workshop on Machine Learning, pp 383–389, Irvine, California, 1987.

One of the examples in the chapter on Interpreters comes from this. If you're interested in Machine Learning, make sure that you have access to a copy of these proceedings.

[22] Timothy G. Lindholm & Richard A. O'Keefe. *Efficient implementation of a defensible semantics for dynamic Prolog code.* Proceedings of the Fourth International Conference on Logic Programming, Melbourne, Australia, MIT Press, 1987.

The "transaction" approach to dynamic data base changes was presented in this paper. Quintus Prolog and SICStus Prolog both use this model now, though the underlying implementations are different.

[23] Lee Naish. *All solutions predicates in Prolog.* Proceedings of the Second IEEE Symposium on Logic Programming, Boston, Massachusetts, 1985.

Lee Naish's paper described some of the problems with the "standard" all solutions predicates setof/3, bagof/3, and findall/3, and described how it is possible to implement well-behaved all solutions predicates in a richer language (explicit quantifiers and coroutining/contstraints).

[24] Lee Naish. *Negation and control in Prolog.* Lecture Notes in Computer Science 238. Springer-Verlag, New York, 1986.

Lee Naish's thesis. Read it for the ideas behind NU Prolog.

Index

The MIT Press, with Peter Denning as general consulting editor, publishes computer science books in the following series:

ACM Doctoral Dissertation Award and Distinguished Dissertation Series

Artificial Intelligence
Patrick Winston, founding editor
J. Michael Brady, Daniel G. Bobrow, and Randall Davis, editors

Charles Babbage Institute Reprint Series for the History of Computing
Martin Campbell-Kelly, editor

Computer Systems
Herb Schwetman, editor

Explorations with Logo
E. Paul Goldenberg, editor

Foundations of Computing
Michael Garey and Albert Meyer, editors

History of Computing
I. Bernard Cohen and William Aspray, editors

Information Systems
Michael Lesk, editor

Logic Programming
Ehud Shapiro, editor; Koichi Furukawa, Jean-Louis Lassez, Fernando Pereira, and David H. D. Warren, associate editors

The MIT Press Electrical Engineering and Computer Science Series

Research Monographs in Parallel and Distributed Processing
Christopher Jesshope and David Klappholz, editors

Scientific and Engineering Computation
Janusz Kowalik, editor

Technical Communication
Ed Barrett, editor